VARMINT HUNTER'S DIGEST
The How-To Book For Varminters

By Jim Dougherty

𝒇 Follett Publishing Company / Chicago

T-0838

Produced by

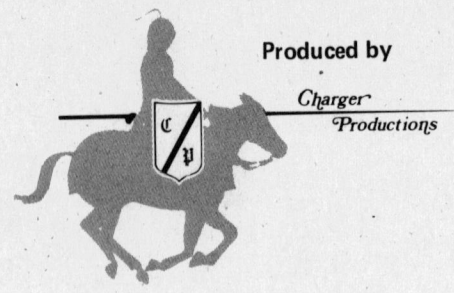

Charger Productions

EDITORIAL DIRECTOR
Jack Lewis

RESEARCH EDITOR
Roger Combs

PRODUCTION EDITOR
Bob Springer

ART DIRECTORS
John Vitale
Felicity Whiter

COPY EDITOR
Rusty Springer

PRODUCTION COORDINATOR
Betty Burris

ASSOCIATE PUBLISHER
Sheldon L. Factor

Cover photography by Tom Brakefield

Copyright ©MCMLXXVII by DBI Books, Inc., 540 Frontage Rd., Northfield, Ill. 60093, a subsidiary of Technical Publishing Company. All rights reserved. Printed in the United States of America. No part of this book may be reproduced, stored in a retrieval system, or transmitted in any form or by any means, electronic, mechanical, photocopying, recording, or otherwise, without the prior written permission of the publisher.

The views and opinions contained herein are those of the author. The publisher disclaims all responsibility for the accuracy or correctness of the author's views and opinions.

ISBN 0-695-80838-9   Library of Congress Catalog Card Number 77-82665

CONTENTS

1. **THE WHY OF VARMINT CALLING** 6
   From a vague beginning, the sport began
   with a sound ecological basis

2. **THE HOW OF VARMINT HUNTING** 12
   Learning the techniques can mean year-round
   sport in almost any location

3. **THE LOUD AND THE LOW** 18
   Different calls, differing techniques — whether mouth calls
   or electronic — can make your hunt

4. **RIFLES FOR VARMINTS** 32
   Choice of rifles is a personal matter;
   Dougherty prefers .22 caliber for good reasons

5. **CONNIVANCE FOR COYOTES** 46
   You must be smarter than
   this wily predator to score

6. **CALLING ALL BOBCATS** 62
   Bagging this predator requires
   special techniques and extra patience

7. **A FEEL FOR FOXES** 70
   Winter is the time for outsmarting this
   creature — and taking prime pelts

8. **...AND THE OTHERS** 82
   It's surprising what unlikely
   game will answer a call

9. **THE UNCALLED FOR** 92
   Although certain varmints cannot be called
   they still offer a challenge to the hunter

10. **THE WINGED ONES** 108
    Protected in some areas, crows still constitute
    a shootable nuisance in others

11. **CAMOUFLAGE YOUR FIREARMS** 116
    We spend time and money to disguise the obvious,
    but a flashing gun can be a dead giveaway

12. **INSTANT BIPOD FOR VARMINT RIFLES** 122
    Here's help, if your aim
    wavers at long ranges

13. **LOADS AND RELOADS** 126
    There are those who insist the
    best varmint loads are home-built

14. **LOVE AFFAIR WITH THE .22 VARMINTER** 134
    Frank de Haas has spent more than three
    decades in evaluating his favorite cartridge

15. **HANDGUNS FOR VARMINTS** 144
    Almost any will do, but some have
    built-in specifics that help

16. **SHOTGUNS FOR VARMINTS** 168
    Consideration of arms and ammo
    can make the difference in success

17. **COPING WITH SCOPES** 176
    A look at the optics needed
    for long-range shooting

18. **OUT OF THE NIGHT** 184
    Some of calling's greatest surprises
    lurk there in the darkness

19. **VARMINT BOWHUNTING** 194
    Getting your critter with bow and arrow requires
    skill and strict camouflage practices

20. **BACKYARD SAFARI** 206
    A tongue-in-cheek look
    at the home varmint scene

21. **MISADVENTURES OF A VARMINT HUNTER** 214
    All was not sweetness and success during the author's
    participation in the annual California-Arizona varmint hunts

   CATALOG OF CENTER-FIRE RIFLES 234

   THE VARMINT CALLER'S TRADE DIRECTORY 246

ABOUT THE AUTHOR

Jim Dougherty is a former World and California Varmint Calling Champion who has captured sixteen game calling titles, including duck, goose, crow and others. Born in California, he now lives in Tulsa, Oklahoma, where he is employed by Ben Pearson Archery. An archer by profession, he has called and hunted varmints with bow and gun on three continents, including Africa. Considered outstanding in the field by his peers, he has a subtle sense of humor, combined with knowledge, which makes his writing not only highly instructive, but entertaining as well.

Chapter 1

THE WHY OF VARMINT CALLING

Jim Dougherty displays a pair of sizeable coyotes taken with one of his favorite rifles in California's Mojave Desert sagebrush.

From A Vague Beginning, The Sport Began — With A Sound Ecological Basis!

FOR AS LONG as I can remember, I have been a hunter, and I have been fortunate thus far in my life to have hunted in a great many places for a wide variety of game. I began hunting as a small boy with my father, a confirmed bird hunter, who took me, a mere toddler managing four steps, on one of his early morning jaunts to a dove field in California.

From there it was the irrigated barley fields of the San Joaquin Valley during waterfowl time where, at an early age, I became enchanted with the conversations of the birds and marveled at the fact that with hard work and patience, conversations could be duplicated and used effectively on a duck call.

Calling any form of feathered fowl or four-legged game is the supreme challenge I consider the epitomy of hunting, even beyond the ability to be able to read animal signs keenly or stalk game to extreme close range.

As a result of that early exposure to duck calling, I became a calling fanatic. As my hunting interest branched out, I constantly looked for ways that a call could aid in the quest for other game. It was only natural, I suppose, that when I first heard one could call coyotes, foxes and other such creatures into touching distance with a wounded rabbit call, I would look to that as a new course in my outdoor education.

I called in my first coyote as a teenager and my most recent one a short time ago. In-between there have been many hundreds of coyotes, as well as bobcats, foxes, cougars, wolves and a host of other critters that find intoxicating music in the tunes played on a varmint call. No matter how many coyotes you have called in, the next one is just as exciting. No matter how much you think you have learned, there is always a new lesson for the varmint

Predator coyote manages to multiply in almost any situation, adapting to crowding in of civilization.

The late Bill Dudley (left) was the world varmint calling champion four times, while his father, Sam Dudley (above), is considered one of the finest callers of all time by his contemporaries.

hunter/caller in dealing with a group of our most cunning man-wise creatures.

I suspect it is incorrect to refer to varmint calling as a new sport. Certainly it has been practiced for hundreds of years in various forms by Indians, frontiersmen, trappers, et. al. Yet as a form of outdoor recreation it is relatively new. Some twenty-plus years ago, when calling really began to gain in interest it was a totally new method of hunting some of the canniest of our wild animals.

I feel fortunate in having, in a sense, grown up with the sport and the fine outdoorsmen I became associated with over those formative and following years.

I began varmint calling with a fellow named Doug Kittredge, an offshoot of our association in the archery business. At that time he operated a large retail archery shop and I was in his employ. Our mutual love of the outdoors had sparked a long-term relationship that still continues.

As our interest developed in calling varmints, we became increasingly aware of others — mostly in Texas — who were into the sport. From the early Fifties, when we first became involved, there developed a relationship with Wayne Weems of Ft. Worth, Texas, and eventually with other call makers and just plain varmint callers.

How the term "varmint calling" actually came about I can't say. It just sort of happened even though the first organized group was labeled the Texas Wild Animal Callers Association.

The predator family of foxes, coyotes, bobcats, wolves, etc., long have been termed varmints, lumped improperly, in my opinion, with such creatures as rats, crows, groundhogs and prairie dogs. It is my belief that our smaller species of predators have long been overlooked as worthy adversaries, and only in recent times have they been accorded the respect, and in some cases the protection, they are entitled to as game animals. The growth of the sport of varmint calling and hunting has had a great deal to do with this increase in status.

It was not until late 1956 that the sport began to gain momentum. At that time, Kittredge and I received a letter announcing the first World Championship Varmint Calling Contest. The event, billed as a rendezvous with callers from all across the country, was comprised primarily of hunters from the Southwest. It was held in Chandler, Arizona, in February 1957.

I do not recall how many contestants were entered — thirty or so — but I do recall that I won that contest and Kittredge took third, bracketing a fine fellow from Waco, Texas, one F.B. Farrell.

In the following two years, Farrell and Kittredge were destined to take first spot accordingly and Doug continued to place in the top three spots for several years, while I never managed a better spot than second in this event after that first victory.

With the growth of contests, it was only natural that organizations would be formed. Shortly after the 1959 event, the California Varmint Callers Association was founded, becoming the third such group in the country. Others followed, as did interest within existing sportsmen's clubs, and among individual sportsmen. The challenge of calling the wily predators to within "handshaking distance," as the Burnham brothers put it, gained a large following.

I'm sure it was the calling contests that cemented the

VARMINT HUNTER'S DIGEST

Serious varmint hunting can be a lonely life when at it, rewards of wide-open spaces more than make up for it.

foundations of the sport and brought it to center stage among the hunting fraternity. These gatherings, held in many states under various banners, drew large crowds. There was the annual world event, a national championship, various state contests and a multitude of combination calling events wherein contestants battled in a variety of game calling categories that resulted in individual division winners as well as the high overall calling champ. In this environment, numerous multitalented outdoorsmen were drawn either to enter or just listen and exchange views while enjoying the camaraderie that existed.

Those who chose the sport were, in most cases, the type of individual woodsmen to whom a different approach had an allure. Varmint callers are a special breed reveling in wide-open elbow-room kind of places. They are adventurers, in a sense, who prefer the challenge of hunting some of our smartest animals in a one-on-one atmosphere where anything can happen and usually does.

By the early Sixties, varmint calling organizations had sprung up throughout the land. The Southwest had the larger organizations due primarily to the geographics of wider open spaces and high-density populations of critters, primarily coyotes. Varmint calling is a desert or prairie operation in country that provides miles upon miles of huntable terrain, where the calling teams could range for days the wandering riverbeds, endless sagebrush flats or the cholla and saguaro-studded hills.

In Arizona and California, the state calling associations flourished, branching out into statewide chapters based in large cities or rural towns. The parent organizations became recognized as accredited sportsmen's associations that worked closely with various departments of state and

In last decade, various varmint-calling clubs in Western states pitted talents against each other, helping to hold predator population in check during annual competitions.

VARMINT HUNTER'S DIGEST

Larry Eliason won this trophy for his triumphs with a predator call in 1960, when he was declared the national calling champ.

federal wildlife departments in providing data on varmint populations, helping in heavily populated areas to reduce depredations by hunting the critters. Thus the groups were providing a service while turning varmints into a source of outdoor recreation.

Good varmint callers were — and are — highly efficient specialists and in many instances the arrival of a few teams of callers provided relief to ranchers and sheepmen who had experienced heavy loss to predators and little control by conventional trapping or poisoning means. Working together, callers lobbied for regulations to aid the sport and fought against certain practices of nondiscriminant predator control. The philosophy was then, as it is today, that the varmints are to be accorded the same rules set for other animal species and that those who choose to hunt them should be entitled to a voice in the future of their particular resource interest.

Admittedly there are times when varmints — coyote populations especially — become burdensome and stringent methods of control are required. It was the position of the callers that, in such cases, they should be allowed to participate in the control and that the use of noxious methods such as poison not be permitted. The voice of the callers across the land played a large part in the final elimination of poison in predator and rodent control.

This brief history of the past of the sport of varmint calling would not be complete without some mention of those who became near legends as hunters and contest callers. Not only were their feats the source of countless campfire conversations, but their dedication went far in promoting calling as a viable outdoor hunting recreation. Some became commercially involved by making calls or

When California-Arizona varmint hunters compete against each other, efforts often spread across as many as four states!

VARMINT HUNTER'S DIGEST

There were trophies in many categories during the heyday of interstate varmint-hunting competitions, but experience shows that the hunting pressure during one such weekend per year did little harm to predator populations hunted over a wide area.

other hunting accessories for a growing market, others simply believed in what they were doing and wanted to see justice for both the hunter and the hunted.

Over the years, in the contests of calling skill held from Michigan and South Dakota to Arizona and the glittering city of Las Vegas, from the small events hosted by sportsmen's clubs to the large scale national and world championships there developed a list who were termed tough by competitors and spectators alike. From Texas there was Rusty Farrell and Bowen Weems; from Arizona the incomparable Bill Dudley, Tom Mills, Dick Beeler, Manuel Sinohui, Delroy Western and Dave Heihuis; from California came Doug Kittredge and a list of callers that always were sure to give the opposition fits, such as Norm Taylor, George Allison, George Wright and Larry Eliason.

Among the call manufacturers and famed field callers were the Burnham brothers, Murray and Winston; Wayne Weems, who developed the Weems Wild Calls, and Jack Cain of Circe call fame. Johnny Stewart pioneered electronic calling, but foremost among them all is Sam Dudley. In my opinion, he is the finest varmint hunter who ever put a call lanyard around his neck and slipped a round up the spout of his .243.

Not only did calling contests provide a chance for us to get together, but manufacturers had the opportunity to perfect their calls by dealing with the experts who provided input in terms of design of barrel shape and mouthpieces, reed tuning designs to match the perfected techniques.

Calling contests of this type were judged affairs scored by a panel of experts, usually five who were separated in individual booths at ranges of twenty-five to one hundred yards from the contestants' platform.

Contestants were judged on volume, tone and technique. The last category most often determined the winner. Maintaining proper tone through the wide range of patterns, a good caller had to run through in the allotted time of a minute, which takes complete skill on the call. Many a contestant has been ruined when the necessary notes were lost or he "blew a reed". Techniques varied, of course, as did the amount of volume a man was able to impart to his call.

Following the first minute, referred to as the long-range portion of the contest, the caller has thirty seconds for the subtle art of the close-range event.

Points are accumulated and the winners eventually determined after three elimination rounds. These are gut-wrenching affairs, as the contests take a good deal of physical preparedness and mental ability in determining what it takes to beat another as the scores for each round are run up.

In addition to calling contests, there were many field contests with the winners being that individual or team that collected the greatest amount of critters in a predetermined length of time. Most often these events were held in areas where predator populations were high, with resultant economic damage to landowners such as ranchers of poultry or sheep. This type of event eventually ran its course as far as large-scale contests were concerned. With the sudden awareness of our deteriorating ecology, the increase in anti-hunting sentiment, and the critical comments of the overnight environmentalists, who suddenly knew all there was to know in spite of what the biological experts in all management phases of our natural resources said, such pursuits were not in the best interests of the hunting fraternity.

Perhaps it is best that the large-scale field contests ended. While it is certain that they did nothing in the way of harm to the predator resource which is resilient and has avoided man's attempts to erradicate him for centuries, the events are not suited to today's social pressures.

Today's varmint callers still are organized in those areas where the big boom had its beginning, but they no longer

Doug Kittredge, one of the pioneers of serious varmint calling, was named the world champion during the competitions of 1959.

represent the majority of the sport. Instead, with the knowledge they imparted over the years, with the development of equipment and techniques and the attention they focused on our small predatory species, they have made the sport understandable and available to future generations of varmint callers.

But in spite of the emphasis on ecology, most of us still have difficulty in dealing with the confusion. An example stands out in the state of Texas, where a few years ago, a bill was introduced in the legislature to make electronic calling for coyotes illegal.

During the same month, a Texas congressman introduced a bill in the federal government seeking a grant of $50 million to cover the damage suffered by his state's sheepmen from coyote damage to the flocks.

There are some things that just don't make sense!

Chapter 2

THE HOW OF VARMINT HUNTING

Learning The Techniques Can Mean Year-Round Sport In Almost Any Location

SOMETIME AGO, a noted outdoorsman who should know better, wrote in one of the hunting books that bobcats are the hardest type of varmint to shoot.

Either this individual was hunting in the wrong places or he doesn't know the first thing about bobcats. I can name any numbers of callers who have gone out in a single weekend in the badlands of the area where Northern California, Arizona and Nevada join and come back with at least half a dozen scalps from these wily predators.

Left: Hunter experiences moment of truth as he has a lined-up coyote in his scope. He still holds short-range call in his mouth, calling the predator in close for the kill.

This writer was supposed to be an authority, and he was right in saying that bobcats are difficult "to find and shoot." But this is because too many hunters are inclined to drive into an area, smoke a few cigarettes while talking it over with a buddy, get out and slam the car doors — then expect to find the bobcats which are already crossing the next county by this time.

Varmint hunting — even for bobcats — can be fruitful if one simply follows the rules. Once, when I was young, I

Before heading for likely varmint grounds, expert varmint hunter checks out his scope and handloads at the range. Accurate facts on actual hunt are noted for future reference.

His face camouflaged with a theatrical grease stick, the hunter is ready to make stalk. In this instance, he tosses handful of dust in the air to determine wind direction.

Left: This hunter illustrates a basic don't of varmint hunting: One never should outline himself on skyline during attempt to call in game. Saving grace is that sun is at hunter's back.

Below: Hunter moves carefully into position where he will make calling stand; keeps below cover, so outline cannot be seen easily; walks heel-and-toe, avoiding rocks and brush.

VARMINT HUNTER'S DIGEST   13

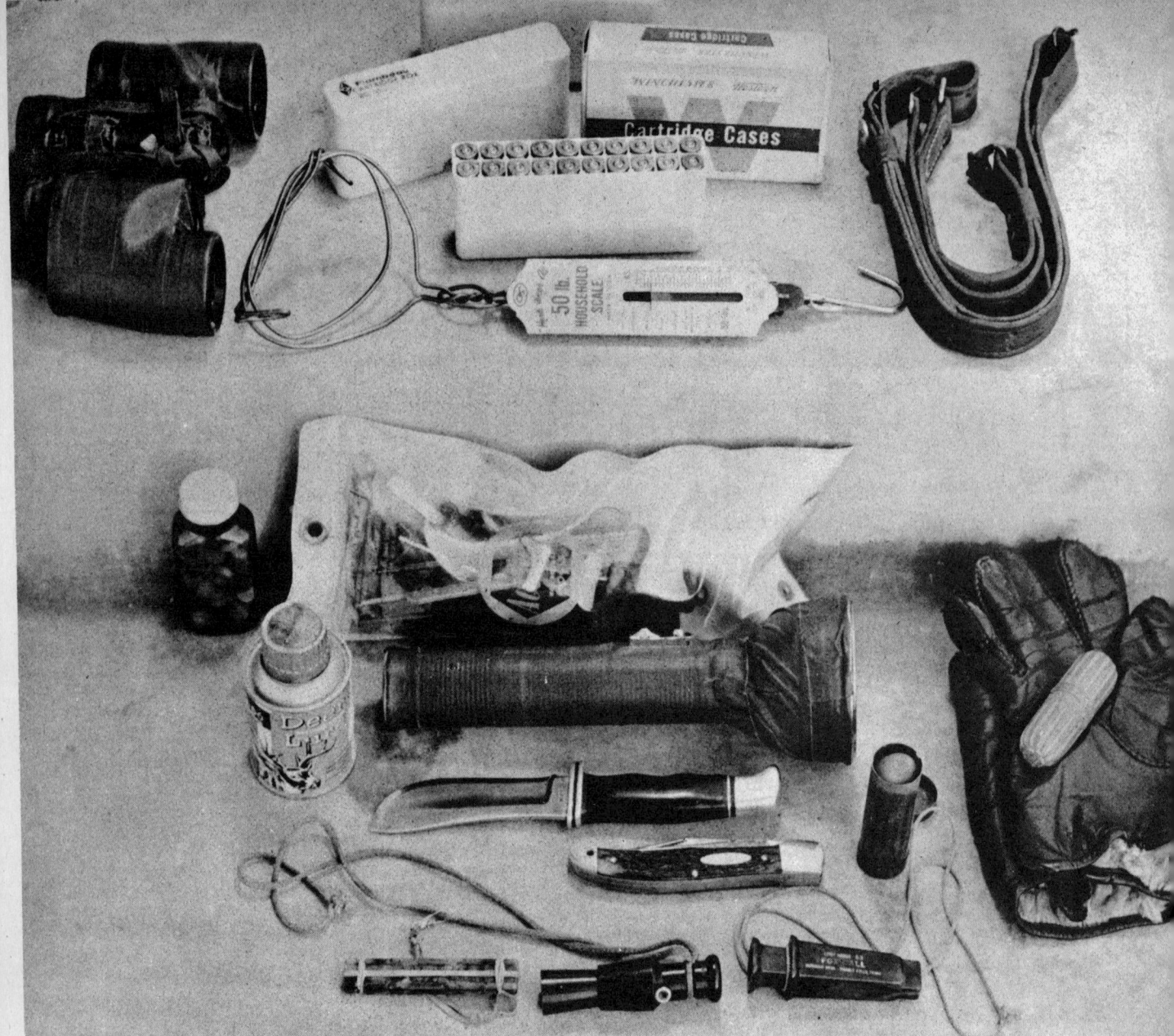

Array of equipment often used in successful varmint hunting by author. Included: binoculars and a flashlight whose shiny metal is covered with camouflage tape; handloads and scales; rifle sling; plastic-wrapped tools for rifle repair in the field; vitamins taken for improving night vision; scent to kill human odor; skinning knives; short and long-range varmint calls; gloves; snake bite kit; cosmetic camouflage stick.

was attempting to work a balky mule, and was getting nowhere. The owner of the mule finally said, "Before you can work a mule, you have to prove you're smarter than he is."

The same goes for hunting varmints. Before you can call a bobcat in close enough to shoot it, you have to outsmart it.

Also, nearly every American sportsman has been brainwashed into the idea that his local hunting season is limited to three months — or less — each Fall. He must be content to go out during that established season, shoot his buck, then be satisfied with less exciting paper punching on an established range for the remainder of the year.

But nothing could be further from the truth. Not only is there game shooting available the year around in most states, but it can be carried out on a minimum budget. One doesn't have to make reservations in Alaska for moose or bear; he doesn't have to go to the expense of a trip to Mexico for desert sheep or fowl shooting.

In virtually any section of the nation in which you may live, there is varmint hunting probably no more than an hour's drive from your home ground. And by following a few simple tips, you can have all of the excitement you want. Hunting coyotes, bobcats and the rest of the predators is as simple as putting gasoline in your car if you do things correctly.

But before we get into the dos and don'ts of varmint shooting, let's take a look at the country as a whole. In the West, of course, we don't have nearly the encroachments of civilization to be found in the other parts of the nation. In the western half of the United States, the following types of varmints are to be found: coyotes; wolves; bobcats; Canadian lynx; grey fox; the desert swift; badger; hoary marmot; cougar; raccoon; rock chucks; ground squirrels,

Learning to recognize paw prints of various types of game is important in varmint hunting. In this case, it's a bear track.

and in the extreme Southwest, jaguar.

This doesn't mean that you will find all of these varieties in any one location, but there is not a state west of the Missouri River that doesn't have some of these which can be hunted the year around.

In the Middle West, one can find coyotes, ground squirrel, the red fox, badger, coon, chucks, and in the northern reaches such as Michigan, wildcats and even some wolves.

The South is sort of limited, although in the swamp and jungle country one can find plenty of wildcats and cougar. Coon and crows are plentiful and entertaining shooting in almost all of these states, however. But be sure to check out local regulations on each species.

And in the East there are varmint problems that many people never heard of. While the coyote, for example, is thought of as primarily a western animal and associated with being buried on the lone prairie, this isn't true. For example, both New York and Maine have been plagued in recent years with coyotes. In addition some of these eastern states have wild dogs, and in Maine, there are "coydogs," which are a cross between coyotes and wild dogs. The eastern area also boasts plenty of crows and fox, and from Pennsylvania northward, there are wolves which have come down from Canada.

But to hunt varmint — and come home with trophies — one must be properly equipped; there is more to it than loading up the old rifle and going off to some hilltop and starting to shoot.

For a small amount of cash, you can purchase a camouflage coat of the type carried by most sporting goods stores. There are some hunters, of course, who will feel this is going overboard, but the coat will pay off in scalps; this I can assure you. One also should have a camouflage hat and gloves. The rest you no doubt have in your closet: hunting boots, rugged jeans and the like.

This is all you need in the clothing department, but let's take a look at the rifle you're going to use. There has been much discussion of so-called varmint calibers in recent years, and most of it doesn't mean much. Any — and I repeat, any — caliber rifle is adequate providing you use the proper loads and can hold them to 1½ inches at a hundred yards. This doesn't mean that I would recommend the .460 Weatherby as a varmint rifle, of course, but I have heard of instances wherein large calibers have been used, only there seldom is anything identifiable left of the target.

High-speed velocities and flat trajectories are the main needs in a varmint rifle, although when you have learned to call in the game well enough, you will find that about seventy-five percent of your shots will be at ranges of under a hundred yards.

Many shooters prefer the 6mm or .22 center-fire calibers. However, the improved versions of the .25 and .30 caliber guns are good. Include in these the .25/06 or the .30/06 using 110 and 125-grain handloads as being quite capable. But going back to shooting a tight group at the century mark, you will find that using the 6mm or .22 center-fires makes easier shooting because of lighter recoil.

One of the greatest flat-shooting varmint rifles I have ever fired or owned is the .220 Swift. Its recoil is light, velocity is high and destruction from shocking power is tremendous. With handloads, speeds of 3700 feet per second can be obtained, yet barrel life is relatively long and the accuracy superb. In spite of its small size, this round can knock down a cougar or a jaguar with no problems.

An absolute must for the serious varmint hunter is a scope; one that has good light gathering qualities and sufficient magnification. My .220 predator pooper sports a Redfield 4X, although I tend to favor a 6X for some ranges.

In order to pinpoint a coyote at three hundred yards, I would suggest a 4X scope with one-minute crosshairs. This makes a less expensive combination that is good under nearly any other circumstance, and is good for both day and night varmint shooting.

Predators are primarily nocturnal by habit, feeding and traveling for the most part after the sun is down and before it comes up. But, if you plan to hunt at night, first check

Groundhogs aren't game that can be called, but with a population problem bordering on that of rabbits, they provide an excellent source of shooting during off season.

Basic knowledge of horsemanship doesn't hurt varmint hunter. This mode of transportation aids access into back country, where varmint population is large, undisturbed.

your local game laws; there are some localities in which this is forbidden.

One can call in varmints during the daylight hours if he is in an area where they are laying up to escape the heat, which is unlikely during much of the year. To determine whether you are in an active area, you must be able to read animal signs, which usually are found in riverbeds in soft sand or along ridges. These predators are smart and invariably pick the routes to travel which are the easiest and most comfortable.

The areas most inhabited by coyotes are rolling hills with sufficient cover for them to move from one feeding ground to another without too much exposure. To find these routes, look for the criss-cross of prints. Also, you will find coyotes in bushes that have packrat nests and which afford cover for ground-nesting birds or for rabbits.

The bobcat prefers a more rocky terrain, free of bushes, for his den, but this animal still inhabits sectors where small game is plentiful. The bobcat is not a traveler like the coyote or his bigger brother, the cougar.

Coyotes feed primarily on rabbits when available, but will eat almost any type of meat when hungry. The bobcat's diet is about ninety percent rodents, as he relies upon his stealthy stalking abilities, while the coyote relies upon his running power and intelligence. The coyote is noted for his ability to plan things out; he has sharp ears, keen eyes and a sensitive sense of smell.

In hunting coyotes, it is a must to do something to kill the human odor. Most sporting goods dealers now handle scent killers in the familiar spray-type can, but I've found that a can of sardines is even more effective. I simply punch a hole in the can and pour the oil over boots and hat. And you know about the odor of sardines; enough said.

Another good odor killing system is to build a small fire and stand in the smoke for a number of minutes. This is an old Indian trick, and one should be certain that all of his clothing has been permeated by the smoke, thus assuring

Rifle scope can be used to glass an area, but binoculars are invaluable. However, outlining oneself against skyline as in this situation is not conducive to drawing predators.

Learning to recognize predator movement on moonlit nights is a must for the serious predator hunter.

that his scent will not act as a personal calling card.

Once this is done, the hunter can move on to a spot which affords good, clear vision with at least forty yards in all directions. One should wait about five minutes before facing into the wind and beginning to call.

There are any number of good varmint calls on the market, but I have found that a two-call system is best. A long-range call can be heard by a human being at a distance of a mile and much farther than that by most varmints. This will attract the animals in.

Then, when you can see the animal from your place of concealment, use the short-range call to bring him in even closer. This can be heard for only a couple of hundred yards, but will draw the animal in even closer.

I mentioned the matter of camouflage clothing earlier, but I have even gone to the extreme of wrapping my gun barrel and other shiny surfaces with green tape to cut down the possibility of glare. Frankly, I'm not certain this is worth the effort, since a good deal of cleaning up is required when one removes the tape. I'm also a great believer in using grease paint to camouflage one's features and hands, but I know varmint hunters who don't do this and still come in with their just share of kills.

Someone is certain to bring up the matter of what to do in snow. Again, I wear the same clothing as mentioned above, since I will undoubtedly take up a post in brush or something else that blends with my camouflage outfit. I think it would be wise to tape the gun with white tape to cut down show of movement and glare from the metal. Some hunters recommend a white suit for this type of hunting.

And in snow, the hunter has a definite advantage over the animal he is hunting. He can pick a spot where his camouflage clothing will blend, but none of the varmints can change their coats to coincide with a winter background. As a result, they show up just that much more plainly against the white of snow. They offer better targets and you can be more sure of good shots at long ranges. Needless to say, if the snow is deep enough, they cannot move as rapidly as under summer conditions.

For the beginning varmint hunter who is properly equipped and who has learned to call in his game, I'd recommend shooting at less than a hundred yards as a starter. I have shot coyotes at up to four hundred yards, but in most cases, one can't see his target at this distance. However, as the hunter's shooting and knowledge of the capabilities of gun, ammo and loads improves, he will be able to make shots at much longer distances.

This may seem repetitious, but I'd like to point out again that most predators are instinctively smart, so use all of the cover possible in making your stalk. Never slam car doors when getting in or out, as this can be heard for long distances in an unpopulated area. Don't smoke in the field, and by all means, never talk while hunting. If you're shooting with someone else, use the punch-and-point system of pointing out game; always move slowly and quietly, and when calling game, look with your eyes, not with your head. By this, I mean that even minor movements of the head or shoulders can call instant attention.

In short, use your ears, eyes and nose — not your mouth — and you will end up with a way of hunting that is exciting, colorful and full of thrills for everyone except that bobcat or coyote!

Chapter 3

THE LOUD AND THE LOW

Different Calls, Differing Techniques — Whether Mouth Calls Or Electronic — Can Make Your Hunt!

Olt Coon Call N-27

Olt Close-Range Predator Call CP-2

Olt Predator Call T-20

Olt Wooden Barrel Predator Call

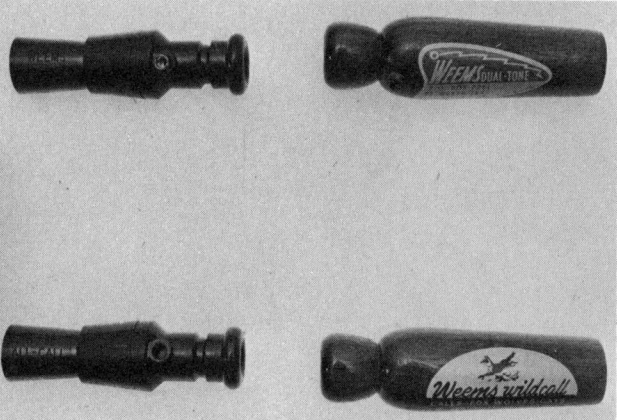
Weems turns out predator calls with both hard plastic and wooden barrels. His Dual-Tone model is the most popular in his line for overall varmint calling.

Burnham Brothers S-4 Mini-Call can be held in the mouth, leaving hands free for shooting. It is high-pitched in tone and can be used to call in coyote, fox and bobcat.

THE SPORT OF calling varmints with a mouth call is about twenty-five years old, which, when compared to most hunting methods, makes it a virtual infant.

While several manufacturers claim to have invented the sport, that is probably just commercial hoopla and a moot point anyway. Undoubtedly, certain of our American Indian tribes were luring fur bearers into club range before the first long hair stepped on Plymouth Rock. The secrets of game calling were no doubt taught to our adventurous frontiersmen-trapper forefathers by their Indian compadres as the white man was evolving and learning the intricacies of seeking out an existence in the New World's living room.

These trade secrets were passed down through many generations and years later, when the hustle and bustle of "civilizing" the country was accomplished, some folks cast a commercial eye at great-grandad's old fur-gathering tricks and turned them into a savings account.

No disrespect is intended. Those that pioneered and promoted the sport have provided a ton of adventurous hours to many thousands of modern-day hunters; anything they gained in return is their due. In my opinion two Texas firms played the biggest role in getting the sport off the ground. My first contact with a manufacturer was Wayne Weems who fathered the Weems Wild Call and very well may have been in a dead heat for varmint call parenthood with the legendary Burnham brothers of Marble Falls. Certainly other manufacturers of game calls were making dying rabbit squealers in those days but Weems and the Burnhams got the movement going. Not too many years after callers began to organize, Jack Cain and Lew Mossinger introduced the Circe line of calls and by then manufacturers were working long hours developing better instruments with added features and sales appeal.

In the beginning calls were simple wood or plastic barrels with metal or occasionally plastic reeds. An exception was the famed Burnham close-range call consisting of a rubber band reed stretched tightly between two thin plastic plates. I'm convinced that calling contests provided the greatest impetus to manufacturers to continually work in developing new, improved calls.

The first calls I came in contact with, regardless of who produced them, were similar in design. Each manufacturer used the same metal reed source — with the exception of some P.S. Olt calls which, as I recall, had a plastic reed in a plastic barrel, and were damn fine fox calls. The others primarily were wood barrels of walnut or maple with each maker tuning the reeds in certain secret and mysterious ways to achieve a wide range of tones. Internal barrel shapes were common with straight or parallel air chamber. I believe Weems was first in experimenting with woods and internal barrel shapes to develop better tone and volume capabilities. His third generation Wild Calls featured a tapered barrel which produced infinitely more volume. Tonal qualities were obtained with varying thickness in barrel material.

Volume in calls is a vital feature equally important to the hunter or contest caller. With contests gaining a great deal of notoriety and winning brands getting consumer demand, it behooved the manufacturer and their pet contestants to develop a better tool. The tapered barrel feature that Weems came up with was the ultimate winner in several major calling events where tone and volume counted heavily when final scores were tallied.

Cost savings at the makers' level were probably as much responsible for the development of plastic barrels in call design as actual improvements in quality. Plastic designs lent themselves to innovative new features such as the Weems All-Call which provided for interchangeable reeds or the Circe Trophy Model with a rotating barrel in a fixed mouthpiece. With this call the user could simply rotate the main barrel/cylinder to change reed pitches from jackrabbit (long range) to cottontail (medium range or higher pitch) to the close-range, mouselike squeaker. The original Circes were made of wood with this feature and are now collectors' items and much sought after by serious hunter callers. Harold Thompson developed some fine quality calls with plastic barrels, the best was his reversible close-range call which could be blown from either end producing different pitches. Thompson's reeds were masterfully tuned and became a favorite with hunters and contest callers alike.

Another innovation developed by Weems was the

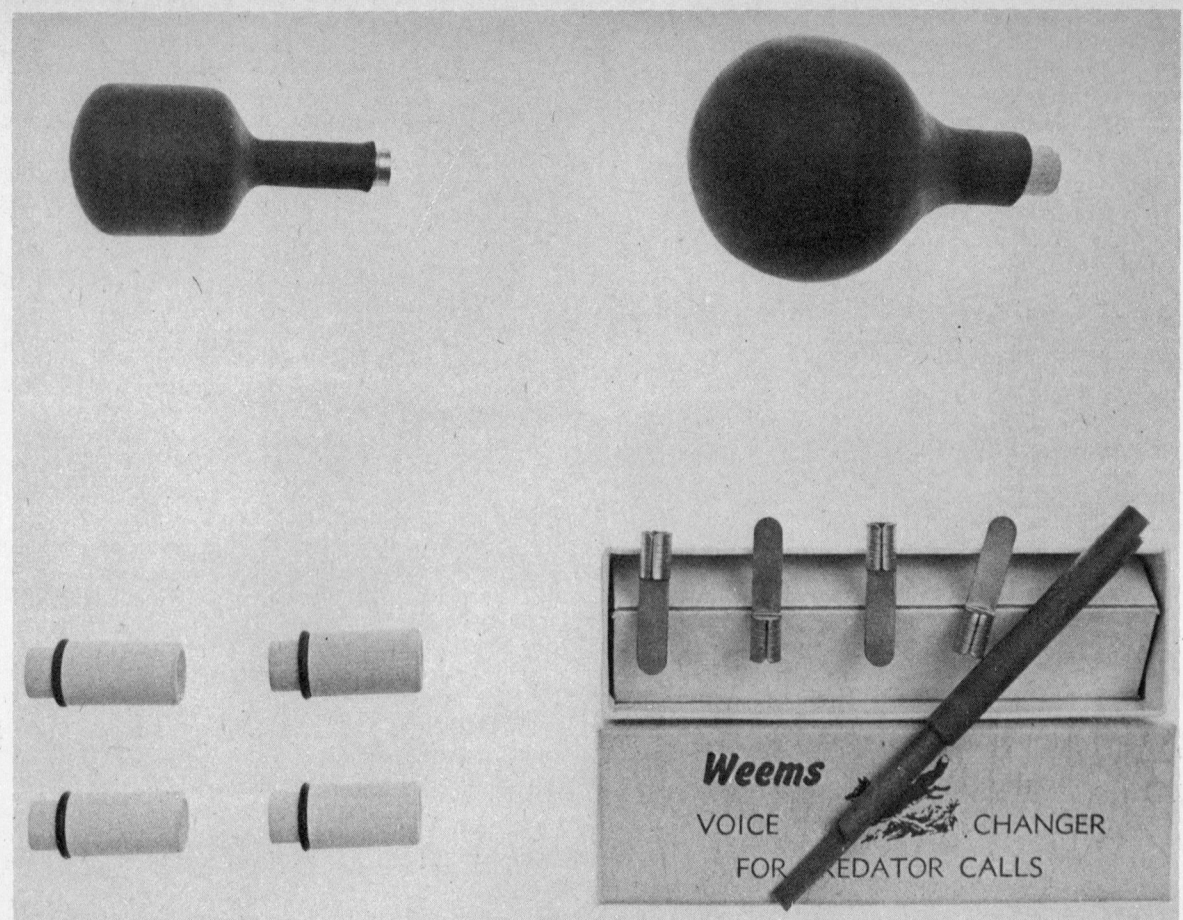

Wayne Weems was the first to introduce a call that used a changer system so that various sounds could be used. The first kit, however, was almost as bulky as the tackle box in which many callers still carry their many calls.

Dual-Tone model which featured a straight voice call with a high-pitch, close-range reed mounted sideways to the barrel. This reed could be cut off with the finger or, depending on the caller's whims, could be blown simultaneously with the main reed producing a stereolike effect that drove bobcats straight to the taxidermy studio.

It is pretty safe to say that every varmint call ever made would call varmints. The secret to success has always been in the individual's ability to make the call in the right place and blow it in a convincing manner. Hunting calls can be either plastic, metal or wood barreled with very little difference in response as far as the animals are concerned. It is really a matter of personal confidence as opposed to the capability of the instrument itself. If a hunter feels better with a wood call, then the wood call is going to get the greatest amount of exposure and subsequent success. In tournament calling it always was and always will be a fact that the favored calls are wood barreled. I do not believe there is any question that better tone, at least as far as the human ear can discern, comes from wood calls. I have called in many contests and judged not quite an equal amount, and have always been convinced that I could tell the difference between a wood call and a plastic one. While this has never affected my judging, the fine and fragile notes obtained in wood calls invariably gathered greater scores from the "human" judges when the subtleties of technique were graded. Over the years I have kept voluminous notes on the reactions of animals in the field to the varieties of audible offerings. I have found days when only a certain pitch would work, perhaps a pitch completely reversed from the previous day's hunt. I have never noted that it made any significant difference if played on a wood versus plastic call. If I was blowing a cottontail pitch on a wood model Wild Call, and my partner the same basic reed on a Burnham with plastic barrel, the results were even. A shift in pitch on either call could be totally ignored.

Overall, from the field man's point of view, the plastic barrel call is tougher and more reliable than a wooden model. Plastic is not as sensitive to changes in the elements. It does not swell or shrink, will seldom crack and is cleaned easily. Wood, on the other hand, heavily finished or not, will react to atmospheric changes of heat, moisture or cold. Admittedly it is the reed that is most delicate but the housing complements the reed.

In the good old days tuning reeds was an art guarded zealously by those who made calls, and purchasing extra or replacement reeds was out of the question. It wasn't long before most callers learned the not-too-difficult art. Changes in pitch are accomplished by the angle of the reed's lip over the plate, and in sophisticated tuning, scoring or denting the reed with a finely wielded knife point. All this accomplished was to vary the coarse or finely pitched tones. When makers do this, they label their calls, jackrabbit or cottontail models which equate to long, close or medium-range pitches. Those of us competing would finely file reeds and do all sorts of neat, intricate little tricks to develop a slight edge in tone; a difference that we hoped the judges would note and like.

Oftentimes we ran the risk of setting one so fine that when the moment of truth arrived, zealous pressure could shatter the thin steel membrane and our individual hopes for glory.

The camouflage-clad shooter is almost lost amid the heavy growth of prickly pear, as his electronic calling unit brings a large bobcat in close for the shot. This type of action is not unusual, according to field reports.

Today, most manufacturers provide reed changing kits as part of their product, complete with a tool to remove the old, worn or broken piece, and simple instructions.

Plastic reed calls are generally more durable than metal. But they are not, in my opinion, as fine in tone or distance carrying capabilities. On the other hand, they are certainly less sensitive to abuse from heavy use or cold weather. Cold weather will affect any type of reed due to the stiffness imparted by the temperature and the buildup of freezing condensation. Metal reeds fail commonly under these conditions. The prepared caller should always carry a good supply of extras.

Using any type of mouth call, regardless of the game it's designed for, takes practice. Surprisingly, the hardest element to master for most beginners is the proper breathing and blowing procedure. Calls are blown from deep within the chest, the air is forced up from the diaphragm, the pressure is controlled by the fingers or palm of the hand encircling the exit end of the barrel, and tone is maintained by a combination of hand position and air pressure. Filling up the cheeks alone with air will not get the job done. Not enough air is available to sustain notes that are developed by maintaining pressure. Deep-rooted gut pressure is the key to accurate calling on a varmint call, or those for elk, ducks, geese or crows. When a caller masters this technique and the ability to let it out in controlled single-phrase blasts, he has learned the secret to volume and tone control. Today there is a wide selection of instructional calling records available to the consumer. Most patterns are similar, with proven procedures that the newcomer should follow. Eventually an individual pattern will develop based on what is a comfortable pace. Contest callers blow hard by necessity; a habit that is often carried into the field. Blowing a call hard over long periods of time is tough work — it takes a lot out of a person.

I recall years ago the morning I first hunted with Sam Dudley. It was the day after a World Championship event in Arizona. A bunch of us had made plans to hunt for three

VARMINT HUNTER'S DIGEST 21

Early electronic callers used a record and turntable to reproduce varmint-drawing sounds, but there were some problems with the units. Today, the tape cassette has replaced the record and has been found more versatile.

days after the contest. I met Dudley and rode in his Scout to the desert rendezvous point some 150 miles south of Phoenix.

The following morning after a predawn desert-style breakfast, the bunch of us split into several groups of twos and threes for the day's hunting. Dudley asked me to make the first stand. I searched for a location as the vehicle slipped through the country. George Wright was with us. He sat on my left, Dudley to my right, both about twenty yards away as I began my series. Fresh from a full day of contest calling and a small amount of training beforehand, I leaned into that call with as snappy a version as a purple-pink Arizona dawn ever heard. My pattern was harsh and demanding, a distance-covering series that when finished left me well tuckered. But two big dog coyotes were down in the yellow ankle-deep grass and I felt pretty good.

Dudley made the next stand after spotting Wright and me some thirty yards on each side of his location, a bit farther than normal due to a natural ridge that formed an inverted broken Y. It was typical of Dudley, putting us where we had the edge and would no doubt get the shooting. When Dudley started calling — the first time I had ever heard him — I almost smirked. His pattern was subdued, artful in its pleading dialogue but a far cry from what I expected, especially after being dealt with severely for the past two years by his son, the strongest caller the sport has ever known. Dudley's call was almost lazy by comparison. To me it didn't convey excitement but it was long on realism. Wright and I dumped three dogs on that stand.

I said something to Dudley about it as we carried our game back to the truck. "Son," he said, "we're going to do a lot of calling in the next three days, no sense in getting licked and wore out in the first few hours. There's lots of country and lots of coyotes. They all hear real good and I'll last a lot longer this way." It was a lesson in style garnished with a good deal of class.

Once the technique of maintaining proper air pressure is developed coupled with standard time-proven patterns, the mouth caller can begin to experiment. Surprisingly, the greatest varieties in tone, technique and style can be accomplished with changes in hand and finger position over the barrel. For instance, grasping the call between the thumb and forefinger and controlling air pressure in the palm of one hand develops a singular tone. Holding the call just the same with less pressure cupped between two hands will totally change the sound and the individual's ability to maneuver it. Folding the call between the palms held almost flat over the mouthpiece, much like a harmonica player controls his instrument, produces a totally different tone pattern and control method. These and other hand positions, when blended with varied pressures controlled from deep within by the stomach muscles, are what makes a caller. Regardless of the type of call, all changes in sound, volume and tone are developed in this manner. Just as the accomplished fisherman meets the challenge of the day with a variety of lure patterns and colors until the right combination is found, the varmint caller must do the same to establish the pattern of the day. To be versatile and observant while maintaining disciplined patience guarantees success.

Whenever callers gather, the conversation gets around to calls and calling styles sooner or later. This is particularly true of contest callers and the armchair strategy can be amusing if not informative. Field calling is different than contest-style calling.

The contest caller has to put everything he knows into a call that lasts two minutes or less. Putting all you know into such limited time allocations is pretty tough.

Calling styles in the field vary greatly with the geographic location of the hunter. For example, Western style calling is long, loud and hard. Eastern and Southern calling is more subdued; by comparison it is almost weak, yet both styles and all the in-between methods will produce with equal efficiency. I suspect that it doesn't matter

Here is evidence that the same type of electronic recording will call both coyotes and bobcats within shooting range.

greatly how you blow your call as long as a few simple elements are included.

Too many callers who experience a noted lack of success fail simply because they are calling in areas where there is no game. It stands to reason that the incidence of success will be greatly enhanced if varmints are in the neighborhood. I have hunted with callers who as far as I was personally concerned had little calling ability, at least as far as style and class were concerned. These individuals racked up some pretty fair scores in the ratio of success per stand, however.

The reasons for this were simple. They were thoroughly woods-oriented. They knew that the game was in the area they had selected to hunt, as they had spent some serious time ascertaining that point. It is too easy to get excited about the potential of any sport and take off on a wild goose chase born of enthusiasm and doomed to failure for lack of preparation.

It is quite simple to take a drive off into the woods or deserts and try varmint calling. There is a fair element of potential success involved in this helter-skelter method. But being a helter-skelter hunter isn't going to get the job done time and time again. The wise hunter will begin a program of investigation; a check with game departments or with local farmers, stock and poultrymen doesn't hurt.

The rewards of this investigation will be an action plan of sorts. You will have come to some basic conclusions relative to the location of the game you want to hunt. In this type of game you can usually get people to talk about and be on the receiving end of some straight answers. It seems as though people are sometimes a little reluctant to give an inquiring lad the true picture on where the big bucks hang out or just how a bunch of turkeys are using a certain hollow, but they seem interested in letting out the whereabouts of a chicken-stealing fox.

The next step is to check it out yourself. Make a tour of the area and see if you can find evidence that substantiates your information. Determine you have been steered into the right country by virtue of sign that is easy to locate, then you're in business.

Such tactics are considerably more important in the East and Midwest than in the desert country of the far West. Foxes have to be psyched out in wood lots adjacent to farm areas and so on with more attention to detail than a western coyote, yet prehunt scouting pays off out here, too.

The type of game you're hunting here will adapt under pressure. They will change their habits and they will change their range. A place that was good last year will not be necessarily an automatic success area this season.

So before you decide that calling isn't all it's talked up to be or that perhaps you are not proficient enough on your whistle, make sure that where you are putting your effort is where the action really is.

Back in the early Fifties, when the calling game was relatively unknown, callers hit the field armed with one or two calls and went to work.

Generally, these calls were alike in pitch; one was simply a backup in case of reed failure. The pitch was usually coarse, loud and geared to simulate a jackrabbit. As the sport began to grow, commercial call manufacturers turned out an ever-increasing array of call models. These were not gimmicks designed to increase the dollar volume of a marketable sport. They were tested and proven instruments made by practicing varmint callers.

It wasn't long before callers began hitting the coyote flats with several calls. Talk of long-range and close-range calls became common around the desert campfires. The virtues of stainless steel versus brass reeds or the tonal qualities of wood barrels over plastic gave aficionados of the sport something to argue about and putter with. In short order, as the number of callers increased, so did their inventory of calling devices.

A caller who once had his entire call selection hanging from a leather lanyard around his neck suddenly found himself laden down with a tackle box containing more than a dozen models, several hundred extra reeds, turning jigs, and jewelers' files. The sport had reached its era of confusion. Callers suddenly were faced with the dilemma of what call to choose, then worried about whether their

Above: Jack Cain (left) shows George Wright how barrels for calls are turned out on a lathe. Right: Unfinished calls don't look particularly impressive as they come off the lathe, but much work is yet to be done on them.

selection was right for the type of country, phase of the moon and barometric pressure.

The one-call era had passed. Callers hit the field with clattering necklaces of reeded goodies rattling about their necks. Splattered with camo face paint and saturated with foul smelling scents, the new caller was about half a step away from being mistaken for a Zulu witch doctor.

When the confusion of one reed began to settle slightly, Wayne Weems threw the Dual-Tone into the hat. This was no gimmick either. Weems had done enough field testing to learn that the call, a common barrel with two reeds that blew simultaneously, really did a job. For a year after they came out I didn't figure that anything else would call a bobcat — depending on the country, the phase of the moon, and barometric pressure, of course!

To make things neater for all the fellows who were ripping their heads off when a rifle scope from a hastily shouldered sporter got hung up in the call necklace, Jack Cain introduced the Circe Pro model. A revolving barrel gave the caller a selection of three reeds with only a twist; long range (jackrabbit), medium (cottontail) and close range (squeaker) all in one call.

Today's caller has a huge selection from which to choose. Almost every major manufacturer of game calls includes at least one varmint number in his line, and there are the increasingly popular electronic rigs available from a host of manufacturers.

The new caller today is confused about which call to buy, which manufacturer makes the best calls. I am constantly receiving letters from folks who want to start calling. "Which is the best call to buy?" they ask.

All calls will work; no call will work all of the time. I believe that all the calls made by any manufacturer will do a good job under the right conditions and if there is an animal there that can hear the call and wants to come in. There is no one hundred percent situation, no one hundred percent call, no one hundred percent caller. I suggest that the serious caller have a wide range of calls, as the angler has baits.

He uses them all, he experiments and he learns. He keeps notes, be observes, he talks to other callers, he keeps calling and he continues to learn.

There is only one perfect call. The call that you use on a particular stand that calls a particular animal. At that point and time, you have the perfect call — depending on the type of country, phase of the moon, and barometric pressure!

Not long ago I heard from a fellow in Missouri who wanted to know what time of day I got on a stand to begin calling. The question was not unusual, but it called to mind the fact that a lot of folks really don't understand daytime calling.

In recent years there has been a strong trend to ignore daytime hunting. Perhaps it is the belief that the animals are nocturnal and therefore should only be hunted at night. In my opinion, this is not true. Varmints, especially coyotes, can be called easier in the daytime. Fox can also be called easily during the day, as can bobcats. The key is not only when to call, but where.

The secretive nature of the bobcat makes him reluctant to leave cover during the day. But it is not unusual to call cats in wide-open country, across large clearings, as long as the cat is not too far from his daytime security cover.

Fox are jittery by nature, but they can be lured into smaller openings, across short flats during the day, while at night they will run across a full mile of plowed field to see what's going on. The coyote will come across greater expanses of open ground during the day. It's his nature; he's a runner and hunter of open ground. He's the king in his range as a rule and relies on his eyes, ears and extreme speed to get him out of a jam.

The first simple solution to daytime calling for cats and fox is to get into the heavier cover. The question, however, is when. It is a fact that they will come to a proper set, so when do you set it?

Surprisingly, you can make your stands almost anytime during the day with a good percentage chance of success. However, the odds go up considerably in the morning hours, with midday being the low. The first three hours from shooting light are the absolute best. The last two hours before dark rate number two. Midday produces, but I personally would rather do something else, like take a nap.

The key to daytime hunting is the weather. Cool fall or winter days are best. Late Summer is the time when callers start to hunt in earnest. The weather is still warm, and by 8:30 or 9:00 the day's heat is building and the sun is bright. The heat puts the animals down just as it does the hunter. They are reluctant to move, especially long distances. If you persist in calling, take your hunt right to the animals, adjacent to thickets and washes for coyotes, and right into them for cats and fox.

As the sun rises, the roaming hunters are working back

to heavy cover. Calling the flats, broad canyons of the foothills, or the edges of farm fields is good sense. Many critters now are overeager; it's been a hard night and not too productive in the grocery department. A well-played call really turns them on. As the day brightens and the weather warms, they step up their pace to their security cover. In the first hours you've got everything going — moving animals, increasing light conditions, cool temperatures. Now you make your stands, hit them for fifteen or twenty minutes, then move quickly to the next. Four stands an hour is possible, but three is more realistic.

During peak movement periods coyotes most often appear between two to seven minutes; fox are the same, perhaps a little quicker, while bobcats seldom appear within the first five minutes and percentage-wise you probably will see him between ten and twenty — if you see him at all.

Gaining experience in varmint calling, when there is no one around to show you how, can be something of a hit-and-miss proposition, but this still is the way that many of us got our start.

A fellow out of Florence, Oregon, told me, "I've been calling varmints for about a year now and have had only limited success. The calls I use are two fox calls and a coon call.

"I seem to be able to call up herds of deer — does mostly — and a few owls, but hardly anything in the way of coyotes, foxes or bobcats. I use camouflage clothing and call mostly at night.

"This area is full of bobcats, coyotes and coons. We have few rabbits and the ones I see are small brush rabbits — smaller than cottontails."

On the surface, it appears that there are two possible solutions.

A change in the pitch in the call often is all it takes to bring in predators. In view of the fact that this gent has been able to call up deer, it might be wise for him to try calls with higher pitches, which would tie in more closely with the sounds of the native rabbits.

Dan Rider of Lompoc, California, used this novel rabbit decoy, complete with sound effects, to lure in this bobcat. He also took rare albino coyote with the rig, which he hopes to develop commercially for varminters.

VARMINT HUNTER'S DIGEST

George Allison displays a fine bag of gray fox, coyote and bobcat he took during weekend outing. Varmint calling, however, does little to reduce overpopulation of predators.

It is not, as a rule, necessary to imitate the rabbit native to the area. In fact, calls work well in areas where there are no rabbits, but where predators are reluctant to show themselves a high-pitched call often works.

The length of this caller's stand might enter into the problem, too. When results are poor, longer stands often are the key. I would suggest trying stands of thirty to forty minutes, particularly in areas that have a lot of bobcats. Coons are not as easy to call as coyotes and cats, however.

Night callers very often have a tendency to ignore wind conditions. This is a mistake and one should be constantly aware of the wind in relationship to his stand. Scent also can help.

I told all of this to my Oregon correspondent and he reported back that since making a switch to higher-pitch calls, he had had success with coyotes and cats that prior to that time had eluded him.

That brings up the old point of new sounds sometimes making all the difference in animal response. Further, it indicates that even in areas where calling is new, experimenting with different call levels is required to get the best results. Sometimes coyotes just don't dig those patented standard sounds.

I recall back quite a few years, when Wayne Weems first brought out the Dual-Tone call. At that time, calling pressures in no way compared to today's high level of competition for results. We were not having any problem with the old standards and daily outings generally produced fifty percent results per stand on coyotes. We sometimes experimented with a new sound at Weems' request more out of curiosity than for any need to improve on a good system.

Calling in the same country and changing nothing but the call, we noted some astonishing results. First, coyotes came in closer and in greater numbers. We credited the greater numbers to the time of year, but the increased closeness was not so easily explained.

Aside from this was the real clincher: the increase in bobcats. We had enjoyed the usual daytime ratio of the odd bobcat appearing now and then to add a little bonus-type spice. All of a sudden, they were popping up everywhere. We rolled three or four the first time out, which was virtually unheard of at that time.

Attempting to blend with his rocky surroundings, Doug Kittredge calls in the snow of the high Sierras of Northern California for predators.

Dan Rider's predator decoy has an internal call and is manipulated by means of string to make it hop up, down. The string also activates the predator call inside.

It seemed that the Dual-Tone was a real cat-grabber and the daylight kitties gave us some hairy moments. In the riverbed terrain we were hunting, visibility was varied from twenty to one hundred yards. Lots of knee-high cover made good blinds and it was no problem to spot a coyote bounding in big and bold jumping everything in sight. The cats, however, played peek-a-boo through the brush with several of them appearing at virtual touching distance before we saw them.

I recall one in particular that gave me a real thrill. Sitting with my back to a tree, I had my Sako .222 magnum lying across my lap, muzzle pointed in the direction I had anticipated action. One hand held the rifle by the pistol grip, while I used the other to call. Perhaps the level of my vision was too high, but I suddenly had that old feeling that I was not alone.

My company was a big cat sitting at the end of my barrel looking at my call hand. At the time, I had no doubt that if I so much as twisted a finger on that call hand, this cat was going to be in my pocket. The problem was solved simply by flicking the safety and pulling the trigger simultaneously. A cloud of dust at my feet set off by the muzzle blast, mixed with thrashing cat and ignited powder, was a small mushroom that slowly enveloped my head, leaving me totally in the dark as to what was going on.

My partner, sitting only thirty feet away, was convinced that I had shot myself and sprang to the rescue. For quite some time after that, we sat in trees and other safer places when calling.

There was just something about that pitch in those first days that really drove the critters goony. More than once we punched coyotes with the business end of the barrel as we jerked, not squeezed, the trigger. George Wright and Don McIntosh respectively shot a coyote and bobcat almost off my back and if they didn't save me from an attack with their gunning, they at least saved me a laundry bill.

Varmint callers have a tendency to become entrapped in the habit of calling too loud and long on each and every stand. The reasoning is obvious and practical: the caller intends to alert and attract everything within a mile radius of his stand.

However, callers become lost in a narrow little rut called volume and have a hard time getting out of the ditch. I have been guilty of this, as have most of my experienced calling partners.

With the rookie callers it really can be a problem, because he hears so much emphasis placed on volume. But a caller, operating constantly with the loud call technique, can scare off almost as many critters as he attracts. Obviously this depends on the country being hunted. Loud calling in tight country is the most commonly committed error. Overly loud calling at night is the second offender in scaring game away.

I recently made a trip with a couple of Kansas callers who used nothing but super-loud calls. Their logic was fairly good, given the wide-open areas and the fact that they were used to hunting and calling in breezy-to-stiff wind conditions. I rolled them into some chapparal and chemise-covered broken country not far from Los Angeles. It was mostly choppy draws and short canyons heavily brushed with four to six-foot cover, bisected by fire breaks and packed with intermittent clearings. It was tight.

Loud calling here was a poor bet. My two friends began to figure this out when on the second stand a coyote appeared, well within a hundred yards, heading in the wrong direction just as fast as his legs could move him. On a later stand, again with the loud pattern, a coyote that came across a ridge out of the next canyon likewise skedaddled when the caller, who was pausing, reopened his series. That particular dog was coming in slow, a characteristic of the coyotes that frequent this type of cover. He was about to cross into a clearing out of the brush that was screening his approach making a shot with a bullet inclined to fragment at the slightest provocation unrealistic. He was in my scope when the ear shattering series, which I could hardly believe, ruptured the atmosphere. It was instant high gear and departure and nary a shot was loosed. I figured that perhaps the only one aware of the coyote's approach was me — although I also figured my partner was aware that I was poised to shoot. I was right and wrong.

He had seen the coyote once and knew I was trying for a clear shot. His intent was to bring him on in for collection. We readjusted after that and they learned a thing or two about close cover calling and the sensitivity of a coyote's hearing equipment. For the balance of the hunt we used nothing but squeaker-type calls. Our success was good as we called up six coyotes during the balance of the day. Two of these, however, came from ranges of six to seven hundred yards, straight in to low-volume, high-pitch squeakers.

The low-pitch and squeaker calls are highly underrated by callers for use as a primary call. They are employed simply as a coaxer in those final seconds before a shot. As cited, the squeaker is effective as a primary call in heavy cover. Where most people are missing a bet is using the squeaker or lower volume calls even in the wide-open spaces. On a quiet morning a coyote will respond to these calls from surprising distances.

A friend up in Alberta has been getting after the calling in what has to be some super-prime coyote country. One Fall I made a trip up there with the idea of trying to collect a bighorn sheep. Dave Richardson was my hunting companion, along with some gentlemen from the game department.

The country was plump with four-legged coyote critters

and we saw several in the first few miles of driving into the mountains. Their tracks in the new snow around camp crisscrossed in every direction. At night, the little wolves serenaded us to sleep and we sighted more than a few as we glassed the upper ridges in search of bighorns. It got to be a distraction; the place was stiff with big, beautiful coyotes with coats seldom seen in the parts of the country where the critters and I have played the game. The idea of collecting one became almost as important as bagging a ram.

On an off day we made a few stands and the coyotes responded with enthusiasm. The only problem was getting one to hold still long enough to become a pelt. None of them did, nor did a sheep wind up as a trophy either, but that's another story.

The offshoot of this bit of background was Richardson's later report. He and the game department types got pretty hyped up on the calling game. The fact that coyotes were bringing their best price in years on the fur market added incentive.

The boys were not doing too badly getting coyotes to respond, but they were having trouble drawing them into good range for a shot. Their problem here is that they are hunting in an archery-only area — a bow zone by Provincial decree — and firearms were taboo. Even outside the area, the crafty dogs were not providing good shooting conditions, staying out and not displaying enough hair in the heavy bush and timber country.

Richardson suggested perhaps they were calling too loud and wondered if that might be the problem. I agreed that the type of cover and the terrain makes loud calling the wrong approach.

The area being hunted was canyon bottoms and narrow valleys heavily timbered and surrounded by granite crags. The sound of a call bounces around in this type of country like a superball and the echoes roll forever. The confusion factor for anything following up the call is considerable. The Canadian's approach was getting some results but the animals were becoming confused, then suspicious. Brushy conditions demand a quiet approach.

With the exception of the opening series when I was calling the country earlier, the balance of the stand was carried out with high pitch calls blown with subdued volume. For that matter, the opener probably was delivered at a volume ratio of fifty percent less than normal; just a quick attention getter, but not loud enough to scare off the game and keep echoes at a minimum.

Over the years we have perhaps placed entirely too much emphasis on the opening series of calling and generally have stressed that this should be delivered with great gusto designed to wake up every living thing for miles around. Not a bad philosophy, it has proved the undoing of more coyotes than a handful. By comparison, far too little has been said about the effectiveness of the close-range calls and squeaker types. They, too, deserve their place in calling as tools to be used at the beginning and not always at the end of a stand.

The problems of calling coyotes in the woods of Alberta bear this out. Sure, drop down to those miles of rolling hills and broad flat plains and one would be well advised to get back to the stuff that puts out the big noise. But in the timber, squeak a lot and you'll get more chances to collect that fur piece.

Dougherty heads for home after a long day in the desert with a prize bobcat that had been raiding small stock on the ranch of a friend. Varmint callers tend to aid in keeping such predators under control in some areas.

Proper techniques for using the call can take time. As explained in text, many beginners tend to call too loud, frightening away the quarry.

There's one more problem. Getting a coyote to come in that heavy bush is only half the battle. If you want to collect him, you have to put him where you can shoot. Stands must be picked with care and they cannot be set to bring a coyote across wide openings as a rule. Desert coyotes cross miles of open country coming to a call; woods coyotes will cross big openings — some of the time. There's something in the nature of these heavy cover inhabitants that makes them think twice about crossing the wide open when responding to a call, so play the odds and keep away from that approach.

Instead, pick your stands along well-defined coyote trails. These will be game trails traveled by all the woods creatures, easy to read. Old logging roads are good and they'll come along the edges at a trot and they use creek beds well, too. Elevated calling positions are good; a portable tree blind can be handy, but a camouflaged ladder placed against a bushy evergreen or broad-based tree trunk takes less time and is an excellent calling location.

So, if you're callin' the timber and heavy bush with nothing to show for it but an occasional glimpse of a sulking patch of cautious fur, call tiny and change your luck.

In recent years, electronic or portable game calling units of various designs have gained increasing popularity among the calling fraternity. Old-line callers still maintain that the mouth-operated call is more efficient than mechanical rigs and it certainly is a greater test of skill.

A mouth-operated call does require more skill to operate than a mechanical unit, but there is a question when it comes to the subject of efficiency. The argument perhaps is predicated on taste, not unlike the fly purist who looks down his nose at one who would have the audacity to dunk a foul, slimy worm in a favored trout run.

The point is a comparison of apples and oranges, for either style is game calling with a common objective. Like the two on the stream who desire to catch a large trout, they share the same desires but have elected to use varied approaches to the same end. I have seen the day when a mouth caller couldn't buy the first varmint, while a man in the same general country did well with a portable tape recorder. And I have seen the direct opposite when the caller with the taped renditions of trembling rabbits in frightful situations would have blown his caller apart had it not represented a substantial investment.

Electronic callers are available in a great many styles today. The majority are continuous tape units run off of transistorized tape recorders with built-up amplifiers. The purchaser of a portable unit has a choice of several types of tapes, ranging from the standard rabbit cries to such exotics as the last gasp of a rapidly expiring woodpecker. This variety of available calls is what brings the portable unit into real focus with the serious callers, who today have to compete with more and more callers and call-wise varmints.

Callers tend to agree that animals become call wary after a season or continued seasons of hunting pressure. There are those who contend that new generations of coyotes, for instance, are taught by their parents to be cautious in approaching sounds. Having more than a little respect for the canny abilities of the critters, I don't doubt this, for I have seen cases where I would have sworn the coyotes really had been to school. On the other hand, there are those who will tell you an area is called out, overhunted and the coyotes all but extinct where there used to be hundreds.

If varmint calling is the only pressure to which they have been subjected, it is more of a case of animal education than overgunning. To erradicate coyotes is no simple task and varmint hunters are just not going to accomplish it.

Electronic calls have two real market sources: the beginner who does not understand mouth-operated calls and the experienced caller who feels the need for a new approach. In other words, electronic calls fit right into the picture; they are made to order for a varmint caller.

Many aspiring callers attempt to lure game with the mouth-operated calls and experience marginal to zero success. They know that animals can be called and blame it on their calling. They become a candidate for a mechanical call. It will not necessarily make them expert callers overnight, because regardless of the bait, you still have to fish it in the right place at the right time. This takes experience more than equipment so do not be misled into thinking that any portable unit will work automatically even if you turn it on in your living room.

Successful calling takes a fair amount of research no matter what you use. The caller who does poorly with a mouth call possibly will not do a lot better with a portable unit except by virtue of continued effort, increased study of the problems and a positive approach, as he seeks the answer.

It becomes simply a matter of success coming to him who works for it. If, by the time you achieve that success, you have been using a portable caller, then you would credit more than the proper share of your new success to the electronic caller. Were you to go back to the mouth calls, you would probably do just as well.

The wide variety of sounds that can be purchased to supplement the tape recorder callers is another story and here is where the experienced varmint hunter finds a need for a mechanical unit. It is tough to develop mouth calls that have such wide ranges of sounds and tougher to learn to use them. These new sounds, however, can make a world of difference when hunting call-shy coyotes.

Moving into an area that has been under tough calling and gunning pressure with an entirely new sound can really open your eyes. Coyotes here may have learned by having their rears scorched by passing high-velocity bullets that a rabbit in distress should be treated with caution. But they can be suckers for a new dinner gong sound in the form of a terror-stricken baby bluejay.

The distress cries of birds work extremely well on coyotes, bobcats and foxes. They work in areas that some hunters would swear on a stack of .243 brass had no coyotes left. The approach is also different, as the style of calling is quieter, the tempo slower and the animal's reaction not quite so audacious. So, who cares? It is better to have them come in a new way than perhaps not at all.

Varmint callers have taken a fair amount of flak over the last few years but no calling group has had quite as tough a row as the electronic crowd.

Those who use electronic calling devices and those who make them have had their backs to the wall for some time and, in certain parts of the land, the fight gets tougher. It's unfortunate, but the electric guys have had about as much hassle internally, if you will, from other callers as they've had from the do-gooders that scream "murder, decimation of the species and diabolical, unethical hunting methods." Doesn't seem to matter what it is anymore; someone's just going to take a poke at you for doing something you like and they don't.

I've taken a pop or two at electronic calls, but directed at the way they have been used, not the concept of those devices which, in my opinion, is good. On the other hand, electronic calls used in what might be termed an immoral manner have caused more than a few problems for serious callers and conscientious sportsmen.

Certain factions among calling groups got in the habit of mobilizing their efforts to such a degree of sophistication that resemblance between their activities and that of the dyed-in-the-wool callers was almost nonexistent.

Then, too, there was the concern that electronic calling devices, when employed on certain types of game, were devastating. Anyone who was in the electronic game when it was first used — then banned, fortunately — on migratory waterfowl will recall their almost unbelievable efficiency. Members of the varmint family are not nearly as gullible as feathered game.

Al Abbot displays an average-size desert coyote in the type terrain which these predators seem to like. A flat-shooting rifle is necessary for the longer ranges of desert.

Problems aside, the electronic call industry has prospered and the equipment has improved. Today's caller/consumer, who wishes to give it a go with the flick of a switch rather than a blast of hot air, has a selection from which to choose that can be pretty confusing.

The best improvement in my book has been the change from records to cassettes, as the latter seems easier to keep in shape with less clutter and damage to the record. One of the biggest problems was keeping records clean and undamaged. When dirty, there was distortion, scratchy noises, etc., that could not help in luring a smart varmint. Once, in a fairly furious crow shoot, an empty hull bounced on the slowly turning record and destroyed the platter for all eternity. There was another time, again on a crow-smoking expedition when, in turning and backing to

and his tackle box of reeded whistles. Playing times average thirty minutes, long enough to make just about any stand, and they can be switched for another thirty or to a different pattern easily and quietly enough so there's no problem there.

One major advantage is the freedom of movement the portables afford. Another point was brought out by a long-time calling friend with a heart condition. Strenuous hunting and calling is tough on a body and if you're a fanatic, you can wear the strongest to the ground. For this fellow, the electronic call has been a lifesaver and he has been able to continue his favorite sport on his beloved desert.

Johnny Stewart, down in Waco, Texas, has a line of some of the most sophisticated equipment and offers a fine

Varmint hunters must remember that use of electronic calls may be adversely viewed by public. Caution should be exercised when using discs or taped predator calls available from suppliers such as Burnham Brothers of Marble Falls, Texas.

nail an escaping high overhead bird, a size 10 boot came down on the center of the whole unit. That really did in the caller!

Portable units today have other adaptations which should be considered when making an investment. There's a good amplifying system built into most. Included are high fidelity for varmint calling and big volume for long-range crow hunting. Most use D2 batteries, are easily portable and lightweight in plastic cases that blunt abuse.

With a portable unit, a caller can outfit himself with a complete range of calling recordings; there's one for every occasion to put you up with the experienced mouth caller

line of calling instruction records and tapes. As a woodsman — the man has few peers — he knows of what he speaks and game calling electrically or mouth-blown is his game. Some of Stewart's recordings are new and different and as effective as any can be. Likewise, the Burnham Brothers from Marble Falls, Texas, have been long-time producers of all things calling oriented; they, too, offer top-quality portable rigs.

The electronic rig is a fine piece of sporting equipment and, wisely used, it will be around for a long time. Misuse it and it could be outlawed. If it goes, so most likely will go mouth calls and the sport.

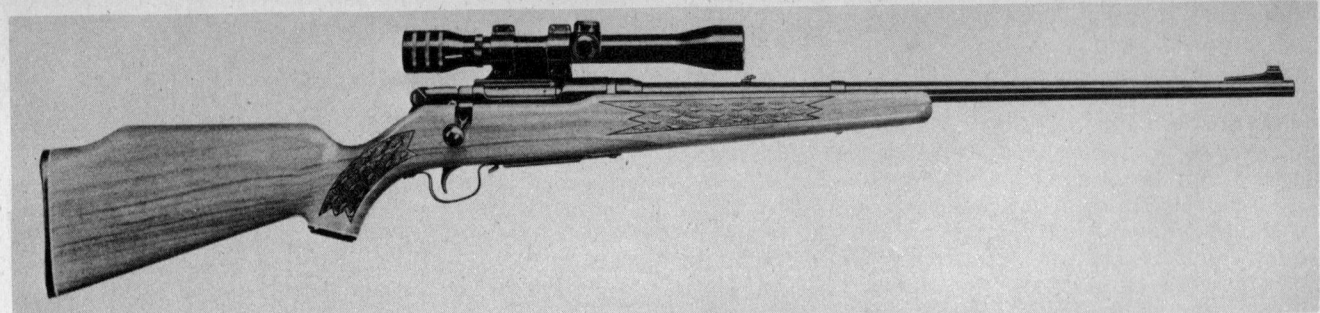

Choice Of Rifles Is A Personal Matter; Dougherty Prefers .22 Caliber For Good Reasons

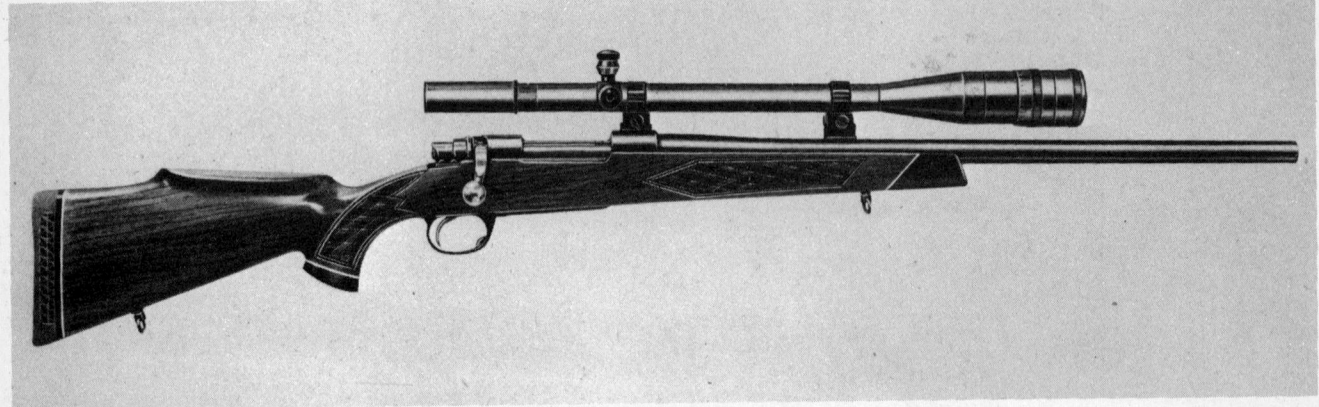

The Savage Model 340-S (top) is available in .222 Rem chambering for the hunter, while the Jana Parker-Hale varmint model (above) is produced in .22-250. Jim Dougherty explains in text why he favors the .22 caliber.

Chapter 4

RIFLES FOR VARMINTS

A RIFLE EXPERT I am not. What technical statements I might make from time to time are most often relatively simple or pilfered from data supplied by the makers, if it is mechanical. If we're talking about mixtures of powder and lead, they are supplied by the professional bullet folks and the GUN WORLD pros like Cotterman and Grennell who have always lent an enthusiastic hand whenever a new rifle came our collective way.

As a user I am somewhat better in that I can shoot them reasonably well in the field and with moderate skill when pinpoint groups are required to determine optimum performance. When it comes to things that shoot, my long suit has always been the bow and arrow and the shotgun. However, I have spent a reasonable amount of time afield with a rifle in the particular pursuit of the category of game which this book is all about, with attention most heavily placed on the order of animals that can be effectively called to the hunter. As a result I have developed some personal opinions based on use and observation.

When it comes to this area I am, and no doubt forever will be, an advocate of the .22 caliber in its varied configurations. If one choice was given I would settle on the .222 magnum as being the ideal cartridge for the calling hunter. Admittedly it has some shortcomings, but what doesn't?

During the many years when, as organized varmint callers, collecting data was in vogue, the .243 led the list of favorites by a healthy margin; and a fine choice it is. In the long haul I suspect my affinity for the smaller bores has been based on its clean killing capabilities without undue damage to hide and hair.

The .222 and the big-brother magnum are not long-range cartridges comparatively speaking. Based on personal hunting experience, and that of many others, it would seem that most shots are inside of fifty yards while calling. Long-range performance is not the issue.

For years I have favored the 50-grain Hornady SX ahead of 27 grains of 4895 as a superb combination for accuracy

The .22 caliber rifle, Dougherty believes, is the most useful varmint rifle for two reasons: if the hunter is good, he'll have only less-than-50-yard shots to make, and for certain game, he wants undamaged fur.

from my Sako with super-instant kill results. As I have always been a collector of hides for a variety of reasons, the tidy results have contributed to my pleasure in the load.

My first varmint rifle was a Model 70 in .220 Swift, a cartridge that received accolades and abuse from a variety of gun experts over the years. It was unquestionably a hot number and my tendency was to keep it as hot as various reload combinations would allow. In not too short order I removed most of the doo-dads in the barrel required for consistency and blew nearly everything I shot with it to kingdom come. I found it disturbing to throw down on a prime coyote, do him in and wonder thereafter where most of his hide had disappeared to.

I like the .22/250 quite well, but usually have loaded it down a bit to almost slow velocities in order to maintain my penchant for sending a critter to his reward while allowing his carcass to retain some dignity. This dialog may seem strange to some and disturbing to others, nevertheless, I have a personal position on this. I know folks who are disturbed if it doesn't rain coyote hair for a week when they trigger a government dog. This has never been my cup of tea, and from a purely greedy point of view makes even less sense today when good coyotes can net the collector up to $65. This is not the basis for my point, but is worthy of consideration.

The .223 has increased in popularity due largely, I suspect, to the abundance of government ammo that seems to be available. I have used this on coyotes and found it satisfactory, although still a bit harsh. Yet this caliber can be neatly set up by the reloader and performs on a par with the .222 magnum.

Tastes vary. That's why we have blondes and brunettes, chocolate and vanilla. The issue of what is the best varmint rifle or load will never be agreed upon. Individuals form opinions based on their preferences in forms of performance. Certainly there are multitudes of combinations that are excellent. For me the combination cited works beautifully and the .22-250 loaded up to normal levels handles the cases where longer range calling and shooting conditions can be expected. Throughout this book we discuss a wide range of options. Choose what suits you best and get out to enjoy one of our finest hunting opportunities.

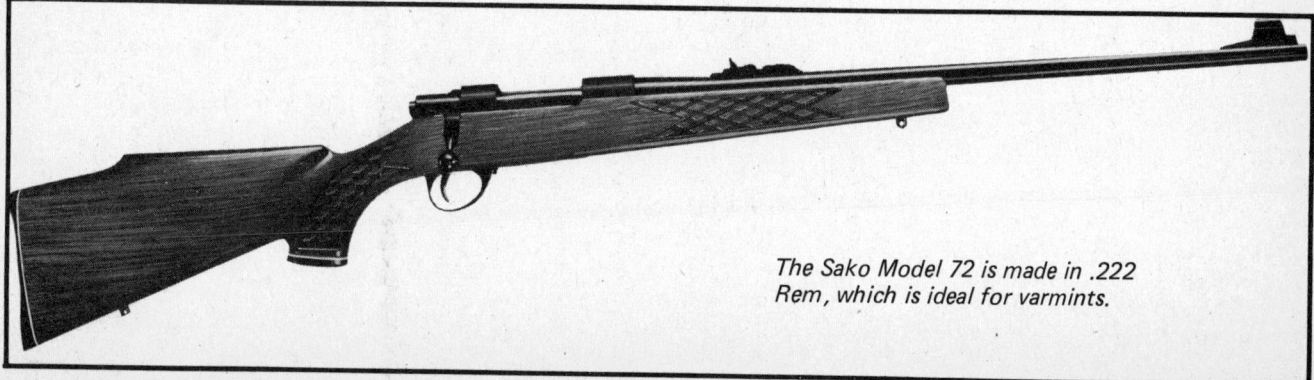

The Sako Model 72 is made in .222 Rem, which is ideal for varmints.

VARMINT HUNTER'S DIGEST

The .30/06 As A Varmint Rifle

THE .30/06 is a time-honored, revered caliber generally thought of in terms of shooting critters on the long side of one hundred pounds, sporting big-game growths of some description on their heads.

Varmint shooting is a pastime that is pursued most often by the rifleman who prefers a little bit of bullet with considerable oomph behind it to make it go fast and do all sorts of super things while in transit, not to mention what takes place on arrival.

Varmint hunting is the rifle game in which we are involved most often when talk around the desert campfire turns to shooting; velocities, bullet performance, sectional density, etc.

Seldom, if ever, does the ol' '06 get much of a mention among the aficionados of the .22 to .25-caliber fraternity whose primary mission in life is pinpoint accuracy on long-range ground squirrels and prairie dogs or putting the lead on a coyote moving fast out across an alkali flat. Among these dyed-in-the-wool types, there is no doubt a tendency to lift the upper lip in a sneer of disdain, should someone in the outfit have the audacity to mention anything larger than .25 caliber, and most often the only time you can say "06" is when it is preceded by that same numerical description of twenty-five; if you happen to be a shooter of a .25/06, you probably are going to be considered to be at the least an extremely cool cat.

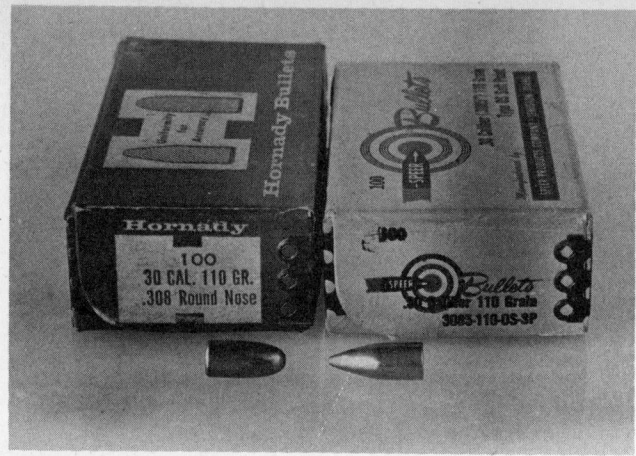
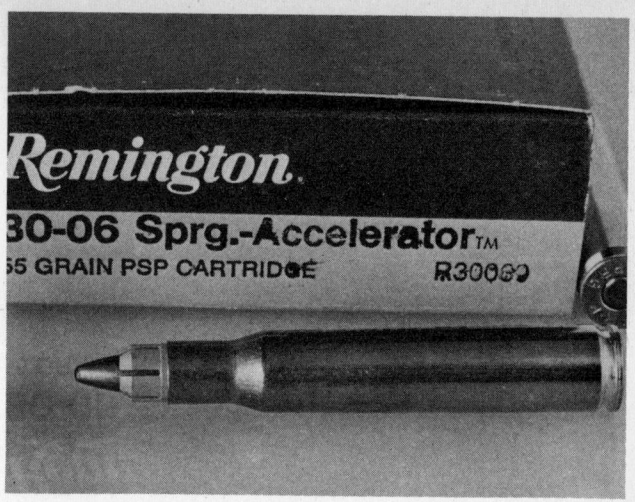

A number of bullet manufacturers turn out .30 caliber bullets in weights that are ideal for varmint hunters. Most are in the 100-grain area, but the latest (above) is the Accelerator, a Remington innovation which uses a .30/06 case for purposes of launching a 55-grain bullet.

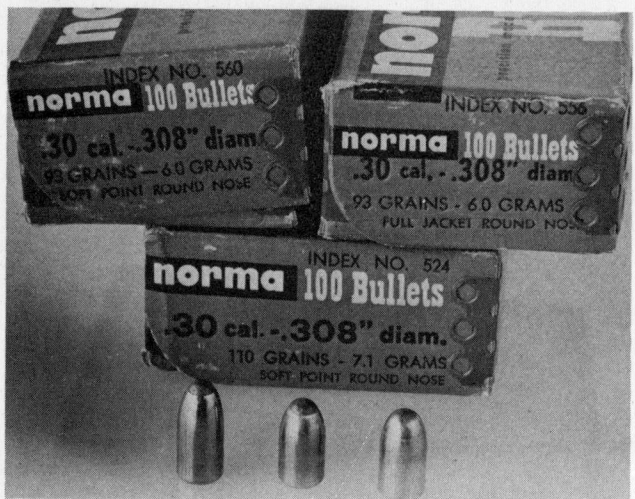

powder-burning individuals usually maintains one time-worn, tenderly loved piece with which they blaze away at whatever happens to be the object of attention at the time. My experience indicates that more of these average American shooters are burning their powder down .30 caliber barrels than anything else, although the steadfast .270 is lying in there pretty close.

The reason for all of this is in answer to the often-asked question: "What is wrong with my .30/06 for shooting varmints? Why doesn't anybody use it?"

Well, the answer to that, pure and straight, is that there just ain't a thing wrong with the .30/06. If the truth were known, there really has been more than an occasional coyote sent to his reward with a boost that began on the short end of some .30 caliber barrels.

Pausing to reflect back better than a decade, when pursuit of the varmints became an important thing to me, I recall that those in our circle of shooting associates, introduced to serious critter busting for the first time, were utilizing old favorites that had been doing their job for years. In most instances it happened to be a .30/06. Would you believe that George Wright and I were shooting .30-30s in the genuine lever-action John Wayne model? Admittedly, we relied heavily on firepower with accuracy being perhaps second on the list of the most important requirements.

A poll of weekend shooters out busting jackrabbits in the mesquite and sand-covered vastness of the Mojave Desert revealed that better than fifty percent of those whaling away with center-fires were doing it with the '06. Bearing in mind that the average shooter is a guy who only gets out on a handful of weekends a year to do his thing, I do not find this to be too surprising. Most of those who have graduated into the varminting fraternity and have, as a result, become hooked on calling were once of this same breed and began their varmint-busting careers armed with the family deer rifle. Once hooked with the sport, the armament refinements come about that have typified the breed of woolly cat who spends long days and even longer nights tooting on a call and staring endlessly across the country that might produce a reward for his efforts.

With some of these thoughts in mind, I pulled a Husqvarna Imperial model out of my gun rack.

It would be a fairly accurate guess, however, that, in spite of all the to-do about varminting and the appropriate firepower, to become a purist at the game, more critters in the varmint category from squirrels to coyotes get popped at with calibers over .25 than under. Among this listing, the '06 probably is standing the tallest in the pile. Twenty years ago or even maybe a bit more, before the .243 became the number one caliber in varminters' gun cabinets, countless thousands of guys were shooting a bunch of rounds tossed out of the "meat sticks" for their off-season shooting sport.

There are now and will continue to be more part-time off-season shooters, who are one-gun owners, than there are true purists in the varmint-shooting game. This army of

Most varmint hunters, knowing their rifles will be scoped, prefer barrels that are without sights. For long moves from stand to stand, sling swivels are a must.

I then formed a rather interesting handful of fodder for the Husqvarna, none of which fell into what is considered varmint ranges as far as bullet weight is concerned, the lightest being 150 grains.

The '06 does not have the flat trajectory and velocity retention capabilities of the lighter calibers, particularly in cartridges with bullets ranging in weights up to 180 grains. So, being slightly bent in the bullet weight department, I slipped by to see Bob Hayden at Sierra Bullet who passed me a handful of 168 HP bullets to concoct to my best ability.

The sexy little rifle was topped with one of Weaver's 600 scopes in the Classic series. The 6-power was my favorite all-around lens size.

It was not so much that I felt this .30/06 was not a rifle caliber suitable for shooting varmints as it was the point that nothing in excess of 55-grain bullets is required really to put a coyote or other member of the order on the ground for keeps with minimum fuss and muss. The larger bullet proportions of the .30 caliber material look to be excessive in the destructive power required to dump animals in the twenty to thirty-pound class. Putting the same material together for popping squirrels and jackrabbits conjured up pictures of instant target fragmentation.

The average shooter who utilizes the '06 as a varminter is a guy who does so to prepare his shooting eye, rifle, scope and sundry loads in readiness for the forthcoming big-game seasons. No matter what, the '06 is not, in my opinion, a varmint man's varmint rifle.

With this in mind, I assaulted the task as though tuning up a rifle on varmints, utilizing the material that would be employed normally on bigger game with bullets in the 150 to 180-grain range. The cartridges for the task — other than the handloads worked up with the Sierra bullets — were factory-loaded Federal 150-grain soft points and an equal portion of Speer 180-grain soft points.

The following Sunday found me sipping coffee with Harold Arnold in the snug warmth of his bunkhouse, waiting for the sun to crack the eastern gloom. Both of us suppressed yawns, while my son hand polished his supply of .218 Bee ammo, hoping a crack at a coyote would come as soon as the old-timers got through with the predawn bull session.

As it turned out, the coyotes in the area were not super cooperative, failing to present a target to lay large amounts of lead upon and, after three stands, we decided that jackrabbits would offer more action, while the warming day would soon have the ground squirrels out in force. Thinning out the latter pests would have some long-range effects on Arnold's wheat crop, which had grown to super proportions and drawn in an abundance of the pesky rodents that put away considerable quantities of a rancher's cash crop.

With my son Jimmy armed with the .218, Arnold toting his favorite .224 and I the bigger, more volatile .30/06, our trio circumnavigated the grain fields, kicking the long-eared jacks out ahead to be harassed by the symphony of "pop - spanggg - ka-whoom" in order of size and authority. Several were hurried on their way before the .30/06 caught up with one topping a slight rise at medium range. The resulting carnage brought the comment, "A little too much gun!"

In spite of the excessive firepower, the Husqvarna was a lightweight delight when it came to the fast swinging required to move the barrel along with and out in front of one of nature's most demanding targets. The weight of the piece, 8¼ pounds, did not seem to deliver unpleasant recoil for this type of shooting. However, when I began shooting from a solid rest at ground squirrels digging up a smooth hill across a 150-yard valley, the recoil naturally became more noticeable. Twice I caught myself in the act of

Good checkering on either a factory or custom rifle often is favored for its positive holding benefits.

flinching, but it should be reminded that I've been spoiled and softened by the gentle nudging of nothing more severe than an occasional belt from a .22-250.

Son Jimmy, however, had not yet developed narrow horizons, when it came to armament, and he found the lightweight easy to handle even though slightly long stocked. He was successful in shooting it quite comfortably and with his usual accuracy, which for several years has had many of his father's friends tearing their hair. This pointed out the fact that, if one does know how to mount and handle a gun properly, the Husqvarna is gentle enough on the smaller shooters and surprisingly easy to handle; food for thought for those wanting to outfit the little lady or the kids with a big-game rifle.

For shooting over ranges from fifty to 250 yards, the Weaver Classic was ideally suited in the 6-power to really snuggle in on shots at targets that, when standing, offered little more than two inches in width and were scarcely more than ten inches high. When it came to holding them in, shot after shot, the capabilities of the Husqvarna gunsmiths were obvious.

Blowing his call, Dougherty clutches the .30/06, while his son watches for a coyote with his old .218 Bee.

VARMINT HUNTER'S DIGEST

A compact portable shooting bench and takedown target frame can be taken afield for checking out the sights on the .30/06 and adjustment for anticipated distances.

I had concocted some handloads with the Sierras which, according to the material available, would give me about a long jump or so over 2800 fps. This was about the same apparently as all the other ammo, although slightly ahead of the 180-grain loads. Still, no correction in hold at the ranges being shot seemed to be required.

It was unfortunate that some loads could not have been brewed with lighter bullets simply to provide more material — and more ammunition for the group to shoot — for by 11 a.m. we were down to the last dregs of our supply. A great many wheat eaters had been sent along their way to the great rodent romping ground in the sky by the combined firepower of the Fearsome Threesome.

As I launched one of the last remaining 180-grain "mortars," as Arnold called them, across the canyon, I asked that individual what his impression of the .30/06 and the Husqvarna as a varmint rifle/caliber might be.

Arnold eased his Stetson up slightly above the center of his forehead, eyes squinting to pick out some trace of a large white rock that only seconds ago had been intact, complete with squirrel sitting atop. Nothing remained saving a drifting whitish cloud that was being borne down the canyon on the rising thermal of a warming day.

Pausing reflectively to remove a wheat straw from his mouth, still staring at the disappearing puff, he replied, "Very thorough!"

When we think of a varmint rifle and cartridge, our visualization is one of a relatively lightweight bullet, traveling at high velocity, with a flat trajectory to extended distances. At the same time, the general specifications include a bullet designed to expand decisively upon impact; preferably, a bullet that disintegrates, thus preventing the hazard of ricochets.

The .30/06 Springfield — one of this country's most common and popular center-fire rifle cartridges — usually is encountered with bullets in the weight class of 150 to 180 grains, with velocities on the order of 2600 to 3000 feet per second, respectively. Such ammunition can be used on varmints, but its performance is less than optimum.

The factory load with the lightest bullet is offered by Winchester-Western: a 110-grain JSP — they call it a pointed soft point — which goes from the muzzle to five hundred yards with velocities and energies given at increments of one hundred yards: 3380/2843/2365/1936/1561 and 1261 fps; 2790/1974/1366/915/595 and 388 foot-pounds. If sighted for point of aim at two hundred yards, impact will be three inches low at 250 yards and eight inches low at three hundred yards; 25.5 and 57.4 inches are the respective drops at four hundred and five hundred yards.

Both W-W and Remington-Peters list a .30/06 load with a 125-grain JSP bullet and ballistic chart listings are identical for this cartridge from either maker, across the board and to the last foot-pound. Velocities — as before — are 3140/2780/2447/2138/1853 and 1595 fps; energies are 2736/2145/1662/1269/953 and 706 foot-pounds. Trajectory of the 125-grain .30/06 factory load is slightly flatter than that given for the 110-grain W-W load, showing 2.5 inches less drop at four hundred yards and nine inches less at five hundred.

Late in 1976, Remington introduced their .30/06 Accelerator load: a novel concept that launches a 55-grain JSP bullet of .224-inch diameter at a muzzle velocity quoted as 4080 fps. Muzzle energy is 2033 foot-pounds and 356 at five hundred yards. That's about half the energy of the regular 125-grain .30/06 load, but the gain lies in the flattened trajectory. If the Remington .30/06 Accelerator is sighted for point of aim at 250 yards, it will be 1.8 inches high at one hundred, 2.1 inches high at 150, 1.5 inches high at 200, and 2.7 inches low at three hundred. In effect, you

Groups fired before and after scope adjustment show the benefits of preliminary target checking before the hunt.

38

VARMINT HUNTER'S DIGEST

With the slightly heavier bullets, such as Hornady 130-grain JSP or Speer 130-grain JHP, the highly popular .30/06 comes into its own as a long-range varmint walloper.

can hunt targets as small as a ground squirrel, with fur in the crosshairs, from point blank range to three hundred yards. It is rare to encounter trajectories markedly flatter than that.

For the varmint hunter who reloads, the .30/06 can be used to good advantage. Speer offers a 110-grain JHP design they call the Varminter, featuring a generous expanse of exposed lead around the nasal orifice. In the few years of its brief career to date, this bullet has won an enviable reputation for reliable expansion at extreme distances. For shorter ranges, Speer's 100-grain Plinker design often can be used to good effect. The rear half of the Plinker is encased in a jacket of the usual gilding metal, leaving the front half with its rounded lead nose fully exposed. For the longer ranges, Speer carries a 110-grain JSP with a spire point designed to minimize velocity loss from wind resistance. A fourth Speer design for the varmint hunter is their 130-grain JHP.

Speer's No. 9 reloading manual gives data for velocities to 3448 fps for their Plinker, to 2865 for their 110-grain Varminter, to 3375 for their 110-grain spire point and to a maximum of 3110 fps for their 130-grain JHP. All of these are maximum velocities and should be approached with caution, as noted in the manual. Accompanying figures show the corresponding tautness of trajectories for the four Speer bullet designs. Assuming the rifle is sighted to hit the point of aim at two hundred yards, the drop at three hundred yards will be 12.9 inches for the Plinker, 20.9 for the Varminter, 6.1 for the spire point and 8.0 inches for the 130-grain JHP.

This points up the marked significance of the ballistic coefficient of the given bullet. The ballistic coefficient is a numerical factor denoting the comparative rate of velocity loss due to wind resistance. The 110-grain spire point, with its ballistic coefficient of .273, will retain its velocity better than the 110-grain Varminter with its ballistic coefficient of .113 or the 100-grain Plinker with its .117 ballistic coefficient. The Speer 130-grain JHP has a ballistic coefficient of .254; slightly less favorable than that of the 110-grain spire point.

Hornady makes a 100-grain Short Jacket in the .308-inch diameter used in the .30/06, comparable to the Speer Plinker, with a ballistic coefficient of .130; a 110-grain spire point (.256 BC) and a 130-grain spire point (.292 BC). The Hornady Handbook lists respective maximum velocities for their three varmint bullets at 3300, 3400 and 3300 fps. A comprehensive series of ballistic tables in the back of the Hornady Handbook gives full downrange specifications for each of these bullets in increments of one hundred yards, based upon given muzzle velocities in increments of 100 fps.

It should be obvious that a certain amount of test firing will be necessary to establish comparative performance of factory loads and reloads out of any specific rifle. Even guns that are nominally identical may not perform identically with the same load. A moderate amount of comparison testing on conventional paper targets quickly serves to pin down the preferences and prejudices of the individual rifle. A portable benchrest and knockdown target frame that can be taken afield will prove helpful in such testing. Space permitting, the target can be moved to various distances so as to make experimental verification of trajectory data from reference sources.

Do not be surprised if test firing shows moderate departure from paper ballistics. Minor variations in factors such as bore dimensions, bore wear, ambient temperature, et al., can contribute to such things. The important thing is to find out where your rifle shoots, what it shoots the best and how to employ it most efficiently. Having done so, let the varmints beware.

The Modern Mountain Men

MOUNTAIN MEN opened the Old West. They hunted, trapped and traded until civilization moved in, then they moved out, since most were loners.

The mountain men of today are the professional hunters and trappers hired to maintain predator control in range country. Often referred to as government hunters, their job is to reduce the predators that harass the ranchers and thus keep the loss of sheep and cattle to a minimum in their assigned districts. Regardless of how they work, most are required to spend a great deal of time alone. Occasionally, though, they team up or pool their dogs for a varmint, if the need arises. These latter-day mountain men aren't loners by choice but by occupation, and the work tends to draw those who can enjoy being alone in beautiful country.

State-employed trappers and hunters of Colorado gather every two years. This compares to the old-time rendezvous of the mountain men in that they compare hunting successes, problems that arise in different areas and they also have a bit of fun.

The old mountain men were noted for drinking and brawling on a nonstop basis. Today's gathering is a working conference. Forty-five or so hunter-trappers from throughout the state of Colorado gather in the high country just east of Gunnison to obtain new department procedures and policies, to compare range problems, and obtain part of their annual allotment of powder and bullets for reloading and .22 ammo. They also find time to conduct unorthodox shooting contests.

During the three-day meet, each morning offers a different shooting contest. The first is with rifles at the odd range of 190 yards. They use this distance, since it is convenient. One year, they shot at fifty-yard, center-fire pistol targets, since the standard two hundred-yard rifle targets hadn't arrived. They fire three shots from a prone position, over grain sack rests, then two offhand shots for a total of five with fifty possible points.

The next shooting event is on a running coyote target at a hundred yards from the offhand position. They get two shots at the target, as it is propelled down the range by an ingenious device. The last competition is with the pistol at fifty feet, slow fire.

There are two divisions: one for the professional hunters and an open division for supervisors and guests. Each pitches a dollar into the pot for each shoot and the winner in each division takes the pot for that event. The winning hunter also receives a trophy.

A favorite headquarters for this gathering is Waunita Hot Springs resort just east of Gunnison.

Alan Wimer of Montrose was the man who set up the course and had the running coyote gadget the year to which I'm referring.

One hunter poked fun at himself, saying he had called in nine coyotes at one stand, but didn't get one of them, since his scope was out of alignment. The big discussion was on what made a good bear dog and who had the best.

The next morning, on the 190-yard range, Wimer was laying out the tarps along the firing line and the feed sacks for the prone shooting.

The other sharpshooters were filing up to register. Registration cost a dollar and one could go for one or all events. Most planned to shoot in all three.

The variety and condition of the rifles of these working hunters was something else. The stocks were in all styles and conditions. As for the barrels and actions, most had their bluing completely worn off. There were a few iron

When government hunters gathered, the talk was of predators and guns.

sights and peeps but the majority boasted scopes.

The professional hunters were to fire first, then the open division competitors. When all had registered, Wimer called for the first group to line up on the canvas tarps that had been laid out.

At most meets, there is deadly quiet as the competitors fire. Not here. When the marksmen moved to the line, the ones waiting offered unsubtle advice about wearing glasses, questioned whether they had powder in the cartridges and said anything they could think of to rattle their opponents. When all were ready, they looked around to make sure no one was in the shooting area and to be certain the wrangler had driven the saddle stock from behind the targets. The horses had been grazing on the hill while the hunters were signing up and it had been decided to move them in case of a ricochet.

The individual hunters stretched out on the tarps, put out their ammo and loaded. They took aim and there was little elapsed time from the first shot to the last. They weren't rushing, but fired fast out of habit. They shot their three rounds prone, then arose and fired offhand. Finished, each fell back behind the shooting line and started harassing others as to whether they had even hit the right target. The targets were pulled, new ones put in place and the next group fired.

When all the targets were in and the totals tallied, Gene

VARMINT HUNTER'S DIGEST 41

At the registration table, each shooter was required to list type and caliber rifle he was to shoot.

Shooters used canvas tarps and feed grain sacks while competing.

42 VARMINT HUNTER'S DIGEST

Most shooters, whether open or hunter class, sported scope sights on their rifles. Off-hand shooting styles varied with and without use of slings. Shooter in foreground was using a newly acquired Remington carbine.

Peters from Rangely, Colorado, had taken the hunter division with a walloping 48 with 2X.

Peters used a .243 Husqvarna loaded with 85-grain Sierra spitzers backed with 36 grains of 4895. His rifle had no bluing on it and the barrel had grooves worn in the steel from riding in the slings in his pickup truck.

Most of the hunters load their own cartridges to save money and to obtain the best possible loads for their rifles. Some of the district supervisors such as Alan Wimer will load all the ammo for the men in their district. This saves the hunters from buying duplicate loading equipment and gives them a central point for picking up their supplies. Wimer uses many pounds of 4831 but is planning some test loads for the .270s in H380. He feels 4831 has a tendency to burn out barrels with the amount of shooting they do. He thinks they may be able to prolong barrel life with the H380, if it affords the needed performance.

Gene Bartnicki of Denver, then the assistant state supervisor of wildlife services, won the open competition using his Model 70 .270 with 130-grain Sierra boattails backed by 58 grains of Du Pont 4831. He won the shootoff from a tie and both shooters used the same rifle in the final shooting. Bartnicki took it with a 46. The open division had more of the custom rifles and shiny hardware than the hunters, but no one managed to shoot as well.

For a cross section of the rifles used, I checked the tally sheets for calibers and makes. The .243 outnumbered anything else, with twelve being used by the professional hunters and eight in the open. The Winchester Model 70 .243 was the predominate rifle in both divisions.

Next in popularity as to quantity was the .270; nine of these were in the hunter ranks and five in the open with the Model 70 again in the majority. From these two popular calibers, the spread went to a wide variety of firearms. To mention a few in the hunter division, there were the .30/06, .257, .300, .300 magnums, .264, 6mm calibers and two .250-3000 Model 99 Savages. One of these had a scope and the other iron sights. They showed signs of much use and the owners were well enough satisfied with the performance not to replace them.

The open division had one slide-action .30/06. The shooter was a southpaw and found it easiest for his type of shooting. There also were Model 700 Remingtons, 660 Remingtons, a Sako and one 6.5x55.

One hunter had a rifle he listed as a Bull Durham. The action came from one rifle, the barrel off another, the trigger from something else and the stock had been whittled on winter nights.

The running coyote event the following day was a bit more like the shooting the hunters usually do; they don't always find an animal sitting and waiting for them. They fired two shots at the cardboard silhouette as it came down the hill.

Al Wimer had designed a propelling device from an old bicycle. The front wheel had been removed and this wheel and the fork nailed to a post. The main frame and back wheel are placed behind the barrier on another post. The distance is about seventy-five yards between them and there is a cable strung above and between. The tires are removed from the wheels and the rope line placed around the wheels, so there is an endless running cycle, much as a moving clothesline as used in city apartments. The cardboard coyote is attached to the lower line and two supports keep the figure in a vertical position; it can't turn

Al Wimer developed this running coyote target from a cardboard cutout, bicycle parts and rope.

Administrators and guests made up the second string of shooters in prone position. After three shots prone, all took two shots offhand. High shooter in open class fired score of 46 out of possible 50.

Rifle calibers used at the gathering ranged from .30/06 to 6mm, with actions including bolt, lever and a slide action for a left-handed shooter. Most popular caliber was .243, with .270 second.

over or flop while moving down the course. Wimer propels the outline by turning the pedals and the coyote moves as fast as he rides in place.

After the coyote reaches the end, Wimer back pedals and returns the silhouette to the starting point to mark and patch the hits. They have an outline drawn on the face and top score is five. They get two shots at the simulated varmint and a possible score of ten.

There were five tied in the hunter class with ten scores and they had to shoot it off. Jay Harper took it for the hunters with another perfect for the shootoff.

Five tied in the open division with Lee Bacus taking a shootoff. Harper used a Model 70 .243, Bacus the same model and caliber.

Wimer tried to keep the target moving at the same rate of speed, but was ribbed about his jerky control. The animal outline moves well and is simple to construct.

The same rifles used the first day were fired on the running target. The coyote outline is about one hundred yards away and shooters stand in the angle of a stone building to give Wimer protection.

The hunters spend a great deal of time away from home, riding the high country to check with the ranchers and herders for trouble areas. It often takes three days to make a circuit. Many of these areas are remote, so transportation is by horse.

The legend concerning Waunita Hot Springs is that opposing Indian tribes would call a truce and all would camp in the area together at the hot springs to bathe in the natural hot waters. It is fitting that the rendezvous, modern style, should be held there.

The pistol meet is standard with fifty-feet slow fire and .22 pistols were predominant with single, double and semiauto actions. The Colt Woodsman appeared to be the favorite. Barney Yeager hit a 36 out of 50 possible to take it for the hunters and Alan Wimer hit 31 to take it in the open division.

After the final speeches had been made and the last tall yarns exchanged, the hunter-trappers packed their sleeping bags, loaded their rifles back into the slings in their trucks and headed out for their particular districts.

The mountain men of old are gone but the modern version of these rugged individuals lives on with the hunter-trappers who have a job of predator control that is often misunderstood by many and not known to others.

VARMINT HUNTER'S DIGEST

VARMINT HUNTER'S DIGEST

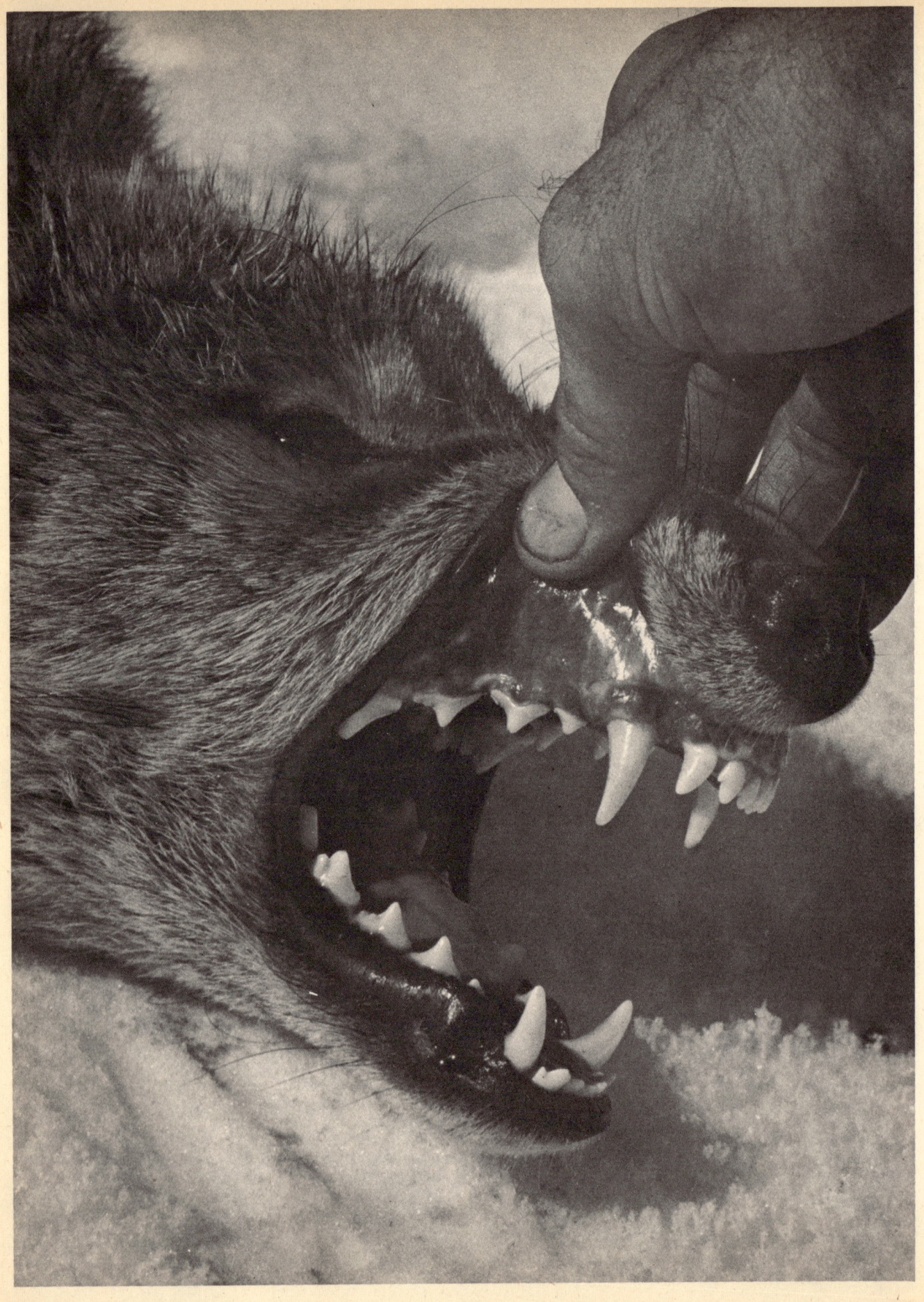

Chapter 5

CONNIVANCE FOR COYOTES

You Must Be Smarter Than This Wily Predator To Score!

Even when startled, a coyote often will pause for a backward glance. This can unnerve a casual shooter.

Left: The teeth of a mature coyote are strictly business against many types of wild and domestic animals.

WHEN THE COYOTE howled, I thought he must be in my back pocket; he was that close.

We had just started the stand, the second of the night, after a four-hour drive from our big city headquarters. It was going on 1:30 of a night that spelled action from the moment we arrived. The desert was pleasant with a light breeze blowing from the northeast, rustling through the sage on the flats around us, cutting through the solid black night that came right down to the desert floor. It was the no-moon time of the month with a billion stars, a good stretch of country awaiting us and this was our second varmint stand.

Holt Dandridge had parked the Scout on the crest of a low swale that lifted slightly above the endless sage flats beyond. This gave us just enough elevation to provide a slight edge for night hunting; the same type of situation that one seeks out for a good daylight stand. We were some distance off the beaten path, even off the unbeaten trails made by other jeeps and four-wheel drive rigs that have been assaulting the desert in recent years.

Quietly we leaned up against the front of the vehicle, seeking the bulk of the vehicle's body to protect us from the breeze that carried an icy edge. I fished a Weems All Call from my pocket, checked the safety on the Weatherby .240 and looked at Dandridge.

On a hunch, I slipped a higher pitch reed into the All Call. Maybe this was done because of the blank on that first attempt where I had used a louder call — my usual selection for coyotes — with a raspy pitch.

The thin-edged shriek cut the night air, the calling series sounding excited, pitiful, but not loud. Volume is a point of great controversy among callers and those who stress it

Left: Dougherty strolls casually along a trail through the brush of Southern California, looking for a likely spot to make his stand and try to lure in a coyote.

Right: Horses can be helpful in getting into the back country of an otherwise inaccessible area. The effort often pays off, where hunting pressure has been low.

As witnessed by this take of six bobcats and only four coyotes, the latter tends to be a tougher adversary for the varmint hunter, who must outsmart his quarry.

have sound logic based on experience to substantiate their feelings. I have, too, for that matter but on more than a few occasions the lightly utilized instrument has been the difference. One never knows what'll work for sure.

It was so early in the stand that we both were in a state of total unpreparedness when the coyote hollered. He didn't yodel, yip or bark. He flat got down deep and brought a long howl up from his very toes right underneath us.

This is unusual. Coyotes often will howl at a caller from considerable distance. They may come in yipping, barking or carrying on in moderation at close range but rarely will they howl right in your face.

"Get on him!" I snapped the words to Dandridge in a whisper. One thing was for sure: with a coyote that close, it wasn't going to be staying long. I never did see the eyes, but Dandridge did when he first dropped the light on the dog that wasn't a full thirty yards away. I didn't need eyes in this case, since the full blast of the light set him off in almost stark white relief against the sage. He turned and headed off in a lope, looking back over his shoulder in that manner characteristic of the coyote.

This was no time to realize that I had not as yet put a round out of the Weatherby. Our spur of the moment departure after dark hadn't been timely for sighting in. The Weatherby had been scoped and sighted in according to the accompanying target. The group imprinted thereon was entirely sufficient for coyotes; even good enough for mice.

I must confess some mild panic at this moment, however. As I have mentioned in the past, my personal scope for night shooting is equipped with crosshairs that check out in the two-minute category and some of my friends often refer to "Dougherty's scope with the two by fours."

Dougherty has found the trail bike to be another aid in getting into hard-to-reach areas, but the noise can tend to spook the game if one does not use common sense.

The Remington Model 700 in .22-250, a wildcat that has gone respectable, is a highly touted varmint rifle.

The Weatherby scope was fixed with wires that were considerably less than two minutes. When you are trained to look at one thing under certain conditions, the sudden lack can be demoralizing. I could see the coyote making tracks for less illuminated ground but I couldn't see anything to hold on him. In desperation I put that thin suggestion of crosshairs in the estimated proper place and

The heavy barrel of the Remington 700 Varmintmaster tends to dwarf the muzzle of the .22-250 model.

jerked the trigger. I did not squeeze; I jerked.

The .240 makes considerable noise, although maybe less noise than I imagined under the conditions. But there was enough to let me know that proper mechanics had facilitated ignition and the projectile had been satisfactorily launched.

Snapping the scope back to the area where the coyote last was seen prior to the shot, I couldn't see his rapidly vanishing shape within the sphere of light.

"Did I get him?" This question alone indicates the poise of experienced calm I had maintained throughout the seconds of action. In short, I had blown my cool.

Dandridge's answer, "Darned if I know," did a lot toward clearing up the situation. So we sashayed out across the desert, looking for some indication of what exactly had taken place at the time of the big boom.

"Here he is." My stalwart brother-in-law had located the coyote where it had been struck dead in its tracks by the combined firepower of Roy Weatherby and the excellence of my own aim. I was admittedly as surprised as the coyote if indeed he had time to be surprised.

The 90-grain bullet prepared by the Weatherby outfit is reportedly moving along across the countryside at about 3400-plus feet per second, when it is turned loose and the sudden materializing of a coyote head in its path sets off a chain reaction of awesome events.

In retrospect, we agreed that my main problem in not finding the hairs was due to the alignment of the light when I was peering frantically into the scope lenses. Dandridge had been off to my side and a goodly amount of light was washing out my sight picture. The crosshairs, themselves, were distinguishable when proper alignment was

VARMINT HUNTER'S DIGEST

accomplished. By my standards they were not sufficient for night shooting but they were not designed with this in mind.

By the time we had fiddled around checking the scope and firing a few shots to double check the gun, we had used up better than an hour. The time was well spent, however, in that I found the gun was shooting a touch high, so we brought it down almost a full inch. This was for night shooting at relatively close ranges as well as the daylight firing that seldom exceeds one hundred yards and, in good cover, is going to average closer to forty. For these reasons I could see no advantage in having a point of impact an inch or so high at a hundred. Get in a hurry and I could miss one through the hair on his back.

The big reason, however, concerns night shooting. In this country, shots at coyotes and cats usually are under one hundred yards. Many times just the eyes or head will be peeked over a bush or rock. With a good light, this gives plenty of material for positive identification, but for shots like this, I like to hold exactly where I want to hit, not shading low or high to allow for trajectory.

By the time we made our next stand, the breeze was a wind. We decided to give it a try anyhow as it was coming in gusts, which still gave us a calling margin. Here it was necessary to go back to the loud call to compete with

When one moves out for the back country, he can live comfortably with a minimum of equipment, if he makes certain he is selecting with proper considerations.

nature. Dandridge took the Weatherby, slipping a round into the chamber, as we sat on a rock that gave us a terrific lookout for 360 degrees. The country was catty looking with lots of cover, including rocks and sandy washes radiating out from our central spot. Wind or no, it looked promising.

After two minutes of hard calling, I pointed the light straight up slipping the switch; the glow cast a faint ring of light out to the sides, a pair of green eyes bore straight down on us, coming hard from sixty yards out.

"Coyote." Whispering the word and indicating the direction by dropping the light slightly, I watched the dog coming in, while Dandridge shifted to line up. The yearling coyote skidded to a halt forty yards out, broadside. The light was depressed and the switch thrown forward to bring all the power into play.

When the .240 went *kahwhoom*, the coyote flew out of sight. At the same time I resumed calling at a frantic pace, moving the light back up and checking the area. I about swallowed my call.

A coyote can pick his way carefully through a patch of prickly pear and never suffer a single scratch on the way!

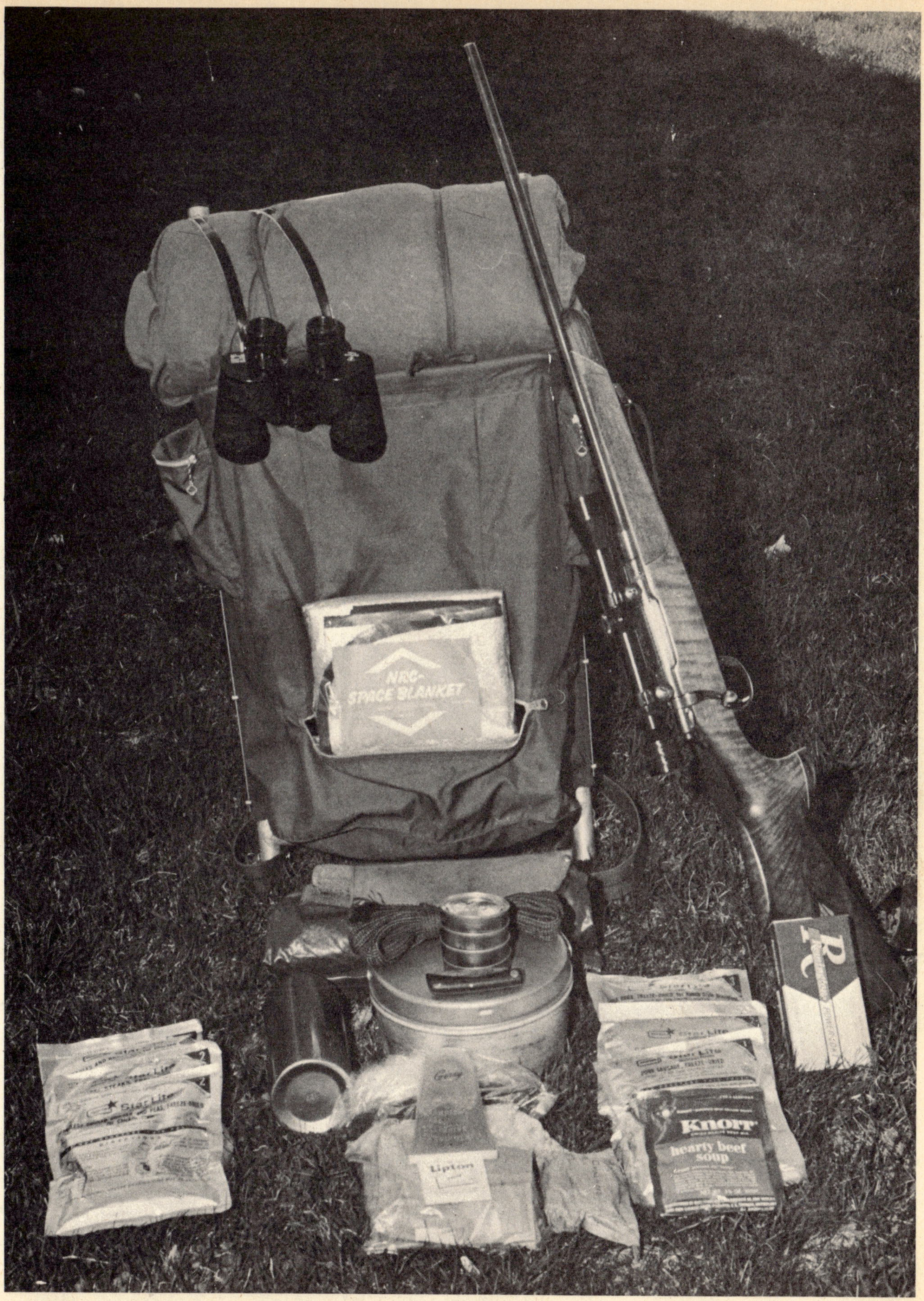
NRC-
SPACE BLANKET
Knorr
hearty beef
soup
Lipton

A flaming pair of coal-red eyes flashed back at us from thirty yards, but ninety degrees from the route of the lately departed coyote. The sharp toe of my cowboy boot advised Dandridge of this new situation. Actually the impact nearly turned him clear around to a position that addressed the glaring eyes that had to be a cat. About the time he was lined up, they went out.

They reappeared seconds later ten yards farther away. With the light up, I tried to tease the critter into committing the wrong move but he wouldn't commit. A quick look, long enough to get almost settled down, then it was gone to reappear somewhere else. About that time, I picked up another set of eyes angling in from another quarter. For awhile it looked like idiot orientation at Camp Runamuck with the role of the idiots equally divided among man and beast alike.

After ten minutes of this mess, the only ones left at the class were the two prize idiots who had not succeeded in loosing another projectile since the first critter had expired.

One of the nicest things about this hunt was the lack of pressure. Over the last couple of years both Dandridge and I have done less calling together than in the old days. Indeed, we had done almost none at all. These few instances had been the contest events where, for the good of the home chapter of the California Varmint Callers Association or some equally stirring cause, we had rousted ourselves out to take part in what can only be described as a series of trying, ego-shattering events.

On this trip, we had no time schedule, nothing pressing; just an adventure in the desert where we could savor the good things. We decided to take a break and fix up a little snack in a spot where we could watch the sun come up and listen to the coyotes herald the arrival of a new day.

Both coyotes taken thus far had been about eight months old, in prime condition and extremely eager, which was good for us. The range was in prime shape. It had been four years since I had visited this country and the conditions were a marvel. The coyotes which we skinned were actually covered with a layer of fat, a relatively unusual occurrence.

Arnold Juenke, Nevada custom rifle maker, tends to check out his own products on coyotes, using a call to bring them in close enough across the coarse desert sands for that telling bullet.

The .240 is an addition to the Weatherby Mark V line and had handled both coyotes in a manner that one could call authoritative. The case has been called a belted .30/06. Ballistically it has to be likened somewhat to a 6mm/06 and in any discussion has to be considered a varminteer with hot properties. It should make an excellent all-around cartridge for game ranging from varmints through medium-size game up to large deer, when loaded with a 100-grain bullet. Velocities for the 100-grain bullet have been checked out to 3438 fps and with the 70-grain bullet utilizing 52.0 grains of 4350 powder they zip along at 3650. Some velocities at the muzzle with the 70-grain bullet have reached 3850 fps, dropping off to 3395 fps at the one hundred-yard mark.

The case is longer than the standard 6mm and .243 and a pocketful of fodder for the rifle is indeed a pocketful, as I found out on our first daylight stand. They were uncomfortable as the devil in a pair of Levi's.

We settled into a cluster of junipers an hour after full daylight to make a stand overlooking an expanse of country gutted by years of erosion. It was an ideal spot and a coyote chose to make the scene less than a minute after my first series of calls. He walked out and turned broadside about eighty yards away.

With all honesty I can say that it has been a long time

Like many varmint hunters, Juenke favors a fixed power scope rather than a variable; this is the Redfield 6X.

since I have missed a coyote, running, standing or flying. I have had a good string going and here was one more as-good-as-collected coyote. I missed that coyote by no less than three feet. In fact that big coyote did not even offer me the courtesy of running. He turned and began to half walk, half trot away.

The Weatherby had removed several pounds of sod from the landscape and now lay forgotten in my hand as I sat there watching the coyote leave, refusing to believe that I had missed a shot that my 10-year-old son would have smoked. But then he's a pretty terrific shot.

Dandridge seemingly was stunned into immobility and the coyote had covered two hundred yards before he decided it wasn't going to fall over and die. The critter escaped, which is as it should be.

By midmorning, when we settled for a siesta in the blue shade of some friendly Joshua trees, we had downed several more coyotes and had had several give us the slip. Dandridge had been doing most of the shooting and our collection rate went up substantially.

We had scouted out new country, found a lot of quail and seen some bighorn sheep sign. We vowed to come back.

If the world were to be hit from outer space with a bomb that eliminated all but one living thing, that would have to be the coyote. Ol' *Canis Latrans* has survived traps, guns, poison and civilization and in most cases is even thriving on these dangers. He is found living in comfort in some of our largest metropolises as well as in many of the most remote wilderness areas in North or South America. Wherever this sly beast is found, he is revered by all who know him as the slickest and most hunted varmint on four legs.

Judd Cooney, who works as a full-time game warden and part-time outdoor writer up in the Colorado Rockies, has some pretty definite thoughts on just how smart the coyote can be.

Several days earlier, a neighbor had asked Cooney if he could do something about the coyotes on the ridge above his place. He had to shoot an old workhorse that had foundered on the hill across the road from his ranchhouse and it hadn't taken the coyotes long to learn that there was 1500 pounds of meat to be had for the asking. A coyote or two doesn't, in most cases, bother ranchers in this area, but this rancher reported that he had counted up to ten coyotes on the ridge above his place the past two mornings and, as his cows were about to start calving, he was worried.

The next morning Cooney was in the ranchyard at daylight and from there soon spotted three coyotes playing on the hillside above the horse carcass.

"The place was perfect for a stalk, as I could stay behind a ridge and get above the coyotes without being seen. I

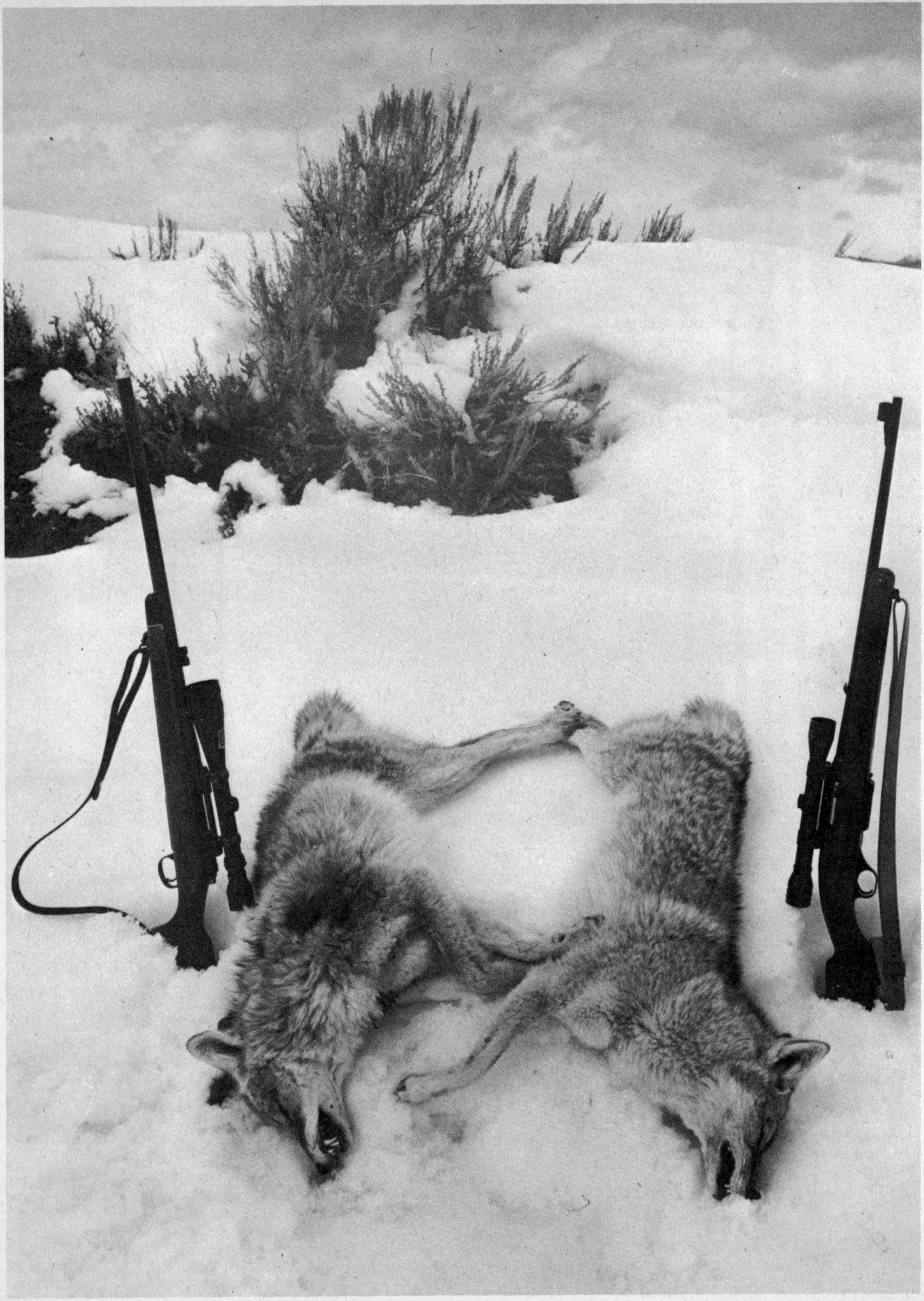

For coyote downing, Judd Cooney, a Colorado game warden, tends to favor the Remington Model 700 in 6mm and the Winchester Model 70, the latter shooting .220 Swift round.

soon had my snowshoes strapped on and my Model 700 HB 6mm Remington loaded with 75-grain handloads. I took my time climbing the hill so that I would come in above the coyotes. When I was halfway to the top, another bunch of coyotes started yapping on the hill above me. I could count four more coyotes on this ridge just sitting and watching me make my stalk."

Another few minutes and Cooney was close enough to the top of the ridge so that he could crawl the rest of the way on the drifted snow. He took off his snowshoes and bellied up to a chokecherry bush and peered through. The three coyotes were across a gully about two hundred yards away. Two were lying down and the other, a big dog, was sniffing around in the snow. Cooney eased into a steady prone position and slowly put the center peep of the 4-12X Redfield on the standing coyote's shoulder and prepared to send him to the happy hunting ground. At the blast of the rifle all three coyotes jumped up and looked. He got two more standing shots and two running shots before he gave up.

"Ha!" Cooney thought to himself, "God's gift to the coyote's educational program has struck again!" These coyotes were, without peer, the most stupid Cooney had ever seen. Two of them, he knew, had their hearts shot to pieces and didn't even have sense enough to realize it. The last Cooney saw of this threesome was when they nonchalantly trotted over a ridge some half mile above me. He was sure the ones behind him on the ridge were spreading the word by now that the guy with the green truck meant them no harm.

If Cooney has learned one thing in coyote hunting, it is never think that you have one of those four-footed scoundrels dead before you can actually put the skinning knife under his hide. The aforementioned episode is by no means the only time any of us blew a setup.

Cooney's favorite method of hunting coyotes in the mountains of Colorado during the winter months is by pure and simple stalking.

This needs clarifying because stalking a coyote is about as far from being pure and simple as you can get. A coyote possesses the finest in detection equipment with no holds barred. His nose, eyes and ears are all tuned to the finest degree of sensitivity and along with this, he has a brain to make use of the information dished out by his senses. He also has the speed and maneuverability to make him one of the hardest to hit beasties on four feet.

The first rule in stalking coyotes is to spot him first. This is ninety percent of the battle, because if Brer Fuzztail spots you first you are not likely to get a good shot, if any shot at all.

Once you spot the coyote or coyotes, you can fall back on all you have learned about hunting. Stay out of sight, keep the wind in your favor, move slowly and quietly and

In the barren desert areas, it isn't always possible to move from cover to cover in seeking a likely stand to call.

Cooney inspects one of the coyotes that he was ready to admit had outsmarted him on a ranch in Colorado highlands.

stay off the skyline. Once you get into position for your shot, take your time and make it good. If you should miss the first shot or there is more than one coyote, don't get up, lay flat and wait, as it is here the coyote will exhibit his one weakness. A coyote, if he cannot see his assailant, just has to stop for one last look.

When a coyote stops for this look he doesn't just look over his shoulder; he almost always turns broadside, and if you have been patiently following him in your scope field, now is the time to center him and touch one off. This little weakness is Mother Nature's way of giving varmint hunters a chance.

Last Winter, Cooney chased a coyote for better than two hours, only to have him give the hunter the final slip on a high ridge and bare ground.

"I was cruising slowly back to the truck when not a hundred yards to one side I spotted an old dog coyote just standing there watching me. I stopped and carefully eased down into the snow around the back side of the machine. One careful shot with the 700 Remington and he was down for keeps.

"As I went over to get him, I found out why he had been so easy to get. He had killed two fat sage grouse and eaten them, then curled up in a patch of sage and slept off his feast until my passing awakened him. When hunting coyotes you have to be ready for the unexpected, because that is about the only thing of which you can be sure."

Cooney's own personal choice has narrowed down to two rifles for all his coyote hunting. He favors a Roberts custom walnut laminated stocked Model 70 Winchester in .220 Swift, topped with a 3-9X Leupold variable scope. He has killed many coyotes with this rifle using a load of 43.0 grains of 4350 powder, Remington primers and the ultra-accurate Sierra 53-grain hollow-point benchrest bullet. This rifle will hold one to 1½-inch groups at two hundred yards consistently. Also this load with the hollow-point bullet doesn't blow a king-size hole in a coyote pelt. The bullet goes in, expands and exits without blowing up too badly.

If you don't care to save the pelts, then switch to the Sierra 55-grain Blitz bullet, which shoots just as accurately but will blow a hole in the coyote that you can stick your rifle through.

"My other coyote rifle, and the one that is fast becoming the coyote gun in my arsenal is the Model 700 Remington heavy barrel in 6mm Remington caliber. This is the most accurate factory rifle I have ever shot and this includes some of the target models. When I first got this rifle, I took it out to the range with the factory-loaded Remington 80-grain Powr-Lokt bullets and shot five groups of five shots each at one hundred yards; all five groups were from one-half to seven-eighths of an inch and this is out of

Using a ridge line as concealment, varmint hunters survey the landscape as man in middle tries to call up a coyote. Group exercises such as this are rarely successful. Two men make a team; more than that constitute a beer party.

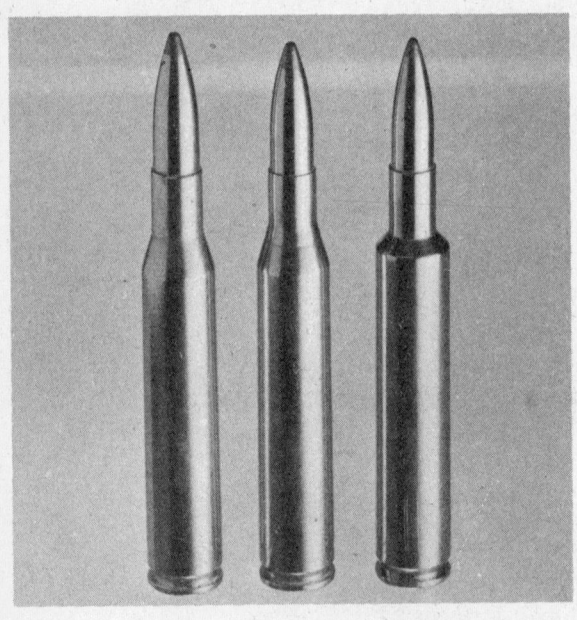

Before taking to the field for varmints, one will do well to check out his equipment on the range. Coyotes call for fast, well-aimed shots. (Left) A variety of rounds are used by varmint hunters, including (from left) the .270 Winchester, Remington .25/06, .25-270 wildcat.

a brand-new rifle. Since then, with handloads of 44.0 grains of 4350 behind the Sierra 75-grain hollow-points, the groups all ran around one-half inch," Cooney reports.

"Last Winter, I topped this rifle off with a new Redfield 4-12X variable scope with the new CH peep reticle. I was somewhat leery of this to begin with, but I really like it after having used it all Winter on coyotes. For running, it is ideal as all you have to do is put the coyote in the circle, then pull ahead until his nose is just touching the outer edge of the peep and let drive.

"There are many other good calibers for coyotes and some of these would be the .22-250, .243, .257, .270, .30/06, .264 and many other of our flatter shooting rifles.

"You'll notice I did not mention the .222, .223 or the .222 magnum. These rifles are used by many hunters in the South and West with fine results but mostly on coyotes that have been called in where the range is under two hundred yards. They are great for this and certainly pack the wallop to stop a coyote at these ranges. In stalking coyotes, I would say the average shot is two hundred to three hundred yards and our coyotes are much heavier and thicker furred than those of the Southwest. Hence they take a whale of a lot more killing power to keep them down for good. The most important thing is to use the rifle and scope combo that you can shoot the best under all conditions.

"Both of my rifles are equipped with variable power scopes and the reason for this is that I like all the power I can get for long standing or sitting shots. For running shots I use the 4 and 6X power settings. I also use the higher power settings for spotting coyotes.

"The only other piece of equipment needed is a darn good pair of lightweight binoculars. The 7X35s or 8X30s seem to work out best for me, as they are light, easily carried and still have good field and plenty of magnification. The 7X50s also are used by quite a few varminters but are a little too heavy to be carried around your neck all day long.

"Some of the other things that help in hunting this varmint in the snow are snowshoes, skis, white parka and something I tried this year and would never be without again: leggings. These fit over your pants to the knee and keep the snow and ice from getting your pant legs wet."

Earlier in this story, it was related how Cooney blew a near perfect setup on three coyotes, but there is a sequel to that story.

"Later that afternoon, I went back up to the same ranch and spotted four more coyotes right back at the carcass of the dead horse. Once again I strapped on my webs and started up the same tracks I had made earlier that

Judd Cooney looks over some of the coyotes he has taken in a single Winter of varmint control as a game warden. Note the white coveralls that he wears during the Winter to help camouflage his bulk against the snow drifts.

morning. I passed the bush I had used previously and slowly made my way to the top of the ridge above the carcass. No coyotes!

"All at once, a small knoll about one hundred yards to my left came alive with coyotes. They all had been curled up sound asleep in a little dip on the hill and I had not seen them until they took off. I calmly sat down, got ready and waited. There was one big, old dark-colored dog in the bunch and I was sure he was the one doing all the yapping at me that morning. He ran up the far hill and sure enough, he stopped about 350 yards out, for a last look back. I settled the peep in the scope on top of his shoulders and let fly.

"The 75-grain hollow-point caught him in the middle of the chest and dropped him in the snow with nary a twitch. I felt better, but I knew that I still had a long way to go before I got the rest of that bunch. They would know I wasn't playing games, as I had that morning.

"I can't say that I was entirely displeased with this task, though, as there are many worse things than chasing after a bunch of coyotes on a nice Winter's day. Working, for instance!"

VARMINT HUNTER'S DIGEST

Chapter 6

CALLING ALL BOBCATS

Bagging This Predator Requires Special Techniques And Extra Patience

THE BOBCAT is a highly prized trophy in the eyes of most hunters. Most outdoorsmen will spend a lifetime in the field, often in good cat country, and never see one of these elusive, beautifully marked animals. Before calling became popular, bobcats were taken either by chance or behind a well-trained pack of hounds.

Many experienced callers have never, to their knowledge, called up a bobcat. In truth, they very possibly have, for the bobtail is a sucker for a call and not nearly so clever as the coyote or red fox. The strength of Lynx Rufus to hang onto his hide is due to his supreme camouflage and his careful method of moving about. Only seldom will a cat come to a call in a full charge out in the open. The bobcat is a stalker, relying on stealth and patience to get close to his quarry before a quick, deadly rush.

While I have seen bobcats do some very un-catlike things at all hours of the day or night, most of the cats I have called were just suddenly there.

Hunting bobcats is easiest at night. While they will stick close to cover and move carefully, the piercing glow of their eyes reflected in a light gives them away. Unlike coyotes who are most often spooky of a light, cats seem to pay it little mind unless it is in country where they have been hunted or called often.

While secretive, I do not think the average bobcat is long on intelligence, certainly not as much as the coyote. Perhaps it is confidence built on their natural camouflage that convinces them that they cannot be seen when danger threatens. I have shot at bobcats, even at close range, several times while the cat never moved. On a stand in California's Owens Valley, a hunter shot at a big ol' tom six times before laying the cat down. The range was not over sixty yards, the country flat and fairly open, consisting of ankle-deep, powdery alkali soil. Each miss was close, blowing considerable dust, earth and brush up around the cat who sat nonchalantly until his movement was up. Such behavior is difficult to fathom.

I have most often preferred higher-pitch calls and close-range squeakers for cats. While every combination works, these seem to be the most reliable and on nighttime stands where the animal's approach can be readily seen, this type seems to move them the fastest.

Bobcats will come uncomfortably close to a caller at night or when well concealed in the day. More than one caller has had a cat jump right in his middle, and while I've not had it go that far, several have been coiled to spring before I was aware of their presence. Such moments are accompanied by the strange feeling that all is not well. I had that notion once just at sundown calling at a pinon and juniper ridge. Shortly after my opening series, I caught a glimpse of a coyote. For a longish period thereafter I kept working a Burnham close-range call with my rifle half at ready. That old feeling came over me but I remained motionless, squeezing subtle notes out of the call looking for the coyote. It wasn't my partner's shot that startled me; one expects that. It was the thrown gravel and expiring hiss in my back pocket. A fine big cat lay stoned out not six feet behind me. The cat had been gathering to spring over the bush at my back when my compadre shot him off. It does pay to hunt in pairs with 360-degree visibility.

I've seen many a bobcat taken after a stand was over. Hunkered down and observing while remaining unseen, the

VARMINT HUNTER'S DIGEST

cats would break for cover when the concealed hunters rose after the completions of a calling series. In known cat country a circular sashay around the stand location is always a worthwhile move. Bobcats frequent all types of terrain and are widespread geographically. In heavy cover, hunting is best done at night, for the slinkly critters are just too hard to spot during the day. If you are confined to daylight hunting, there are some steps that will increase your odds. First, make long stands, from thirty to forty minutes. Be well concealed with as much visible command over the areas as possible. Keep your calling subtle. After the opening series of several minutes, use the higher-pitch close-range calls and as time goes by, keep the call weak but pleading. Observe the birds. The presence of a bobcat drives most birds berserk. They will carry on nervously, often diving or fussing in the cat's vicinity. Detail everything around you and watch for a change and keep a special eye out for the gentle twitching of a short stubby tail that will have a bit of white on it and will be moving constantly as the cat stalks in.

It is not unusual to call several cats at once. This generally occurs in the desert country and I think it ties in to the breeding periods when several cats will be running together. The most bobcats I have ever had on one stand was five. I've had four on another and three many times. In the case of the five, it turned out to be a female and four males, three of which still count in the top ten of the heaviest cats I've bagged. It was unusual to collect all five who were gathered on a large isolated knob in otherwise flat country. We brought them off the knob and a hundred yards across the flats to another rock pile not twenty yards from where we were set up.

When a cat is reluctant to come in, as often happens in desert country where, because of a height advantage, he is sometimes reluctant to leave, the caller can easily walk to the cat. This happens in situations where you may be paralleling a ridge hoping to call animals off this natural passageway. Walking carefully toward the cat while calling and keeping the light well in front is most often a surefire way to cut the distance to comfortable ranges.

The use of scents is often discussed among callers. I believe it helps, certainly it shouldn't hurt, but in the case of the bobcat, who has a relatively poor nose it is not a critical issue. Bobcats are the only member of the callable critters I've had come in straight downwind on more than one occasion.

No, the bobcat is not difficult to collect, yet he is one of the most sought-after hunting trophies and his hide demands top prices in the escalating fur market. The real challenge in cat hunting is that offered by an individual animal.

Back in the Fall of 1963, my brother-in-law, Holt Dandridge, and I made a stand along an old deserted road that probably saw no more than five cars a month. The stand location was a familiar one, marking the fifth time we had hit this exact spot in almost as many months. Our

Dougherty displays more proof that bobcats will answer to same call as coyotes. All were taken in desert-type terrain. Note that the cats are almost as large as the coyotes. All were taken with .222 Remington mag.

Left: Murray Burnham of Marble Falls, Texas, displays the pelt of 27-pound bobcat called in during Mexican hunt.

VARMINT HUNTER'S DIGEST

The distaff side does its share of varmint hunting these days, too. This huge bobcat was taken with .22 rimfire, using iron sights. It's hardly the ideal varmint rifle, but does prove that the lady knew how to use her call!

reasoning was basically sound. Some five months earlier I had made a stand in this spot at the suggestion of a sheep trucker who in the warmth of an all-night coffee spot passed the word that he had seen "a huge ol' bobcat, 'bout the size of a young tiger, cross the road." On that first occasion, some ten minutes or thereabouts after the stand began, the big cat showed up on a far hill and wouldn't come any closer than three hundred yards no matter what we tried to say to him about dinner. The effort failed but we catalogued that cat for future reference. Sooner or later we would give him another try.

Intervening attempts had all met with defeat. No cat showed up, although on one stand we did have a flicker of eyes for a moment. Both Holt and I were fully convinced that the big cat still claimed that particular piece of real estate as part of his home range.

Knowing that we were after a particular cat had some bearing on how we set up for the stand. There was the possibility that some other total stranger, like a coyote or a fox, could come rolling along. We suspected not, for in the aforementioned blanks there just wasn't anything else taking the trouble to look us over.

The country wasn't the type where you would expect to find lots of critters running heavily. Sparse cover, steep rocky hillsides, lots of dirt and sand, and not much else. We pretty well figured we were dealing with one old tom and this ridge was the center of his home range. Sooner or later we would all be in the same vicinity at the same time.

The open country meant the shot, if any, would be on the lengthy side. We took our most powerful light, a couple of sandbags, set them up on a rock that offered benchrest facilities and got to work on the call.

It took the old boy a full fifteen minutes to show up and when he did, he perched on top of the farthest rock pile and sat and sat with only an occasional turn of his head. No matter what, nothing in our bag of tricks would move the

Dougherty, a renowned bowhunting expert, has taken his share of bobcats with the bow, but it is tough to do.

Hiding beneath coyote skin cap, Jerry Mills was able to call in this bobcat in broad daylight, but calling at night is easier.

Bobcats will take to the trees in search of nests, young birds, author says.

cat. The range was pushing the long side of two hundred yards, a bit touchy at night if you have a tendency to twitch your trigger finger as I do under stress. The decision was made to take a shot. After all, this was an opportunity, such as it was, that had been a long time coming. Besides, it's damn tough to collect bobcat hides if you don't at least offer up a token shot once in awhile. To make the story come to a happy ending, at least for the Dougherty-Dandridge duo, it shall be noted that the 50.0 grain pill from the Sierra people ahead of 27.5 grains of 4895 caught the cat about four inches under the chin. His honest weight of twenty-six pounds makes a pretty healthy bobcat.

The recounting of this thrill-packed chain of events is not designed to impress you with the unerring skill of my marksmanship — although you may draw that conclusion if you like! — rather, it's offered up as an angle that will occasionally pay off.

You will recall that we felt the area we were calling was key to that particular bobcat's home hunting grounds. It followed that the cat would hunt this area of his home range on some sort of regular schedule, providing he was still alive. I confess that we did not know what that schedule was. Blind luck certainly entered into the timing, for on the occasion cited, we happened to make our stand when the cat was within hearing distance of the call.

The home range of a bobcat consists of only a few

The famed Burnham brothers, Murray and Winston, racked up this array of bobcats during two nights of hunting. When areas become overpopulated with such predators, the effect on birds, small game calls for a needed reduction.

square miles. Within that area he will set up housekeeping, live and die and probably never venture too far away with the exception of a possible trek in search of love or whatever it is that bobcats go looking for at certain times. The basic tactic that we applied was persistence. We knew, or more honestly, felt, that the cat was still about. We were not calling helter-skelter across the desert looking for a random critter to show. We directed our effort towards one particular animal that logic told us was still in the area.

This tactic, particularly on bobcats, is a good one to follow. If you have spotted a cat in a certain spot, chances are very good that he can be called at that spot in the future. This can apply to any type of cat sign that you locate; tracks, scratches, etc. It is not necessary to actually sight the cat as long as you know one is in the general area.

Then select the most advantageous calling site and begin to hit it on a regular basis.

Over the years there have been a good many cats honored by calling teams with a special identity and vast strategies planned to bring them to earth. To locate one solitary old tom such as the Caliente Cat and keep after him is specialized varmint hunting that adds a certain spice to an already tangy pastime. There is a certain regret as well as a deserved sense of accomplishment in collecting a cat after you have tried for a long period of time. Usually such cats are collected after many long hours of unrewarding effort. The final reckoning gives you a well-earned trophy that properly belongs on the den wall to remind you for years to come of a particular challenge you were able to meet. Such incidents add a considerable measure to an exciting sport.

Chapter 7

A FEEL FOR FOXES

Winter Is The Time For Outsmarting This Creature — And Taking Prime Pelts!

THERE ARE ONLY two things wrong with varmint hunting in the snow — it's cold and it's wet. Proper equipment will solve the discomforts of these two problems in short order making the prospects of a wintery coyote or fox hunt as pleasant as a summertime hunt with the added spice of potential greater action.

Like fishermen, the majority of hunters are fair weather enthusiasts, discounting, of course, the wildfowlers who are a separate breed of hardy souls. This self-indulging trait of avoiding possible discomfort is costing a lot of us some pretty exciting moments and for no good reason.

Varmint calling is at its peak during the winter months, beginning in late September and running through early February, before it slows down to a standstill that carries over into late Spring. Winter affects all mammals, including man, in some manner. Man becomes content in many cases with sleeping late and enjoying a strenuous afternoon before the one-eyed monster, lapping hot toddies and helping his favorite football team get the touchdown, something they probably wouldn't be able to do without his help.

Varmints, being mammals, also are affected. Their constantly gnawing gastric cavities work overtime and to ease

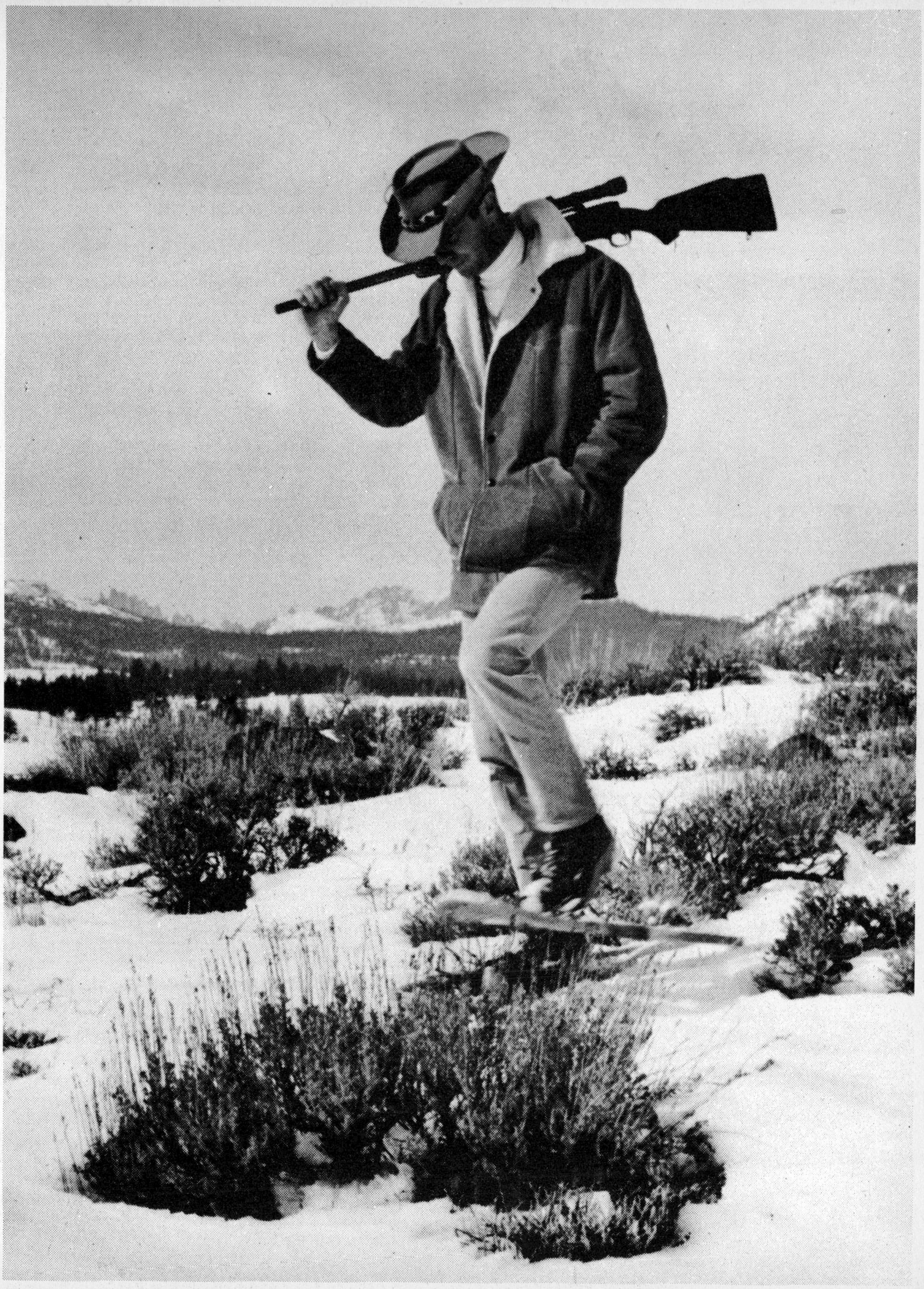

First step to successful fox hunting in the snow is to find animal signs such as tracks at left.

the pangs they too must keep at it. If you're one of the sort who enjoys his winter hunting in plying the pages of the gun magazines with a restless trigger finger, this may serve to light a fire under you: There's a good deal going on outside your winter retreat. You can get out and put out the fire that has the critters running a twenty-four-hour food patrol and salve the spasms of that restless finger.

No matter what part of the country you call home, there are some critters in your hunting neighborhood: coyotes, bobcats or fox and all of them have to eat. The ol' varmint call sounds pretty good anytime and particularly enticing during the Winter when the animals must hunt harder and keep their stomachs fuller to keep up body heat and energy.

It's not as difficult to locate the varmint population now, either. Any place they cross the snow, they have to leave a track as long as the crust has not developed over a few cold days. If this is the case, wait for another snowfall and bomb out of bed early for a change. Head for the hunting grounds and look for tracks. In short order, you should be able to figure just how the animals are working.

Now that you have arrived, there are two ways of going at this. One method is unique and Winter offers the only chance to put it into operation. This is the game of walking up the varmints. Should the snow be deep and powdery or soft, snowshoes are an essential part of your equipment. Granted, you can walk in snow with rubber or waterproofed leather footgear for a fair piece, but you may have to walk longer and further than any fair piece before you get within range of the game you seek. Use snowshoes. Traveling as light as possible, this is a made-to-order game for the man with a long-range varminter such as the .220 Swift, the .22-250, right on up to the .264.

Should you get on the short end of the track, it will not be too long before you sight your game. Range then will depend upon the terrain, but in coyote country it will most often be from one to three hundred yards. You can see him a long ways off, and likewise, he can see you. Sometimes, of course, you can be suddenly startled by a fast exploding target breaking from a draw or a brush pile at close range. This is especially true when working on foxes. Should you hit it right, you sometimes can come onto the game as it takes a midday rest. I know of hunters who have walked them down in this manner and taken them with bow and arrow — quite a feat.

Walking up a varmint is a pastime for the hardier souls; if you can locate a partner to share in this physical fitness program, your chances of success are greater. Two hunters working a trail with the persistence of good trail dogs cut down the tracking time considerably. One should stick to the track while the other plays a circling game in the antici-

Hunter uses white camouflage parka to call in snow. Weather increases fox's appetite.

Proper calling and camouflage may entice wary but hungry varmint to within close rifle range.

pated direction of the animal's travel. This hunter should take advantage of whatever rises in terrain are available, using binoculars in an attempt to locate game.

Clothing here is as important as it is in calling. White parkas, coveralls or pullovers fashioned from bed sheets will make you almost invisible from any direction to the sharp eyes of a varmint that constantly watches his back trail. Coyotes, in particular, have a habit of traveling in groups during the white months. It is quite common to get on a single track and find that it is joined by one to four additional animals. When this happens, the prospects of increased action are enough to spur the trackers on to greater extension in order to catch up and get shooting.

Should you jump a group like this, your work will be cut out for you when the moment for throwing lead is at hand. A coyote boring through soft snow is a slower target than his summertime counterpart, as he has to fight the snow for traction. This in no way makes him any easier to put the lead on, as his bouncing gyrations for evasive tactics are akin to a fish leaping out of water and about as easily hit.

If you are not inclined to spend a day making like a snow plow in hopes of catching a coyote with his tail down, there is the tried-and-true varmint call to do the work for you.

Calling tactics for winter hunting are pretty much as under other circumstances but with a few refinements.

The biggest problem in calling when the temperature has dropped to cold, freezing hash marks on the mercury stick, is the call itself. Calls get cold, too, and have a tendency to freeze up on you right at a crucial moment. Keep them out of the air, inside a breast pocket or similar holding place where body temperatures will keep the reeds warm. You should carry two or three with you and use only one at a time. Moisture from your breath as you blow the call will solidify in short order, causing the stiffened reed to shatter, or at best, to stick shut. The use of gloves is great to keep the fingers warm but will deaden a call's clarity and tone. Learn to call one-handed and keep the trigger hand in a glove. If possible, use a call with no wooden housing around the reed as the wood swelling with moisture, then freezing, constantly alters the call's tone up until the glorious moment when it cuts out with a terrible squawk. The Burnham Brothers and Thompson wildlife calls are two that have all-metal and plastic parts.

The dramatic photos on these two pages are courtesy of North Dakota Game and Fish Department, illustrating some successful winter fox-hunting techniques described in text. Final sequence is below as fox is hit and falling.

VARMINT HUNTER'S DIGEST

Stands should be selected as at any other time of the year, and sign on the ground should be evidence enough of animal activity in a given area. Clear, frozen mornings are notoriously quiet, and the snow on the ground will act as an additional sounding board putting you in a natural echo chamber of sorts.

Unless you are certain that a prospective fur piece is some long distance away, calling should be done with less gusto than during the dry months. Many callers use only coaxers or squeakers at this time of year. As the audio range of the varmint is perhaps the best in the animal kingdom, one is quite able to pick up a high-pitched squeal from half a mile away and course it right down to your waiting gun barrel.

If everything is totally white, there is nothing that will serve you better in the way of camo gear than the all-white ensemble. Regular hunting shades can be used though, as long as the hunter situates himself to take advantage of them, using a brush or rock pile or the base of a tree.

Covered with white and lying prone in the flats is an excellent way to secure a critter at close range. The normal caution displayed by varmints when crossing openings at other times of the year is greatly reduced, because their line of vision is increased when all is white. Anything out of place is noted easily and they have become mentally resigned to traveling the white flats for a few months. Lying down, the caller-hunter looks like any other snow-covered lump to the probing orbs of the edgy predator. Boots, pants and gun barrel are harmless objects as long as the caller remains motionless; the greatest camouflage in the world is suspended animation.

Winter hides are prime pelts and, depending upon the area and the market during a given season, the hunter can make himself a pretty nice pile of change; enough to pay expenses or maybe pay for the new varminter he has been fondling at the local gun shop.

Fast-opening bullets of the thin jacket type should be used if you plan on skinning out the animals for commercial purposes. A hide that looks like a doughnut will not bring much of a price. The Hornaday 50 and 55-grain SX (super explosive) are terrific choices for the hot-shot .22 shooters. Shotguns are excellent if the ranges are going to be under forty yards. A good combination would be one of the over/under rifle/shotgun rigs, the most common being in 20-gauge and .22 magnum. Factory short magnum loads in No. 2 or 4 are adequate and the rifle cartridge should be tipped out with hollow-point ammunition.

Winter calling also opens the door on the sneaky, skulking bobcat. While foxes and coyotes are bold in their approaches to a call, the cats are always cautious in coming to the stand and, during the summer season, are difficult to locate among the scattered rocks and brush with their slow movements and perfect camouflage.

Sneaking in on the snow-covered ground, a bobcat looks altogether different from what the caller has been trained to expect — it looks like a bobcat.

In good bobcat range, the walking-type hunter has an even better chance than with coyotes and foxes due to the cat's reduced hunting circuit and his lazy personality. In the Northwestern states, cats are hunted down in this manner with a high degree of success. Cat callers will not find the bobtails in the open flats but along the sidehills and brushy draws that offer as much cover as possible. Still, odds are raised in the callers' favor even when calling in this type of country, as the snow has a grand habit of flattening out the countryside. In the varmint kingdom, nothing makes a nicer trophy than a winter cat with a hide full of prime fur.

Of them all, though, the fox is the prime winter target. The Midwestern states have had an ever-increasing fox population in recent years and many states are paying bounties to induce hunters to pursue these animals, as their depredations upon pheasants, grouse and other birds have reached an alarming point. This makes it a double picnic for the caller, as the fox is the easiest species to sucker into range with a call.

There's a lot of sport to be had in this game of winter calling and the possibility of additional bonus of prime pelts or bounty money should be an added incentive to pick up your gun. As you go out the door, don't forget your call.

In many Midwestern states, fox pelts are bringing a good bounty price.

With Or Without Bounties, Winter Fox Hunting Has Its Own Rewards

COLD, WINTERY WINDS watered his eyes as Denny Ballard peered through the barely open window of his truck. Outside, Mother Nature had prepared a beautiful Iowa day for armchair quarterbacks, ice skaters and the hardiest of the winter hunting clan — the fox hunter. Between pop tunes, the announcer on the truck's radio warned of chill-factor temperatures as low as minus ten degrees, camouflaged under bright, sunny skies.

"My sidekick and I had been cruising the snowy back roads of Johnson County since dawn and knew, regardless of the weather conditions, we'd soon be able to find a red fox curled up on the lee side of a protective hill, soaking up the warm rays of a winter sun," Ballard recalls.

Don Roberts poked his shoulder and pointed.

"Hold it! Right over there. It's got to be a red!" Roberts hissed.

Ballard eased over to the side of the road and set the brake. Three hundred yards from their position, balled up on an open, snow-covered hillside, lay a red fox. A closer look through his seven-power binoculars told Ballard the red wasn't asleep. His head was up, looking the hunter straight in the eye.

"If the fox held, it would be a tough stalk. Drifted snow complicated the only concealed avenue of approach along a fence line. I won the toss for a try on this red and quickly laid a simple battle plan. Roberts would drive the truck slowly ahead and drop me at a shallow cut in the road. From there, I could make a crawl along the fence to a good shooting point atop a hill two hundred yards from the fox.

"After negotiating the first fence, I uncased my Ruger 6mm rifle and locked a hand-loaded varmint cartridge into the chamber. My white suit and ski mask would help conceal my approach, but I'd have to stay low. The snow was waist deep and soft. It felt like I was crawling through soap flakes. My elbows penetrated to the ground and my feet flailed helplessly. By the time I reached the hilltop, I was exhausted."

Mr. Fox had lowered his head to a sleeping position as Ballard rested his rifle for the shot. A fence post helped steady his position against the sharp, icy winds that must have come straight from Fairbanks. He wiped his teared eyes and slipped out of his mittens for the final squeeze.

The two hundred-yard shot, if successful, wouldn't set any record for distance, but Ballard wasn't interested in just toppling the fox. That prime red pelt would bring upwards of $40 at the fur buyer's, so it would have to be a head shot or nothing.

"At the roar of my 6mm, snow erupted just over the fox's head and he spun out of his curl and disappeared over the hill. I'd held too high for the downhill shot."

Back at the truck, Roberts congratulated Ballard for a fine stalk, then bad-mouthed him for missing the shot. The shooter countered with excuses that ranged from cold fingers and an unsteady position to the sun being in his eyes and the wind wrong. There was little doubt, though, that the exhausting one hundred-yard belly crawl had contributed significantly to his miss.

The problem of stalking red foxes across open, snow-covered terrain had plagued this pair on previous hunts. They begin searching the broad farmlands of eastern Iowa for foxes as soon as the snow falls, preferring to use center-fire varmint rifles. Most riflemen load up hollow-pointed bullets for use on fox in this area. They're the safest bullet to use, because they'll disintegrate upon contact, leaving little danger of ricochet. Red foxes, they had found, seek out wide-open, bare hillside for winter naps and it's common knowledge among varmint specialists that the lee side of the hills, about one third of the way down, is where to find them. Like Eskimo dogs, reds feel more at ease curled up away from cover and with their tails across their noses, than back in the brush. About the only way to close the distance on a hillside red is to belly crawl, as related before.

"I hit upon the idea of using a toboggan as a vehicle for

VARMINT HUNTER'S DIGEST

sliding in on red fox while sledding with the kids one Christmas. A little tyke on a white, plastic toboggan nearly cut me down as my boy and I climbed a hill for a rerun. His light-colored snow suit and toboggan made him almost invisible.

"By New Year's Day I had a five-foot, hardwood toboggan ready for the trial run. A coat of white paint and plenty of wax looked perfect. The pad cover was white, too, making the complete outfit well camouflaged. By laying my rifle on the pad with the muzzle under the curl, I could lay, belly down, on the sled and push myself along using a swimmer's breaststroke. When it came time to shoot, the toboggan's curl formed a dandy rifle rest. I checked the little equalizer thoroughly and found that my front-view profile was nearly invisible from a hundred yards. Roberts and I were all set to hunt New Year's Day," relates Ballard.

The first stop was at Frank Stockman's farm just east of Iowa City. This farm juts into a vast, three square mile section that had always yielded three or four foxes per season. The hunters split up to hunt individually for sleeping foxes. They'd course into the wind about a half mile apart, searching with binoculars the likely looking bedding grounds for targets. If no game was spotted, they would meet on the far side and loop through another end of the section. This parallel hunting method gives one hunter a chance to maneuver for a shot at a fox his partner misses or jumps prematurely.

Front curl of the white-painted toboggan makes a handy rifle rest. Hunter is dressed in white, minimizing visibility.

VARMINT HUNTER'S DIGEST

Varmint hunter is almost invisible with low profile behind toboggan. Text describes propulsion method similar to swimming.

"I topped each hill carefully, glassing the far slopes before much more than my head had appeared above the horizon. My little toboggan tagged along behind me, tied to my belt with a short length of rope. The first opportunity for a trial slide came just as I had eased over the top terrace on one of a broad series of hills. I saw him without my binocs. A big, bright red fox lay several hundred yards away on a hillside, content, for the moment, and unaware of my presence.

"My route for the slide was a little uphill, but the going was easy compared to a normal crawl. The little toboggan inched ahead and I kept my arm movements slow and deliberate. I hoped that I'd be able to close to within easy rifle range before the shot.

"Even though the red devil's head was down, I wasn't sure he was asleep. It could be that he was wide awake and was watching me swim up the hill to him. I took no more chances and stopped at an estimated 150 yards. I rested my rifle on the toboggan's curl. The position couldn't have been more comfortable. With my crosshairs centered low, between the two black triangles marking the fox's ears, I touched off an 85-grain hollow-point. Ker pop! My first toboggan red was in the bag," recalls Ballard.

Since that initial kill, Ballard and friends have used the short toboggans to shoot many more foxes with rifle and camera and it's apparent to them that the method is tops for approaching bedded red fox. High-powered rifle buffs like to try the long shots many times, but the red fox in the

This prime red fox pelt is about to be loaded aboard the white toboggan to begin the trip to the fur buyer.

Midwest sports a valuable coat during the winter months and it behooves the serious hunter to get in close for the head shot, saving the pelt for the fur buyer.

Until recently, the fox was considered an undesirable species in Iowa that depredated rabbit and pheasant populations and slaughtered farmer's chickens, ducks and swine. State law required that all county governments pay bounties on fox scalps and other vermin in order to encourage sportsmen to hunt the destructive devils. But bounties, it was found, did not help limit fox populations or any other pest species and in 1965 the mandatory payment policy was changed.

County governments were given the option, at that time, of paying bounties on individual varmint species from their own treasuries, if population seemed out of hand. Many counties continued to pay a $2 fee to hunters for killing foxes. During one of the last years of the county-paid bounty system, over $72,000 was spent by participating counties to control varmints.

"In 1968, the last year my home county paid bounties on foxes, just over $1600 was awarded to successful fox hunters for red scalps. Now, most bounty practices have been terminated, because conservation commission figures show that hunters will pursue foxes, bounty or not, and that the red fox may not be such a culprit after all," Ballard reports.

The image of the red fox in Iowa has changed considerably in the last five years mainly due to the research work of the state's conservation commission. They've found that red foxes make few inroads on other game populations and, since modern poultry and swine raising has moved indoors, farmers rarely lose livestock to marauding reds.

In July 1970, the State Conservation Commission announced the appointment of red and gray foxes to the game species list. A September-to-March hunting season was put on foxes, enabling the species to rear young during the vulnerable spring and summer months without fear of death from unscrupulous den diggers and pup shooters.

The Hawkeye State's serious varmint hunters roll their own ammo for increased performance while stalking open country reds. The .222 Remington, still popular as a two hundred-yard varmint fetcher, groups 50-grain pellets well within a fox's vitals using 20 grains of No. 4198 powder. Severe winter winds, while rarely deterring veteran fox hunters from the hunt, can upset the route of the .222's light bullet. Many hunters, therefore, have substituted the .243 or 6mm Remington pushing an 85-grain jacketed or boat-tailed hollow-point to buck tricky crosswinds.

"I've used 38 grains of No. 3031 in my 6mm Remington with good results. The 85-grain, at 3000 fps, expands rapidly and puts fox-size varmints down for good," Ballard says.

Fur buyers have put a tempting price on red fox pelts and have challenged Midwest shooters to present one-piece hides for top dollar. Slipping up on bedded reds using a hardwood toboggan has spelled the difference between good pelts and bad for Ballard and has added a new dimension to fox hunting.

The short hardwood toboggan serves not only as a stalking vehicle and a benchrest, it also is perfect for hauling game.

VARMINT HUNTER'S DIGEST

Chapter 8

...AND THE OTHERS

It's Surprising What Unlikely Game Will Answer A Call!

THE USE OF a varmint call is most commonly related to the hunting of coyotes, bobcats and foxes. What is perhaps not as well-known as it should be is the wide range of appeal varmint calls, with varied techniques or standard calling methods, have on a wide range of game animals and birds, carnivores and herbivores alike.

It would be logical to assume that mountain lions respond to a call, which they do well. Many callers have been rewarded with the sudden silent approach of one of these big cats while calling for bobcat or coyote. I suspect that the reason more lions are not taken by callers is simply because most serious calling is done outside of prime lion habitat (i.e., in lower elevations such as open desert country). However, lions have been taken in this type of cover, usually when adjacent to higher elevations (above 6000 to 9000 feet) and most often when the occasion coincided with deer herds being on the lower winter ranges.

A hunter seriously interested in calling for lions would have to make several commitments. First he would have to concentrate on the higher rugged mountain country. He would have to spend hours detailing and scouting the country with a topography map and preselect areas that would allow the greatest coverage of his call over good lion holding cover. Then he would have to pass the other targets of opportunity such as bobcat that presented themselves, and he should make stands of no less than an hour's duration. This type of hunting is ideally suited to weekend backpack operations, far off the roads, deep into the lions' living room so to speak.

I am convinced that a lion will come to a call as readily as any other predator. Lions, however, exist in lesser quantities than the smaller predators and cover a large range in the course of their daily lives. The hunter, too, must cover a lot of lion country, be patient and wait until chance puts him within hearing of a susceptible cat.

One year, during the California field championships, a large female mountain lion was called and collected by Jack Slaney.

Although lions have been called up and taken over the years by a handful of lucky callers, this was the first to be taken on a major hunt.

The state championships took place on a wildly wet and windy weekend two hundred miles north of Los Angeles in the Owens Valley. It was another storm in a continuing series. Although the weather reduced attendance to teams from California's fifteen chapters, there still were plenty of callers ready to accept this additional challenge.

Slaney made the stand of his life at night in California's Sierra Nevadas at an elevation of 6500 feet. He first picked up the eyes of two critters some five hundred yards out. One cat was hesitant, while the other made a straight-in, hard-galloping approach.

The big cat came in to within twenty-five feet of Slaney, who, by this time, knew full well what he had going for him. One bullet from his .264 magnum put Jack Slaney in the company of the relatively few men who not only have called a lion, but remained cool enough to prove it.

While not regarded as a predator in the sense that lions are, bears are called quite often with a varmint call and there are hunters, particularly in Arizona, who have developed bear hunting with a call into a sport. A great deal of similarity exists between lion and bear hunting for the

Cougars are protected in many areas, but most states have open seasons. A varmint call can be used to bring the big cats into position for that shot.

Taking advantage of the terrain and concealment during a varmint calling stand can put the shooter in position for a wide variety of game animals that are not considered as call answerers, when one considers varmint populations.

caller. Scouting is a must, but bear sign and locations are easier to dope out than than the whereabouts of a cougar. The country where bear and lion are found is similar, since both are creatures of the high country, and both respond to a call in a similar manner with a careful, almost sneaky, approach being the norm. There are cases of bears boiling right in on a caller ill tempered and full of fight. In most instances, the caller was set up close to a kill or bait that was considered by the bear to be personal property.

I have called a few lions and one bear. In each instance, I considered the event to be accidental, but those of my acquaintance who call them with as much regularity as can be expected offer up the theory that higher pitch calls, preferably the dual-reed variety such as the Weems Dual Tone work best on bear, while cougars seemingly prefer the coarser, jackrabbit-type pitch. I would suspect this is based on the fact that the varmint call pitched in this fashion could appear to simulate a young deer in trouble to a lion. In the case of other respondents, it may well represent the universal distress call and thus tend to attract the varmints.

I recall a letter from a fellow in Canada who was about a degree away from frothing at the mouth over the fact that every time he blew a call lately a black bear ambled in to see what was going on.

Calling in the forest country of Ontario, famed for its bear population, never looked too intriguing to me. I have been in there — hunting bear — and the country is about as dense as any South American jungle. Although there seems to be a fair lynx and fox population, judging from the sign I saw, I never liked the way the country was laid out from a caller's point of view. Squealing up bears is nothing new, however. It has been going on for quite some time with better success than one would be inclined to believe.

Sam Dudley of Phoenix calls up a bunch every year as do many other Arizona callers. Dave Neihuis was one of the first Arizonans to figure out that bears liked a call and did a pretty thorough job on them for several seasons. Murray and Winston Burnham reported calling in bears a good many years back.

The point is, however, that a varmint call works on bears and more than a few bruins have been converted to rugs, because they liked the sounds of the wooden whistles.

Bear callers don't seem to agree on a definite style. Some claim the call should be loud and tough, while others maintain that high-pitched calling such as the style bobcat specialists prefer does the best job. All this indicated to me that any good style probably will get results. The key is to have a good bear area figured out.

Bear are not too difficult to figure out. If you have some in your country, it shouldn't take much in the way of reconnoitering to develop a good game plan. According to most I've talked to who have called bear, the approach is slow, the bear standing up and doing a fair amount of looking around. The exception seems to be calling in close to a kill or bait that one bear figures he owns. Apparently that bear will come in lickety-split — which should be interesting!

A lion can appear when you least expect it. I am reminded of a night hunt made several years ago in the mountains of California's coast range. The country was thickly covered and conditions were perfect, with no moon, just enough breeze to diagnose wind direction, and a remote but passable four-wheel road that wound upward into the high country. My partner who had provided the lower private ranch access to the road wanted a bobcat badly and had contracted me for a weekend hunt to put one in front of him. In those days, when I was doing a bit of this sort of thing to pick up a few bucks, I had an understanding with my clients. The shooting was to be theirs unless by some chance I called up a lion, in which case I claimed the shot. My partner was using a customized .222 Remington of his own creation topped with a variable power scope with a post. By 11:00 that evening he had two cats, one a real beauty of a tom that would go an honest twenty-five pounds, and a strikingly marked smaller cat. Both had been taken uphill from our calling positions at ranges in the hundred-yard vicinity, a common enough occurrence when critters come from uphill. With the advantage of height, it seems that animals are less inclined to come close as opposed to coming well from the downhill side. Both cats had been shot straight through the chest exactly where he was holding. With the little fast-opening bullet, the hides were unmarked, making for neat, undamaged trophies.

It was about midnight of an ebony, star-studded night when we picked up a set of eyes coming with good speed on a line parallel to our elevation. Based on the movement, I thought it was a coyote. I whispered to my partner to get set and continued coaxing to the eyes which would vanish

Black bear is another type of game animal that Dougherty has found will answer to a varmint call. The author has one such animal to his credit as a result of calling.

Game wardens report that cougar follow deer herds and in the course of a hard Winter can do endless damage.

and reappear, coming closer all the while. There was a small ridge directly in front of us some twenty-five yards away, which dropped off into a small ravine, between us and the approaching critter. Easily visible, his eyes flashed brightly in the perimeter of the light, and vanished into the draw. My partner flicked off his safety while we held motionless and ready for the critter to top out close in front. The eyes suddenly appeared on the ridge, intense with a violet hue; I flicked the soft flood to full spot and dropped the beam on a big lion broadside, right in our lap.

I give credit to my partner as a gentleman. Because my little Sako was out of reach, he tried to push his gun on me. There was no time for a switch. "Shoot," I hissed. The cat was walking away rapidly, still broadside, but close to heavy cover. The little .222 snapped in the quiet air, and the cat walked out of sight simultaneously. To make a long story short, we failed to find any sign and returned the next morning to search again, convinced that my partner could not have missed. But he had and the chance of a lifetime was lost, as have been several others for me when the long-tailed cougars came avisiting.

It is my position that any meat-eating animal will respond to a varmint call. Raccoons are frequently called with standard pitch varmint calls as well as calls tuned to imitate the chirring call of the animals themselves. The Burnham Brothers are famed for their ability to call coons in the heavily populated Southwest around waterways with calls that mimic the distress of seagulls and other feathered creatures. Over the years, my calling partners and I have called many coons with calls in the high-pitch range, such as the standard cottontail models.

When a raccoon decides he is interested, he comes with an intensity most commonly associated with a runaway team of horses. We have had the little bears literally run over us, and I recall an account related by George Allison, one of California's premiere callers, about one that ran over

VARMINT HUNTER'S DIGEST

him one night while he was hunting with a bow. As Allison put it, "The critter came on so hard and tough that when I shot, the arrow never left the string." That's close.

On another occasion, I was in the Deep South, just prior to turkey season, and my companion was one of those dyed-in-the-wool turkey hunters that get goose pimples, when they see a duster made from turkey feathers. Since his early days as a barefoot lad, he'd lived for nothing but matching wits with what is probably our most magnificent game bird.

He also had developed several effective calls that worked on the heavy bobcat population in his area, not that he was too interested, mind you, but he passed on the observations and theories he had, probably to pacify me a little in that he failed to see how anyone could really want to call up a bobcat, when he could chase it with a good pack of dogs his brother happened to have. And that brother lived and breathed just to hear those dogs.

Ol' Pete allowed that this maybe was all right and he "tagged along to tote the corn" primarily, because they ran at night and the turkeys were all on the roost anyhow.

Pete quite naturally had called up the occasional predator, while talking to turkeys. There happened to be a "thieving varmint in the area who was turkey hungry" and the old guy acknowledged that, if he was armed, he knocked 'em off without a thought.

"Hell — they was feeding on my turkeys!" All the turkeys in this area, incidentally, were referred to as "my birds."

What made the story interesting, however, and proved that deep down inside Pete could get slightly interested in something besides the wily gobbler was his discovery and subsequent pursuit of a call he stumbled on that "made raccoons act as though they had a head full of humming birds."

Importance of this discovery was that Pete was getting the coons to scurry in at all hours of the day.

Pete was working on a squawk box that he had intended to give to a friend, as he wasn't a "box man himself, being a confirmed yelper," which means that his calls were mostly mouth operated. Well, this box apparently was one of those that hasn't the proper wood density to get good tone. Pete kept fooling around and finally figured that he had a box that would make a good but not great hen call, so he decided to forget it and start over. He wasn't about to give a friend an inferior call.

A couple of days later, he was driving down the road and saw a small flock of turkeys up ahead dusting in the powder of a country road. The bad box was the only call in the truck, laying on the dash where it had sat in the sun.

"I never gave it any thought. Didn't even recall it was that ol' poor box. I just snatched her up and slipped into the woods to make a circle out to where I knew this little group would be working."

Glassing a likely area can help the varmint caller to determine the route of approach his quarry may use.

Dougherty checks out a king-size raccoon that he called in with a variety of calls, using a light for his shot.

Seems Pete got all set and, after he let things "kinda flatten out and the red birds quit hopping about trying to tell on me, well, I gives the ol' poor box a lick. Why, the sound that came out woulda curled your hair.

"All I got out of that box was kind of a grating twitter. Didn't sound like anything ever meant to be uttered in the good Lord's woods. I waited a minute and tried again. I got real good hand position on the box and slide striker, but it was about the same as the first; real poor sound, the kind that makes your skin crawl, like a fingernail on a blackboard.

"Well, I says, what the hell, and I'm about to throw it away, 'cause I knowed them birds has headed back up the hollow on the first lick, but I figure I'll see what's wrong. I'm looking at it and sliding the slate across the sound board when, wham, this ol' boar coon 'bout climbed right into my lap, skeered me about two early days into my reward."

Pete got over the shock and, later on, his curious nature about this sort of thing began to irritate a spot back in his head. A few days later, he tried to make the same sound in a small brushy creek bed where he knew coons were denned for the day.

"I didn't know if I could even make that sound again. I was kinda hoping I couldn't, you know. Well sure 'nuff, it come out about the same, as close as I could remember. I give her a touch about once a minute and all of a sudden I got a coon splashing through the creek to get to me an' another coming out of a big ol' oak up the river like he had his tail afire. Pardner, I had me a coon caller's coon call."

Pete spent a lot of time studying that call after that. As close as he could figure, it had to do with the way the edge of the box had warped in the sun and never got another that quite sounded the same.

We drove on for awhile and finally I asked Pete to show me the call. Protocol probably demanded that I wait until it was offered, but he was off the subject and back on his birds again.

"Funny thing about that ol' box. I finally give it to my brother, the one with the hounds, and he took to totin' it out after coon at night. Got so he called up a coon, then set those ol' hounds loose. It was a real banger for training young pups.

"Time went by and one day I asked him for it. It was kinda still on my mind, you see, why I couldn't make another. He said he burnt it up one night on Red Ear Ridge. Tossed it right in the fire. Asked why, he said it was no good. His cold trailin' dogs hadn't had to hunt in months and, with the coons right there, when we turned out, he had developed nine strike dogs an' every dog in his pack turned into a sight runner.

"Besides, the races were shorter and there wasn't hardly much anticipation of wondering if he'd find a good track. Besides they was so busy running coons and getting to the tree it was causing a lot of good corn to go unattended, so he burnt it — kind of glad he did, too. I'd as soon leave coon calling to you varmint guys."

Here's another tidbit I happened upon while talking to a fellow from Tulsa. The subject eventually got around to hunting and he does a little calling, specializing in coon, but has a rather different approach I'll pass on. He has done some past calling for coon with calls designed for same. By his admission, there were noisemakers better-suited for Halloween and New Year's parties. He had found — by what set of circumstances, I'm not quite sure — that a duck call was a real coon-calling machine.

He uses a regular duck call and makes it growl, which is no difficult task, if you fool with it a bit. His theory is that raccoons are more interested in answering a call that plays on their fighting instincts and defense of young tendencies. My experience with coons is that you can't really rely on responses of the intensity that coyotes or fox display.

The sound is, in his opinion, much like that of a fighting mad-boar coon and this sounds right to me. The coon's response is one of determination. In short, they come in looking for trouble, and shooting quick, as well as straight, is a requirement.

Raccoons fall under a variety of categories and hunters should check into game laws relative to their taking before they are hunted. Areas around waterways are always best and nighttime is the key for these animals which are mostly nocturnal.

Wolves are blessed with extreme senses in matters of self-preservation and most of the successful wolf callers of my association claim that it is very hard to get them close. I agree, based on experiences I've had in Canada and Alaska. In all instances, even with excellent terrain, cover and wind, I could not get the big fellows inside of a hundred yards. Had I been armed with a firestick, the results may have been different, but in those few experiences, the stands were made while I was bowhunting for other game such as moose, caribou or bear.

What has always fascinated me about the use of a varmint call is its ability to entice animals of a nonpredatory or nonmeat-eating disposition. Bull elk have been called with a gutteral pitch call and deer come with alacrity, particularly in the Spring, when I suspect the does

The javelina has a reputation as being a vicious game animal, but actually will depart at high speed if he is surprised or frightened. However, the animal appears to have a curiosity which will bring it into the call.

feel a fawn is in distress.

Perhaps the most interesting form of nonvarmint varmint calling is the little collared peccary of the Southwest most commonly known as the javelina. Why they come is a mystery but when they do it is with total commitment, and when they choose not to, the exodus is carried out the same way. Marion Marshall of Arizona has guided many a bowhunter for javelina and put the pig in the archer's lap. Many times when hunting coyotes in the Arizona desert or the thick brushland of Texas, we have had javelina and coyotes coming at the same time with the little pigs huffing and puffing and carrying on with a vicious clattering of teeth.

Some years ago I was bowhunting for javelina in southern Arizona, east of Nogales. It was January, a beautiful time on the desert which carries a green hue, garnished by sprinklings of short-lived wild flowers. I was contouring a hill, working slowly towards a distant saddle, when I spotted several javelina feeding ahead and below me two hundred yards. Eventually I got within fifty yards of the outside members of the herd which was feeding below. As I sat and studied the herd, I became aware that there were perhaps thirty head of javelina in the bunch, well spread out, and that I was unable to work in closer due to the steep hill covered with gravel-like marbles. The pigs were unaware of my presence, and rather than take a poor shot, I decided to make a call.

The results were amazing. As I leaned into the call, I became aware that the closest pigs spooked badly, while those farther away turned towards me coming fast. It was chaotic when all members of the herd met in the bottom of the draw. They sorted it out, to their advantage not mine, and lined out in that steady mile-eating trot. Through my binoculars, I watched them go clear through the distant saddle without stopping and we never found that band again. I have no explanation for the behavior of that particular band. Obviously some wanted to come and some did not; understanding javelina can be difficult. Calling javelina has become a standard hunting method in the last ten years, offering good mixed bag opportunities when the chance for a coyote, cat or fox is added in. The most preferred calling style is deep throated, raspy and loud with long, drawn-out notes. I suspect that other styles work, too, but I have seen this method produce with the most consistency.

On an earlier occasion, Doug Kittredge and I were bumping about down around Tucson, Arizona, snapping a bunch of primers at coyotes and the odd fox. Kittredge has a hell of a distinctive calling style that's virtually guaranteed to make coyotes drool.

On this trip he had something else going for him, as Kittredge called up the first javelina the pair of us had ever seen in the wild. Now that was a real conversation piece for quite a spell; imagine a javelina coming to a varmint call. The javelina is a pig-like fellow found in Arizona, Texas, Mexico and parts of New Mexico. A peccary, actually he's a vegetarian that roots around the Sonoran-type desert chomping down on succulent cactus, needles and all. The javelina enjoys a funny reputation; some consider him dangerous due to the fact that he carries some pretty wicked teeth around in his mouth that could be tough to get along with if they were planted in your leg. They are, however, hardly dangerous game, but they are fun to hunt, pretty good on a platter and impressive as hell on the wall.

Over the years a few more stories on javelina answering a call circulated in calling circles and pretty soon, it became obvious that they could be called up regularly. General calling styles are hard-blown squeals. It apparently sounds like a youngster in a pickle and the pigs come running, whether to help out or watch, no one's quite sure about that. At least it's fairly obvious that a coyote's intent is to eat the source of all the commotion. It seems there is no middle ground with the little desert pigs when they hear a call — they either come in hard or split for distant parts, but they don't stand around and just listen.

At this time, real students of the javelina's habits were soon working out extremely successful calling styles and during the seasons that followed a new hunting method was born. Previously, the general method was to locate good pig country and hoof it until the game was sighted. Spotting a pig is tough; they are just darn hard to see, even if you're looking right at one. The little guys look just like a bush and have a horrible habit of remaining motionless for long periods of time, particularly if they feel danger is in the area. Many a time I've hunted them for days, knowing full well they were right there with me and never seen a hair.

The calling angle changed this. At least, it seems to work well enough to make it a profitable diversion from miles of desert wandering.

Based on the javelina's interest in a call, I have experimented for years on the wild boars found throughout the country, from razorbacks to Russians and the mongrel varieties of feral hogs in-between. So far, however, they have not expressed an interest in my attempts to lure them to a premature end. One nice thing about the javelina game is the peccary's home range is always good coyote, cat and fox range. Nothing wrong with calling up a coyote now and then. Been quite a few occasions when pigs and critters come together.

In the part of the country where a lot of us hunt, the wolverine is something you read about. Personally, I've never had an opportunity to call one in, but Max Blackham, a Utah dentist, testifies that this vicious little creature can be brought in with a mouth call.

"It was that dying squeal from the predator call that made the wolverine concentrate his senses in my direction," he recalls. The prior squeal had not attracted him. It had been a long hard Winter. A two-month spell of sixty below weather coupled with cold snaps dropping down even lower had made food as scarce as elephant tracks in the Sahara Desert. This particular wolverine was out for one square meal and the sound of a dying rabbit made the ribs from both sides shake hands with each other. This time of year, a constant twenty-four-hour a day search goes on for food.

"He turned straight at me and, with head high and eyes my way, a nonwavering course was set on his automatic pilot. At this point, I had a couple of big problems. One of them was to hold still while he covered the next two hundred yards. I was lying on the stock of my rifle and did not dare chance a move to free it to where I could shoulder the gun. The other was that my guide and outfitter, Louis Brown, was not too far away, walking up the bank of the Yukon River trying to find me."

Colonel Roy Crawford of Fresno, California, and

Silence is a must, when calling. Unusual sounds such as the click of cartridges can send game running. This belt cartridge carrier introduced by Federal several years ago can be an aid in having cartridges handy but still silent.

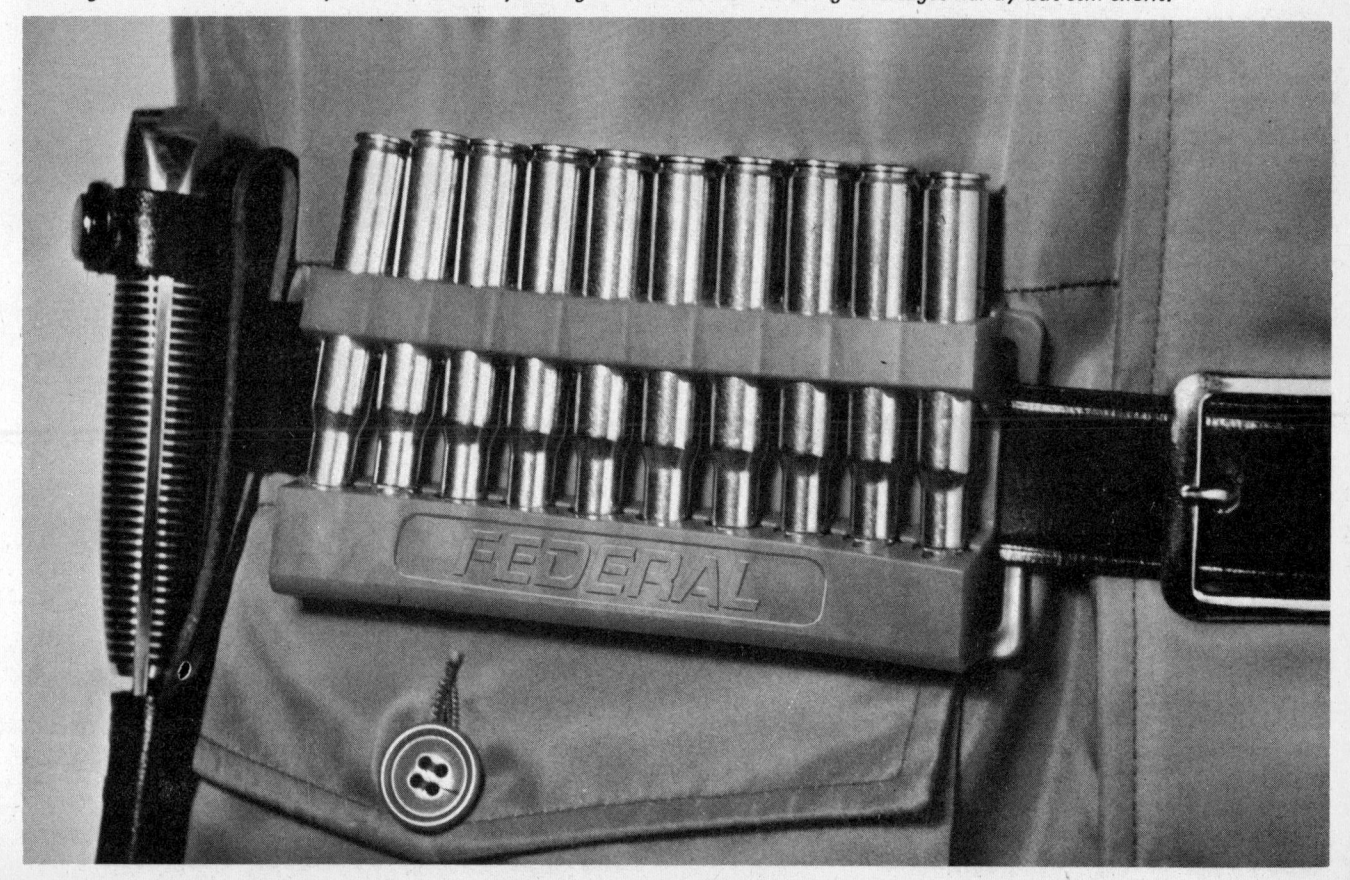

VARMINT HUNTER'S DIGEST

The wolverine, found for the most part in Northern climes, has been immortalized as a cute creature by Walt Disney and others, but the fact is that the predator is a killer that appears to slay for joy as well as for food needs.

Blackham had just touched off four rounds each at the wolverine at about four hundred yards. The two were really out for spring grizzly, so all they had was large caliber rifles designed for old Ursus. Crawford had a .308 Norma magnum on a custom job and Blackham had a .338 Winchester magnum on the old-style Model 70 Winchester. Both had Redfield 3X-9X variables for scopes. Smaller caliber, flatter shooting rifles would have been better, yet the hunters felt fortunate to not only have seen a wolverine, or king soldier, as the Yukon Indians call them, but to throw a little lead in his direction.

"Both Crawford and I were a little hurt that he was not going into one of our trophy areas at home, and while consoling each other, we walked back toward our tent. We were camped on the bank of the Yukon River about two hundred miles upstream from Dawson City. We hoped to complete a 250-mile spring grizzly hunt by floating the near 250 miles between Minto and Dawson City. We already had put thirty miles behind us the day before. Grizzly sign was more than abundant," according to Blackham.

"My quickening heartbeat seemed to cause my still body to jump while I was trying to lie so quietly. I did not know where Brown was and I did not know if he could see the wolverine — and I sure did not want Mr. King Soldier to see either of us. This might be my only chance in an entire lifetime to collect such an animal."

As Blackham and Crawford were lamenting their failure of missing this prize, the former again saw a movement on the edge of the island where they previously had tried to long tom the beast. The original sighting of the wolverine was made by Harry Baum, the Indian guide.

"I just happened to have my Circe jackrabbit predator call in the pocket of my shirt. I grabbed my .338 magnum and made a dash up the bank of the Yukon River that should have qualified me for the Olympics. I'm usually a bit slow in a foot race but this time I fairly flew to my stand behind a small pine tree in a clump of grass situated on the very bank of the river."

The wolverine covered the next one hundred yards on a steady lope, with the characteristic mid-body humping, coiling and uncoiling. His mind was on a fast rabbit fricassee — until he suddenly stopped. He threw his nose high as though testing the air. The wind was quartering off the hunter's right shoulder.

The wolverine acted like a cold-nosed hound trying to wind a bear and it worried Blackham that the wind might gust toward the animal.

"The time was right for the next calling attempt. I tried to make it sound like Mr. Rabbit was on his final breath, and that was all it took. The wolverine homed my direction like he had a built-in radar set. And I felt like he was going to stay right on the beam. If he did, I was sure to get my kind of shot.

"Between us was a nice big open ice pack and he was now coming out on it. He would soon be within 150 yards. 'Brown, please get lost,' I sort of mumbled into the long yellow grass in front of me. But you should never sell your guide short. Most of them have spent a lifetime in the north country and if you do not know what you are doing they usually know for you. Unknown to me, Brown could see what was going on and had settled back into the trees about a hundred yards down from my position.

"I now had to chance some movement to get at my rifle which I had blundered under me. And it was farther under than I had originally thought. I had to roll nearly over to free the rifle and get it out in the clear. I'm confident that I rolled into good visual position as seen from the wolverine's standpoint. I do not know if he saw me, but if he did not, he had just missed the one and only chance he was ever going to get from me.

"I felt a little overgunned about now but it was all I had. The load that was going to be used was my private handloaded bullets. A 210-grain Nosler with a Winchester 8½ x 120 primed, Winchester case that had 72.0 grains of Du Pont 4350 powder with approximate velocity of 2965 fps (average forty-five shots) was apparently good grizzly medicine."

The wolverine was now about 150 yards away; he stopped, turned broadside and posed. If he was going to make a last mistake in life, he sure was not going to make it a small one. He held perfectly still while Blackham lined up the crosshairs and began the squeeze.

The Yukon silence was broken and the wolverine's mistake was indeed his final blunder. He really was not a large animal but was a beautiful dog male in full winter coat. He must have weighed about twenty-five pounds. It was mid-May and still plenty cold.

"I figured that the big magnum would really pulverize this smaller animal, and I was almost afraid to inspect the damage. To my delight, I found a small hole about the size of a dime in the lower rib cage on one side and one about the size of a dollar directly through and out of the other side. That cannon is a fair varmint gun after all, I thought to myself after the damage check.

"As I stood over him on the ice pack where he had dropped, I felt more than lucky because I'd not only had seconds on him but had also the opportunity to try a predator call — which I would have enjoyed anyway.

"I admit I am not up on the facts about the wolverine but I would bet there are not too many of us members in the We Call Wolverine With A Predator Call Club. I do realize that the wolverine is a bold rogue and quite fearless in any given situation and this, in part, may make him a real top animal for the caller who prefers to use calls for hunting. And as scarce as they are to the hunter, this might be a better than usual way to collect a wolverine."

Birds of prey respond well to a call which provides the caller with super opportunities for photography or just plain relaxing observation. Many times at night we have been literally attacked by great horned owls and even the smaller species such as barn or screech owls. Once, when I was calling in the middle of the day, a huge bald eagle stooped from high overhead and sat in the branches above me not six feet away. When calling, the hunter will do well to watch the birds, for many times they will tip him off to a four-footed approach. Hawks and ravens will fly in with an approaching coyote and, magpies, crows and jays will tip a hunter off to the unseen visit of a stealthy bobcat.

Whatever the motive, food or curiosity, the varmint call has a strange hold on most of our wild animals and many of the birds. You should never become complacent. And always expect the unexpected, be it the magical appearance of a bobcat moving like a vagrant breeze or the sudden bounding materialization of a wild-eyed whitetail doe — such is the charm and magic of the calling game.

There are records of a number of cougar being called in by bowhunters as well as by the more familiar rifleman.

Chapter 9

THE UNCALLED FOR

Although Certain Varmints Cannot Be Called, They Still Offer A Challenge To The Hunter

ALTHOUGH CONSIDERED a year-round sport, varmint calling — and shooting — has its off-season in some respects. There is a period that is observed by the well-informed varmint caller during which he does not hunt. The reason is pure and simple conservation.

From February through late June, for example, the coyote is raising a new family. Conscientious callers back off and allow the proud parents to teach the youngsters the rudiments of growing up to become fair game in their turn. During this time, accredited varmint-calling clubs and associations emphasize to their members that they should hold their fire.

So the dedicated rifleman must seek out new fields to conquer with his pet smoke pole. The fields are there if you know what to look for.

When the question was put to me as to what I might shoot during this hiatus, I suggested, "Why not picket pins?"

The so-called picket pin is the ordinary ground squirrel, a rodent that creates a good deal of trouble for farmers and stock raisers by digging up fields and pastures. Reducing this particular population might be considered a minor boon to humanity and it would rightly test the capabilities of the .243. In recent months, incidentally, they have been

Idaho rock chucks don't grow as big as this camera angle would suggest, but their numbers make up for it. This species, with woodchucks, ground squirrels and prairie dogs, can literally take over the ground of farm or ranch.

Ralph Whited uses a pair of binoculars to check the action as Sue Dougherty settles in on a ground squirrel target in the Sierra's mountain meadows.

reported as carriers of the dread bubonic plague!

The eastern slope of the High Sierra in Spring is one of nature's better works of art. Here, with the snow melting off the high peaks and filling the trout streams to brimming, things take on a penetrating, bright feeling of newness. It is to these Sierras, though, that thousands upon thousands of city-bound dwellers flee in Spring and Summer, hoping that some of that feeling will rub off.

This, of course, leads to some problems. For example, the National Park Service estimates that one eventually will have to make a reservation — with a wait of up to two years — before he'll be able to find room in a park to pitch his tent.

The idea of having to stand in line to commune with nature is one of those things that gives me a dull ache about the wishbone, but it hasn't reached that point yet and it's to Mammoth Mountain and vicinity that I retreat, when I want to combine relaxation, trout fishing and gun testing. It's still one area where all three can be properly accomplished.

There are several varieties and variations of ground squirrels, picket pins, et al., and each can offer a terrific challenge to the rifleman who wishes to keep his abilities tuned up and burn some powder.

A phone call from my den to Mammoth Lake brought the news that the little rodents were out after the snows of Winter had run off the lower meadows. In fact, testified my informant, there was a certain piece of pasture where they were creating all sorts of problems by digging more holes in the landscape than ever could be put to practical use. After all, a cow or horse has only four legs, and after the members of the herd had stepped in that many holes to break that many legs, there still were a lot of holes left over. This was bothering the local ranchers to no end, proving that there may be even a few troubles in paradise. This was, in short, a situation seemingly tailored for the .243 Husqvarna that rested in my rack.

With this encouragement, I put down the phone, then told my wife to pack her boots and hunting gear.

My helpmate, Sue, is not one to go completely out of her head over another rifle. She's had a fair share of assorted armament pass through our abode, where rifles, shotguns, handguns, bows, arrows — even an occasional bean blower and dart — have at times been shown deference over the contents of the family bean pot. Generally she makes the usual wifely noises concerning my favorite toy, then returns to more realistic pursuits such as guarding the family cookie jar against the cold war constantly pressured by our sons.

It is only on rare occasions that she becomes even slightly enthralled with a rifle in spite of the fact that she joins me for a jaunt afield from time to time. It's one way of getting away from the kids, at least.

But when the pert little Husqvarna was pushed into her hands for inspection from the female's point of view, she let it be known that this was one gun she intended to shoot. I'd had the now-obsolete model since 1966, but this was her first real introduction.

To handle this gun is to touch richness, and that may have been a contributing factor to my wife's interest. The wood is European walnut and superbly hand-finished. In fact, it's so well done that someone wanted credit for his workmanship. Thus a small tag attached to a sling swivel proudly announced that the job was accomplished by one Alex Liljeqvist, apparently a dedicated Swede who spent long, loving hours in an effort to achieve perfection. After

Dougherty settles into his favorite military-type sitting position, bracing elbows on knees to take on a rodent.

initial inspection, more than a decade back, I could understand why this gent felt proud of his handiwork.

This one was called the Husqvarna Imperial lightweight with the price starting at $214.50; a respectable sum in those pre-inflation days.

Less scope, it scales in the vicinity of 6½ pounds, and the action is of the familiar Mauser design. Both action and barrel are of Swedish carbon steel with the latter having something called hammer-forged rifling. Overall length of the little rifle in the .243 caliber is 41¾ inches, while the barrel from chamber to muzzle is 20½ inches. Twist ratio is 1:10. The stock is of the Monte Carlo design and, as suggested earlier, the checkering is finely done with no runover around the edges of the design where the artisan can get careless and allow his knife to slip.

It has a fully adjustable trigger that is deeply serrated for positive squeeze when you're on target, and there is a latch in the forward section of the trigger guard that releases the trap door magazine.

The one facet that I found somewhat trying in the beginning is the safety, which is designed well enough, but it's on the right side of the gun and almost in the vee of the hand when you're grasping the pistol grip. There may be another, easier way of doing it, but I found that I might be well set in on a ground squirrel, ready to fire, then would have to loosen my hold and switch my thumb over the top of the stock to release the safety with a light forward push. This meant getting settled in again for my shot. Since the picket pin is a nervous little beast, he wasn't always so cooperative as to wait around while I went through the required safety steps.

In fact, ground squirrels in any form do not offer much in the way of a target, and when the range reaches out to a couple of hundred yards or more, things can get just a might tight.

There's a novel rear sight on this rifle. It's a three-piece arrangement with the center leaf remaining upright and alleged to be wedged into the rifle barrel to shoot accurately at a hundred yards. The forward and rear leaves fold down, but can be raised with a mere flick of the thumb. The front one is marked for the two-century mark, while the rear leaf is for three hundred-yard shooting.

For obvious reasons, I ignored the iron sights and installed a 4-power Bausch & Lomb scope, which may be perfect for the critter shooter, but it becomes somewhat demanding as a rodent reducer. A 4-power is just about right for nailing a running coyote to his tracks, but when it comes to popping a crawling *citellus* at the two hundred-yard mark, one has to squint a bit.

Getting the scope and barrel to coincide didn't take a lot of valuable time, since I bore sighted the rifle in my kitchen. A few minor adjustments of the mount in the field showed me that even with factory ammo, I could shoot groups of 1-1/8 to 1½ inches at a hundred yards, firing ten-shot groups.

The ammo I had on hand was the standard Remington factory load featuring the 80-grain pointed soft-point bullet. There is a multitude of beautiful loads that can be concocted for the .243 and Dean Grennell was irritated that time didn't permit the fashioning of some of his favorite squirrel loads.

Grennell's favorite general-purpose load for the .243 Winchester consists of the 75-grain pill, motivated by 40.0 grains of IMR-4320 powder. The velocity is a comparatively modest 3300 to 3350 fps and the 40-grain charge of 4320 is somewhat below the maximum levels listed in most reloading manuals: Speer, for this powder and bullet weight, specifies 42.0 grains as maximum — to be used with caution — for a muzzle velocity of 3450 fps; Hornady sanctions charges up to 41.6 grains of 4320 for their 75-grain secant-ogive hollow-point, rating the velocity as 3400 fps from a twenty-two-inch barrel. Lyman says 42.0 grains is the maximum for a velocity of 3450 fps.

Most of the loads listed for this caliber in the reloading manuals are developing pressures toward the upper levels of practical usage and any attempt to cheat a few more feet per second of velocity by padding the powder charge is almost certain to result in loosened primer pockets and the other signs that all is not as it should be. Moreover, the .243

Sue Dougherty loads the .243 Husqvarna. A favorite with varmint hunters, the rifle no longer is being manufactured. Those who possess this model guard it with a great deal of care and even jealousy.

The snow still clings to the peaks of the High Sierras, but this doesn't keep the ground squirrels from their attacks on lower pastures. The rodents do a great deal of damage to land, crops, causing erosion problems.

case frequently displays considerable tendency to stretch and thicken at the neck and both of these conditions, when present, can boost breech pressures to the danger point and beyond — even when the bullet and powder charge are perfectly conservative and safe from a properly dimensioned case. Accordingly, case length should be checked and held to the specified dimension of 2.045 inches and trimmed back below that length when the measurement reaches approximately 2.047 to 2.049 inches.

A bullet should be used to check the mouth of the fired case before resizing, to test for thickened case necks. This affords a quick and convenient check but, if the bullet can't be inserted base-foremost into a fired case, you might also wish to measure the outside diameter of the case at midpoint of the neck. Normally, fired cases will measure somewhat more than .276-inch at this point, depending upon chamber dimensions of the individual rifle, but one sometimes encounters loads which do not expand the case mouth to chamber dimensions so that the plug check with the bullet base is not an infallible indication of a thickened neck.

However, if the bullet base won't go into the neck of a fired, unsized case, and if the outside diameter of the case is the same as typical fired cases from the same rifle, then — very definitely and most imperatively — that case must either be throat-reamed or discarded.

With sighting in and scope adjustments taken care of, we made for the preselected meadow to wait out the burrowing rodents that should be showing themselves. On the edge of the sage-bordered meadow, Sue and I set up,

Picking up ground squirrels or rats isn't a good idea these days, as they have come to be suspected of being carriers of bubonic plague, which is making a reappearance.

while Ralph Whited, who had accompanied us, began spotting with a pair of Bushnell 7X35 binoculars.

Our combined armament at this point consisted of a Sako .222 magnum, a Ruger Blackhawk .357 magnum and, of course, the Husqvarna, not to mention ammo for each. The Ruger handgun can hardly be considered a long-range squirrel gun, but for those that pop up within fifty yards, it constitutes quite a demoralizer — even when you miss.

Ground squirrels, not being very large, require little lead to total out their careers. The 80-grain bullet proves effective.

As the first dirty digger of the day presented himself, I quietly closed the bolt, assumed a comfortable sitting position, and pushed off the safety before I settled the crosshairs on the squirrel and obliterated it.

"Right in the eye!" I boasted. Considering the fact that there was little left of the squirrel, it was a claim that would be difficult to disprove.

As the day wore on and the shooting continued, my wife laid shot after shot neatly where it would do the most good — or harm, depending upon viewpoint. Her most observant comment was, "Isn't this just a little too much gun for these little critters?"

Caliber-wise, the .243 is the ultimate for game ranging from varmints to medium-size types, I feel. The varmint-calling fraternity seems to favor this cartridge and the wide selection of bullet weights makes it the ideal rifle for the man who wants one gun.

I had an opportunity to use the .243 during a trip to Idaho, firing it upon coyotes, bobcats and a big mule deer. I used the 80-grain bullet with a load of 48.0 grains of 4831. In each instance, including the deer, these were one-shot kills.

The Husqvarna magazine well holds five rounds and allows an additional cartridge in the chamber, and there are no sharp edges in the magazine that can create hang-ups or cut one's fingers.

My wife made no bones about the fact that she considered the rifle her own. The long tapering forend fits the smaller female hand perfectly. However, this model being the lightweight, the recoil against Sue's shoulder over a long morning of continuous popping did become a bit taxing. Recoil is a bit more than the .218 Bee with which she is more familiar.

Whited and I also ran a fair share of lead through the bore. When it was time for lunch, the three of us had accounted for sixty-odd picket pins with the Husqvarna. That meant the remainder were going to have to put on an additional shift to get their holes done on schedule.

But a note of caution: In view of the reported outbreak of plague in the Western states, it's a healthy idea not to handle the rodents — alive or otherwise!

In the flat valley country, Sue Dougherty discovered that she made her best shots on small targets from prone position.

VARMINT HUNTER'S DIGEST

99

The Big Ones Grow Up Idaho Way

"HE'LL GO BOONE & Crockett. Easy."

Steve Herrett had rendered this judicious verdict, standing in the foyer of the Herrett-Hilton and, somehow, incredulously, managing to look insufferably dapper in pajamas and cowboy boots.

It was early of a Sunday morn and the sky over Southern Idaho was the pellucid azure of sapphire. Dean Grennell had awakened early and, feeling it a shame to waste such glorious environment by sleeping, had dressed for a solo outing. Scarce a hundred yards from the luxurious camper truck, he had encountered Owen Barton, afield in the dawn's brilliant sunlight with a pickup full of salt blocks for distribution across the numerous acres of the Diamond A Ranch. As a matter of record, the salt blocks did not get put out until later in the week.

"We had stood there swapping small talk, Barton and I, and he had swept his good right eye across the skyline and picked up a rock chuck in plain view; plain, that is, if you have the game-wise eye of an Owen Barton. As a result of a childhood accident, his left eye — while appearing normal from the outside — is all but useless," Grennell explains.

After a bit of patient guidance, Grennell also saw the critter. With arrogance, the hoary-whiskered monarch of the bluff surveyed his domain and took in the kindling warmth of the early sunlight. Grennell twisted the ring that zaps the magnification of the 3-9X Leupold Vari-X II scope to its upper limit and examined the grizzled varmint who had spent his life gorging on the lush grass and excavating pitfalls to imperil the unwary feet and legs of Barton's horses and cattle.

"I came within an ace of inching off the trigger of the cherished old Ackley-Niemiec without further ado and caught myself within scant ounces of let-off," Grennell recalls. "Suddenly, it had occurred to me that it would be akin to strafing the pup on a Victor record or — heaven forbid — the little girl on the carton of Morton's salt. For, there in the bleary focus of my freshly awakened eye, was a trademark fully as familiar to reloaders as Leo, the MGM lion. A rock chuck pinned in the crosshairs of a scope reticle has been the trademark of RCBS for several of the recent decades. Indeed, though it's none too widely known, the initials stand for Rock Chuck Bullet Swage," the

Rock chucks may look cute to the casual viewer, but they constitute a threat to farm and ranch lands in the West, since they multiply rapidly.

Behatted Steve Herrett and Dean Grennell survey a deep canyon, seeking a colony of rock chucks in the depths.

product with which Fred Huntington launched his enterprise down in Oroville."

Steve Herrett and Hugh Farmer, Grennell's hunting partners, had been awakened by the hubbub and Barton's son, Bob, had driven up in his jeep, pausing to spectate the proceedings.

With a mental apology to the patient — or perhaps merely overconfident — rock chuck, Grennell began taking up the pressure on the trigger again. After the protracted firing of the previous day, the sight picture had become sheer instinct and he nestled the center of the reticle on the point between the chuck's tummy and the supporting rock. Sighted for point of aim at about 220 yards, the impact is a trifle high at 150 and the target was some sixty feet or so above the marksman, likewise requiring a touch of underaim. The sight picture looked precise and satisfactory as the .25/06 emitted its piercing blast, shattering the tranquil quiet of the morning to echoing splinters and leaving the Bartons with one less noxious pest to support and worry about.

VARMINT HUNTER'S DIGEST

It had turned out to be a trait of the .25/06 to send the little 87-grain capsule of lead and jacket metal at clocked velocities of around 3350 fps.

"So I stuffed a handful of fresh Remington factory loads in my pocket and forded a small stream to climb the steep slope to the top of the bluff for a closer look at the retired rodent. The rifle weighs a touch under twelve pounds, having been put together with the specifications that it should be capable of top-notch shooting firstly, and more or less portable, secondly. But I didn't begrudge the extra weight, because Barton spotted a second chuck for me to dust off on the way, which the .25/06 did with the deadly dispatch that is its outstanding characteristic," Grennell recalls.

At the time the test rifle was put together — in 1967 — if you fancied the .25/06, you had to build your own ammunition for it. This rifle carries a twenty-six-inch Ackley barrel, with a 1:10 twist in a Mauser-type action then being built for Ackley in Japan. Al Niemiec, of Highland, California, had devoted a lot of skilled and patient hours in fitting and sculpturing the stock from a choice blank of screw bean mesquite and the result of the combined operations is a rifle that would hold its zero, come drought or drizzle, with total reliability.

By mid-1970, Remington had added the .25/06 cartridge to their line — an act of benevolence both welcome and overdue — and commenced to produce their Model 700 bolt-action rifle with chambers cut to fit the latest addition. The barrel offered as standard is twenty-four inches in length, with 1:10 twist. This seems to be the ideal pitch of rifling for the .25/06, capable of excellent accuracy with all of the various weights available in this diameter, from 75 to 120 grains.

Grennell's Ackley-Niemiec, with the same rate of twist, has punched out 1.5-inch groups from one hundred yards with five rounds of 75-grain bullets, plus five rounds of 117-grain bullets.

Until a few years back, the reloading manuals refrained from providing any reloading data for the use of 60-grain bullets, or cast bullets in the .25/06. So, having a rifle of that persuasion, plus chronograph, the hunters undertook to fill in the gap. In the tests, they took the 60-grain Hornady to 3802 fps and the 60-grain Speer to 4016 fps and, at the same time, took the Lyman number 257420 cast gas check from a mere, loafing 629 fps — on 1.5 grains of Bullseye — up to 1694 fps (weight, in linotype metal, is 75 grains) and the Lyman number 257325, a nice-looking, round-nosed gas check at 112 grains in lino metal, from 1007 to 2267 fps.

In the wide expanses of the Idaho mountain country, a pair of binoculars becomes a must in attempting to find any type of game, whether rodents or elk, as Herrett discovered, or when attempting to find the rock chucks.

Ranchers such as Owen Barton carry binoculars in their vehicles as just another necessary tool for ranching.

VARMINT HUNTER'S DIGEST 103

Steve Herrett and his .25/06 make an adequate team for the long-range shooting in his native Idaho mountains, but they are dwarfed by the grandeur of the terrain and the skies. The .25/06 is a favorite in such situations.

While the parameters of performance could be extended, certainly, it was felt that this expanded the versatility of this great caliber by a considerable degree.

Reloading tests with the 87-grain Remington Power-Lokt bullet in Remington primed .25/06 cases developed load data that will drive the bullet to velocities all the way up to 3773 fps from a twenty-six-inch barrel. This is good for a rousing 2750 foot-pounds of muzzle energy, although it was decided that 3676 fps represents a practical upper velocity ceiling for bullets of this weight.

When you get down to the point that is both nitty and gritty, most of those super-speedy loads exact a toll that is rather extortionate, from the standpoint of long-term accurate life expectancy of the barrel. The rifling at the chamber end is apt to melt away like the snows of Winter in the warm rains of Spring. And one basic, bedrock operating principle reads like this: When you luck onto a gun that shoots well, don't mess it up.

"For this good and sufficient reason, after working up the recipes that will produce paces in the region of upper three thousand to lower four thousand feet per second, we refrained from making up any large quantities of loads to those performance levels," Grennell recalls.

Some several weeks previously, the rifle had been zeroed in for the Remington factory loads and, true to its track record, it showed every indication of holding that zero with dogged determination, until someone spun the knobs on its scope. Arriving on the Diamond A, with its teeming hordes of rock chucks, there were no facilities for extended range target work, and about the only yardstick was to aim at a chuck and find out if you had hit him or missed him.

If you hit the chuck, the result was more apt than not to verge upon the sheerly spectacular. Bob Barton zapped several of the little rascals with the Ackley-Niemiec .25/06 and, in the process, developed a sort of incoherent awe for its potential. On at least one memorable occasion, the results could not have been more devastating if he could have induced the chuck to swallow a number seven blasting cap and detonated it in the hapless critter's gizzard. One thing was certain: The retired varmint suffered no pain at all.

In anticipation of the planned safari, Grennell had made up several test batches of other loads for the legendarily reliable Ackley-Niemiec. But, firing from ranges of four hundred yards and beyond, none of these displayed the pinpoint predictability of the factory loads — for the simple and obvious reason that it had been zeroed with the factory jobs. Since the hunters had a hundred rounds of the lovely tailor-mades, Grennell soon went back to using the Bridgeport handloads on an exclusive basis, and misses became a rare and noteworthy event.

He reports, "I soon encountered fresh proof of a facet of the .25/06 which had been unmistakable since my earliest encounter with this rather remarkable cartridge: When properly zeroed, you have to be one helluva long way from any target before you start holding over it. Almost all of the missed shots occurred when I peered through the sights and figured, well, that's so far away that I'd better hold a trifle high.

"So I'd skim the back of the chuck's neck with the crosshairs and ease the trigger off and Steve Herrett, monitoring through his spotting scope, would regretfully inform me that I had shot over: 'You just skimmed over the back of his neck,' he'd say. Finally, I learned to keep some fur in the crosshairs, no matter how far away and, as of that moment, misses became almost rare enough to rate front-page space in the local paper."

Herrett, who turnes out superlative handgun stocks in his plant at Twin Falls, Idaho, had added an invaluable accessory to his spotting scope: iron sights. In a varmint-shooting situation, you're apt to be working with a large hunk of terrain, most of which looks about the same as the rest of it. If the naked eye, or a sweep of the binoculars, turns up an area suspected of harboring a rock chuck, it is quick and easy to line up on it with the iron sights, peer through the eyepiece and get a good, close view of the area. Contrawise, if you are trying to steer a partly blind neophyte varmint shooter to the specific area, you can snarl, "Look down the iron sights, stupid!"

"Herrett, being a gent of the old school, did not put it in just those words, of course. But it was more than slightly humiliating to scan the talus and scree for invisible varmints, only to have them suddenly materialize, huge and obvious, when I finally got my unseeing eyes aimed in the proper direction," Grennell recalls.

"This is a phenomenon which continues to baffle me: the business of game vision. There are some people, not necessarily overly keen of eye, to whom anything capable of moving under its own power is as screamingly visible as if outlined by a neon sign. But, to a city dweller, unaccustomed to watching for anything smaller than a hurtling Volkswagen, the pesky thing remains invisible, until someone steers your eyes to it, hits you across the head with a two-by-four, and screams, 'See? See? See?' in your ear.

"Given a super-capable combo such as the Ackley-Niemiec and the Remington factory fodder, any idiot can hit just about any target that is within about two counties from the shooting spot. But it takes a hunter to find the game in the first place. And that's where skill takes over," Grennell philosophizes.

By mounting rifle sights atop his sighting scope, Herrett is able to get on target faster and find an area he wants to glass more quickly. He aligns the general area with the sights, then makes more minute inspection.

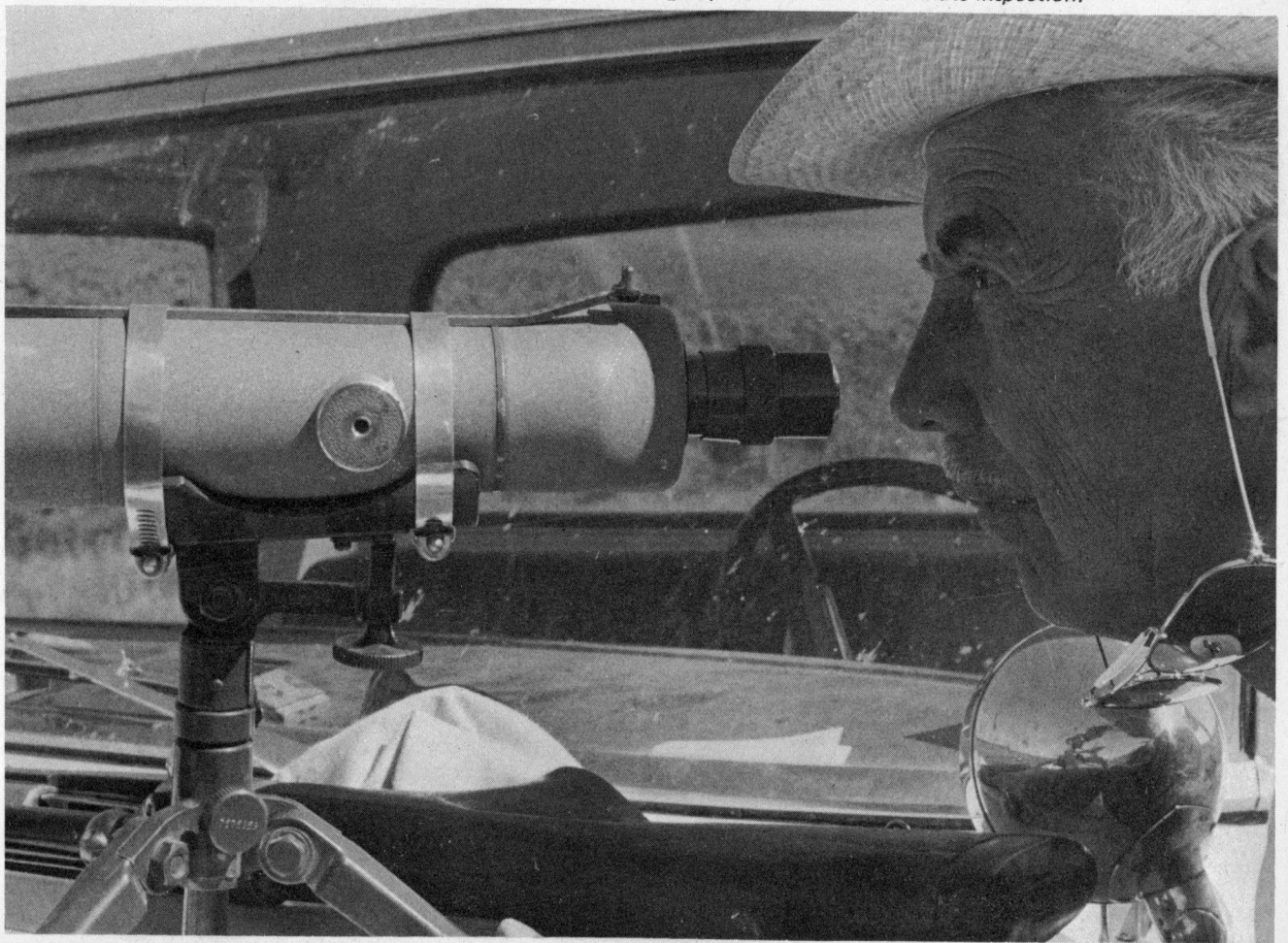

VARMINT HUNTER'S DIGEST

The .270 Weatherby magnum Mark V is a fine varminter.

Sako Vixen in .222 magnum is author's favorite.

Marlin lever-action .22 started Dougherty on squirrels.

Years ago, when I lived in California there were miles and miles of good ground squirrel territory open to shooting with any combination we chose to use. Today these squirrels still exist in numbers but so close to California ranch-style housing that laying it on them with a .22-250 or even a .22 LR is out of the question. My buddies still pursue them with bow and arrow in some limited areas but by and large the sport is all but over. I'm sure this condition exists over a large portion of the country, yet a varmint hunter who seeks the test of pinpoint long-range shooting on digger squirrels or prairie dogs can still locate shootable populations. One simply has to travel farther and work harder.

As a youth I hunted ground squirrel heavily with bow and arrow; excellent practice for bigger game as it required patience to get close and fine shooting to be occasionally successful. I shot at so many squirrels and jackrabbits with a fine old Marlin 39A in .22 LR that the barrel eventually went and that takes a lot of rounds. There was a time when I was a fair hand with a rifle, especially that little Marlin, due simply to lots of hours spent shooting sitting squirrel or running jacks. While it still seems unbelievable to me, on a three-day Memorial Day weekend I did in 1036 ground squirrels with that 39A. No wonder it eventually went smooth.

For many years my varmint shooting at critters in this category was restricted to the .22 and the bow and arrow. It was not until I got seriously involved in calling the bigger stuff that I made the move to the hotshot center-fire rifles. My first step in this direction was a Winchester Model 70 chambered in .220 Swift. When compared to that Marlin, with its hold high and allow-for-drift ballistics when plinking at squirrels that were out there a ways, it was a revelation.

My hunting buddies in those days were armed about the same. While we all had several shotguns, our big-game arsenal was primarily archery equipment, although everyone had a .22. When the calling bug bit us our attention was directed to new firepower channels, and we outfitted outselves with a variety of rifles in various calibers from the .257 Roberts, .250-3000 and .222 Remington to, in Doug Kittredge's case, a .270 Weatherby magnum. We obtained these pieces in order to shorten the odds on the coyotes that evaded our arrows with frustrating frequency and seemed to absorb .22 bullets as though they were bionic. It was only natural, as we moved through different calibers reloading and fine tuning, that we would gravitate

Ground squirrels are plentiful targets for the novice varmint hunter. Farmers and ranchers encourage depredation.

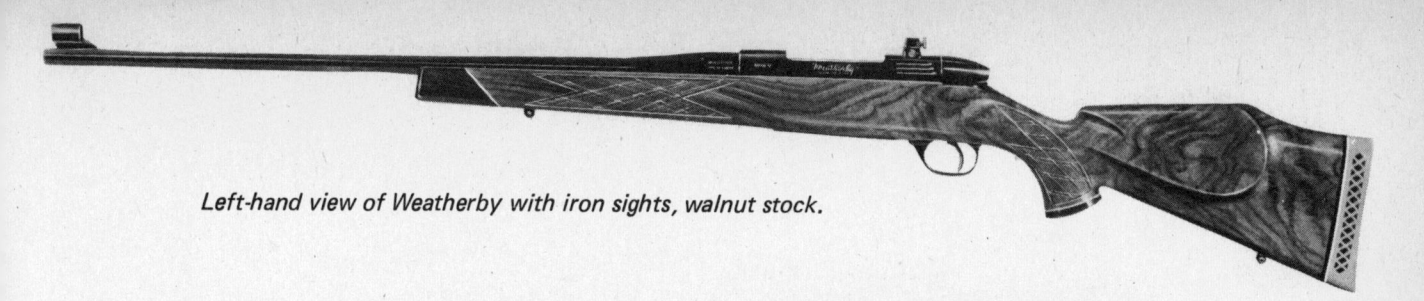

Left-hand view of Weatherby with iron sights, walnut stock.

to the range of the ground squirrel colonies for shooting practice and experience. While hunting of this type is fun, it is truly more of a precision shooting game than it is hunting. Given a choice I would still prefer to sneak through the brush and dry creek beds or belly down a fence row in hopes of getting a close-range shot with a bow or open-sighted .22.

Having hunted prairie dogs, woodchucks, rock chucks and ground squirrels extensively with both rifle and bow, I have found that they can be pursued effectively in both manners. The bowhunter must be cautious and patient. His shots will be few and his target difficult, but no matter what the game, this is the bowhunter's constant dilemma.

Broadheads are most effective on the bigger rodents such as the chucks, while blunts or field points suffice on the smaller targets. Other than the demands in bullet construction and powder loads for accuracy, if the shooting is going to be past 150 yards, it has never seemed to me to make a lot of difference what bullet configuration is used when the moment for missile and rodent meeting takes place. Whatever you hit them with seems to work marvelously. Kittredge's .270 Weatherby was some exception in those earlier years, requiring some time for the dust and gravel to settle before results could be confirmed.

Of all the variety of smaller varmint hunting to be had, my favorite has always been the wide-spread, long, lean black-tailed jackrabbit and the phantomlike antelope jackrabbit of Southern Arizona. Jackrabbits can be hunted in a multitude of ways from high vantage point observation in desert country with spotting scope and heavy barrel rifle to walking them up with bow, shotgun or rifle and taking the challenging runners as they highball to safer parts.

Years ago we discovered a method of hunting jackrabbits quite by accident that was remarkably successful for a short period each Spring. We learned that during the peak mating months the same call used so effectively on predators held mysterious fascination for the long-eared hares. To be most productive the call would be a simple series of squeals without all the scrambling excitement one seeks when attempting to draw in a coyote. The jacks, primarily males, would come aloping to the call, sometimes as many as a dozen in number. They would flop their ears, stand on back feet and occasionally do complete back flipping cartwheels. It was a unique way of hunting ideally suited to a bow or pistol shooter.

I recall a time in late February along the California-Mexico border. My partner Bob Jeske and I had wandered through the back country calling coyotes with little success when late in the afternoon we came upon a lonesome bean field of perhaps eighty acres carved in the middle of surrounding brushland. At the far end of the field sat an old tractor some hundred yards from the brushy corner situated perfectly with the prevailing wind to use as a blind. I was carrying my favorite Sako Vixen in .222

magnum while Jeske toted a custom 6mm. Each of us carried only a few extra shells beyond what we had loaded in our guns; three in my clip, five in the 6mm.

Several minutes into the stand I caught a flicker of movement, then another. My first thoughts were that a pair of coyotes was coming through the beans. Not so. They were jackrabbits. Jeske nudged me and pointed. Here came several more. Forgetting the coyote possibility we climbed to the top of the scrubby rows of beans. Quite literally we were surrounded by jackrabbits. We shot all the shells in our possession, then made an ammo run to the truck. When we returned there was not a rabbit in sight. Within three minutes of calling they began to reappear. According to my notes from that day dated February 19, 1960, we dumped thirty-one jacks. A good day's hunt.

Ground squirrels and others of the uncalled for may be hunted with either rifle or bow and arrow.

VARMINT HUNTER'S DIGEST

Chapter 10

THE WINGED ONES

Protected In Some Areas, Crows Still Constitute A Shootable Nuisance In Others

IF YOU'RE LIKE me, the last day of the scattergunning season can be kind of traumatic, downright sad in fact. It comes just about the time we have finally established a rapport with the shotgun and it shoots where we look, which just happens to be where we've finally started pointing it. Those remaining winter months look kind of bleak with nothing more exciting in store than weekend football and basketball on the tube and the monthly meeting of the rod and gun club, made up of fellows as down in the mouth as ourselves.

Well, there are several solutions to the scattergunning bug and the cold gray months of Winter happen to be as good a time as any; perhaps better. First item on the agenda would be crows.

There are a few problems concerning crow gunning now

VARMINT HUNTER'S DIGEST

Jim Dougherty, shotgun over his shoulder, seeks out a likely spot for ambushing crows that plague some areas.

that need to be considered in view of their status under recent federal regulations. Be sure and check with your local game department for correct interpretation of the rules and seasons. Generally speaking, crow hunting still is going on as usual, the key being the crow's role as a predator reflected in his habit of eating up agricultural efforts, involved in this type of practice he will probably be a legal target.

Here in Oklahoma, we have a wintering crow population of upwards of ten million birds on the Fort Cobb reservation alone, crow shooters quite naturally figure this is not a bad area to begin operations. In fact and fable, the crow is a cagey customer, perhaps not quite as educated as some would have you believe but a downright clever bird.

Stories have spread on their ability to count, which is downright silly. I personally know for a fact that crows cannot count beyond five. There are stories of crows being able to tell the difference between a man carrying a stick or shotgun and some hunters claim they can reckon and fly just outside the effective range of low or high-base loads. Such birds obviously know the difference in range capabilities of a rifle and shotgun, and rumor has it that sentinel crows remember license plate numbers in order to tell hunters from harmless picknickers on wooded roads as they fly their daily survey of parked cars.

There are naturalists who claim that a sentinel crow who fails in his responsibility to the flock is placed on trial by his peers, found guilty and pecked to death for negligence.

All of this leads to the general premise that crows are downright smart and difficult at best to lure within effective range of anything less than a guided missile, in which case they probably scatter tin foil. I'll take a front seat in the testimonial to crow intelligence panel. I do believe they are sharper than the average bird, but I base their ability to survive more on pure inherent caution than absolute brain power.

No matter what your analysis, crows are clever adversaries that offer post-season wingshooting in many areas, where controlling their numbers serves a worthwhile cause.

The classic way to gun crows is over decoys aided by a good mouth caller, who must be a pure artist at crow conversation. The electronic call also is popular. In areas of heavy concentrations such as the aforementioned Fort Cobb, calls, either electronic or mouth-operated, and decoys generally are a waste of time. Crows within the immediate vicinity of the Fort Cobb roost have had every trick known to man thrown at them. They just don't buy standard crow tactics anymore.

Personal experience and conversations with veterans tells me that in areas where large concentrations are roosting, there is no way to take the birds in the classic manner anymore. Smart gunners wait for tough, rough, windy days and pass shoot the birds on their way out of the roost area. On a calm day, a Fort Cobb crow will lift off the roost at daylight, circle to three hundred feet or more and head to feed. He comes home the same way, along with 9,999,999 other crows, give or take a million. Come a windy day that crow won't circle up quite as high. In fact, he and those other fellows will be forced to come off the roost low and stay that way on their way to the feeding grounds. As a result, those who shoot at Fort Cobb wait for the weather to bring them to shooting.

The farther out the bunches of crows range, the smaller the flocks. Most claim these flocks to be individual bands that travel together throughout the entire migration. It is when the huge flocks break up that the crow hunter preferring classic gunning methods can get in his licks.

This is generally a setup along a flight line up to twenty miles from the roost area, bordering feed areas which are most often corn or similar-type grain fields, stock feed yards, hog farms or garbage pits and dumps.

Decoys should be set prominently in fingers of woods that border feed grounds in close proximity to the flight line. With this type of condition, the shooters will get opportunities at small flocks of crows until midafternoon when they begin to gather for the long, high return to the roosting grounds. If the mouth call is used, it should be in the hands of a proficient crow caller. More than one caller helps, too.

Crows are not inclined to pay heed to faulty notes. They answer with a call that alerts all others that something's fishy, and off they'll go to where the climate's not as hostile. Electronic callers are ideal, much preferred by today's serious crow hunter.

An incoming crow looks for all the world to be as big and tough as the largest Canada goose, it's all camouflage for a small frame covered with lots of big feathers. Ideal loads are the same used for doves and quail — 7½ and 8s, although some shooters prefer No. 9 shot. Personally, I lean the other way and usually will carry some of the more authoritative 6s, particularly if there is some medium to long-range pass shooting involved.

Decoys are a must for good gunning and, while many

Crows have outstanding eyesight and usually can spot a trap, unless the cover and camouflage are utilized by the caller to the greatest advantage he finds possible. (Right) Bob Fuller utilizes an outcropping of sandstone for cover, while waiting for Dougherty to call crows in.

types can be purchased in the local sporting goods store, simple handmade silhouettes will do. We fashion ours from wire clothes hangers which easily can be bent to a basic crow shape. Cover the frame with black cloth or crepe paper if it won't be wet and put 'em out. The straightened hanger hook protrudes from the bottom of the decoy, ideal for sticking in the ground, fence post or for wrapping around a limb. Lightweight and easy to carry they also move suggestively in a breeze making them more effective.

The old owl decoy is still an effective way to drive crows nuts. For years we used a stuffed owl, a veteran of many a crow hunt until he expired in a puff of dried feathers amid a rather hot shooting spree when a back-peddling crow crossed in front of the old deek about the time a load of 8s caught up with him. Now we use a fiberglass cast of a great horned owl, well-painted and almost as effective, probably

Fuller displays the black bandit downed with the Browning 20 gauge during the day of crow calling. He is considered one of the TV industry's top field gunners.

just as good but we had a soft spot in our hearts for that moth-eaten old owl.

Crows will respond well to standard varmint calling but not in the reckless hell-for-leather fashion that regular crow music exerts. We have found, however, that a new twist often is the key to success on birds that have become shy due to heavy pressure.

A proven method is a combination of both varmint calling mixed with the excitement of hard-rocking crow fight conversation. Generally this is done with a regular opening series or two on the varmint call before the crow calling joins in. It's an effective angle that will produce fast action regularly. In the Western states springtime is still too early to do more than think of the forthcoming good calling months, another sixty days before serious critter pursuit gets into high gear.

A good many years ago, we hit on a good calling-shooting game that is generally chockful of action; particularly if you like the feel of a shotgun working your shoulder over and get a charge out of tricky wing shooting. The answer to our early season varmint assaults is the magpie — a strikingly pretty bird with obnoxious habits generally classed as undesirable whenever they can be found. Changes in status however do come about, so a check with regulations is in order. In California, for instance, the yellow bill magpies are totally protected.

By June, the young birds are fairly well on their way to independence following the trail of their elders who lead them on predatory forays that raises billy hell with a wide variety of song and game bird eggs and young such as quail, pheasants and water fowl. Young small game such as cottontails, also fall victim to the attacks of the black and white bandits. All in all, the magpie is a crusty character inclined to ruthlessness and the proper subject for a little corrective lead poisoning from time to time.

I like magpie shoots as it allows us to get out into some of our most favorite calling country, good time to get in some pre-coyote hunt scouting and secure a reading on how the desert critters are doing by checking for signs along the back roads and taking a census of early morning coyote conversation.

Our strategy for calling magpies is to hunt the heavy groves of cottonwoods or similar trees along canals and river beds that offer good concealment and are favored haunts for the feathered varmints. Calling is straight loud coyote patterns with a harsh call that has a tendency to peak out on a high pitch. The straight calling is supplemented by occasional bursts created by "chirring" into the call, what I guess would be best defined as a squawk-squawk pattern done by fluttering the tongue. All of this added together excites the birds into sometimes flocksized, screaming, suicide charges. The idea is to terminate the charge with a stack of No. 8 shot on the beak. The shooting is fast and tricky as the birds dodge through the trees, lots of lead in the air is a good solution to the surprisingly erratic and fast flight. We have experimented slightly with decoys and I believe they would add to the overall success, but they are not as effective as crow decoys.

Gunwise I prefer improved to modified choked 410s or 20-gauges with no longer than twenty-eight-inch barrels, for the oftentimes quick shooting that requires a bunch of maneuverability. It's lots of fun, good sport that will help maintain some of the touch that you started to develop last fall. It satisfies that trigger finger itch as well as getting the lungs back into shape for the serious calling days ahead.

Mid-winter crow shooting and spring magpies are challenging sports guaranteed to keep a fine shooting edge built up. Make sure you check the regulations in your area, round up a handful of clothes hangers, some calls and a couple good companions, it'll be time well spent.

For example, I recall one specific outing in California a few seasons back. Bob Fuller — of TV series *Emergency* fame — and I didn't have doves in mind on that particular Sunday morning, when we first arrived at my secret dove spot. Dove season wasn't quite due, but the whistling ghosts of the fields all were zipping about and we had cause to think ahead a few weeks. Our trigger fingers were having mild fits, causing us to stop our hurried walk to the cover of the cottonwoods to swing the guns, tracking a few of the tantalizing targets.

I had cause to remark to Fuller that come dove season the warm nights probably would have been chased off and the birds would be absent, but we would sure be here to make sure.

At the time, Fuller was fresh back from a demanding movie schedule in Europe, and somehow my editor, Jack Lewis, had brought up the subject of crows and, as things generally happen, it caused a chain of events that brought Fuller and I together that morning. It then also was a dandy excuse to get out and burn up a little powder, since there was a new Browning autoloader hanging about that — in its light 20 gun frame — simply demanded to be shot. Well, you know how it goes. Fuller wanted to snap some caps, particularly after hefting the twenty and, at the time, we didn't have anything more serious on our mind but some late-season bass fishing anyhow. With the prospect of the dove season close at hand, we decided that the twenty, some shells and a crow or two would make a hell of a morning.

The cottonwoods offered great cover at their bases for hiding from the sharp eyes of the group of crows sitting in

After the initial round of crow shooting, Robert Fuller moves out to gather up the birds he has downed with the Browning 20-gauge automatic he was trying out.

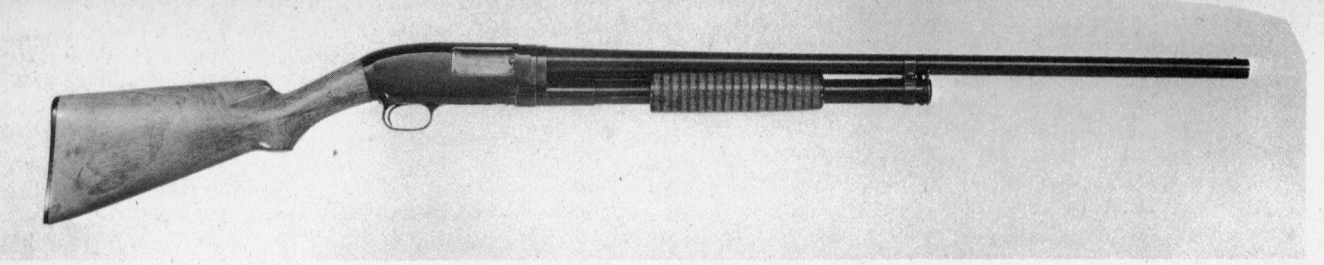

Robert Fuller's personal favorite when it comes to shotguns is the old Winchester Model 12, only recently revived.

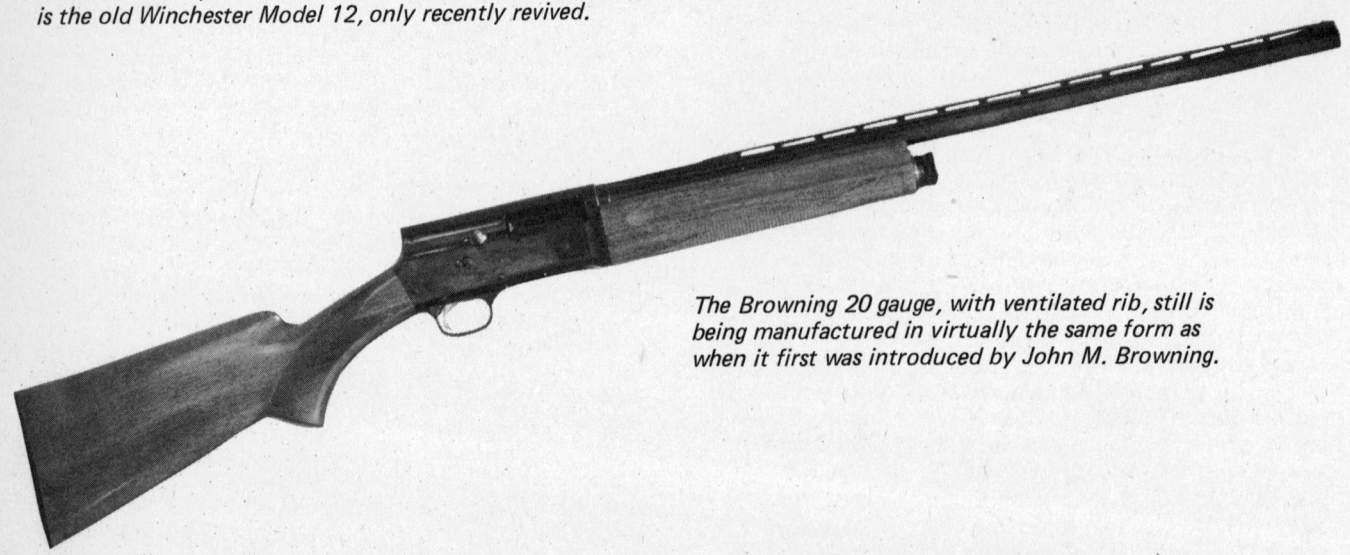

The Browning 20 gauge, with ventilated rib, still is being manufactured in virtually the same form as when it first was introduced by John M. Browning.

some eucalyptus trees a quarter mile distant. Fuller got himself settled covering the approach that those birds would most obviously make, while I covered the other side and set up my portable calling unit.

Our plan was the hit-and-run tactic we often employed to good advantage. No decoys were used. Simply set up and hide carefully, turn on the caller, supplement it with a mouth call and wait for action, which usually is not long in coming.

I had Fuller highly enthused on the hot action that was about to commence. As a matter of fact, I had myself in a pretty frame of mind and with Fuller's signal of being ready, I punched the button on the recorder, cutting loose with the call simultaneously. After five minutes it became obvious, even to me, that something was amiss. Not a crow from the distant bunch had moved out of the tall and leafy security of the trees. A pair had ventured to extreme long-gun range at the first stage of the ruckus but did not come close enough for us to try a shot. We figured that something better would develop, but nothing did. My only explanation for this was that we had been observed entering the cover of the trees and that crows are indeed clever critters. All the while, doves kept wheeling into the trees overhead, filling the air with the gentle whistle of their wings as they darted by. It was still early, causing no alarm: After all, success has to be won and every stand cannot be a huge triumph.

Over this particular California valley where we were, there are many good locations that are natural choices for the hit-and-run crow-hunting technique. Without much delay, Fuller and I had parked the truck and deployed ourselves in another cunning ambush preparatory to punching the "on" button for the second time. This time a pair of birds came on in from a half mile away, rising and falling in the characteristic flight pattern of a charging crow, closing fast, and now inside of deadly range. Fuller had his back to the pair, but at the signal to rise and commence firing, he made a noble effort to do same while sliding a short distance downhill.

The results were not good. Fuller can handle a gun with the natural ease of one who has done more than smoke rustlers and injuns for the silver screen. He's a born shooter and has done a great deal of the real thing. Perhaps that's what was wrong with this particular episode: It was the real thing and therefore there was no time for a retake.

Neither of us looked remotely impressive. In fact, I doubt we even impressed the one crow that succumbed to my sloppy second barrel. He probably had a last thought involving his rotten luck in being swatted by a golden BB in the hands of a complete incompetent. Fuller had not gotten a round out of the forward end of his twenty's barrel, having been in the process of a rather complicated physical maneuver. The sole glory of having failed to double on a pair inside of twenty yards was all mine. True gentleman that he is, Fuller did not mention this fact but did have a comment or two relative to the wet and slippery grass that had impeded his progress. It was not, as you might have gathered, a well-executed exercise.

On the bright side, however, it had to be considered that a crow had indeed been brought to bag, therefore raising the hunter success to a stupendous .500 per gun which in this day and age isn't anything to be scoffed at if you're talking about goose statistics.

Continued calling from this particular point failed to yield anything more productive than another single that came hell bent from another direction and was subsequently crumped by one well-placed charge from the little twenty. Fuller, having been blooded, was no longer quite as disgusted with the condition of the turf while the success ratio was doubled.

Not more than two miles away, there stood another fine grove of eucalyptus, the topmost portion of each tree holding several of our desired targets. The grove, stretching in a line fully half a mile long, looked like a natural for a slight change of tactics. Fuller positioned himself at one end, his camouflage jacket making him almost invisible in the tangled shadows, while I poured the coal to the Chevy in a circuitous route that put me at the opposite end. Our plan here was to walk slowly towards the center in hopes of pushing crows toward one another. The crows seemed reluctant to leave the trees in spite of the fact that we were present and blazing away. After the first barrage, wherein I neatly took two bushels of leaves off one tree with both upper and lower barrels of my Browning and nary a feather, I proceeded to call the crows back for a second chance that resulted in one crumped bandit and another wing-tipped fifty yarder that plopped into the weeds, calling beautifully on his own.

Down the line I could hear Fuller carrying on as if he were protecting the wagon train all by his lonesome and doing a respectable job. My elation at finally getting a good thing going was short-lived, abruptly I was interrupted by a gentleman in an official-looking car who politely explained to me that we were killing crows inside the limits of a new boundary line for a neighboring prison. Neither the fact that he was an ardent fan of Fuller's, to whom he had just recently spoken *in person*, nor the fact that I presented my genuine deputy credentials altered his decision. It impressed the hell out of him but it didn't change the fact that we could no long shoot crows, or anything else for that matter, in this particular row of trees. Well, scratch one more spot. The rapidly growing giant of civil authority once again had taken a shooting spot from my list. It was somewhat nostalgic in that I had been shooting in that row of trees then for fifteen years and suddenly, by virtue of its proximity to a prison some five hundred yards distant, it could no longer be gunned.

The fact that the prison had been there for all those fifteen years and not a single hunter had engineered a mass jail break apparently didn't have a thing to do with the decision.

We had, however, collected several crows — or almost. They seemed to be stuck in the trees by virtue of our rapidly increasing run of really good luck. I did find the wing-tipped bird who promptly took a swipe at me in a frenzied flop and nearly succeeded in drilling me right in the eye with a pile-driving beak.

Getting run out pretty much soured the program for awhile. Fuller is a real supporter of the shooting American and has given extensively of his time in combatting gun legislation spawned by mass hysteria. Our bitterness was salved slightly when we stopped at another location where permission to shoot always has been granted the man who properly approaches the owner. We were told to go ahead and, although still upset personally over the loss of one of my favorite spots, I was happy to learn that this location hadn't been lost, too. It was ironic to a point in that this fellow raises thoroughbred race horses and is a nonshooter himself, yet he always has allowed me into his place to shoot crows, doves, pheasants or anything that I might care to pursue on his land. It appeared to me that he was running a far greater risk than the prison.

The pens for the horses were full of crows which brought our excitement level back up to a high point. Naturally, we couldn't shoot near the stock but we could set up on a hill overlooking the area and attempt to bring the birds to us from that point. It didn't work wonders, but it did work. We drew several singles into the natural blind created by a fallen and weather-washed adobe building and there were a few birds passing the blind on their way to the pens, which created a little action; not the crow shoots that most of us experience or read about, but relatively steady gunning that gave a pair of guys a chance to talk between birds. A wing-tipped single was placed in a nearby tree as a decoy, but he did not bring his brothers into our cunning trap in undulating black waves.

Noon was upon us, time for a stop at a nearby store for some groceries to appease the gnawing at our middles and some conversation with the locals. A couple of tips were passed our way in answer to our questions regarding crow handouts.

The hit-and-run crow tactic works especially well during the middle of a hot day. By now the birds were all in the shelter of high, cooling groves waiting out the day until it was time for an afternoon foraging flight. We found such a location along the river and quickly set up the recorder, stepping back to stand silent against the trunks of towering cottonwoods. A trio came boiling in, screaming for a fight. Wings closed in a steep dive, they piled over each other pulling out as they flared in our faces. It took five shots to account for the group. Fumbling to reload as several others wheeled above was accomplished first by Fuller who dumped one more high flyer who wig-wagged down in a long arc to terminate his predatory existence in the river.

As quickly as it had begun, the action stopped. Several birds circled a hundred yards above us for a minute before flying off calling alarm. It wasn't a total bust but all that day we seemed to be unable to get any amount of birds boiling over a set such as we usually do: one or two and that was that. Perhaps it was too early in the year as the bunches sighted never seemed to number more than ten birds, more often five or six. This indicated family groups to me and perhaps they have a greater tendency to remain cautious.

Nevertheless, we did have some shooting, albeit sporadic, but the prime reasons for getting out had been accomplished. As a bonus we had located two more fine dove spots which almost might make up for the loss of the row of eucalyptus trees.

The electronic and tape recorder-type callers for use on crows have made crow shooting easier for the not-so-proficient mouth caller. Further, they create a wave of excitement among crows that usually brings the black bandits in to the set of waves. Although we did not experience this type of reaction today we still brought in enough birds to satisfy the basic desires to hear a shotgun go off. Most of the portable units feature several records or tapes for calling crows and other game such as coyotes and bobcats. The crow records that seem to be best for us are fight or distress signals set up by several crows. The joining in on tape of what sounded to be several hundred after the first few minutes usually will attract even the most reluctant members of this wary tribe.

I don't know that mouth calling is necessary as a supplement to a good portable unit but the practice is good and it does give one the feeling of being a contributor to the cause. Dyed-in-the-wool crow gunners would no doubt consider this unethical as hell but the recorders are not designed with such experts in mind. I do know mouth callers who can take more crows under worse conditions than a record or tape unit can under good conditions, but these people are, quite obviously, exceptions to the rule.

For the occasional crow buster the portable unit is ideal to aid in the shooting program and will provide a lot of off-season sport. Fuller and I certainly felt this way. As I remember it, we had a good day's outing that honed the rusty edges of the bird shooting eyes and gave us a jump on doves. Lord knows one can't be too prepared for them.

Chapter 11

CAMOUFLAGE

YOUR

FIREARMS

VARMINT HUNTER'S DIGEST

SOME OF THE things hunters do make little or no sense as far as I am concerned. Mind you, I'm not knocking the hunter — I have hunted from one end of the country to the other and in a few other spots in this world — but some things just puzzle me completely.

Take the duck or goose hunter: He gets duded up in camouflage pants and mud-colored hip boots, dons a camouflage jacket and cap, smears camouflage paint on his face, wears camouflage gloves and even sticks two camouflage bandannas in his pocket, then uses a brightly blued shotgun! Okay, so duck hunters are as crazy as trout fishermen.

But the fellow who stalks the wily turkey and collects than one or two hunting trips, and getting the old stuff off and putting new material on became a chore.

Local duck hunters use a variation of this method, wrapping strips of burlap around the barrels of their guns and taping the burlap into place. This works reasonably well on doubles, but the idea falls flat on its face when you try that stunt with a pump or an autoloader.

Then, there were a few Teflon-coated and OD-painted guns on the market, but few hunters bought them and this idea also passed on. Bob Steindler, the Midwestern gun scribe, is one of those who seems to agree with me. "Living in an area where duck and goose hunting is a way of life, I had shopped around for a good way to camouflage my

We Spend Time And Money To Disguise The Obvious, But A Flashing Gun Can Be A Dead Giveaway!

his Thanksgiving dinner is a real hunter! He, too, gets decked out in clothing that darn near makes him invisible; clothing that breaks up his outline so that it's hard to spot him if and when you encounter him in the woods. But he too carries a gun that's visible one hundred yards away.

Varmint hunters, especially those who use calls adroitly, have to stay hidden so that the incoming varmint won't be able to spot the danger. Again, we — yes, I hunt ducks, geese, turkey and varmints plus a few other critters — get all decked out in camouflage clothing, but nothing is done to make our guns less visible.

If you hunt in snowy territory, you wear white and the gun you pack on these trips is camouflaged, even if the camouflage job consists only of a coat of white paint or some two-inch-wide tape wrapped around the gun. Why not camouflage your gun for other types of hunting?

Of course, a number of camouflage methods have been tried on guns over the years but, until recently, I never encountered one that was really satisfactory. First, there was camouflage cloth that was wrapped around the gun and glued into place. The wrapping never lasted much longer

duck gun. I figured if I could ever find a good method, I'd later use the same camouflage system for my combination turkey gun, and maybe a varmint rifle," he tells me.

I listened to what Steindler had to say, and while he used a shotgun for his experimentations — and that's what you'll see pictured here — there is no reason at all that the same general techniques should not work well with that varmint rifle you take afield with the idea of doing some damage to the predator population.

Needless to say, anything you can do to convince that coyote or bobcat that you're not there at all is going to be to your advantage. Camouflaging your firearm should be a definite help.

But I seem to be taking over what Bob Steindler has to say about his project. Let's let him get on with it:

"Before the last hunting season, I doped out a way of camouflaging a gun and what I found out about it while tackling the job sold me on the idea of dressing up a couple of my other guns that way." Basically, you can do the job in three evenings, providing the various layers of paint and gunk dry completely in that time. You will need the following:

Shotgun tubes and other firearm barrels should be plugged before beginning to spray with nonreflecting material. Plastic wads, usually on hand with the shooter, are ideal for shotguns; shaped wooden dowels are for rifles and handguns.

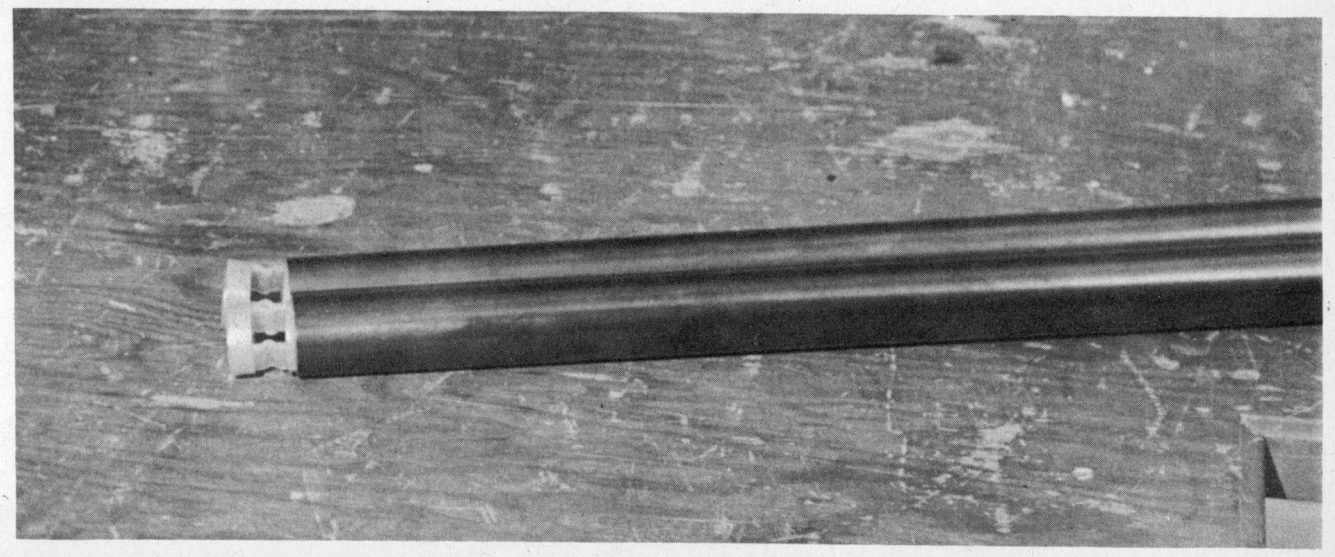

VARMINT HUNTER'S DIGEST

Most satisfactory method is to use plenty of newspaper covering while working out of doors. Spray materials dry rapidly in air.

LPS Instant Cold Galvanize. Depending on the gun, one or maybe two cans will do the job. Steindler used just a tad of the second can on the gun illustrated, but put the rest of the second can to good use by spraying the bottom of a trash can that had seen better days.

Rust-Oleum paint in brown, green and yellow in eight-ounce cans; Steindler found the brush-on paint easier to use than the aerosol spray, since the brush allows you greater control of the paint applied.

Krylon, an acrylic spray coating, one or two cans.

Total cost of all the materials mentioned is under $10. The LPS Instant Cold Galvanize and the Krylon spray are best applied out-of-doors, unless you have adequate space and ventilation in your workshop. If you do use the Krylon spray indoors, be sure there are no open pilot lights or the possibility of any sparks near the area you're working in — and refrain from smoking, since the vapors from Krylon spray may ignite explosively.

"Depending on the type of action on the gun you want to work on, your camouflaging job will vary a bit. I don't suggest getting spray or paint on the action bars of a pump gun, for instance, and an autoloader will require a slightly different treatment than a bolt-action gun," Steindler says.

On bolt-action rifles, it is best to treat the wood separately from the barrel action. The barrel channel need not be painted or treated, but this might be a good time to see if the barrel channel is waterproof. If not, a sealing coat of shellac or varnish can be applied.

The ejection port of a varmint bolt action is not big enough to worry about camouflaging, but the bolt handle should be treated. Remove the bolt from the action and spray only the bolt handle — you can either mask the remainder of the bolt or, with careful spraying, cover only the bolt handle. To prevent binding of the action, the bolt itself, of course, should not be treated.

Gas vents on the action should be plugged with a match or toothpick before spraying or painting, and the ejection port should be plugged or masked before you begin operations. Smoothbore barrels are best plugged with a suitable plastic wad with plastic shot collar to avoid getting any spray into the barrel, and rifle barrels can be plugged with a dowel whittled to fit like a cork. If the dowel is permitted to project a few inches from the muzzle, the dowel also will serve as a handy handle while manipulating spray can and gun at the same time.

The side-by-side shotgun was camouflaged without being stripped or taken down, and single-barrel shotguns of the top break variety need not be taken down either, Steindler discovered.

As long as you avoid a too-enthusiastic application of either the LPS or the Krylon spray around functioning parts, they still will operate properly. The safety, top lever, triggers and sling swivels on the side by side were checked for smooth functioning after both spray applications and there were no problems. With semiautomatic pistols, be sure that the slide, hammer and magazine release, as well as the safety, are fully functional after each spray coat.

"You may wonder about the sling swivels on the side by side, but I like a sling on a shotgun — especially a duck or goose gun. A sling leaves my hands free for a bag of blocks, lunch and shooting box."

Before you actually begin to camouflage the gun, take a look at the sundry pieces of camouflage clothing you own. Note that not only the design, but also the colors vary — especially the background color. Colors on the current military camouflage suits contain quite a bit of green, the coloring being designed to match the verdant jungle growth of Vietnam.

Select your paint and the paint pattern to match your clothing and also the area where you'll be using the camouflaged gun. The color best known as dead grass does not match the gray-greens you encounter when calling coyotes in Texas and, conversely, the green used by the varmint hunter will not match the muddy-brown of the Maryland goose hunter's terrain.

Begin the job by cleaning the gun internally and externally, being sure to remove all traces of gun oil, grease, solvent and dirt from all external parts of the gun. If, for instance, some dirt is left in the checkering, you will find it almost impossible for the LPS galvanize or the paint to adhere. If the checkering has filled in with dirt and the accumulated crud of ages, use an old toothbrush to remove all foreign matter. Before using the LPS spray, be sure that no dust has collected on the gun and that all parts are bone dry.

The LPS Instant Cold Galvanize is said to rustproof any metal for three or more years. This spray is not a paint, but actually bonds with the metal to which it is applied, setting up an electromechanical action that fuses ninety-five percent of a pure zinc compound to the steel. This LPS product prevents rusting underneath the camouflage paints, and the zinc deposit effectively withstands over 3000 hours of saltwater exposure.

Holding the nozzle about a foot from the gun, spray lightly in long, sweeping strokes. Keep the spray can in constant motion when applying the LPS, or you'll end up with heavy blobs of the galvanize in some spots. The spray will be dry to the touch within five minutes — at least on a bright breezy day with low humidity.

This quick drying enables you to turn the gun over within a short period of time and complete the spray job on the other side. Check the functioning parts — if the gun has not been taken down — after half an hour has elapsed, then let the work dry overnight or at least six hours.

"For the most durable job, I favor two separate but light applications of the LPS Instant Cold Galvanize, letting each application dry the recommended time," Steindler tells me.

"The Rust-Oleum paints come next. Our local hardware store had only three of the basic colors: yellow (659), chestnut brown (977), and forest green (1282). Once the paint in these cans has been thoroughly mixed, you can begin to blend your own colors by mixing varying amounts of yellow with brown and with green.

Yellow mixed with dark brown gives you a color very close to dead grass, and yellow plus forest green gives you a light green, the final color depending on the ratio of the two basic colors used when making the mix.

The yellow/brown mix, when combined with the yellow/green mix, gives yet another color suitable for the camouflage job. Yellow alone is not suitable for use as a camouflage color, and the dark brown and deep green should be used sparingly.

When you start painting, remember that the basic idea behind a camouflage job is to break up the distinctive outline of an object, and an irregular placement of paint splotches is better than a uniform distribution.

Never work with a brush that is too full of paint, and in such areas as the checkering, use the dry-brush technique. Here, the fibers of the small brush contain just a little bit of paint, for if too much paint is used, you will fill in the checkering. Use the same dry-brush method around screwheads, taking care not to fill in the screwhead slots, on the serration of the safety and similar points.

There is no need to use too much paint on this job. The LPS spray serves as a base and, if you have done a reasonably even job in spraying on the galvanize, can serve as a background color for your camouflage painting.

The Rust-Oleum paints do a good job in covering and a single coat of the various colors will be sufficient. I found it easiest to start at the butt of the shotgun, using a camouflage jacket as a guide for some of my splotches of

Using a camouflage jacket or vest as a guide, the hunter begins pattern with various colors of Rust-Oleum. Text describes method of applying paint to difficult areas.

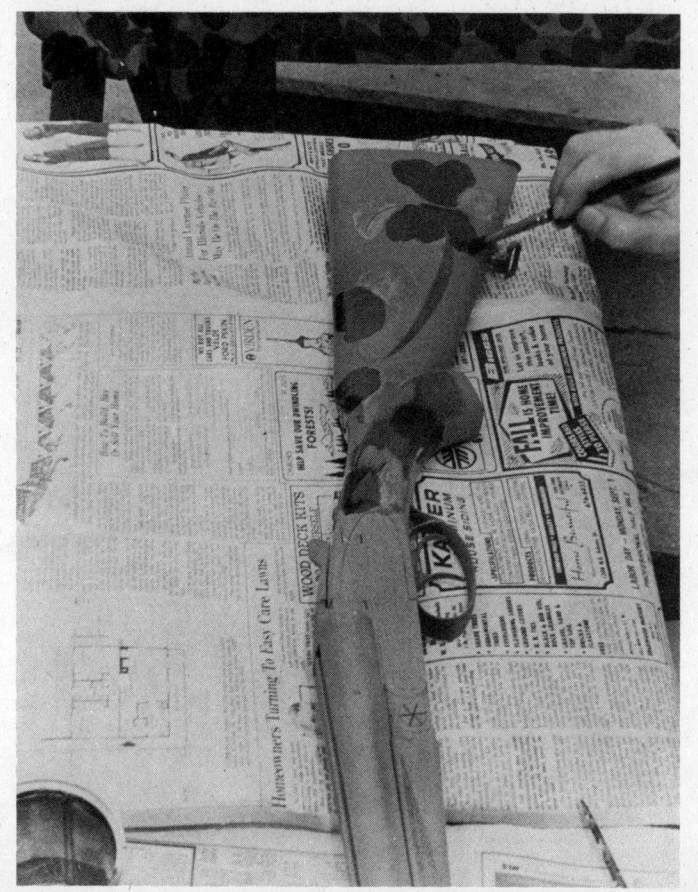

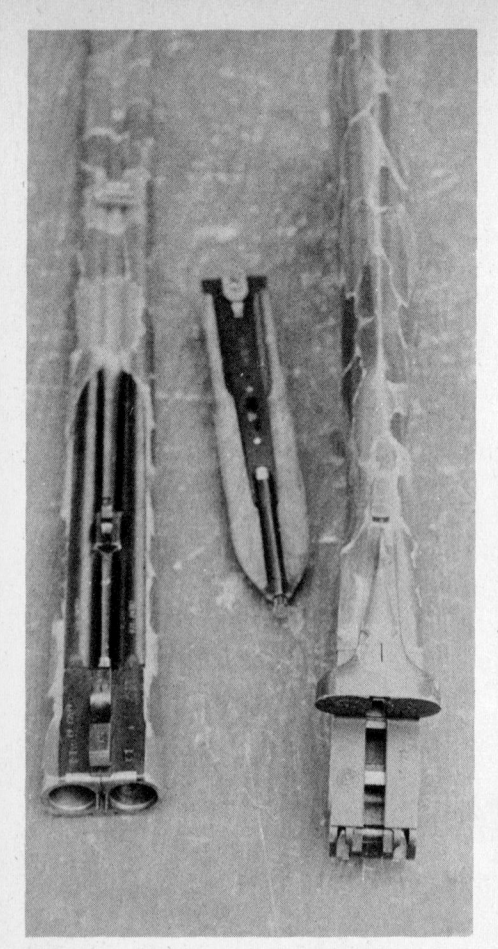

Untreated parts of double-barreled shotgun are clearly visible while painted portions seem to disappear. Paint didn't seep into or under parts.

paint. Keeping in mind the basic aim is to break up the outline of the gun, carry some of the splotches of paint over the comb, and from the cheekpiece down into the butt stock.

Whenever wood meets metal or metal meets metal, bring the paint almost to the junction of the two meeting parts, then continue the paint splotch in the same way on the other side of the junction. In this way, there is no chance for any paint to run down inside and gum up the works.

As you proceed toward the muzzle, you'll find that you refer back to the camouflage jacket less frequently and are proceeding at a faster pace with the various colors. Just be sure to vary the size and shape of the various color splotches, as well as the juxtaposition of the colors.

After paint has completely dried, two coats of Krylon spray — waiting 24 hours between coats — are applied to cloud shiny camouflage paints.

120

VARMINT HUNTER'S DIGEST

If the humidity is low enough, you may find that the butt is dry enough to the touch for you to start the other side in a short time. If not, leave the painted side uppermost and finish the job as soon as the paint has dried sufficiently.

You may have used Rust-Oleum in aerosol spray cans for other jobs and found it easier and faster to apply to such things as outdoor furniture. But in camouflaging a gun, it is too difficult to control the amount of spray when you're working with small splotches of color, and you may end up with too much paint on critical areas of the gun. Although there is a broad spectrum of colors to choose from, especially in larger paint stores, the colors are too clear and bright for the effect you want to create, and blending of the liquid paints is the only answer.

As soon as all of the Rust-Oleum paint has dried thoroughly — and this will vary with the temperature and humidity — spray the entire paint job with the clear acrylic. Usually, twenty-four hours is sufficient time for the Rust-Oleum to dry, but in our area of high humidity it took longer.

When using the acrylic spray, be sure to cover all areas that were painted. The Krylon provides a permanent protective coating for the Rust-Oleum paints. It dries clear and stays that way, sheds dirt and effectively seals all porous surfaces.

Unpainted sections of the gun, such as the recoil pad, need not be sprayed. Use the same technique with the Krylon as you did with the LPS spray, long sweeping motions with the nozzle of the can about a foot from the surface of the gun. The trick with the acrylic spray is to get enough spray on the surface without creating runs or sags.

For best results, the manufacturer of Krylon suggests that this be applied when the temperature is between seventy and eighty degrees. When the temperature is within this range, the Krylon dries almost immediately and you can place the gun on a flat surface and give first one side and then the other a light application of the Krylon.

Check the functioning of the gun after the first application of Krylon, then inspect it carefully from butt to muzzle to be sure that all painted areas have been covered. In good light you will be able to detect a subtle difference in areas still not covered by the Krylon. Apply a second light coat of the Krylon, paying particular attention to the uncovered spots you have noted.

"Once the last treatment has dried, check the functioning again, then take the invisible gun hunting. Of course, I can't promise anyone that he'll bag more ducks, call in more coyotes, or collect his Thanksgiving gobbler the first hour out, but such a camouflage job is just one more item that will work in your favor," Steindler contends.

And like someone once said: It sure can't hurt anything.

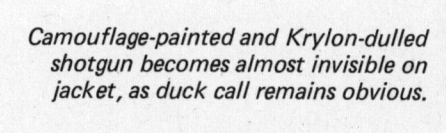

Camouflage-painted and Krylon-dulled shotgun becomes almost invisible on jacket, as duck call remains obvious.

Chapter 12

INSTANT BIPOD FOR VARMINT RIFLES

Here's Help, If Your Aim Wavers

THE LITTLE GRAY MONSTER moved around his mound on the opposite hillside, estimated at 150 yards, but try as I might, the rifle wouldn't hold steady enough to bring him down. Squirrel popping makes an enjoyable afternoon of hunting and an excellent way to keep the eye and rifle tuned together. The problem I was having wasn't unique, at least, for me.

I had borrowed a Leupold 3X9 variable to learn whether I could justify the price. I found I liked the optics, but when I racked the power up to nine, it just wouldn't stop moving on the target. The hillside where I was shooting offered little choice of shooting position. I had tried to find a slope where I could assume the favored prone position, but the slant of the hill didn't allow that. The best I could manage was sitting position, which is not the best for my shooting.

There had to be a solution, so I retreated to my shop, where I rummaged around for means to alleviate this unsteady sitting problem.

Beneath a pile of hardwood I found a variety of half-inch bolts varying in length from six to sixteen inches. That would be great, if there were something to put them into and make a portable bipod.

Cached in another area I found a length of leftover copper pipe with half-inch inside diameter. A quick check proved the half-inch bolt would fit nicely into the pipe. This gave me a variable length rest but how to hold it together and make the height adjustable?

You should never rush into ideas like this, so I slept on it for several days. We decided to have a barbecue on the patio and when I brought out the barbecue basket I had found my attachment for the bipod. The basket has two round metal rings that have a thumbscrew tightening bolt that fastened the basket to the spit. After about an hour of rummaging and test fitting, my wife asked how the barbecue fire was going. I told her to get something from one of our popular instant eateries since our barbecue basket had fallen apart.

I had disassembled the basket, discarding all but the two retaining rings on the end. These were cleaned and buffed to give a smooth surface, removing the welds that held the wire frame of the basket and making them more presentable. This gave me the components for my instant bipod.

The copper pipe measured thirty-eight inches, so I cut this in half, making each leg nineteen inches. The basket ring was held in place with a vise, while the copper and metal ring were soldered with a torch. By cleaning both units and using an excess of flux, I managed to get a good bead on the solder joint and one that would be more than strong enough. The wing-type lock nut was kept in place while soldering to prevent any of the solder from running into the threaded area.

When the sections had cooled enough to handle, I measured three inches down from the top and drilled a three-eighths-inch hole on both sections. This would be my pivot point and all it required was a bolt inserted through the first pipe, a washer, the second pipe, another washer between the pipe and nut and a lock nut over the first one. This gave me an adjustable bipod that could be carried easily into the field and give me the support desired in prone or sitting position.

Here's all you need to assemble your own instant bipod. Items include aluminum tubing, bolts, washers, solder and parts of a barbecue basket. All are inexpensive.

There is usually a rock that can be used or you can take off the hat for a prone rest, but this would solve all those problems. The next thought that came to mind was the highly polished finish of my .270 Winchester. If I put that copper pipe next to the finish and fired enough, I would scratch or rub the finish. This was solved by inserting a piece of plastic flexible tubing, called Tygon, over the ends of the upper fork section. This not only gave me the protection I wanted for the rifle finish, but also afforded a nonslip surface to prevent the rifle from sliding on the copper pipe. This simple addition actually solved two problems.

To try out the bipod, I removed the bolt from the rifle and sat down in the garage. My neighbors don't worry too

Hacksaw is best used to cut the metal tubing cleanly, after you measure the desired length. The overall length of the bipod is left to the individual.

VARMINT HUNTER'S DIGEST

After cutting, drill a bolt hole at least four inches from the end, making sure the hole is bigger than the bolt. If no drill press is available, use a hand drill.

much anymore. From a sitting position I could raise the bipod to the desired height and obtain a solid rest that held steady even at the higher powers. The bolt head was left on the half-inch bolts and they slipped on the concrete. I moved to the yard where I would have a surface more comparable with my shooting area and found the unit satisfactory. The bolts remained in position when carrying, stayed in the locked position when set and could be carried in that position. I would be ready to take a sitting position with the legs in the extended angle. If you have uneven ground, one leg can be set higher to allow for terrain variation.

This had worked almost too smoothly and with no problems in assembly. One minor variation might consist of cutting off the bolt heads and grinding the bolt end to a sharper point for use in rocky areas. The bolt heads do slide on rock surfaces. After a field test of the unit, I was still happy with it, but thought there might be a way of making it lighter overall. This copper pipe unit weighed in at two pounds fourteen ounces.

Digging around in the pipe section brought out a piece of aluminum tubing, heavy wall, that fits the half-inch bolts snugly. There is no feasible way to solder steel to the aluminum without exotic equipment and that I didn't have. I ruined another barbecue basket to obtain the metal rings and thumbscrews. By putting the ring on the bolt and inserting the bolt into the tubing, I had a snug fit. When I wanted a longer leg I could lower the rod, set the collar or metal ring on the bolt, and allow the tubing to seat against the base of the ring.

This gave me a bipod without anymore work than cutting the tubing and removing the rings from the basket. The tubing measured thirty-four inches, so it made two sections of seventeen inches. I lowered the pivot point for the crossbolt to 3½ inches to give a wider rest area at the narrower angles of the legs. The ends again were covered with the sections of plastic tubing to prevent scratches and provide a nonslip surface.

Both units utilize sixteen-inch bolts and they both ended up with the same overall length of twenty inches in the telescoped position. The weight of the aluminum tube unit didn't change much, but came out at two pounds six ounces, a half pound lighter than the copper pipe unit. Either unit will extend to thirty-two inches from the base of the bolt to the pivot point which forms the X rest for the rifle. They both work well in the field.

With the aluminum unit, the bolt had a tendency to slip out of the tubing while being carried in the down position. There is nothing to hold it in but friction and a center punch with a wood block backup to dimple it would give more friction and a more stable rest while carried.

Tom Larson and I took both units and tried them at our favorite squirrel hill. The legs dropped down to give the required height on the sidehill shooting and we easily adjusted them to allow for variations. We moved to another area and I tried the copper unit from the prone position and it worked beautifully. With the legs in the full up position and the angle of the pivot point stretched way out, the bipod gave me a comfortable position with no strain on the back of shoulders.

We found that if we wanted to glass an area with binoculars, it was a simple matter of placing the butt of the rifle on the ground. The forend didn't slip on the plastic tubing and the entire unit stood in place as if fastened to the rifle. A few minutes work with some scrap material can give you the same unit or perhaps even a variation of this.

One added advantage I hadn't thought of was in picking up game. If you reverse the copper pipe unit so the bolts on the tightening rings are inside, you can place the tightening screw under the animal, pick him up by squeezing the legs together and carry them to a collection point.

The best part involves the minimum materials and work.

Use plenty of solder when you attach barbecue ends to the copper pipe, keeping pressure on the tubing.

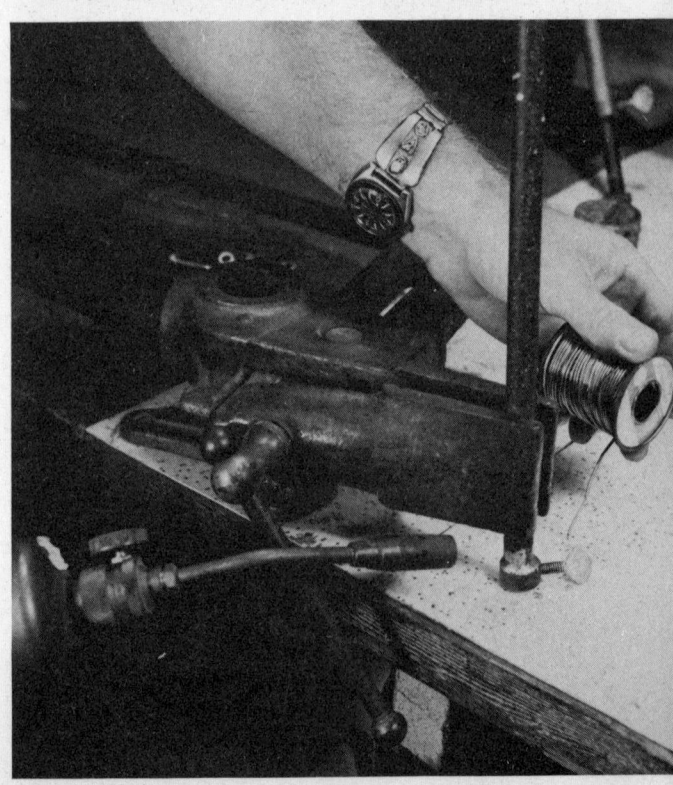

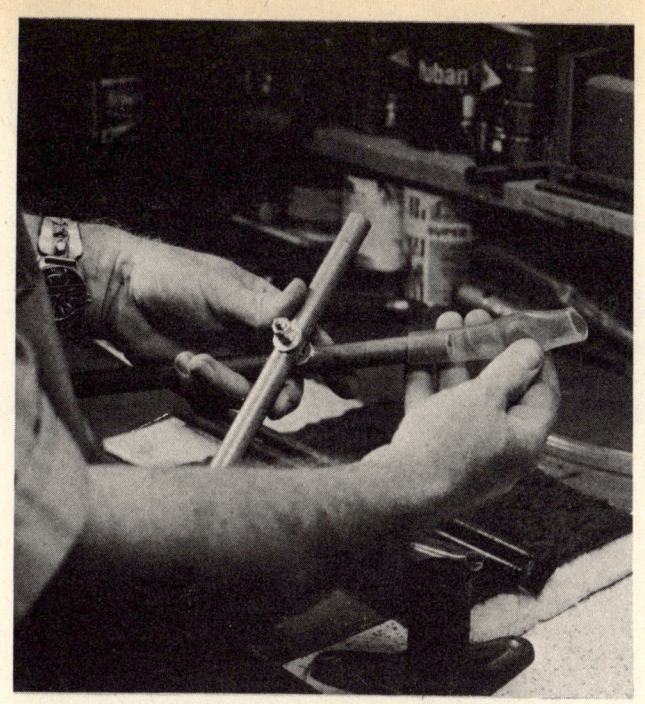

Insert the bolt through the two pipe sections with a washer on each side, and one in the middle. Then place protective plastic tubing over the ends of the pipe.

The final step is placing the half-inch bolts in the ends of the tubing. These will render the bipod immobile after setting it up in the field.

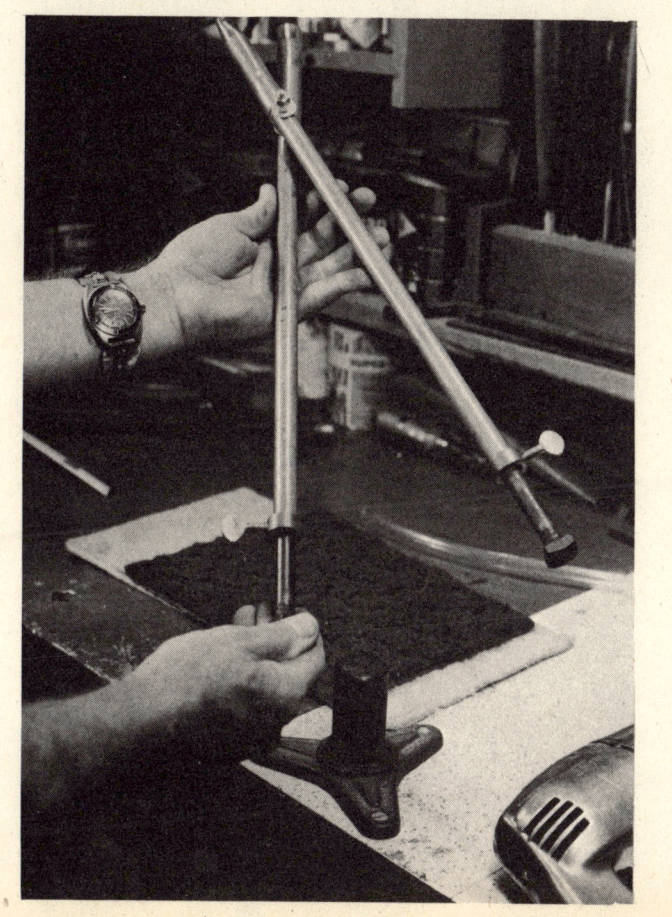

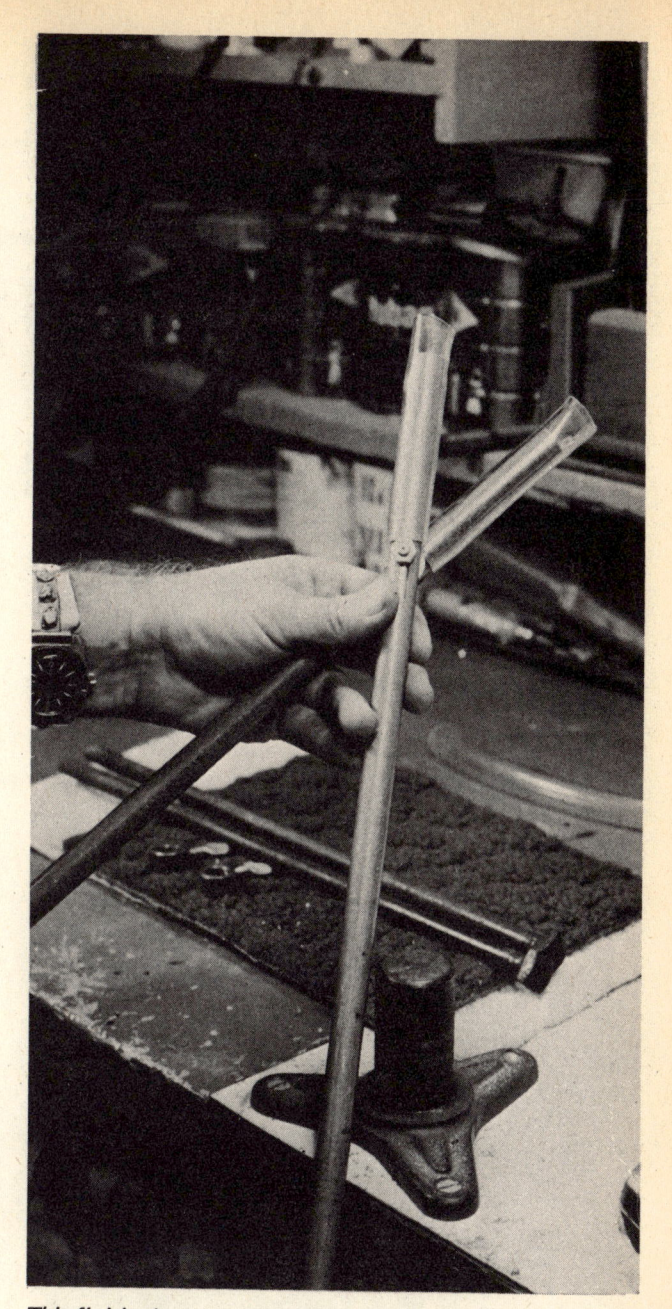

This finished cross-section shows plastic tubing cut a bit long to prevent stock from getting scratched. An extra bolt can be added through pipes to act as lock-nut.

One drill, a hacksaw and some solder will give you the copper pipe unit and you don't need the solder for the aluminum tubing unit. One could make the unit from regular galvanized water pipe, but this material will add even more weight. You could buy the copper for less than a dollar from a scrap yard, but unless you can find a substitute collar unit, you might have to put out a few dollars for the barbecue basket. Be certain it has the round collar type assembly, not the square ends found on the flat baskets.

You can make it longer, shorter, extend the pivot lower to make the angle wider for a larger beavertail forend rifle or any method you might find you need to modify. The best ideas often cost little in materials.

You may not hit any better, but at least you will be steady on the target.

CHOOSING THE RIGHT cartridge for varmint hunting would be easy if you could always count on being close to your quarry. But it rarely works out that way and we are drawn by necessity to the longer-range, flatter-shooting types. At this point it becomes a matter of not only the right cartridge, but also the right reload.

Factory loads are good and, with some rifles, provide satisfactory performance. There is still a better than even chance that the varmint hunter can work out something just a bit better by loading his own. The fact remains that each rifle is special and, so being, different from all the rest, regardless of apparent similarities.

LOADS AND RELOADS

Chapter 13

There Are Those Who Insist The Best Varmint Loads Are Home-Built!

The coyote, such as the one below, is the object of much of today's varmint-hunting activity. Proper loads help.

A 50-grain Sierra Blitz in caliber .224 and a Gardiner hollow-point .224 are compared at left. Below, a Gardiner 87-grain soft-point bullet next to a .257 Roberts loaded with an Omark-Speer soft-point bullet of 100 grains. Text contains technical evaluations.

To learn more about the care and feeding of high-power varminters, I called on Dan Cotterman whose experience as a reloader and experimenter goes back to the days when, as he recalls, "A bunch of the boys could make the dawn scene up in Southern California's Summit Valley with a hundred rounds of reloads apiece and pop ground squirrels so fast they'd be out of ammo before noon.

"The situation has changed today," Cotterman admits, "at least as far as Summit Valley and a lot of other places are concerned. The government poisoners and what you might call evolutionary spookiness among the ground squirrel population have combined to thin the critters out to where what used to be a 150 or two hundred-yard shot is now almost twice as far out. The rifleman and his sighting gear, to say nothing of the reloads he uses, just have to be a little sharper."

I was quick to point to the fact that some pretty precise reloading was going on, even before the Summit Valley boom years that followed World War II. Yet I had to agree with Cotterman's contention that, in many instances, ranges are a lot longer these days. That is, unless you're calling them in the way you do with coyotes, bobcats and the like. Otherwise, I still haven't met a ground squirrel or a chuck that'll come when you call him.

Cotterman, in recommending larger cartridges for smaller varmints, points to the fact that "there's no loss in scattering flesh and fur halfway to the next zip code when you're shooting small varmints. If you happen to be a trophy hunter, maybe you can find a taxidermist who likes to do mosaics. And the old reckoning about smaller bullets costing less and smaller hulls being cheaper to fill doesn't hold up anymore. Figure it for yourself. By the time you mount a varmint safari and make the long drive at today's gasoline prices, you'd be wasting your time to worry about the cost of a few reloading components.

"There's an advantage in using the rifle you're going to take with you in the Fall when deer season rolls around. The .30/06 or even a larger-caliber rifle as a varminter during the off-season is not so much a matter of being overgunned as it is a matter of keeping in practice for the time when each shot will really count.

"Granted, the rifle — '06, .270, .257, one of the hot sixes, whatever — will be the same one you're going to carry afield for larger game. Chances are, however, that the reload will be different. In the first place, the bullet will be lighter and of different construction. A change in bullet weight will call for the use of something in the nature of a faster-burning propellant.

"That's where the emphasis has to be placed as far as the innards of the reload are concerned. The individual characteristics of rifles has already been brought out. For that reason, we have to realize that charge weights that give

Loaded cartridges are, left to right, .221 Remington Fireball with 50-grain soft-point bullet, .222 Remington with 50-grain Powr-Lokt, .223 Remington with 55-grain Powr-Lokt, and .22-250 Remington with 55-grain Powr-Lokt bullet. Cotterman believes the latter cartridge is the ultimate varmint round with good reliability.

Probable varmint rounds below are, from left, Federal .243 with 80-grain bullet, Remington-UMC 6mm Rem with 85-grain hollow-point, Federal .25/06 with 90-grain hollow-point, and Federal .270 Win with 130-grain soft-point bullet. Each is useful.

good results in one rifle may not be ideal in another. The idea, therefore, is to shy away from the usual practice of showing charge weights right down to the tenth of a grain. Instead, it seems far better to list certain powders that have, in my experience, given good results with specific cartridge and bullet weight combinations. It is hoped that the varmint reloader — or the seasonal hunter who sharpens up on varmints during spring practice sessions — will find it easier to come up with an ideal load.

"The powders chosen for this sampling of deer rifle-type cartridges are all of the spherical type. The reason for my choice is simple: Spherical or ball powders are easy to work with when reloading because they pour freely from container to hopper and can then be thrown from a powder measure with a freedom that is almost liquid in nature. Because of this fluidity, the arm of the measure moves with ease and there is never the need to force the edge of the drum within the measure to cut through a powder granule, as is often necessary with stick-type powder granules. As a matter of further advantage, there is more consistency of charges, especially when using less than maximum charges in large cases. Finally, it has been learned that most spherical powders burn at a lower flame temperature. When shots are frequent, as with varmint shooting or range testing, an advantage in longer barrel life can be seen."

A slight change in the specifics of reloads will make the same rifle suitable for use on anything from the smallest varmint to the largest U.S. game animal you're likely to meet. If you have one or more rifles set aside for varmints only, you'll still find that working within recommended weight ranges of certain spherical powders will lead the way to that ultimate load.

"The hot sixes provide a good starting point. They're good on deer-size game animals and dynamite for varminting. Recoil is light and, given the right reload, they'll shoot where you look. Of the two most popular sixes, those being the .243 Winchester and 6mm Remington, I always have preferred the latter because of its slightly greater capacity and shoulder angle and because its longer neck allows a little more versatility with bullet seating. Otherwise, it's fair to say that either of them has a high potential for accuracy as well as being effective on deer-size game," Cotterman opines.

"Both the .243 Winchester and the 6mm Remington respond well to doses of Hodgdon's H-380 or H-450 with the 80 or 90-grain bullets that suit them so well to the task of varminting. If you're reloading the .243, you can begin with 41.0 grains of H-380 with 80-grain bullets, then gradually work up to about 45.0 grains. In using 90-grain bullets, the H-380 charge weight should be cut back a grain so that you'd be starting with 40.0 grains with a working maximum of 44.0 grains. Velocities for the 80-grainers will range from roughly 3200 fps to 3400 fps while the 90s will get out at from 3000 fps to 3250 fps. The slower-burning H-450 calls for a range of charge weights that will begin with 45.0 grains with 80-grain bullets and end at a maximum, or near maximum, of 49.0 grains. The 90s, when propelled by H-450, will have charge weights beginning with 44.0 grains and top out at 48.0 grains. Velocities will run from about 3000 fps to 3200 fps.

"Before going any further, I should qualify statements about velocities with a reminder that the best anyone can do is come up with an estimate that is based on previous chronographings with similar loads. Differences in barrel lengths and other characteristics that are a part of your rifle's individual personality can cause a variation in bullet speeds. Bullet seating depth and powder temperature, as well as primer type and a number of other factors can also change breech pressure, hence velocity.

"The low-high span of charge weights has been calculated to provide a range within which the best accuracy can be found. Going on past experience, a good guess would be that groups will be best with the lighter charges. Start with the lowest charges with, say, two different bullets of the same weight. Test in bunches of ten loads while giving the barrel a few minutes to cool between three or five-shot runs. If you decide to go to a slightly heavier powder charge, load another couple of groups of ten using a charge weight increase of no more than half a grain. Above all, remember that each rifle's pressure potential is different. If

Remington's Accelerator round launches a 55-grain .224 caliber bullet assisted by the .30-caliber sabot (left). It is compared to standard .30/06 loaded with Winchester 100-grain Silvertip bullet. Sabot separates in flight.

When disassembled, the Accelerator round shows the propellant to be of stick type, finely cut, nearly spherical. Propellant measures 55.8 grains.

VARMINT HUNTER'S DIGEST

129

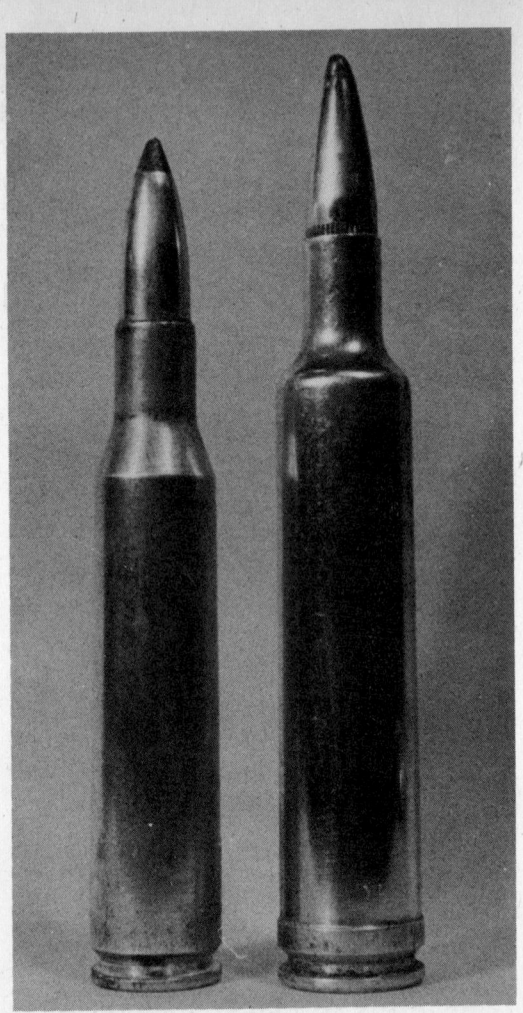

Two more excellent varmint loads shown are, from left, .257 Roberts with 100-grain Omark-Speer bullet and a .257 Weatherby magnum with a Hornady 100 grain.

you see anything like a punctured primer or run across an empty that is hard to extract, back off and figure your rifle's top load is at least five percent less than the one that caused the trouble.

"Moving up to the 25s, we have three that seem to run the ladder from hot to outrageous. The still-hot .257 Roberts flourishes on ball powders. The same is true of the somewhat hotter .25/06 and that ultra-25, the .257 Weatherby magnum. The Roberts, with 87 to 100-grain bullets and good sighting equipment, is one of the finest varminters around. Start with 42.5 grains of H-380 behind the 87-grainer. Velocity will run above 3050 fps and the accuracy you get may convince you not to load for anything hotter. However, it is possible, with proper caution, to work on up to around 46.5 grains when using H-380 with 87-grain bullets in the .257 Roberts. Stepping up to 100-grain bullets, you can still use H-380 in the Roberts. Try a starter load of 40.0 grains. This bottom load will produce about 2900 fps with the 100-grainer. Then, if you feel you need more speed, you can work on up to 43.5 grains with H-380 and the 100s. At this point velocity will be up around 3350 fps and, considering the better flight of the 100 when compared to the 87, those long-range shots will be a lot more feasible.

"There are lighter bullets for the 25s in 60 and 75 grains, but I don't consider them practical when it comes to accuracy. Not to be lured into madness with visions of super velocities, we'll find all the shocking power we need

The variety of bullets for varmint loading and reloading is rather extensive, as illustrated by the nine below.

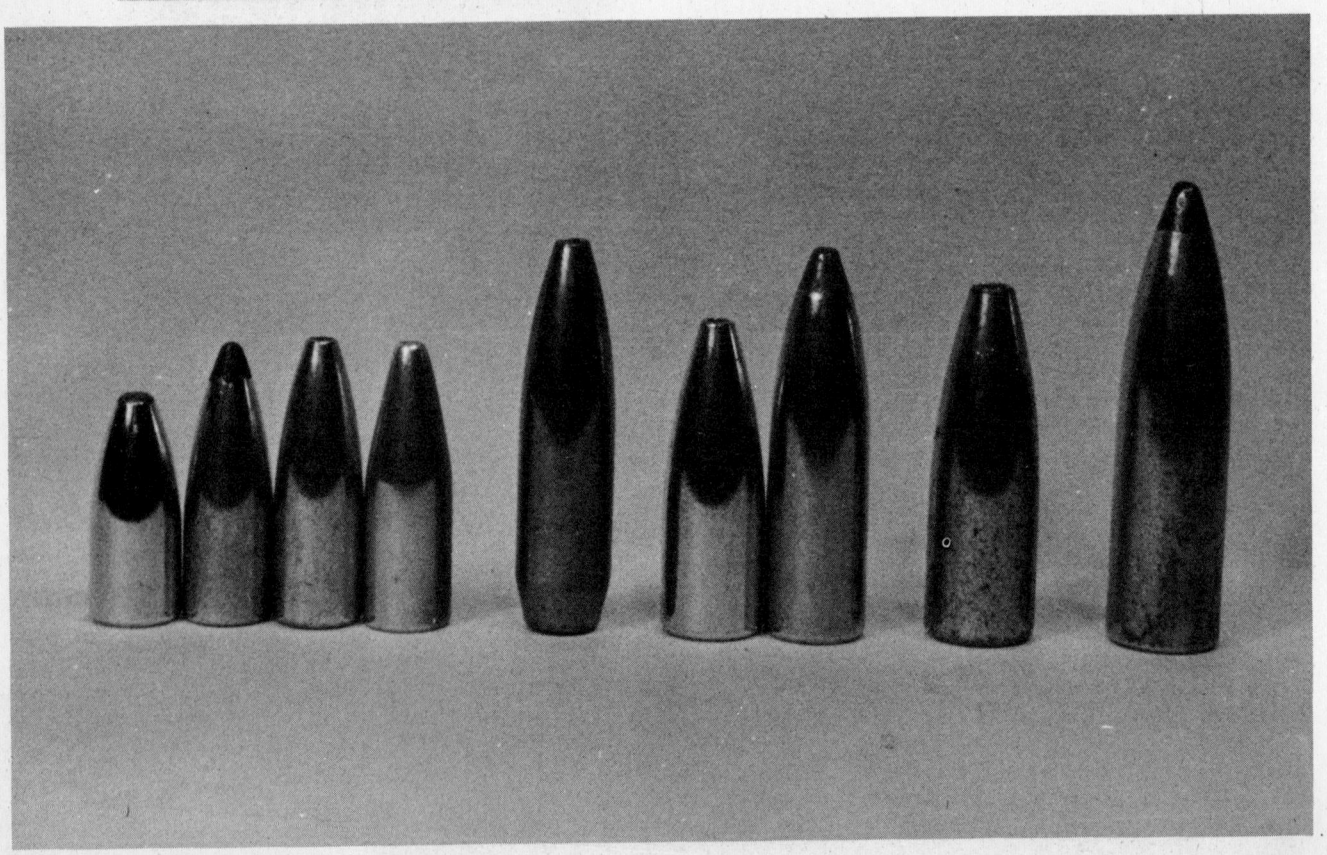

VARMINT HUNTER'S DIGEST

with the 87s and 100s. The .25/06 handles them about as well as anything going. Sticking with H-380, a charge of 44.5 grains will propel an 87-grain varmint bullet at around 3200 fps. Top loading with the H-380/87 combination comes to 48.5 grains for a 200 fps boost in velocity. I feel that, with 100-grain bullets in the .25/06, it's best to go to the slightly slower-burning H-450. Here a load of 48.5 grains will get the 100 out at between 2700 and 2750 fps. If accuracy is not lost in so doing, the load can be brought up to 52.5 grains with a matching bullet speed increase to well over 3100 fps.

"I've found that bullets in the 100-grain-and-up range provide the best accuracy in the .257 Weatherby magnum. However, it may be that other rifles will yield good accuracy, even with 87-grainers. If you like 'em hot, you can use the 87s ahead of H-870 (slowest of the sphericals) and have a fair chance at acceptable accuracy while maintaining relatively high velocities. Start with 75.0 grains of H-870 and you'll be putting an 87 out at almost 3100 fps. This, of course, isn't as much as you can do with the 87 in the little Roberts, buy you can work carefully on up to 81.5 grains using the same H-870 for a velocity of around 3600 fps, 300 to 400 fps above the Roberts and, incidentally, a couple of hundred better than the vaunted .25/06.

"The Weatherby hot-shot .257 usually performs well with 100-grain bullets. You can stay with H-870, using a load of 73.0/H870/100 and come forth with a respectable 2900-plus fps. From the outset, this about equals the performance of both the Roberts and .25/06. The advantage in the .257 Weatherby's larger case capacity comes to fore when we see that we can move on up to an H-870 charge of 79.5 grains with the 100-grain bullet. Now bullet speed ups to about 3450 fps. If this level of performance can be reached without having your groups open up and without unwholesome pressure signs, you'll have achieved that long arm every varminter should have. The rest will be up to you.

"The .264 Winchester has to be included any time talk about hot-shot varminters comes up. Again, I'll skip the ultra-light bullets because I've found that accuracy good enough to satisfy the long-range varmint hunter is not to be had with them at other than fairly low velocities. The .264 is best loaded with 100 to 120-grain bullets. I like to use H-450 with 100s in the .264. A good starting point is 64.0/H-450/100. Velocity will be around 3150 fps, not the most sensational. If accuracy is good, however, it's a good place to level off. If, on the other hand, more velocity is practical, 69.5/H-450/100 can be approached. Velocity will then figure at well over 3600 fps. Something to write home about.

"The use of H-450 in the .264 sustains in the loading of 120-grain bullets. The load, 61.0/H-450/120 is low-scale, yet will exorcise varmint medicine at around 3000 fps. A heavier charge that reads 66.0/H-450/120 takes bullet speed up to between 3350 and 3400 fps. The velocity-retaining properties of this long, thin bullet are good, making a muzzle speed of anything over 3000 fps entirely adequate for distance shooting.

"Like the .257 Roberts, a lot of older cartridges provide the basis for quite excellent varmint loads. The .270 Winchester, for example. Here's one that's nearly half a century old, yet capable of being loaded so as to run right alongside many of the newer hot shots. The .270, with 100 to 130-grain bullets ahead of H-380 will get the job done, even at today's varminting ranges. Start with 49.0/H-380/100 for about 3200 fps. If necessary, you can ease up to 53.5/H-380/100 and get almost 3400 fps. Also in the .270 you can try 47.5/H-380/110 and about 3200 fps. The 130-grainer, usually reserved for deer, goes better with H-450; thus 54.5/H-450/130 for around 2750 fps. The latter is a starter load and should be worked cautiously toward a top of 59.5/H-450/130 whereby velocity will be about midway between 3100 and 3200 fps.

"Back in the more modern category, Remington's 7mm magnum is, in my opinion, winner in the best-of-sevens series that's been raging for the past few years. Take the 7mm Remington magnum hull, one of several good 120-grain varmint bullets available, and begin with 64.5 grains

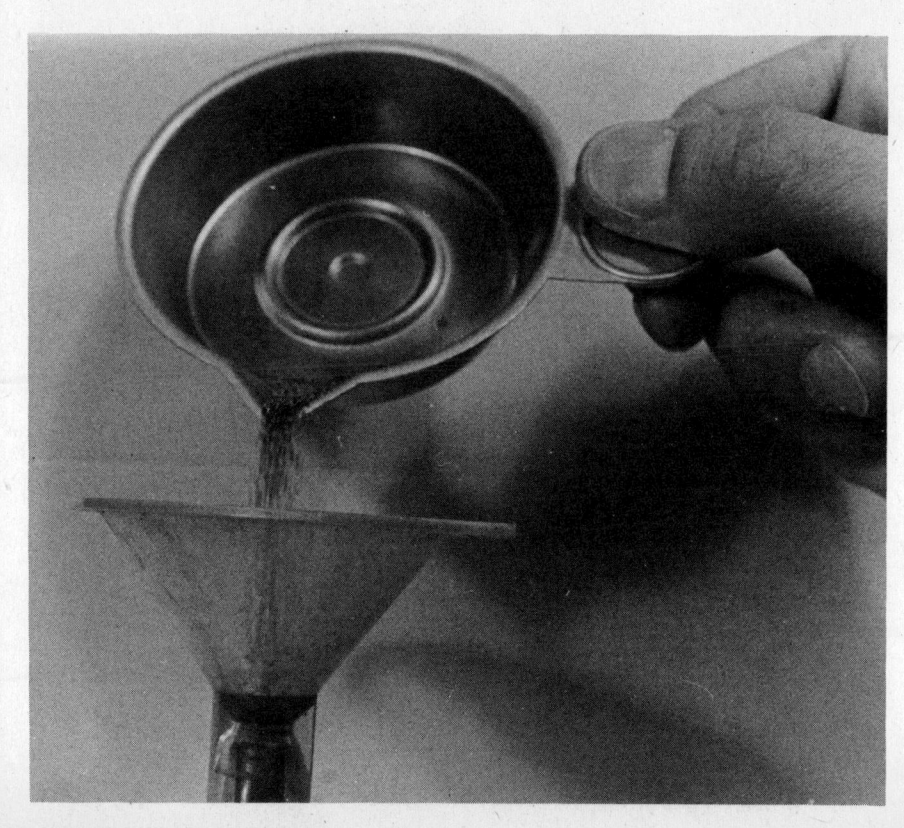

The spherical shape of H-380 flows easily through funnel into case.

of H-450. Velocity will start at a respectable 3150 or so fps. Higher speed is possible by working up to 70.5/H-450/120 where velocity moves on up to almost 3400 fps. If you'd like to try 130s in the Big Seven, H-450 remains as a good source of power. Slightly reduced charges, beginning with 61.5/H-450/130 will result in a bullet speed of between 2850 and 2900 fps. Then with 66.5/H-450/130, about 3200 fps is attainable. Velocity retention with either the 120 or 130 in 7mm is excellent.

"The timeless .30/06 took on new life a short time ago with the introduction of Remington's new sabot load. This one, the Accelerator, is said to launch a 55-grain, .224-inch bullet through the barrel of an '06 by means of a shoelike casing that drops away as soon as the bullet leaves the barrel. Velocity is said to run at something in the neighborhood of 4100 to 4200 fps.

"Meanwhile, with the new Remington creation temporarily falling beyond general reloadability, we have to consider its potential with .30 caliber bullets. I like 125 and 130-grain bullets for '06 varminting. Using H-380 you can start with 51.0 grains behind either bullet weight for speeds of between 2800 and 2850. Then easing up to 56.0 grains of the same H-380 will bring velocities to something in the 3100 and 3150 fps category. More sensational speeds can be had with 100 and 110-grain bullets. However, as with other lightweights showing high speeds, accuracy usually will not come until the load has been reduced to mere plinking effectiveness.

"If you reload for a cartridge in the 6mm or higher caliber that hasn't been covered herein, it'll be no problem to apply the same reasoning I've used to develop ball powder reloads in years past. Quite simply, it's a matter of checking a manual for a starting point. If varmints are your objective, pick a light-jacketed or hollow-point bullet of medium weight and begin accuracy testing.

"Medium-weight bullets have better staying power when it comes to retaining those high muzzle velocities. This, of course, means less correction for drop at longer ranges, and we were talking about stretching the effectiveness of varmint loads, weren't we? There's the further advantage of better resistance to downrange breezes.

"For those who insist on trying light bullets in the heavies, there is hope in the discoveries of GUN WORLD'S reloading wizard, Dean Grennell. Reporting on .30/06 varmint loads in the July 1966 GUN WORLD, Grennell indicated that he had been able to get good accuracy with a charge of 54.0 grains of Hodgdon's spherical H-335 and 110-grain bullets. You might try dropping down to about 52.0 grains of this propellant and working up to the 54-grain load to see what kind of results your rifle produces.

"Load development, regardless of caliber, has to include some attention to primer selection. Ordinarily, a change of primer types will not salvage the accuracy of a reload that is wrong in some other respect. Nonetheless, the primer is a powerful factor when it comes to a matter of whether or not the best results are to be had from a given propellant. For this reason, it is important to use magnum primers when dealing with fairly high density charges of slow-burning powders in large cases. In this regard, the H-450 and H-870 types are considered slow in the likes of the .25/06, .257 Weatherby magnum and larger cases."

Cotterman's report brings us to the varminters of lighter caliber, the sub-sixes, we'll call 'em. Among these is the fabulous .222 Remington. Now in its twenty-seventh year of existence, the Triple Deuce was touted by Edson Hall in the pages of the 1953 GUN DIGEST, Seventh Edition. Hall, working with a Remington Model 722 bolt action with a 6-power scope, reported spectacular results during a crow-shooting excursion. I figured I'd try one of his

Dan Cotterman prefers the use of free-flowing rifle powder such as Hodgdon's H-380 for varmint reloading.

favorite loads when, a few years later, I got my first .222. The recipe called for 26.0 grains of 4895 under a 50-grain Sierra bullet. Having no Sierras in that type on hand, I substituted the 50-grain Speer. Results, after some range testing, were determined to be satisfactory for ground squirrels at ranges of up to three hundred yards. One foible was encountered, however: The .222 case didn't want to accept a quantity of 26.0 grains of 4895. I kept at it, despite the difficulty, and was finally able to coax the desired amount into the .222's little boiler room. Needless to say, this amounts to a compression load in that you'll be squashing the powder down as the bullet is seated. I have since found that a .25.0/4895/50 combination works about as well. Twenty-five grains fills the .222 to its mouth, but you're not tucking the stuff in with tweezers.

Other tried-and-true formulas for the .222 include the use of IMR 4198, IMR 3031, H-335 and Winchester's special spherical for the .222 Remington, BR-748. I have come to favor the latter (which came into being after Hall's

Careful workmanship, attention to detail and a well-supplied reloading bench will result in better hunting.

early .222 write-up) because it's easy to work with and because, after some testing, I found that a quantity of 25.0 grains of BR-748 would result in a velocity of around 3100 fps while producing good varminting accuracy. It takes about half a grain more of Hodgdon's ballish H-335 to produce similar velocity results with the 50-grainers.

The Triple Deuce's big brother, the .222 Remington magnum offers more in the way of velocity performance, though it'd be a tall order to top the smaller version's accuracy potential. With the .222, 50-grain bullets are preferred; however, the .222 magnum will give similar bullet speeds with the 55s which will hold velocity, and energy, much better. Here you can go with 26.5 grains of H-335 for a muzzle velocity of about 3100 fps for the 55-grainer.

J.E. Gebby's contributions to the development of the .22/250 were more or less immortalized in the name he copyrighted for it, the Varminter. This round, concocted over sixty years ago from the .250/3000 Savage, animates the entire concept of varmint hunting by presenting us with an ideal cartridge for reloading. It seems to be a thing of near-perfect balance for top .22 varmint shooting.

The .22/250, now the .22/250 Remington, isn't fussy about diet and will accept a number of powder-bullet combinations. If, like Cotterman, you would rather work with powders that have that liquid-flow behavior during the reloading process, you can have a ball with sphericals in the .22/250. Some of that H-380 you may have on hand for varmint loading the bigger bores will work well.

Taking 55-grain varmint bullets as a preferred weight in the .22/250, you can begin your loading with 34.5 grains of H-380. I have no velocity figures for this particular load, but suspect it to be above 3400 fps. Chronographings of 55-grainers ahead of 35.5 to 36.0 grains of H-380 indicate speeds of from 3450 to 3575 fps. Obviously, velocity depends on the rifle, as well as a number of other conditions, so take the figures given as approximations. Good accuracy has been recorded in, for example, the Remington Model 700 with 36.0 grains of H-380 and either Speer or Sierra 55-grain varmint bullets.

The tedious and painstaking effort of putting together better long-range varmint loads is sometimes lost through wrong practices during range testing. It's a good idea to be absolutely certain that optical sighting apparatus is right and that your wood isn't pushing your barrel around before you start blaming a test reload.

You also can avoid frustration on the range and in the field by being careful with each step of the reloading process. All can be lost through improper case resizing. In that regard, those who advocate neck sizing only as a means to improve accuracy may not understand all they know. Full-length resizing of fired cases seems to have produced better accuracy in the finished product for the simple reason that it assures more positive bullet alignment. Backing a die out a turn or so in order to resize only the neck may create an off-center situation for the seated bullet.

Getting everything right the first time isn't what long-range varmint reloading is all about, at least not as far as the high degree of accuracy you'll need is concerned. You'll be late to the supper table more than once by the time you arrive at that ideal combination for your rifle. It'll be worth it, though, because what are a few cold pork chops when compared to the satisfaction of a perfect varmint hunt.

Chapter 14

LOVE AFFAIR WITH THE .22 VARMINTER

Frank de Haas Has Spent More Than Three Decades In Evaluating His Favorite Cartridge!

Ruger's No. 1 Special single shot is gaining favor with varmint hunters. It's available in a variety of calibers.

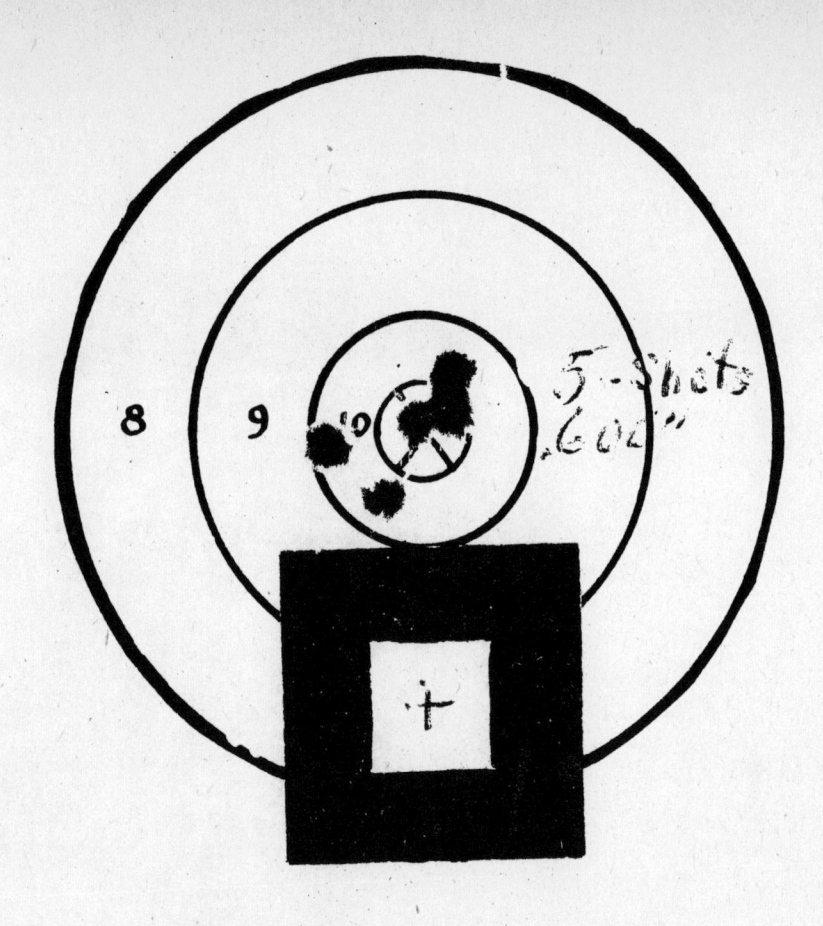

Rifle _de Haas - Miller Prete #2_
Ammo _22-250 34gn 4895-52 Sierra_
Range _100 yds_ Date _7-28-72_
Fired by _F. de Haas_

"I HAVE HAD a long-time love affair with the .22 Varminter cartridge, and I guess that as long as I live there will be a rifle of this caliber in my possession. In my last thirty-five years of shooting many center-fire rifles, I have fired more .22 Varminter cartridges than any other; with it, I have taken more varmints than with any other. My respect for this cartridge has ever increased and I still think it is the finest .22 center-fire varmint cartridge ever developed"

That's the opinion of Frank de Haas, who is considered one of the nation's authorities on rifles and has a book or so to his credit to back-up his references.

Brother de Haas, himself an ardent varmint hunter, sits out there in the wilds of Iowa, where he does a lot of hunting and a lot of rifle building. From the latter, he has learned a good deal about how to make a rifle shoot right and it's not surprising that he has developed some pretty definite tastes for loads over the years.

The .22 Varminter first came into some prominence in the mid-Thirties. It was merely the .250-3000 Savage cartridge case with its neck sized down to hold a .224-inch diameter bullet and, because of this, it now is known as the .22-250. Jerry Gebby was one of its main promoters and he named the cartridge the .22 Varminter, later having this name registered. When Remington introduced this cartridge commercially in 1965, they called it the .22-250 Remington.

Originally a wildcat, the .22-250 has gained wide acceptance in recent years among many shooters.

There was much written about the .22 Varminter in the Thirties and Forties, and no little controversy developed. Some riflemen praised it; some damned it. Using the same rifle, one writer found the rifle and cartridge accurate and devastating on varmints such as crows and woodchucks, while another expert complained it was noisy, hard to reload and only so-so in accuracy. Soon after the first reports came out on this cartridge, United States and Canadian gunsmiths began making reamers for the .22-250 case and building rifles for it. Soon many more reports were published; reading them objectively today, they were generally favorable.

"By 1940, I was a confirmed varmint hunter and my special target was the crow. I also hunted ground squirrels, prairie dogs, jackrabbits and foxes. My first successful varmint rifle was a Winchester High-wall in .25-20 single-shot caliber. This was followed by rebarreling the same rifle to the .22-R2 Lovell, whose cartridge was the .25-20 single-shot case necked down to .22 caliber. The .22-R2 Lovell was doing a fine job for me and I was content with it until one summer day on an edge of a large prairie

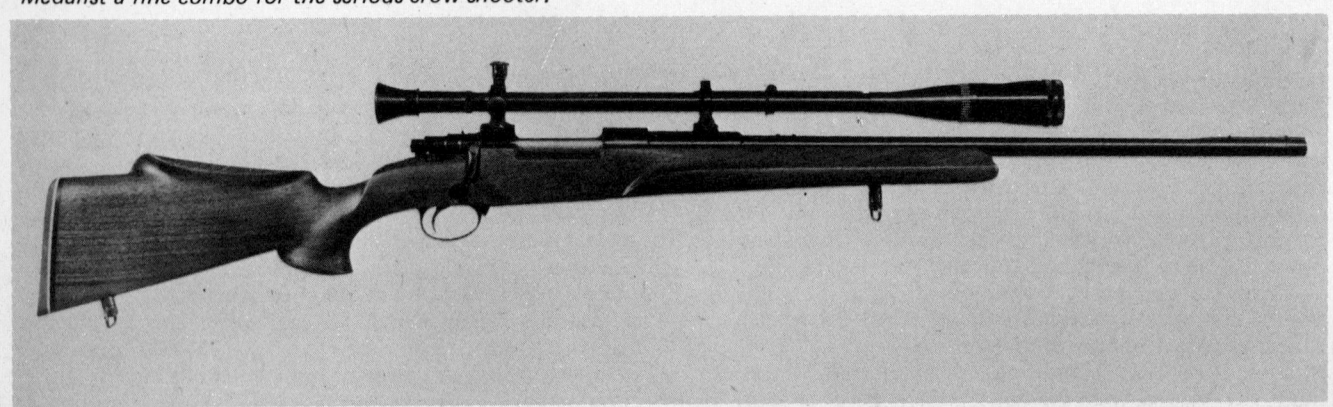

Fitted with Lyman Super Target-spot scope, de Haas considers Harrington and Richardson Model 370 Ultra Medalist a fine combo for the serious crow shooter.

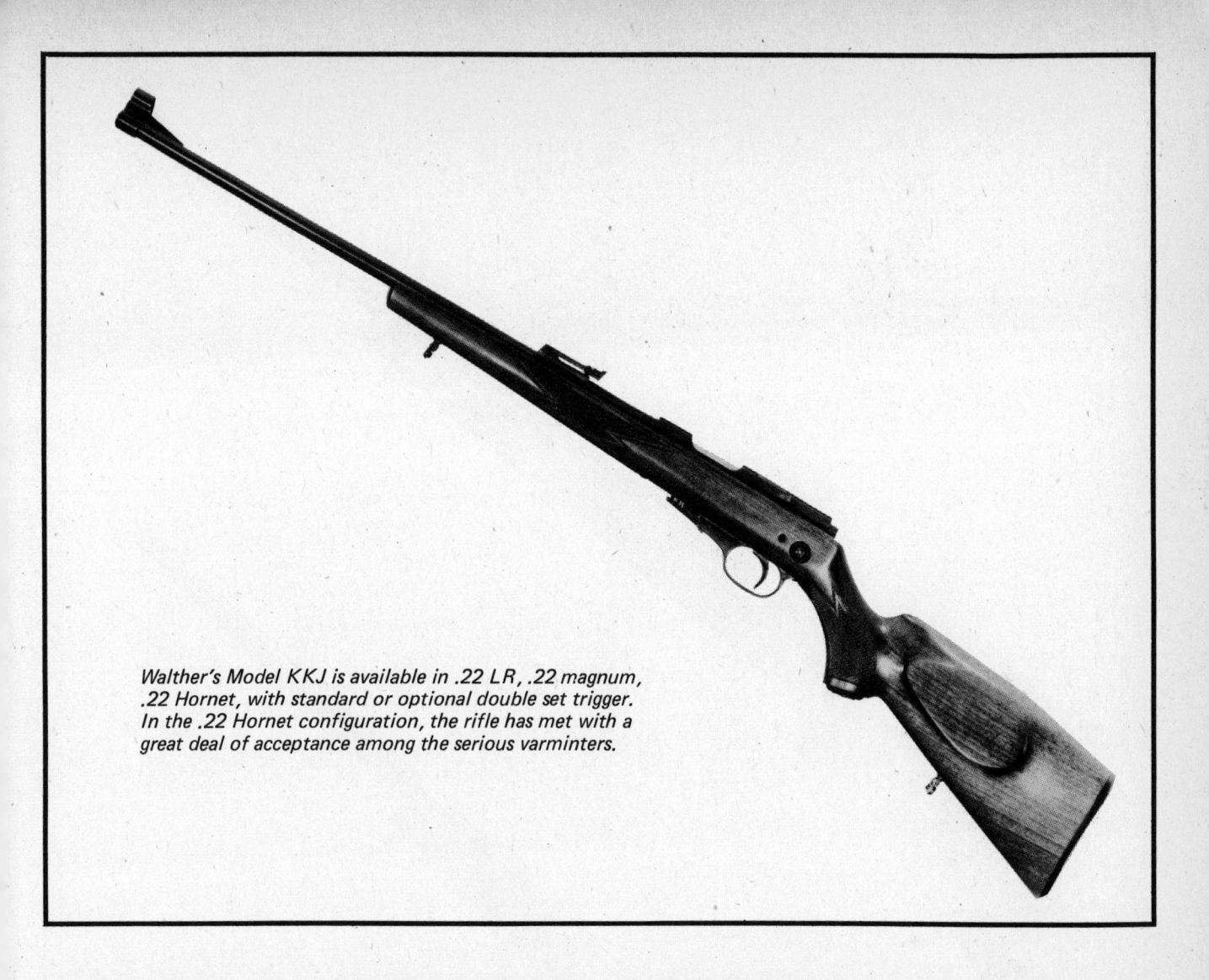

Walther's Model KKJ is available in .22 LR, .22 magnum, .22 Hornet, with standard or optional double set trigger. In the .22 Hornet configuration, the rifle has met with a great deal of acceptance among the serious varminters.

dog town in Kansas, a wildcatter friend let me fire his .22 Varminter at a few dogs. The rifle itself wasn't much, but that cartridge made by Lovell sure seemed puny.

"I was determined that my next rifle would be a Varminter and this came about sooner than I had expected. My wildcatter friend told me about an old Kansas farmer who had a small collection of guns for sale; among them were two Model 98 Mauser military rifles. We bought the lot of about ten guns for about $5 apiece and, after selling the excellent Spencer carbine that was included in this bunch, my 98 Mauser and my share of the other guns cost me nothing.

"My 98 Mauser turned out to be a Czech VZ-24. Arriving back home in Iowa, I ordered a .224-inch groove diameter barrel with 1:14-inch twist from John Buhmiller in Montana. When the barrel arrived, I turned it down and threaded it to fit my Mauser action. I then drove to the small village of Hudson, South Dakota, where Marion Havelaar, a young gunsmith fresh out of the Air Force, lived. He had a new set of .22 Varminter chambering reamers. He chambered and fitted the barrel and also made up a case-forming die. I made up the other dies myself to reload the cases. A Bishop stock, a K-2.5 Weaver scope with an 8X Litschert attachment in Tilden mounts and a new GM single-set trigger completed the outfit. After loading some cartridges, I drove back to Hudson and Havelaar and I sighted-in the rifle, shot a few test groups, then busted a few hillside rocks and jackrabbits."

Frank de Haas fired that first Varminter rifle a great deal. It was amazingly accurate and he soon settled on a load consisting of 35 grains of DuPont 4320 powder behind any good 50 or 55-grain bullet. He used mostly Sisk bullets at that time and liked the 55-grain bullet best. He prowled the countryside with that rifle at every opportunity and word began to spread among local shooters that that lanky de Haas had some magical smoke pole with which he could drop crows at unheard-of distances.

"One early winter day, after I had used this rifle for a year or so, a young farmer who had heard about my crow rifle dropped in. He was a hunter who wanted a crow rifle and who had never used anything except a shotgun and a .22 rimfire rifle. My asking price for my Varminter seemed too high for him, but I suggested he take the rifle out with the thirteen remaining loaded cartridges I had for it and pop a few crows with it that afternoon," de Haas recalls.

A couple of hours later he was back, all smiles. With those thirteen cartridges, he had dropped eleven crows, missing the first two at less than 150 yards because he thought he had to hold high. On the next crow he held dead on and then he was in a groove. He promptly bought the outfit and de Haas set him up for reloading.

"I missed that first Varminter, but I soon made up another. If it turned out to be accurate — which was usually the case — someone would buy it. And so it went. I'd build a rifle for myself and use it awhile; then someone would want it more than I did. Fortunately for me, most of these

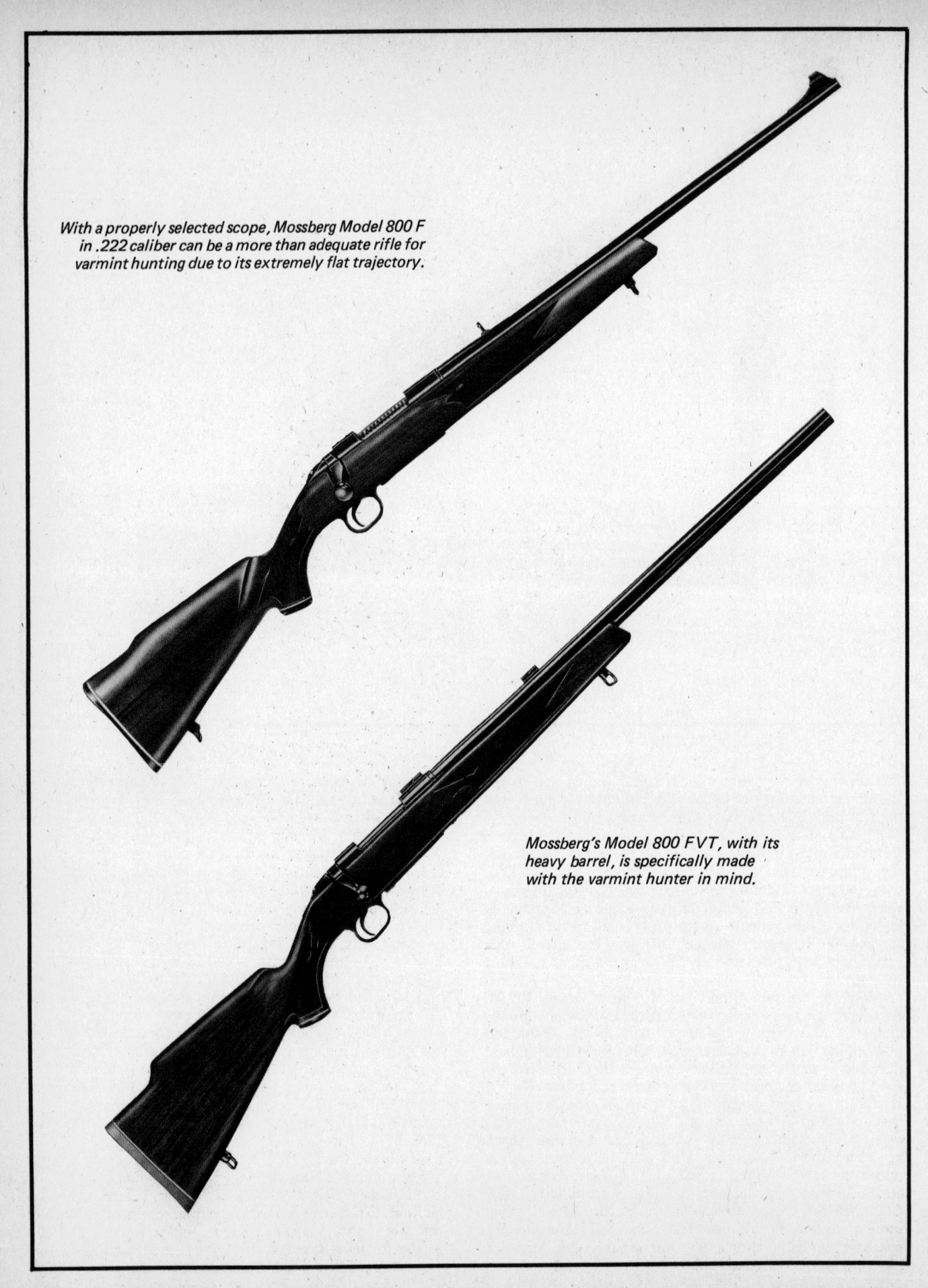

With a properly selected scope, Mossberg Model 800 F in .222 caliber can be a more than adequate rifle for varmint hunting due to its extremely flat trajectory.

Mossberg's Model 800 FVT, with its heavy barrel, is specifically made with the varmint hunter in mind.

Varmint cartridges favored by de Haas include (from left) the orphaned .225 Winchester; the .22-250 Remington, his seeming favorite; the .224 Weatherby magnum, the smallest of the Weatherby magnums; and the .220 Swift, which appears to be undergoing a revival with varmint callers.

rifles went out of my hunting territory. I never built these .22 Varminters alike, although most had twenty-four to twenty-six-inch medium-heavy barrels and sporter-type stocks. They were built on various commercial and military turn-bolt actions, with fancy figured stocks, fitted with a good scope and usually with a set trigger.

"An almost surefire method I had for getting a sale was to demonstrate the accuracy of the rifle and the potency of the .22-250 cartridge. To begin with, I always had used it for a year or so and had fired it many times, mostly on targets. By that time the bore was lapped, I knew which bullet and load was most accurate in it and, above all, I had the rifle properly sighted-in and always ready to go.

"Then when a customer came around, we would simply go out and find a crow or two for him to drop. If there was little or no wind and if the prospective buyer knew something about rifle shooting, I usually could give him the instructions needed to drop the first crow we spotted. If this happened and if he'd then pace his steps as he walked out to get the crow, the sale would be cinched. After that there would be another .22 Varminter booster and I'd get busy making another."

Frank de Haas also built rifles for others on order, mostly varmint rifles chambered for a number of different cartridges besides the .22 Varminter. These included the .22 Hornet, .219-Zipper, .219 Improved Zipper, .219 Donaldson Wasp, Rimless Wasp, .220 Swift, Improved Swift and .222. Of these, the closest rival to the .22 Varminter was the .219 Improved Zipper.

There were times when he owned a fully equipped ready-to-go rifle in each of these calibers, but when it came time to pick a rifle to use for an early morning's crow hunt, he would almost invariably choose one chambered for the Varminter. "There were times for periods of up to perhaps a few months when I had no .22 Varminter in my gun cabinet, but at other times I had several.

"Right now I have four .22 Varminters; my old standby on a VZ-24 Mauser action with the Miller single-set trigger, a Ruger Model 77V, a Browning M-78 single-shot, and my deHaas-Miller single-shot. All four are ready to go and I can count on any one of them to place its first shot within a crow-sized target at 250 yards.

"I have used a lot of different bullets in my .22-250 rifles over the years. At first I used only Sisk bullets and I can remember purchasing a thousand of them when I could

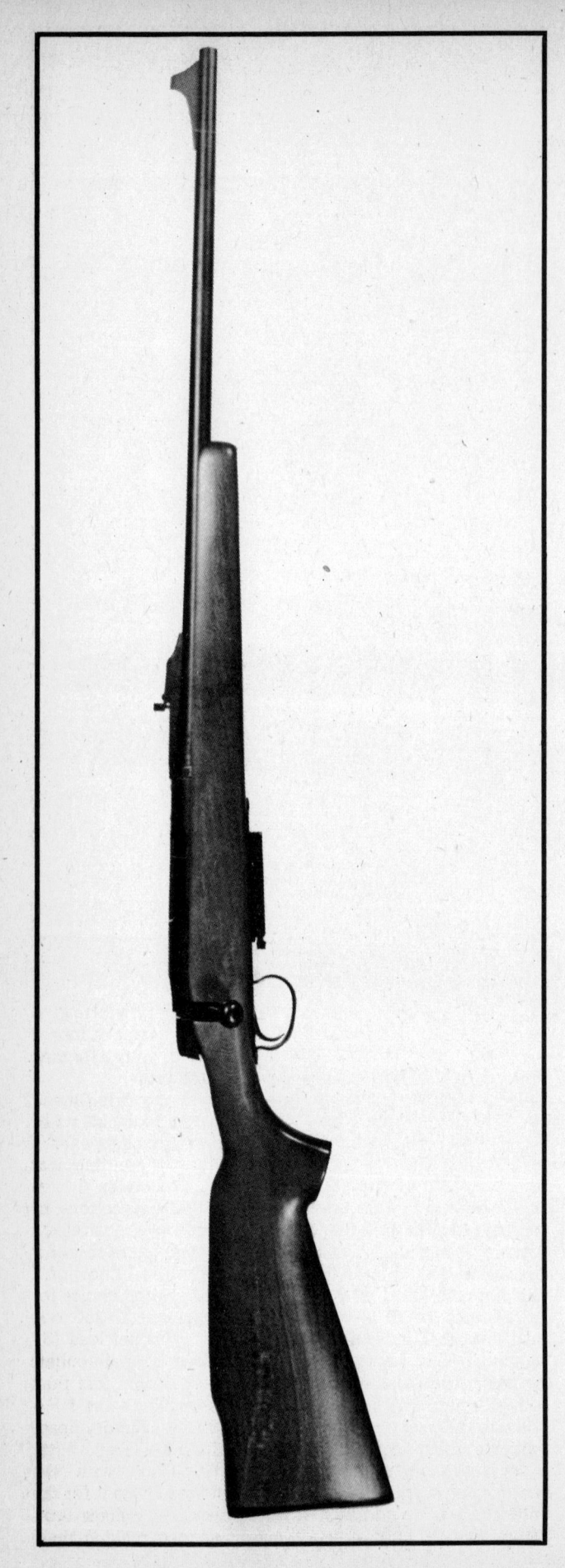

The Remington Model 788 is considered the lowest priced rifle available today to handle the .22-250 cartridge. Many owners have reported exceptional accuracy from this rifle with commercial rounds.

little afford it. By 1945, practically everyone was out of bullets; at that time I traded for a set of Banta bullet dies and began making my own. At first I used fired .22 long rifle cases for jackets, but only the copper cases worked well and not many of these could be found. I then obtained 5000 copper jacket cups and we were back in business. I say we because I was joined by George Meyer, a fellow shooter and gunsmith. He owned a huge pair of muscled arms, and in one long evening's work, after I had previously cut the lead cores and had seated them in the cups, he and I pumped out nearly all 5000 of them, with him furnishing the power to my heavy Pacific press. We had splendid success with these home-brewed bullets and got the best accuracy from them if we soft swaged them, leaving them hollow-point instead of making them with a lead point.

"With better times, I began to use Hi-Precision, Hornady, Speer, Jordan and Sierra bullets. I soon picked a favorite, the Sierra 55-grain semi-pointed. For target work I like the Sierra 53-grain hollow-point."

After trying many load combinations in many .22-250 rifles, de Haas settled on two powders; namely, 4320 and 4895. His all-time favorite load is 35 grains of 4320 with either the Sierra 53 or 55-grain bullet. Equally a favorite is 35 grains of 4895 with any 50 to 55-grain bullet. If, on testing a new .22-250 rifle with these two loads in combination with either the Sierra 53-grain HP or 55-grain semi-pointed bullet, the rifle does not show good initial accuracy, the chances are it never will be accurate. "I generally do not waste much time on such rifles. I either get rid of them if they are commercial rifles or install a new barrel on them if they are rifles I built."

Some varmint shooters using the .22-250 caliber rifle prefer to use light bullets, driving them as fast as they can. An acquaintance uses 40-grain bullets with loads that drive them over 4000 fps. Frank de Haas tried them on several occasions, but never could get the accuracy desired. Another shooter he knows likes the 60 and 63-grain bullets in his .22-250. He has used both in several of his rifles — all having the standard 1:14 rifling twist — and gotten exceptional accuracy from them. However, even though accuracy was good, he could not make consistent hits and kills on varmints with them as with 50 and 55-grain bullets.

"One deer hunter I knew used the .22-250 cartridge successfully on deer using 55-grain bullets. However, he hunted and shot deer the same way he would shoot a woodchuck; that was by making a successful stalk or still-hunting them, then placing the shot with pinpoint accuracy in the brain or neck vertebrae. He never lost a deer at which he fired with his .22-250 and all dropped in their tracks. Even so, I don't recommend the .22-250 as a deer caliber.

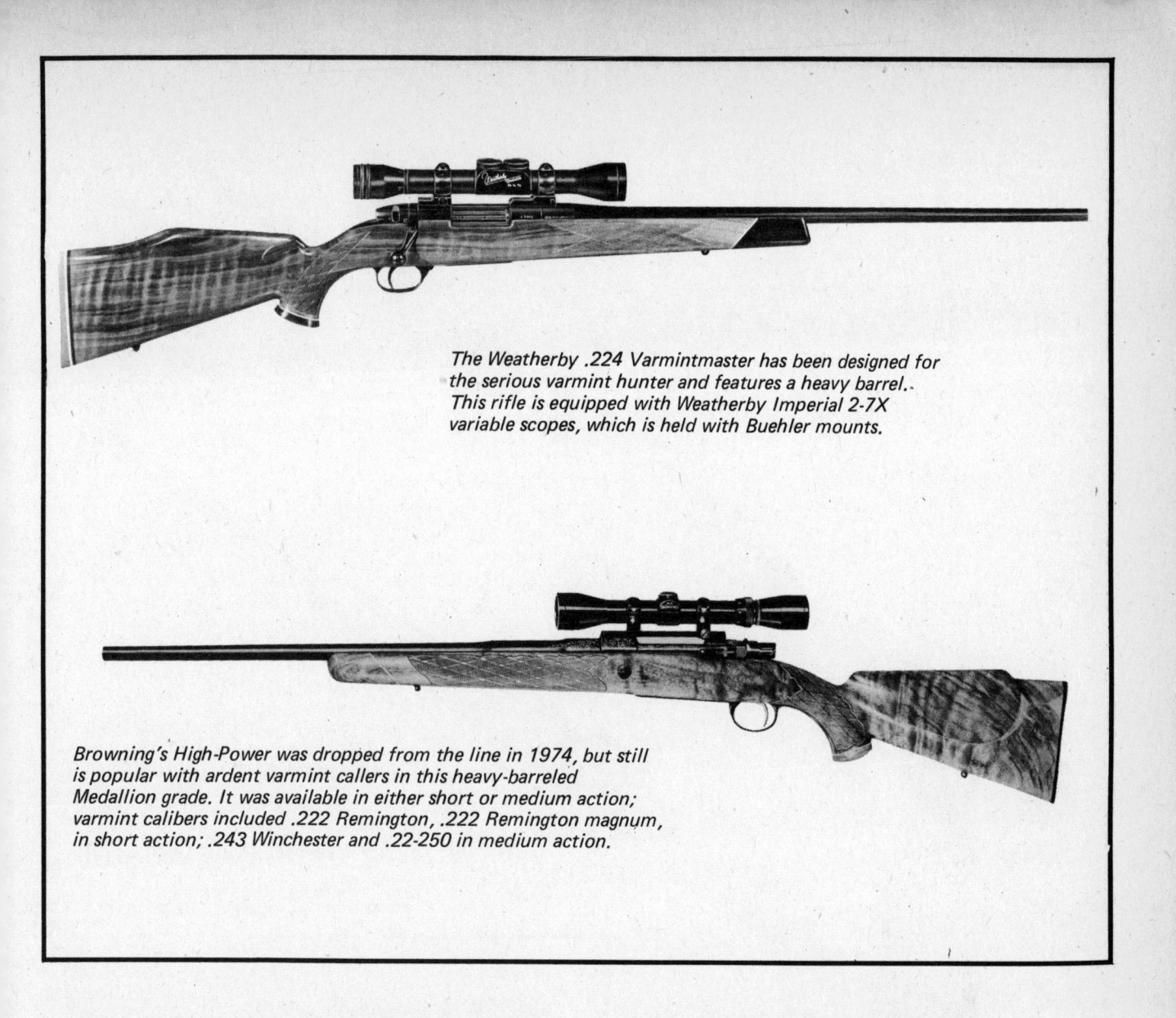

The Weatherby .224 Varmintmaster has been designed for the serious varmint hunter and features a heavy barrel. This rifle is equipped with Weatherby Imperial 2-7X variable scopes, which is held with Buehler mounts.

Browning's High-Power was dropped from the line in 1974, but still is popular with ardent varmint callers in this heavy-barreled Medallion grade. It was available in either short or medium action; varmint calibers included .222 Remington, .222 Remington magnum, in short action; .243 Winchester and .22-250 in medium action.

"Speer makes a fine 70-grain .224-inch diameter bullet but the 1:14 twist in most .22-250 barrels is too slow to stabilize it properly. I have yet to try a barrel with a 1:12 twist needed to stabilize this bullet, but I do know from experience with other calibers and twists that a .22-250 barrel with a 1:12 twist would likely be just as accurate with all lighter weight bullets as a barrel with the slower 1:14 twist."

Besides using various makes and models of M-98 Mauser actions on which to build .22-250 caliber rifles, de Haas has used Models 1903 and 1903A3 Springfield actions, Model 1917 Enfields, Type 38 Japanese Arisaka 6.5 actions, FN Mauser and Sako Forester actions.

The M-1917 Enfield action is a bit big for this cartridge, but the others are quite good. The short Mexican M-98 Mauser action is perhaps the best choice of the Mausers. He never bothered about blocking off the rear of the magazine box on any of these rifles, since he seldom used the rifle as a repeater. In most cases, if the cartridges are loaded toward the front of the magazine or to the rear, one or two of them will feed properly and that is all the repeat shots he has ever needed.

The .22-250 cartridge is not big, but it is potent. It is now normally factory loaded up to about 50,000 copper units of pressure (cup). A lot of handloaders will load it even hotter than this and, even if you don't want to load it hotter, the load that you may find best in your rifle may exceed this figure without you knowing about it.

"In loading many of these cartridges and firing many rifles in this caliber, I have experienced a few incidents of high pressures and case failures. Whenever this happened, I was mighty glad that the rifle I was using at those times was built on a strong and safe action. For this reason, I have never built a .22-250 rifle on any pre-98 Mauser actions, or on any other doubtful actions. However, I have rebarreled a couple of fairly late Model 99 Savage solid frame rifles for this cartridge and, unlike some other gunsmiths I know of, I am not wholly satisfied that this action is a good choice for it. I fired both of these rifles with my own pet .22-250 load and everything seems to be up to snuff. This pet load (35 grains of 4320 with either the Sierra 53 or 55-grain bullet) is not particularly hot (I estimate it to develop less than 45,000 cup breech pressure) and according to the NRA Handloader's Guide, it is milder than the factory load, which is about 48,290 cup.

"I have always been so well pleased with the performance of the .22-250 cartridge that I chose it for the prototype of my own rifle, the de Haas-Miller single shot. Dean Miller of St. Onge, South Dakota, is making these

Ruger Number 1 Special Varminter is manufactured for varmint hunting currently in .22-250, .25/06 calibers. It comes equipped with standard target scope blocks.

Browning's Safari grade was dropped in 1974, but was made in the same varmint calibers as Medallion grade.

rifles on strictly a custom basis. It was sort of a test rifle, and the first Summer I had it, I fired it over a thousand times at targets. I tried many loads in it besides my own pet load and the rifle, as well as all loads, gave satisfactory results. However, for top accuracy in this rifle, I found that a load of 33 grains of 4895 with the Hi-Precision 53-grain bullet was tops. The smallest five-shot one hundred-yard group was only .425-inch.

"The .22-250 cartridge is easy to reload and will digest just about anything and everything. I have always liked Du Pont's 4320 powder for this round, but recently I've found that 4895 is just as good. I have also used a lot of 3031 and 4064 powder in it. Recently, a friend of mine was testing his Model 700 BDL Remington Varmint Special in .22-250 caliber and fired a couple of near .500-inch five-shot one hundred-yard groups with a load of 40 grains of 4831 powder behind the 55-grain Hi-Precision bullet. While I have only used Du Pont powders in loading the .22-250, other shooters are getting results that are just as good with a number of other powders with burning rates similar to those of 4320 and 4895, such as powders made by Hercules, Winchester-Western and Norma.

"I would advise .22-250 shooters who reload to start with factory-loaded ammunition for new .22-250 cases rather than making the cases from some other caliber brass like everyone used to do before this cartridge became a commercial one. Years ago I used to make .22-250 cases from everything from .250 Savage to .300 Savage, .270, .30/06 and .308 brass. However, doing this today is just not practical, and except for using the .250 Savage brass, it was never advisable."

It used to be that the only way to obtain a .22-250 rifle was to have it made by a custom gunsmith or to build it yourself. Twenty-five years ago, it wasn't as easy to build your own rifle as it is now, for now there are a number of commercial actions available for which commercial threaded, turned and chambered barrels are also available,

Savage's Model 110C, currently available in .243 for the varmint hunter, originally was made in .22-250 and .25/06 as well, when it was introduced in 1966.

or barreled actions with the barrel already fitted, chambered and head spaced.

If you want to build a rifle, it is best to get the assembled barreled action; then all that is left to do is to make the stock for it or fit a semi-inletted stock to it. If you have an action for which a threaded and chambered barrel is available, it is best to have a competent gunsmith set up the barrel in the action, check it for head space and make any needed corrections.

The .22-250 is so popular that almost every arms manufacturer that makes a center-fire turn-bolt rifle has one or more models in this caliber. Here are some of the commercial bolt-action ready-to-go rifles available in .22-250 caliber: Browning High-Power B.A., BSA Monarch, Harrington & Richardson Models 300 and 370, Ithaca Model LSA-55, Mossberg Model 800, Remington Models 788 and 700, Ruger Model 77, Savage Model 110, Sako L-579 Forester, Smith & Wesson, Weatherby and Model 70 Winchester.

There are also several other foreign rifles available in this caliber such as the Mauser Model 3000, Mauser Model 660, Mark-X, HVA Carl Gustaf, FN Mauser, Parker-Hale and others. Most of these — foreign and domestic — are available in several grades and styles, including some especially made up for varmint shooting. There are also some falling block single-shot rifles available in .22-250 caliber, including the Ruger No. 1 and Browning M-78.

"Don't look for a lever-action, slide-action or semiautomatic rifle in the .22-250 caliber; they are just not made. The .22-250 is a varmint cartridge and these fast repeating rifles just are not varminters," de Haas opines.

"I have owned and tested only a few of the commercial .22-250 rifles made but, even so, I am safe in saying that most of them right out of the factory box are capable of 1.50 minute-of-angle accuracy. That is accuracy good enough for the serious woodchuck and coyote shooter. With a bit of tuning up or breaking-in, and/or with selected handloads, most of them will do even better. The various heavy-barreled varmint models can be expected to give less than MOA accuracy with factory loads and perhaps less than .750 MOA with good handloads. This last is the kind of accuracy the serious crow shooter needs and demands.

"For hunting, I always have sighted-in my .22-250 rifles so that the bullets strike about three-quarters to one inch above the aiming point at one hundred yards. With a scope — and every good Varminter rifle needs the best scope one can afford — mounted about 1.5-inch above the bore, such sighting-in will give dead-center hits at two hundred yards, and on crows you have to start holding over a bit at 250 yards and beyond.

"After shooting the .22 Varminter for over thirty years, I hope I can use it for several more decades. Even thirty years hence, I am convinced it will still be the best and most popular .22 center-fire varmint cartridge around."

That's the contention of a true expert.

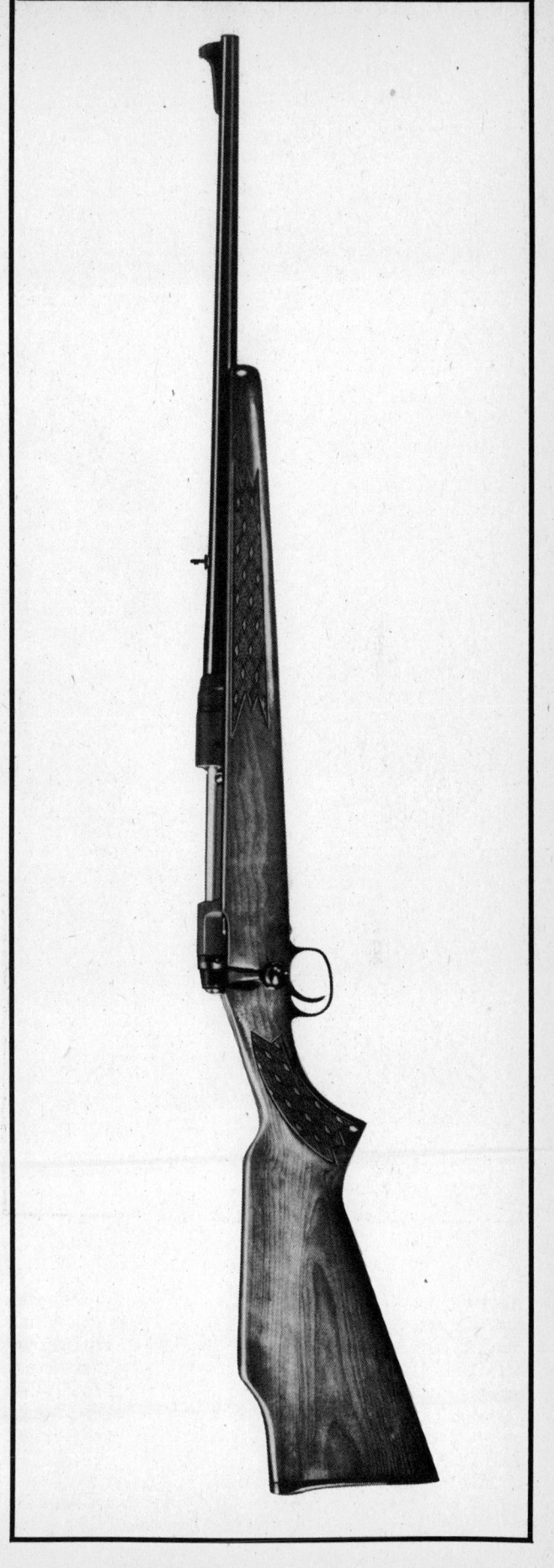

HANDGUNS FOR VARMINTS

Chapter 15

Left — Sherry Moon used a Charter Arms Pathfinder with 3" barrel in .22 WMRF to bag this jackrabbit in California desert.

Jerry Mills used Remington XP-100 in .221 Fire Ball to collect this fine bobcat trio.

Almost Any Will Do, But Some Have Built-In Specifics That Help

TO BE USEFUL and practical for varmint hunting, the handgun must be capable of scoring accurate hits upon the intended target at typical distances and it must deliver sufficient punch — as evaluated in terms of the intended quarry — to anchor the target cleanly, without causing undesirable suffering.

The suitability of the handgun depends upon the proposed varmint and, to some extent, upon the hunter who plans to use it. Pistols and revolvers chambered for the ubiquitous .22 long rifle cartridge can be and have been used with outstanding success by hosts of varmint hunters on a surprising variety of species. Within recent times, the introduction of the Omark/CCI .22 Stinger cartridge has boosted the capability of guns chambered for the ever-popular .22 LR round.

It should be emphasized that the .22 Stinger is intended for use solely in guns of good quality, manufactured since the introduction of the high-velocity .22 LR cartridge — circa the early Thirties, that is — with chambers and bores having dimensions that correspond to domestic standards. In addition, the gun must be in good mechanical condition.

The .22 Stinger has a case about .10-inch longer than that of the .22 LR, but overall dimensions of both

High velocity, flat trajectory and exceptional accuracy make the Auto Mag a favored number, particularly in the .357 AMP chambering, as in the photo at left.

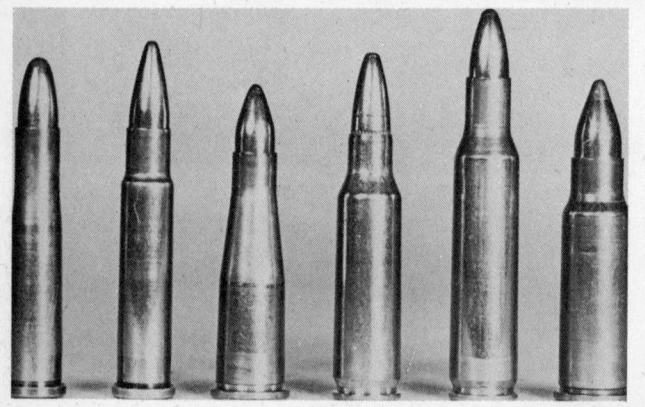

Top, Omark/CCI .22 Stinger can be fired in standard .22 LR guns and delivers velocities about 300 fps faster than .22 LR. Above, from left, .22 Hornet, .22 K-Hornet, .22 Jet, .221 Fire Ball, .222 Remington and .256 Winchester magnum are six popular loads for handguns. Right, Hugh Farmer uses a ski pole as field shooting rest.

A Conetrol mount and rings hold this M8-2X Leupold scope to Thompson/Center's Contender, here with .30 Herrett bull barrel.

Above, typical 5-shot groups off the bench at 100 yards with .221 Fire Ball XP-100. Left, factory nylon stock, with thumbhole stock by Fajen. Below, T/C Contender with Thompson/Center's 1.5X Lobo scope on T/C mount.

cartridges are essentially the same. Velocities vary with the individual gun, of course, but typical performance figures are about 1250 fps for the .22 LR against 1600 fps for the .22 Stinger. The latter packs a bullet weighing about 33 grains, of a specialized design, with a five-sided cavity extending through slightly more than half its length. It tends to expand quite decisively, meanwhile holding good, average accuracy in terms of typical .22 LR performance.

The .22 Stinger does not quite equal measured performance of the .22 magnum or .22 WMRF — two terms for the same cartridge — although it comes surprisingly close; within about twenty-four foot-pounds, when compared in a six-inch Ruger Single Six revolver fitted with auxiliary cylinders for both the .22 LR and .22 WMRF.

Whether working with .22 rimfire handguns or the more potent center-fire calibers, accuracy is a prime consideration. First you have to score a hit and, secondly, it

VARMINT HUNTER'S DIGEST 147

T/C Contender in .218 Bee, with custom bull barrel and M8-2X Leupold scope in Conetrol mounts puts all its hits in one ragged hole off the bench at distance of 25 yards.

must be an effective hit. The bullet must deliver enough foot-pounds of transmitted energy to be effective, and the location of the hit is at least equally critical.

Several factors weight the odds in the handgunning hunter's favor: Accuracy and flat trajectory — a product of relatively high velocity coupled with favorable aerodynamic shape and proportions of the bullet — plus cross-sectional area of the bullet, its capability for expansion upon impact and its weight.

Most of the pertinent factors interlock and balance against each other. To get high velocity, you may have to sacrifice some bullet weight. But, if you sacrifice bullet weight, it may carry a corresponding loss in ability to retain velocity. Bullets with a nose profile that have maximum impact effect tend to lose a lot of their zip from plowing through the air. Ideally, a bullet should lose velocity rapidly within the target medium, meanwhile losing as little as possible en route to the target.

So, as you're beginning to see, the problem tends to break down into a confusing series of trade-off

New Insta-Sight, by Thompson/Center, positions a reticle in same plane of focus as the target, does not magnify image and can be adjusted for windage, elevation.

Right, cast wadcutters were modified in obsolete C-H Swag-O-Matic press to cup-point shape for expansion. Below, Midge Dandridge draws a bead on a jackrabbit with Browning Model BDA 9mm double-action auto. Lower right, Speer's 140-grain JHP for .38 or .357.

Speer shot loads are highly effective in .38 Special, .357 mag or .44 mag, as discussed here.

VARMINT HUNTER'S DIGEST

149

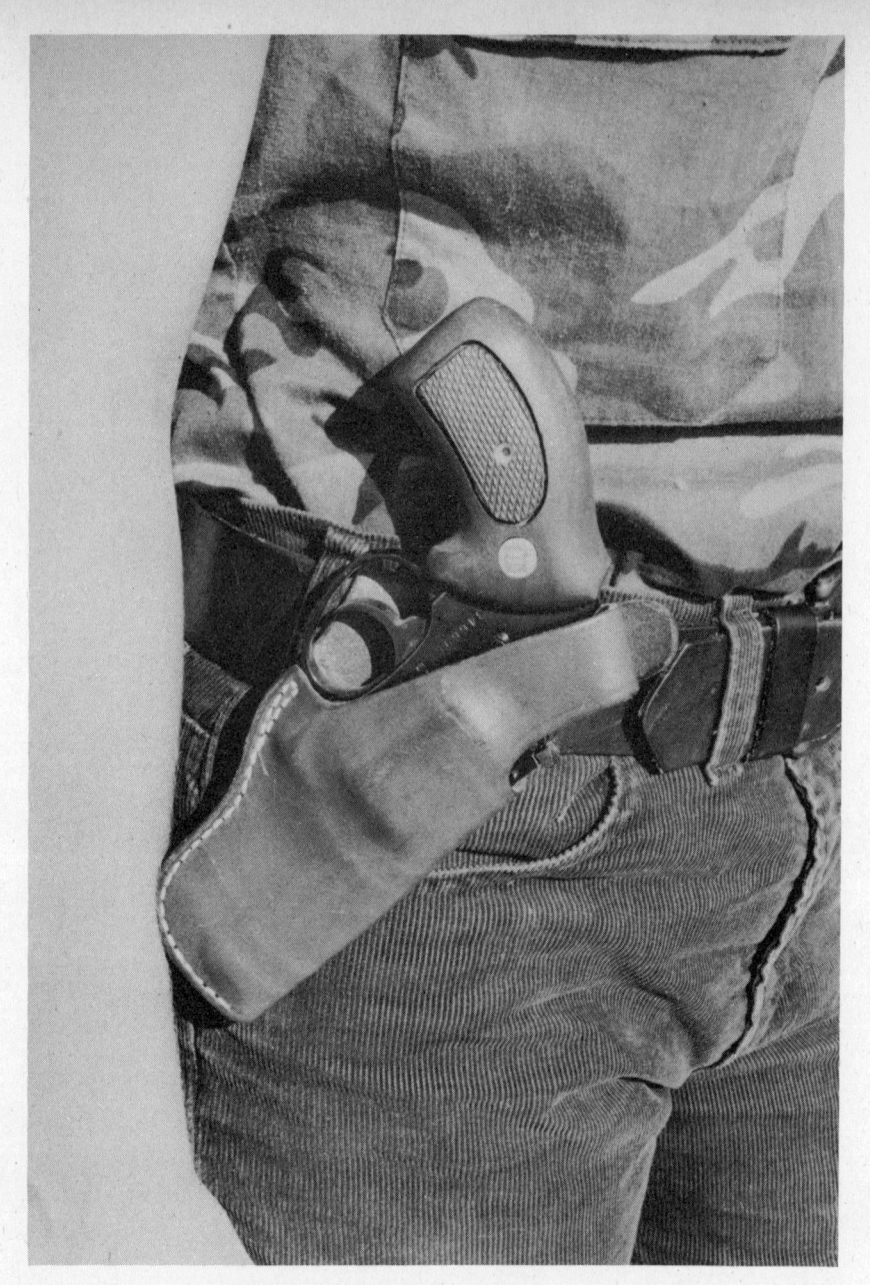

Bianchi holster, here for Charter Arms Bulldog or Pathfinder, does not impede movement and is fast.

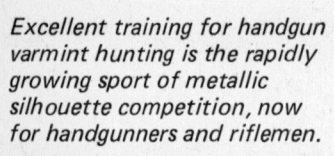

Excellent training for handgun varmint hunting is the rapidly growing sport of metallic silhouette competition, now for handgunners and riflemen.

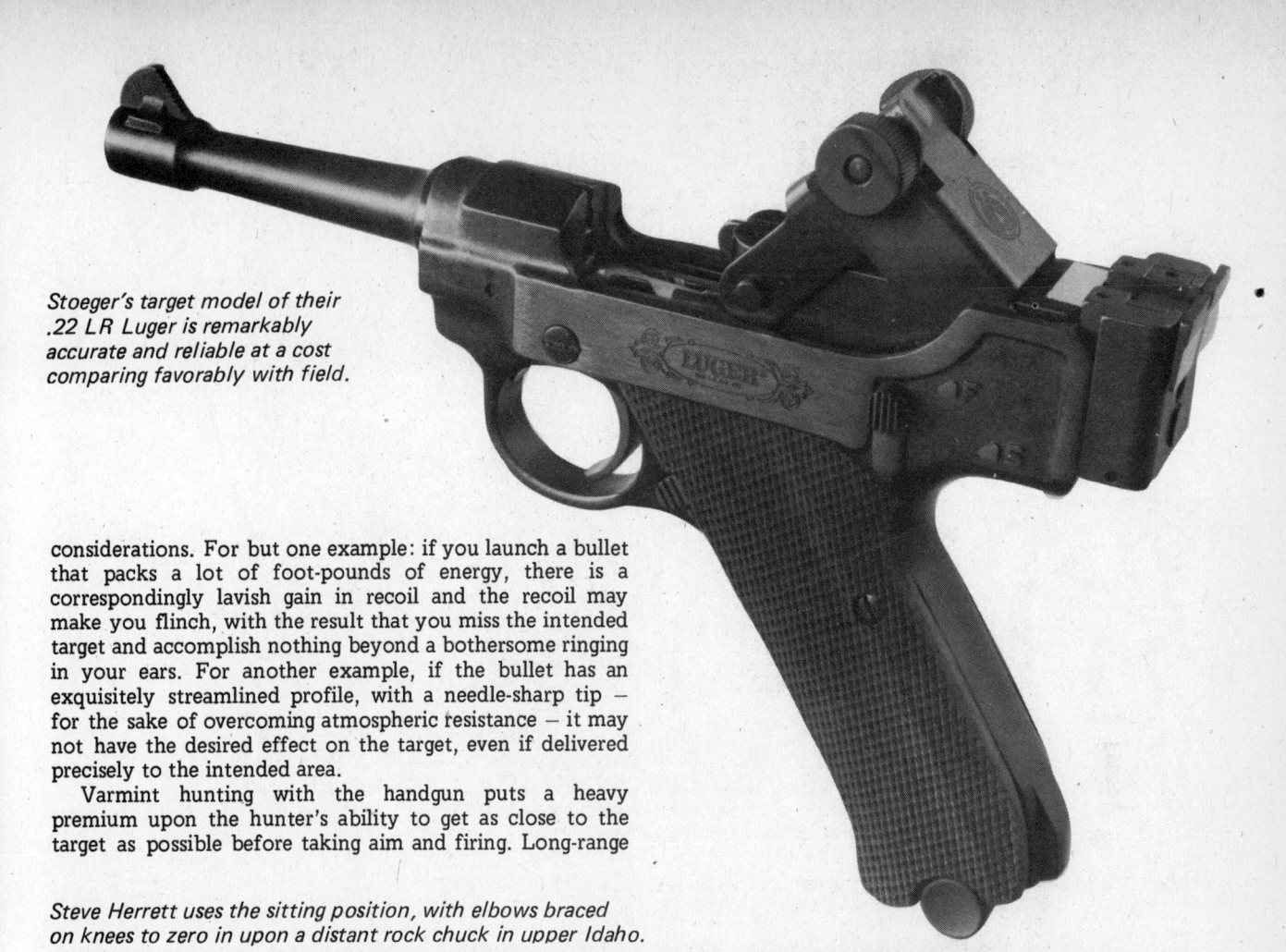

Stoeger's target model of their .22 LR Luger is remarkably accurate and reliable at a cost comparing favorably with field.

considerations. For but one example: if you launch a bullet that packs a lot of foot-pounds of energy, there is a correspondingly lavish gain in recoil and the recoil may make you flinch, with the result that you miss the intended target and accomplish nothing beyond a bothersome ringing in your ears. For another example, if the bullet has an exquisitely streamlined profile, with a needle-sharp tip — for the sake of overcoming atmospheric resistance — it may not have the desired effect on the target, even if delivered precisely to the intended area.

Varmint hunting with the handgun puts a heavy premium upon the hunter's ability to get as close to the target as possible before taking aim and firing. Long-range

Steve Herrett uses the sitting position, with elbows braced on knees to zero in upon a distant rock chuck in upper Idaho.

VARMINT HUNTER'S DIGEST

T/C HotShot loads, in special Contender barrels, offer high degree of pattern capability to the handgunner. Stock on this gun was an experimental Herrett prototype.

Jerry Mills made this bipod as an aid for long-range shots with his Remington XP-100.

Although the hunter above is using a scoped handgun, hunting in heavy, brushy cover may favor open iron sights.

hits are possible, but they occur infrequently, despite impressions one may gather from exposure to accounts in the firearms press. Shooters — definitely including those who write for such publications — tend to remember their surprisingly lucky shots and let the memory of misses filter away beyond recall.

There is one handgun with accuracy capability so noteworthy that it must be regarded as constituting a one-gun class of its own: it's the Remington Model XP-100, chambered for the .221 Remington Fire Ball cartridge. Draw a line one hundred yards long and then, starting with one end of the first line as your point, draw a second line that diverges from the other end of the first line by 1.05 inches at the open portion. That is one minute of angle, commonly abbreviated at 1 MOA, with 60 MOA equal to one degree of angle. For some reason, 1 MOA has come to be regarded by marksmen and shooters as a sort of mystic talisman; a benchmark against which accuracy standards are judged.

It would be rash and foolhardy to state that any Remington XP-100, with any load, can be relied upon to hold 1 MOA at one hundred yards. On the other hand, it is realistic and valid to say it's not uncommon for skilled marksmen, firing well-tuned XP-100s, with good scopes

Hugh Farmer displays positive proof that his novel ski pole rest, shown on page 146, does its work quite well.

VARMINT HUNTER'S DIGEST 153

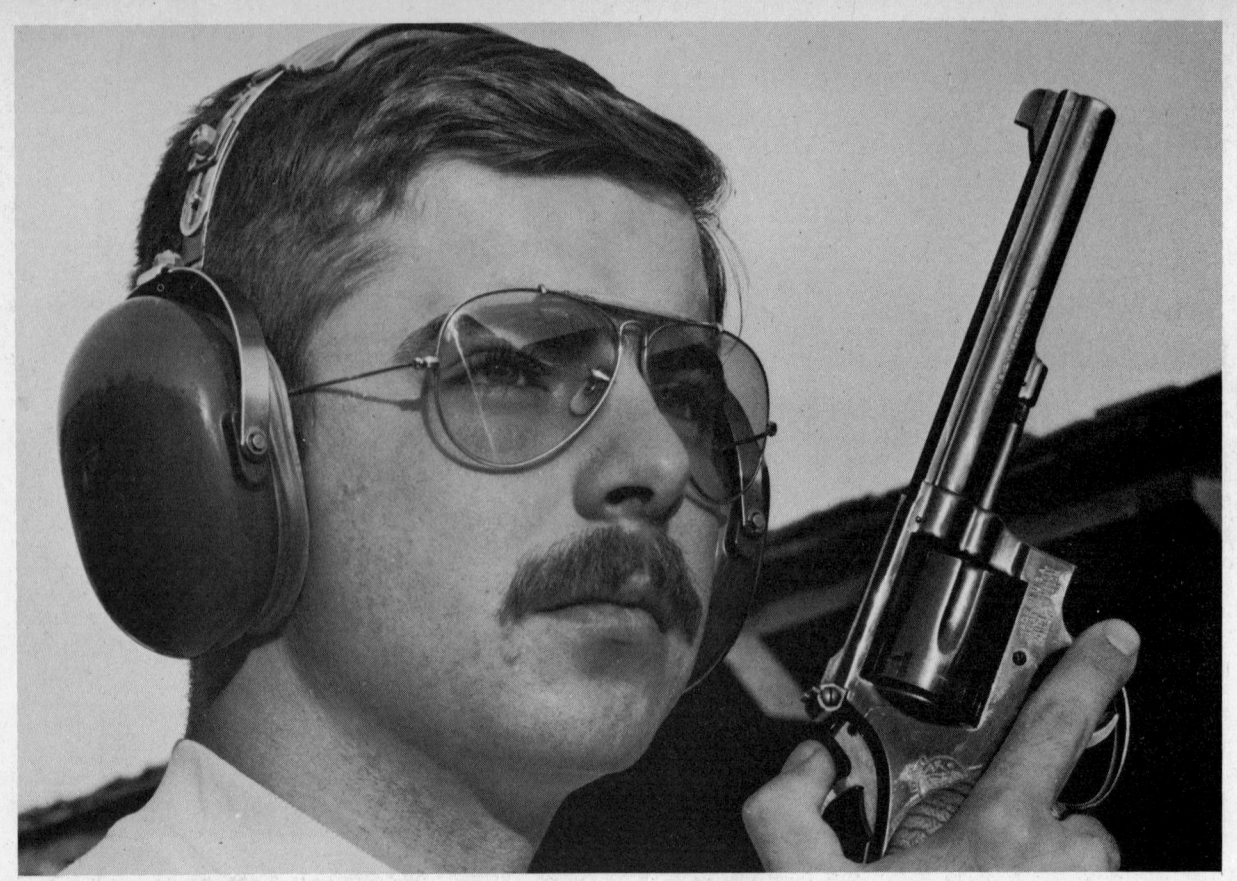

Firing handguns can present varying amounts of hazard to shooter's eyes and ears. Habitual use of shooting glasses, such as pair of Bausch & Lomb above, with ear protectors such as David Clark earmuffs, can be highly beneficial.

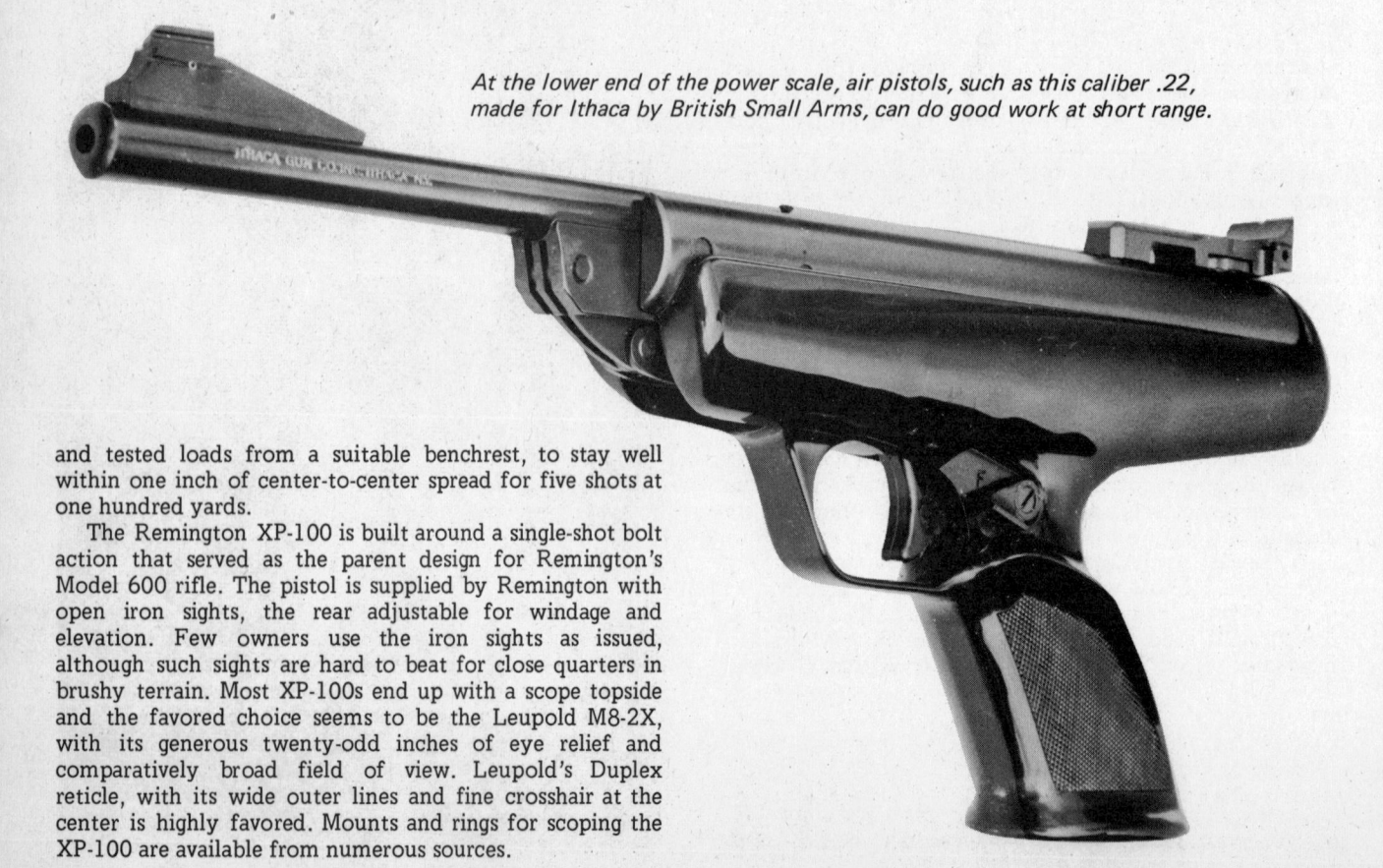

At the lower end of the power scale, air pistols, such as this caliber .22, made for Ithaca by British Small Arms, can do good work at short range.

and tested loads from a suitable benchrest, to stay well within one inch of center-to-center spread for five shots at one hundred yards.

The Remington XP-100 is built around a single-shot bolt action that served as the parent design for Remington's Model 600 rifle. The pistol is supplied by Remington with open iron sights, the rear adjustable for windage and elevation. Few owners use the iron sights as issued, although such sights are hard to beat for close quarters in brushy terrain. Most XP-100s end up with a scope topside and the favored choice seems to be the Leupold M8-2X, with its generous twenty-odd inches of eye relief and comparatively broad field of view. Leupold's Duplex reticle, with its wide outer lines and fine crosshair at the center is highly favored. Mounts and rings for scoping the XP-100 are available from numerous sources.

Bob Milek bagged this ground squirred at a distance of about 75 yards while conducting tests to find a bullet capable of good expansion at typical velocities of the .22 K-Hornet, for which the T/C Contender in the picture is chambered. The intact condition of the digger indicates that the bullet used for this shot did not expand. Note the scoped-gun holster.

Another favored handgun for hunting varmints is the Thompson/Center Contender. It's a single-shot design that breaks open for loading by upward/rearward pressure on the tang of the trigger guard. An unusual feature of the Contender, adding much to its versatility, is the availability of readily interchangeable barrels in a wide variety of calibers. Changing barrels and calibers is a quick, simple matter of removing the forend and pushing the pivot pin from the receiver. A circular insert in the face of the hammer can be pivoted to activate either of the two firing pins, when shifting between rimfire and center-fire cartridges.

Thus, the Contender will handle ammunition across the span between the diffident .22 CB cap and roaring might of the .357 Herrett, with several high points along the way such as the .30-30, .44 magnum and the .30 Herrett. Specialized barrels will handle the Thompson/Center HotShot loads, available in .357 and .44 calibers or, by

Browning's Challenger II .22 LR autoloader, introduced in 1976, is the first Browning produced in the USA. Colt pre-WWII Woodsman .22 LR auto was designed by John M. Browning and built by Colt until discontinued about 1976. Left, a Contender for the .44 T/C HotShot load was used to bag this running jackrabbit at a distance of 30 yards.

removal of the internal muzzle choke tube, the .357 HotShot barrel will handle conventional .357 magnum ammunition and the .44 HotShot will fire .44 magnum. Respective capability for .38 Special and .44 Special adds further to the versatility.

Federal law specifies payment of substantial transfer tax, registration and allied red tape on smoothbore handguns. Since they are rifled, the HotShot barrels do not fall under this restriction. The muzzle choke tube has pronounced lands and grooves that are parallel to the axis of the bore — not spiral cut in the usual manner of rifling — and these serve a dual purpose, arresting the rotation of the shot capsule and shredding the tough plastic envelope to release the shot pellets. As a result, the Contender HotShot barrels perform favorably in comparison to a conventional .410-bore shotgun, both in pattern and weight/velocity of the shot charge.

When firing the larger sizes of ammunition in the Contender, the recoil tends to seem rather severe. Custom makers of handgun stocks, such as Steve Herrett, have developed Contender stocks that help to minimize such discomfort. Herrett developed the .30 Herrett cartridge and, later, the .357 Herrett cartridge, both based upon the .30-30 WCF rifle case, shortened, with its shoulder relocated and squared outward. T/C offered a specialized version of the Contender for the two Herrett rounds, featuring a bull barrel and a forend that is held to the

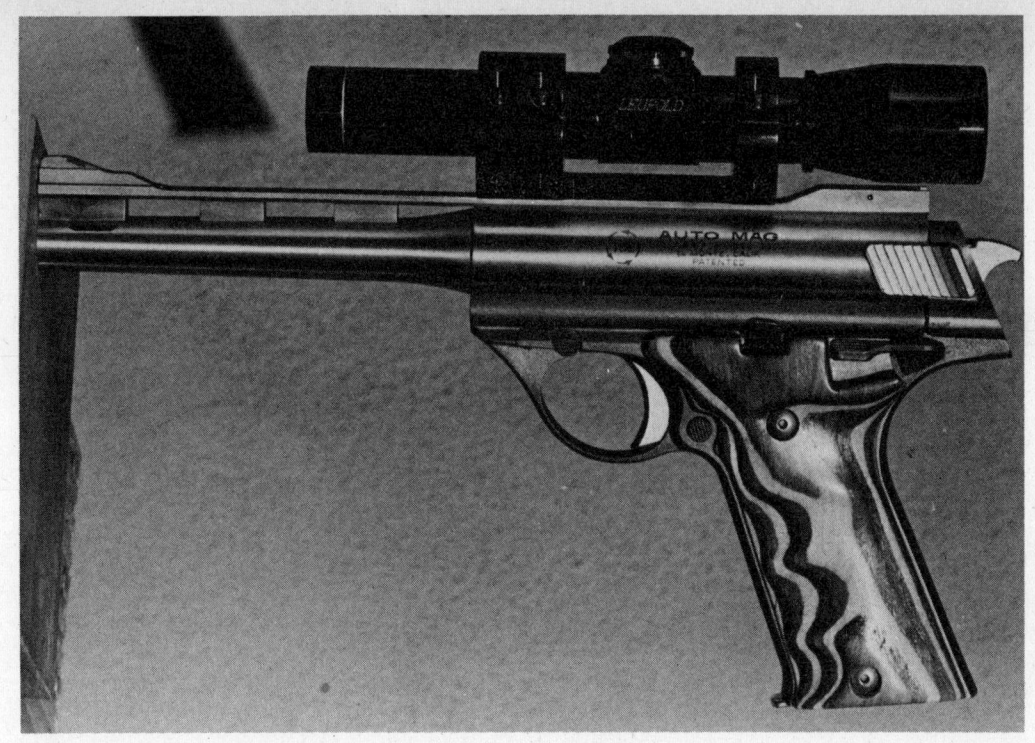

Herringshaw Maxi-Mount carries a Leupold M8-2X scope on this .357 AMP Auto Mag, consistently grouping less than 1.5" at 50 yards off the benchrest.

underside of the barrel by a sturdy screw. This counteracted a tendency of the heavier calibers to shed the forend, when recoil forces acted upon the spring-loaded detent inside the forend.

Ten inches is standard for Contender barrels and it's rare to encounter them in other lengths. Although barrels are offered in .222 Remington chambering, that otherwise excellent cartridge does not perform at its best in a barrel that short. One of the most suitable of all .22 center-fire cartridges for the Contender is the .218 Bee, with its generous rim and a powder capacity that seems to work out to ideal proportions.

Slightly up the scale is the .256 Winchester magnum, another good performer in the Contender. It handles jacketed bullets of .257-inch diameter, from 60 to 87 grains in weight and the case is, essentially, a necked-down .357

Machine rests, such as this design by Lee Custom Engineering, can be used to good advantage in establishing which of several loads group best in a gun.

VARMINT HUNTER'S DIGEST

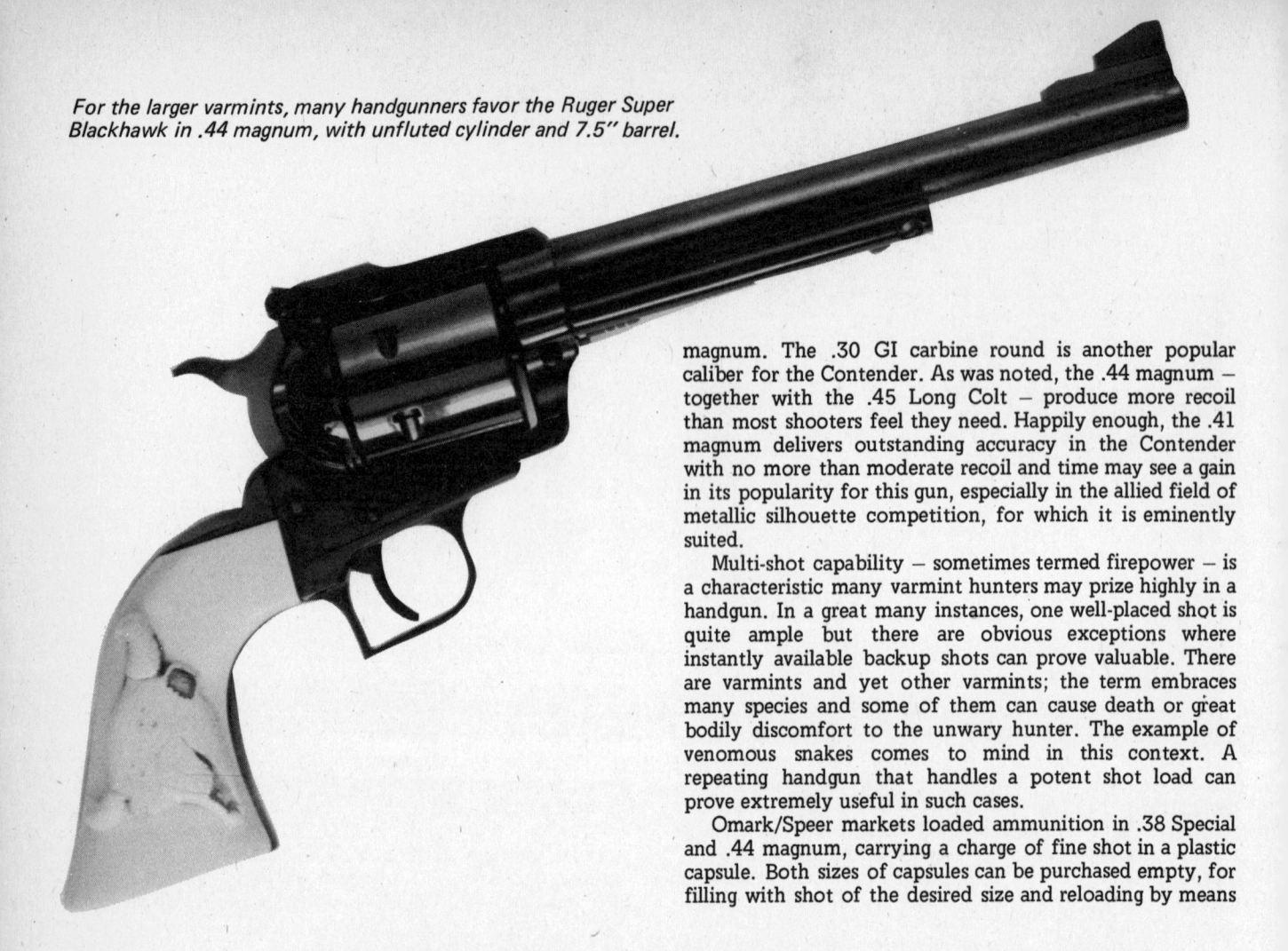

For the larger varmints, many handgunners favor the Ruger Super Blackhawk in .44 magnum, with unfluted cylinder and 7.5" barrel.

magnum. The .30 GI carbine round is another popular caliber for the Contender. As was noted, the .44 magnum — together with the .45 Long Colt — produce more recoil than most shooters feel they need. Happily enough, the .41 magnum delivers outstanding accuracy in the Contender with no more than moderate recoil and time may see a gain in its popularity for this gun, especially in the allied field of metallic silhouette competition, for which it is eminently suited.

Multi-shot capability — sometimes termed firepower — is a characteristic many varmint hunters may prize highly in a handgun. In a great many instances, one well-placed shot is quite ample but there are obvious exceptions where instantly available backup shots can prove valuable. There are varmints and yet other varmints; the term embraces many species and some of them can cause death or great bodily discomfort to the unwary hunter. The example of venomous snakes comes to mind in this context. A repeating handgun that handles a potent shot load can prove extremely useful in such cases.

Omark/Speer markets loaded ammunition in .38 Special and .44 magnum, carrying a charge of fine shot in a plastic capsule. Both sizes of capsules can be purchased empty, for filling with shot of the desired size and reloading by means

From left, .22 K-Hornet, .22/30 M-1 carbine, .218 Bee, .22 Jet, .256 Winchester magnum, .32 S&W Long, .32-20 WCF, .30 Herrett, .38 S&W, .38 Special, .357 magnum and .357 Herrett. Herrett wildcats are based upon the .30-30 case.

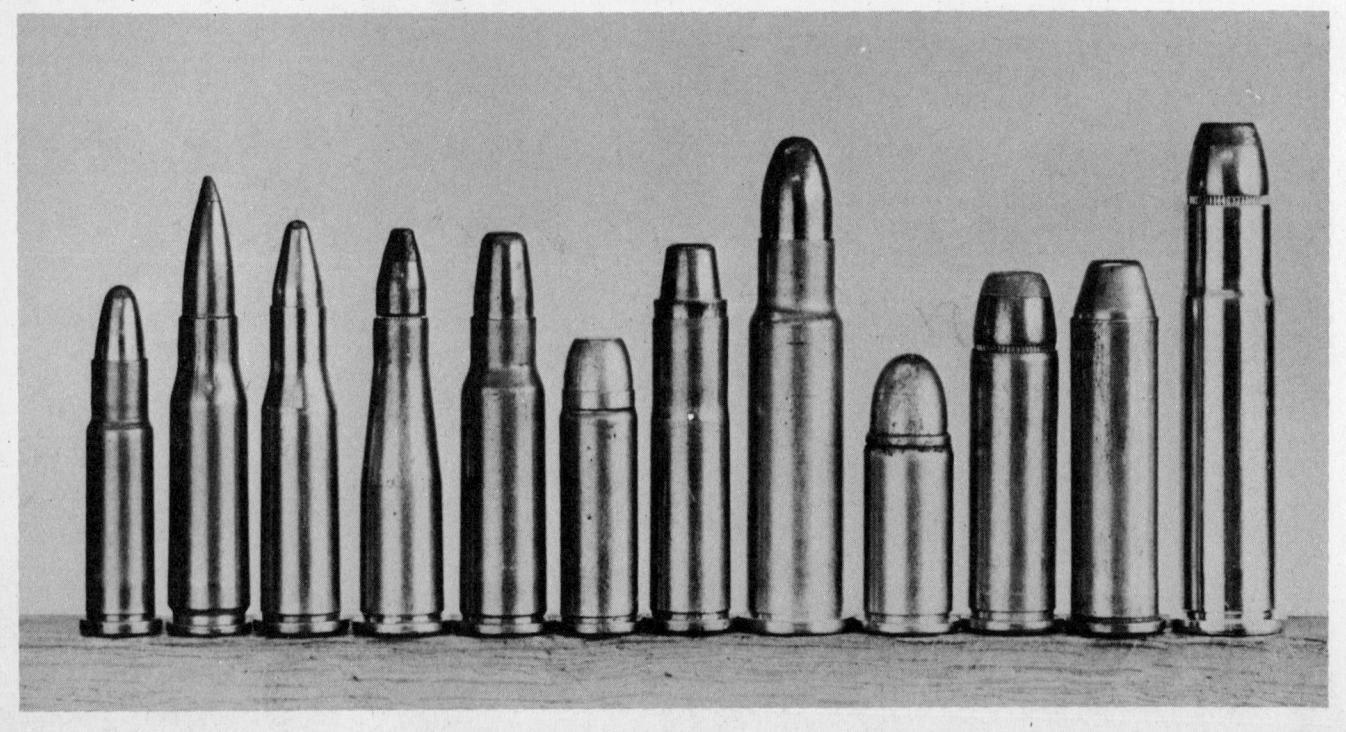

No longer offered as standard, the 6-inch barrel Thompson/Center Contender, here in .22 LR, came even with tip of forend and made a handy rig.

of conventional metallic cartridge presses. There is a substantial cost saving in reloading with these capsules and, if the shooter has a .44 Special revolver, the .44 capsules can be put up in Special cases, permitting their use in .44 magnum guns as well, just as the .38 Special factory loads can be fired in .357 magnum guns.

Just up the banks of Idaho's Snake River from the Omark/Speer plant lies their sister operation, Omark/CCI, makers of exceptional shot cartridges for use in rifles or handguns chambered for the .22 LR or the .22 WMRF/magnum. The shot pellets are enclosed in a plastic capsule, giving the load essentially the same outside contours as conventional, one-bullet ammunition. Thus, the .22 LR shot load can be hand-cycled through autoloading pistols chambered for that round, although the recoil usually is not sufficient to work the action in autoloading mode. With revolvers, no problem is encountered in this respect.

Turning from such specialized areas as the single-shots and the shot-firing handguns, there are a great many makes, models and calibers of handguns that can be used in varmint hunting to good effect. As mentioned, it requires on the part of the hunter a judicious evaluation in terms of the size of the varmint, the distance from which it is apt to

From left, .30-30 WCF, .30 Herrett, .357 Herrett, .38/45 Clerke, .357 AMP, .44 AMP, .44 magnum, .44 and .357 HotShot, made up in .44 and .357 magnum brass. The .38/45 can be used in M1911 autos by installing a custom barrel, utilizing original magazine, with cases formed from .45 ACP empties.

VARMINT HUNTER'S DIGEST

be taken and the peculiar traits of the given species. For illustration, you do not need 1 MOA accuracy capability for shooting rats in a dump because most such shots will present themselves within distances of a dozen paces and speed is a major factor. Dump rats are elusive targets, usually moving at a rapid pace and it's not the place for a scope-sighted handgun.

Single-action revolvers are by no means ruled out and many have been used with highly satisfactory results. Ruger's line of single-actions, including the caliber .22 Single Sixes, the now-discontinued Bearcat, the Blackhawks and the redoubtable Super Blackhawk are great favorites, together with the same maker's double-action Security Six and Speed Six. Colt's single-actions, produced in varied forms almost continuously for over a century, have won many devotees among varmint handgunners, not to slight the extensive line of Colt double-action revolvers and autoloading pistols. Smith & Wesson continues to offer several handgun designs well suited to the varmint hunter's needs, including such outstanding examples as the K-22 and K-38 Masterpieces, the heavy-frame magnum revolvers in .357, .41 or .44 and the petite revolvers of kit gun dimensions.

Even that unique and unlikely design, the Auto Mag, can turn in outstanding performance against varmints, particularly with the .357 AMP barrel in place topped by a scope mounted and zeroed carefully. The scoped .357, fed with selected loads, will group well under two inches at fifty yards and its velocities – approaching the 2000 fps level – give it an awesomely flat trajectory. The big trouble with the Auto Mag, in these latter days, lies in its scarcity and substantial cost, which tends to range upward of $500 a copy.

Varmints can be taken with almost any imaginable configuration of handgun – and, quite probably, have been. The characteristics of the given varmint species tend to dictate the suitability, or unsuitability, of any particular handgun. Once the basic parameters of performance have

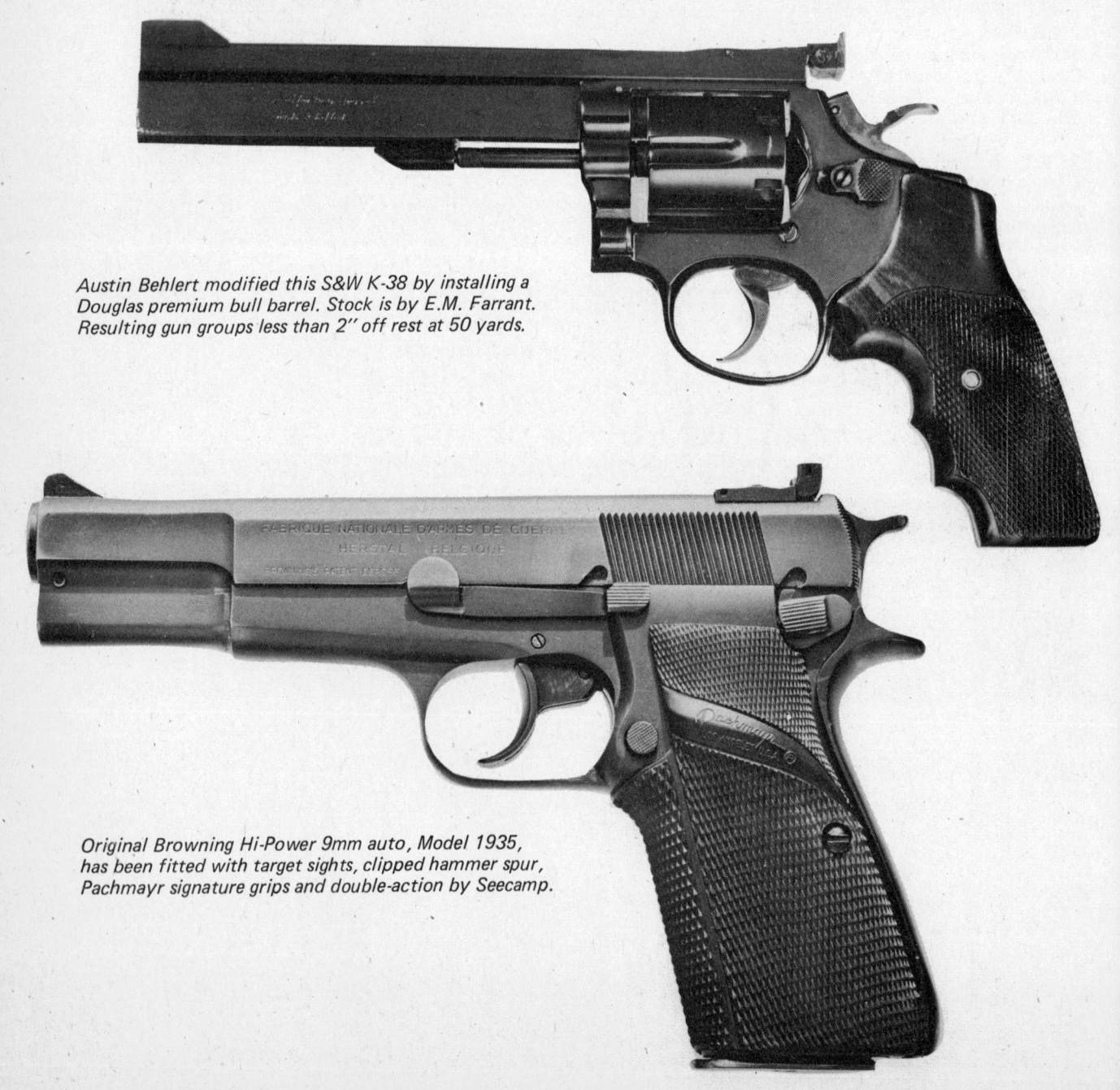

Austin Behlert modified this S&W K-38 by installing a Douglas premium bull barrel. Stock is by E.M. Farrant. Resulting gun groups less than 2" off rest at 50 yards.

Original Browning Hi-Power 9mm auto, Model 1935, has been fitted with target sights, clipped hammer spur, Pachmayr signature grips and double-action by Seecamp.

been settled upon, selection of an appropriate hardware choice becomes a much simpler decision. Accuracy is a prime criterion in nearly every instance. Power, range, impact effect, rate of fire and similar factors are pivotal around the primary purpose envisioned.

In any event, once a handgun — or battery of handguns — has been selected, there remains the needful but not necessarily unpleasant — chore of optimizing effectiveness. Some amount of test-firing is all but mandatory, for purposes of determining a realistic level of capability that can be delivered. Handguns chambered for rimfire ammunition, such as the .22 LR, obviate considerations of reloading — and the need to retrieve fired cases. Even the rimfire handguns, however, respond with surprising variations to changes in diet. A thoughtful program of test-firing, trying out as many different loads as possible, is certain to indicate that some loads group much more tightly than others. Once the preference of the individual gun has been established, the varmint hunter can lay in a supply of that particular make, type and lot number to assure extended interludes of optimum capability.

Handguns chambered for center-fire ammunition can handle reloads in addition to factory fodder and, again, it is beneficial to test as many loads as possible in quest of the best one or two candidates. Once tentative results have been established, the selected load(s) can be put through further tests at several appropriate distances to determine the trajectory and the amount of hold-off required for compensation. The sights can be set for point of aim at some appropriate distance and a drop table can be made up to be attached to the gun or memorized. When used in conjunction with an optical range finder, such data improves the odds for successful hunting most usefully.

So, too, will any aid to steadier aim. Bipods, sandbags or even a ski pole can help to dampen out the distracting shimmy and tremor that is so demoralizingly apparent through a scope and only slightly less so with iron sights.

Hunting varmints with a handgun is neither easy nor simple — no one said it was supposed to be — but it offers a unique and stimulating challenge that seems to enjoy ever-growing appeal.

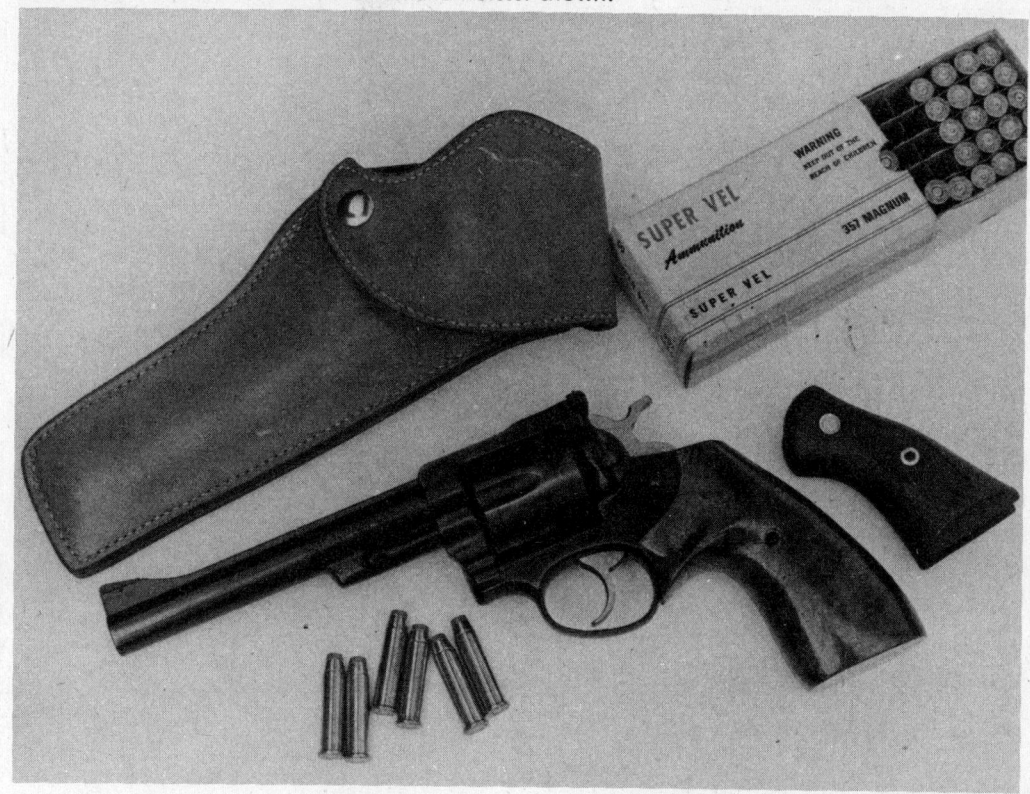

Ruger's double-action Security Six, in .357 magnum is an accurate, powerful handgun at a comparatively moderate cost. Herrett custom stocks and Safariland holster shown.

Pivoting the circular insert on the face of the T/C Contender by half a turn enables it to switch between rimfire and center-fire loads.

VARMINT HUNTER'S DIGEST

Varmint-Trying The .45 Auto

SEVERAL OF US were discussing Sierra's jacketed hollow cavity pistol bullet designed for the handgun hunter. I hadn't given much thought to their use in the varmint fields, until pictures of a big dog coyote began forming in my mind with what these jacketed hollow cavity (JHC) bullets might do in the moment of truth.

Sierra offers these bullets in the following calibers, weights and styles: .38 caliber .357-inch diameter, 110-grain JHC, 125-grain jacketed soft-point; 125-grain JHC, 150-grain JHC, 158-grain jacketed soft-point; 9mm .355 diameter, 90-grain JHC and 115-grain JHC; .41 caliber, .410 diameter, 170-grain JHC; 210-grain JHC; .44 magnum, .4295 diameter, 180-grain JHC and 240-grain JHC; .45 caliber, .4515 diameter, 185-grain JHC.

Something came up, though, and I asked Jerry Mills, another varmint hunter who has been known to experiment with the unlikely, if he would carry on.

A few days later, with bullets in hand, powder in the hopper and a goodly supply of brass in .45 ACP, 9mm and .38 Special, the experiments began. Dean Grennell furnished loading data he already had worked up. This data and nearby range facilities reduced the time in finding the most accurate loads for the aforementioned calibers.

Mills is quick to admit that his pistol shooting leaves something to be desired. However, after many loads were tried, he did manage a score of 93 with his accurized Model

The Sierra JHC designed for use in the .45 ACP round weighs 185 grains, much more than average varmint needs.

Cross-sectioned .38 bullet shows unique jacketed hollow cavity design. Called the JHC at time of introduction, it is intended for maximum expansion and stopping power. (Right) Varmint call clenched between his teeth, Jerry Mills steadies the Star 9mm for shot at nearby coyote.

1911A1 Remington .45 auto, firing slow fire at twenty-five yards. This particular load is 4½ grains of 700-X behind the 185-grain JHC for a muzzle velocity of 750 feet per second. The other pistols involved were as follows, listing the most accurate load for each: Colt Cobra, with two-inch barrel

VARMINT HUNTER'S DIGEST

utilizing 7.0 grains of Unique behind the Sierra 110-grain JHC, for velocity of 950 fps. The second load was 6.5 grains of Unique behind the 125-grain JHC for 850 fps. The third pistol was a Star Model B, in caliber 9mm, with five-inch barrel utilizing 5.0 grains of Bullseye and the 90-grain JHC for velocity of 1450 fps.

The second load for the Star is 5.8 grains of Unique behind the 115-grain JHC at 1225 fps.

All loads qualified accurately enough to be used for hunting. However the Colt Cobra was not taken into the field due to the short barrel, although the loads listed can be devastating when used within their limits. Not all the load data furnished by Grennell was used; when hunting is the primary objective, one tends to find an accurate load and head for the field, with due respect to velocity and energy variables obtainable through time and trial.

Mentions had been popping up on the local scene about the use of a red light when hunting varmints at night. One particular comment concerned the claim that a red light reduces the chance of spooking a varmint coming to the call and changes the whole effect of night hunting.

In the West, where the shooting range is likely to be in excess of a hundred yards at night, Mills' test was made before and after the moon had risen. The light was covered by red cellophane. This may not be the most desirable experiment, but adequate to draw some conclusions. Before moonrise, the red light was at its best, having less dilution from an outside light source. This means that, as the moon began to rise, the additional light broke up and dissipated all afterglow from the red light. This reduced the ability to illuminate both in distance and circumference, which in turn eliminated the use of a scope; the crosshairs could not be defined well enough to shoot by. The eyes illuminated by the red light always appeared red, regardless of species. Were a light tint used such as a rose-colored lens, the benefits may increase to a point that a colored light would be more practical for night hunting at longer ranges.

Bushnell has an illuminating dot around the crosshair intersection of their Scope Chief rifle scope. This dot is energized from a small disc battery located in a separate housing behind the vertical and horizontal adjustment housing. Featuring a silent off-on knurled knob switch, red, green and white dots are available; the last was used in our test.

With this scope mounted on a Remington .22 magnum, Mills' hunting partner, Carl Simonelli, took a stand at about 10 p.m. in a likely looking spot for bobcats. Mills, himself, was hidden a few yards away. Within fifteen minutes of calling, a cat was stalking our position. Simonelli worked the handlight slowly, keeping just enough of the afterglow on the eyes to illuminate them, turning on the scope light while bringing the rifle to bear. Then he uttered something unprintable, ending in, "I can't see the eyes."

Mills took the rifle while squeaking softly on the short-range call. Looking through the scope, he found that the white dot gives off a reflective light beyond the circumference of the dot. However, if the red or green dots were used and additional reflection was eliminated, a real plus factor would be had for dusk, night and predawn shooting.

The first of Mills' two trips to the field for varmint hunting tests of Sierra's handgun bullets was made with Gary Freeman. The two left Los Angeles on a Saturday afternoon for a four-hour drive to where most of their hunting is done in California's high desert country. Hunting is good here, the country is big and you can forget about running into other people who can remind you of the outside world.

"By eight o'clock that evening, we had finished final sighting-in adjustments with both pistol and rifles. I had brought along my old standby, a custom Model 70 in .220 Swift, utilizing 37.0 grains fo 3031 behind a Hornady 53-grain HP. This is an accurate load, giving me great confidence in hitting what I shoot at and where I shoot at it.

"By nine o'clock, the midsummer sun had set, filling the desert canyons with darkness. We sat sipping coffee, just enjoying the fresh air when the howl of a coyote drifted in on the evening breeze. That was all it took. We packed up Thermos jugs and readied ourselves for the night's hunt."

It is next to impossible to shoot over pistol sights at night, so Mills and Freeman planned to look for areas that indicated predator activity abundant enough to justify daylight stands. This would be accomplished by checking dry sand washes for tracks and dead baiting with predators' natural prey. Bobcats usually like to make their own kills. However, a coyote will eat carrion more often than not.

Mills combined skillful use of his mouth call with the potent loads from his .45 auto to take this big bobcat.

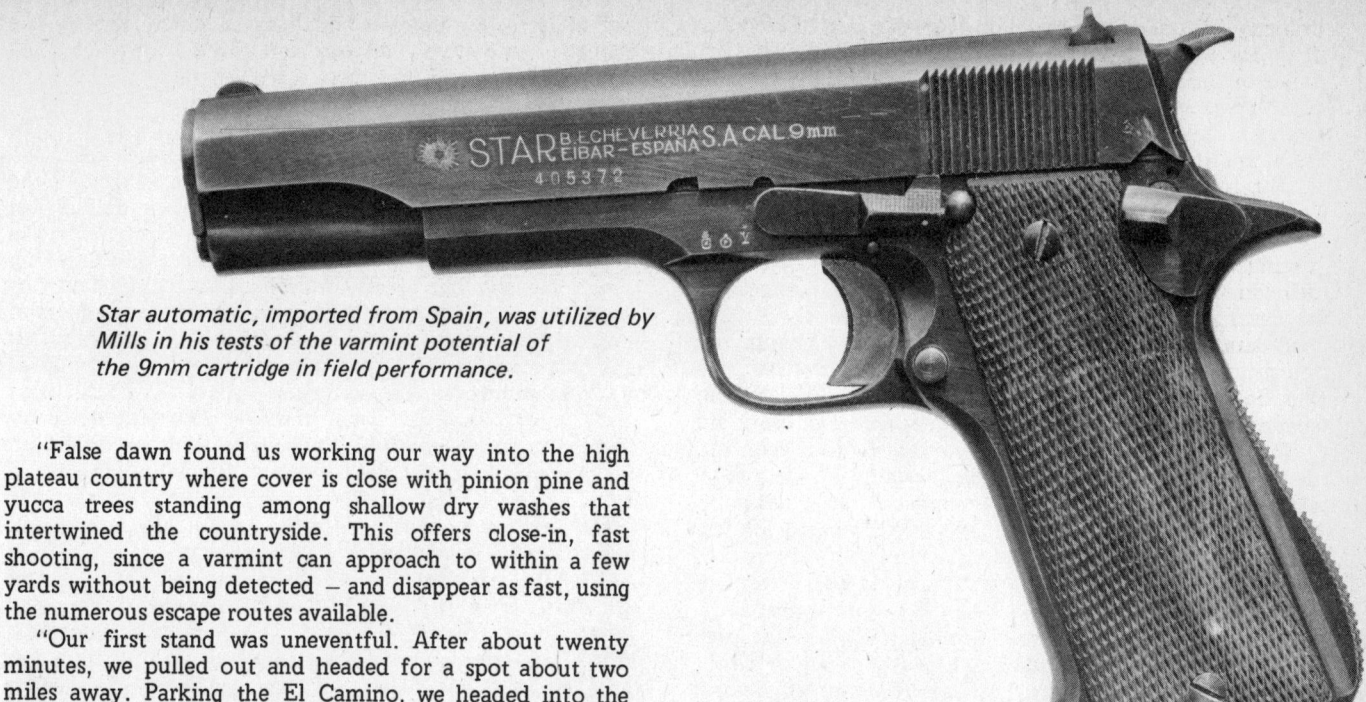

Star automatic, imported from Spain, was utilized by Mills in his tests of the varmint potential of the 9mm cartridge in field performance.

"False dawn found us working our way into the high plateau country where cover is close with pinion pine and yucca trees standing among shallow dry washes that intertwined the countryside. This offers close-in, fast shooting, since a varmint can approach to within a few yards without being detected — and disappear as fast, using the numerous escape routes available.

"Our first stand was uneventful. After about twenty minutes, we pulled out and headed for a spot about two miles away. Parking the El Camino, we headed into the wind with the sun at our backs, cutting a course away from the car about half a mile before taking up a stand. With Freeman on my left, I faced into the wind and began calling on the Weems' Dual-tone All-Call.

"Minutes passed that seemed like hours as they always do when you are tensed up looking for the slightest movement that may be a predator or just a jay squawking insults at you from atop a pine."

Then, without warning, a coyote appeared forty yards below and to Mills' right at the foot of a dry wash. The hunter could see only part of the wild dog through the pines, but as it stared, Mills froze in position until the coyote decided that there was no apparent danger. Then he turned and headed up the wash to the right.

"As soon as he was out of sight, I brought the .45 auto to rest with elbows on knees for a solid hold. Set now, I squeaked the short-range call once and he crested the small ridge no more than seventy-five feet away. This was perfect and I had him in the bag before the trigger was ever squeezed. Or so I thought."

With the sound of the first shot, Carlos Coyote wound up that tail and was high rolling back down the wash, out of sight using all available cover. He broke cover about where Mills first had spotted him. For the sake of pride, Mills threw another ineffectual shot after him.

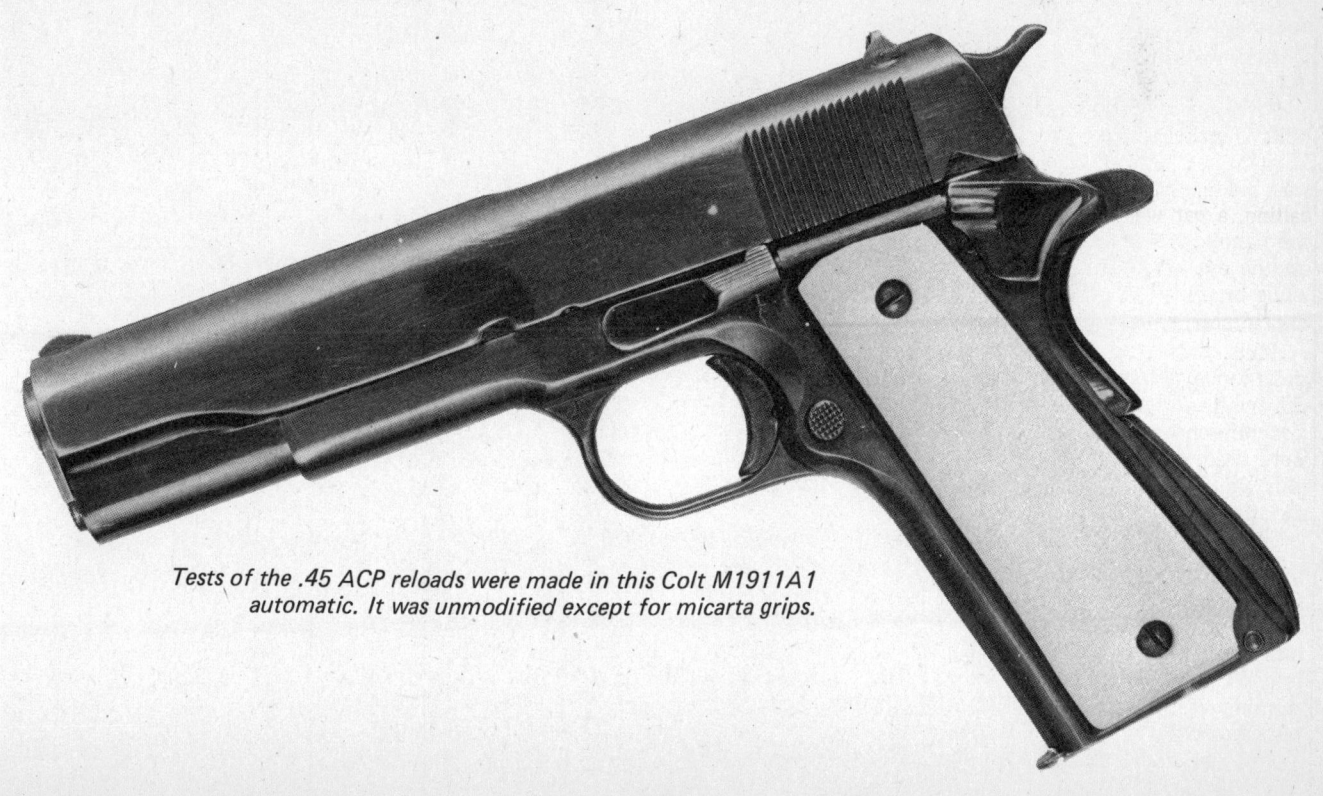

Tests of the .45 ACP reloads were made in this Colt M1911A1 automatic. It was unmodified except for micarta grips.

VARMINT HUNTER'S DIGEST

"Back at the car, we shed our undergarments, proof that the desert warms up mighty fast once Summer sets in. This was good country, so we decided to shorten the distance between stands. Stand number three found us holed up under a pinion tree about a quarter-mile from a big rock outcropping with enough visibility to see any approaching predator within fifty yards.

"We sat and listened for awhile before calling. When the calling began, all went still. Only ten minutes passed before a good-size bobcat showed, looking like she meant business. The cat paused behind some rocks and again I brought the .45 auto to rest with my elbows on my knees.

"I squeaked on the call and she headed right up the chute, coming straight in. If the cat did not detour, she would be in the middle of my chest. It didn't look as if she were going to stop, then the cat came to a stop no more than twenty feet away. I had been following her with my sights the last few yards. Carefully, I squeezed the trigger of the .45. The 185-grain JHC entered the chest, virtually exploding all life. The bullet made its exit behind the last rib on the right side eliminating recovery for expansion examination."

The next stand looked like it would be productive when a coyote came into view about two hundred yards out after only a few minutes of calling. Then, when he was within fifty yards and hidden behind some brush, Mills set up for a shot. The idea was to let him come to a point directly across from the shooter's position, then use the short-range call to bring him up close enough for a shot. The next time the coyote was seen, he was going back the way he had come, in no hurry, yet three hundred yards out. All the calling and coaxing had little effect on him.

Two weeks later, Carl Simonelli and Mills went back to the same area. This time the moon and weather conditions were perfect. On their way out, a coyote crossed the highway in front of the Jeep Wagoneer. Both men smiled and agreed this was a good sign.

"We settled down to some serious varminting with headlights and our favorite varmint busters, again leaving the pistol shooting to daylight hours. A few stands failed to produce any action, so we headed for another area about thirty miles away. The move paid off."

Simonelli was calling when a set of eyes appeared about sixty yards out. By the way the eyes moved in, Mills felt certain it was a coyote; Simonelli let him get to within forty yards before lowering the boom with his rifle, a Remington .22 magnum. The dog was still moving when the bullet hit him far back. He went down, then got up and tried to move away from their position.

"I was packing the .45 auto for just this type of situation. With flashlight in hand I hurried to the spot where the coyote was last seen. The brush was about four feet high, affording good cover in which to hide. He might have made it, but he was mad and ready to fight. With a deep-throated growl, he came around a bush with teeth bared.

In spite of the pork pie hat, Mills used this prone position to fool several wary coyotes and bobcats in the high desert country of Southern California. He was able to prove to his satisfaction the .45 auto's potential.

"I was close enough that, when my light found him, he was blinded. I put one 185-grain JHC through the neck, while my second shot took him through the head and that was that."

The pair took the rest of the night off and got some sleep to be fresh for the morning hunt. Since Mills had taken two varmints with the .45, it was decided that Simonelli would take the next shot with the 9mm Star, regardless of the way a varmint might decide to come in.

"We were up long before the first signs of false dawn. Eating a breakfast of bacon and eggs, we finished our coffee by first light. We had camped high that night, so we decided to make stands on our way to the desert flats some forty miles south. Simonelli had parked the Jeep in an inconspicuous gully and we were walking out a small finger overlooking a valley when two, maybe three, coyotes started to howl," Mills recalls.

"We didn't know whether we had been seen, so I began calling and the coyotes stopped howling. With that, our hopes faded.

"We were about to give it up when a coyote broke cover thirty yards away. He saw us and came to a sliding stop, but before he could make up his mind, my partner put a 115-grain JHC through the front shoulder and another through the side. The stopping power of these bullets on small game is impressive.

"Our next stand resulted in a coyote being taken with the .45 auto and two or three stands later we put another coyote to sleep. This certainly was enough shooting to draw some pretty conclusive evidence in that Sierra has made progressive advancement in pistol bullets," Mills reports.

The jacket thickness is thin enough to allow complete expansion, yet thick enough to resist shedding at high velocities such as is the case in the 9mm 90-grain bullet at 1405 fps. We melted down a 185-grain .45 JHC to find that jacket weight to be 32.5 grains, lead weight, 152.5. All bullets miked out in agreement with Sierra's claim.

Mills' hunting partner, Carl Simonelli, holds tangible proof that jacketed hollow point, designed for hunting, can perform adequately in the wilds against the coyote.

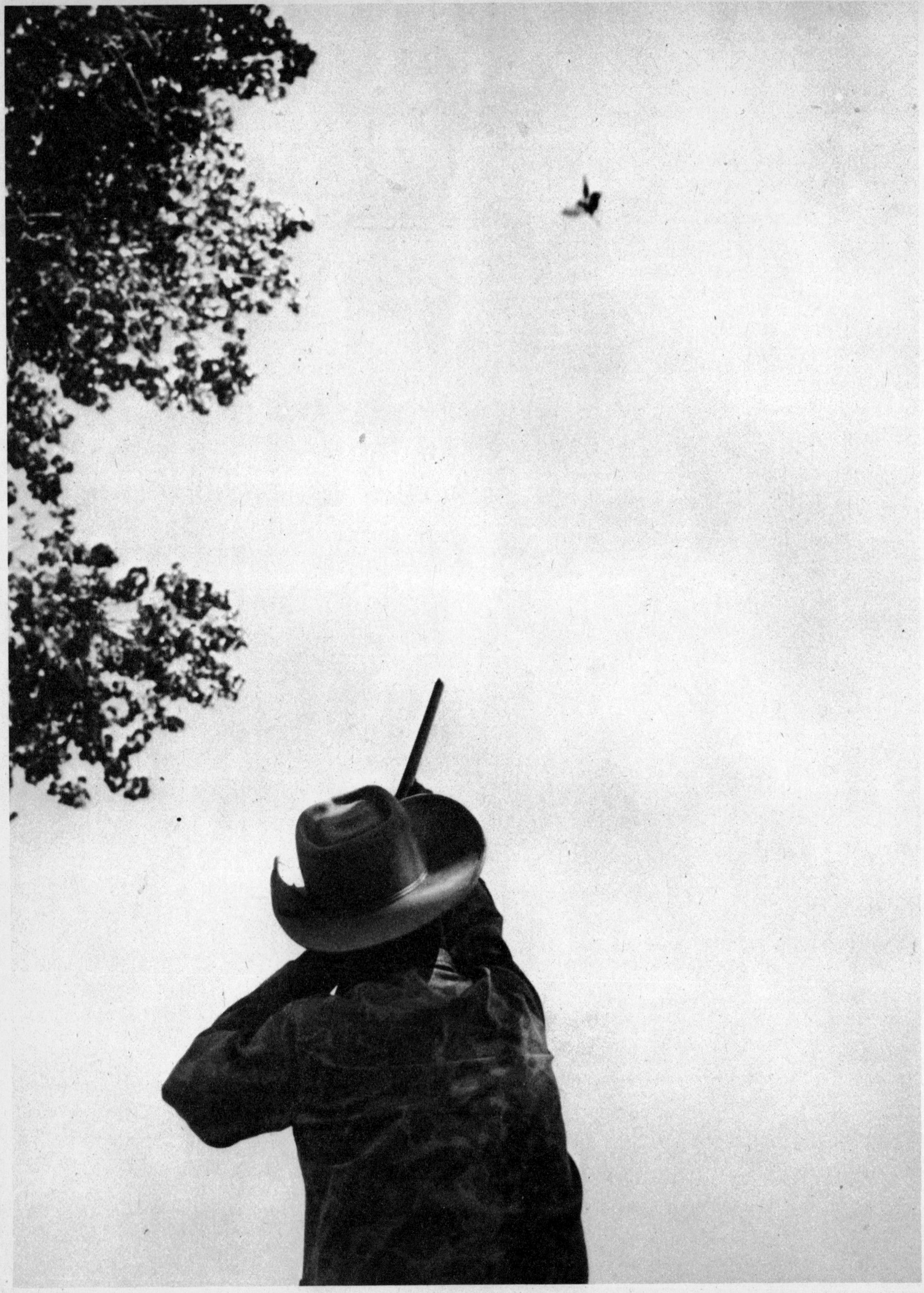

Chapter 16

SHOTGUNS FOR VARMINTS

Consideration Of Arms And Ammo Can Make The Difference In Success

A WEEK AFTER I was married, I came across what would have to be considered a deal on a used Browning superposed choked full and modified in immaculate condition. I took it home, feeling I had stolen the piece but wondering about the wisdom of the purchase, considering that Sue and I could pretty much count our worth on our combined fingers.

Three days later I had to make a sales trip to Arizona by car. I departed with the Browning, a handful of 4s and a couple of calls. Somewhere out of Wickenburg with the evening shadows getting longer on the desert, I spotted a coyote standing near a thicket not too far off the highway and pulled over a half-mile down the road. I slipped on a camouflage jacket, my call lanyard and hat, grabbed up the shotgun and two 4s, and dashed out into the greasewood and mesquite. The country was sparse, with no cover. I laid down flat with the scattergun pointing forward and got on the call in a hard-pushed opening series. Two minutes later I spotted the big dog coming hard, raised to my knees as he went by thirty yards out attempting to shift into overdrive, and rolled him up like a beach ball. I didn't purchase that Browning to shoot coyotes, but since that first shot poured

There have been plenty of nursery rhymes about the magpie, but these scavengers can create problems in the areas where their numbers increase too greatly.

through the spout, it has collected a passable bunch of hair, as have a wide range of shotguns in my personal collection.

Generally speaking, the shotgun is not what the desert hunter chooses as a varmint equalizer, but there are many places in which a scattergun is the varmint collector supreme, and never doubt for a minute that they cannot be effective.

Sam Dudley, the dean of varmint callers, had an old Winchester 20 gun that he called Singing Sally. The singing perhaps was caused by a sweeping uphill curve in the barrel; the results of Dudley bending the tube over the head of an especially eager coyote that quite literally wanted to take Dudley on. He never fixed that piece; instead, he just learned how to hold low and touch her off.

George Wright, Dudley and I were calling on a piece of thick Arizona real estate one day; the type of country where one member of the group should have his hands on a scatterpiece. I elected to take Sally out on a stand and set up on the extreme right in the midst of the brush. No sooner had Dudley started calling, I heard the pounding of feet drawing close from the right quarter. A big dog came screeching by flitting through the brush twenty yards in front. "No sweat," I thought as I rose, swung and touched off one, two and three, getting nothing but dust and scattered twigs. "At twenty yards you have to hold three feet low," said Dudley afterward. "You see, she shoots a might high." I left Dudley to the peculiarities of old Sally

In many areas, jackrabbits are considered vermin, tending to spoil crops when the population becomes too heavy. A shotgun and correct loads solve the problem.

VARMINT HUNTER'S DIGEST

The positive action of the slide-action shotgun has found great favor with varmint hunters, who go after crows and other winged predator types found in many areas.

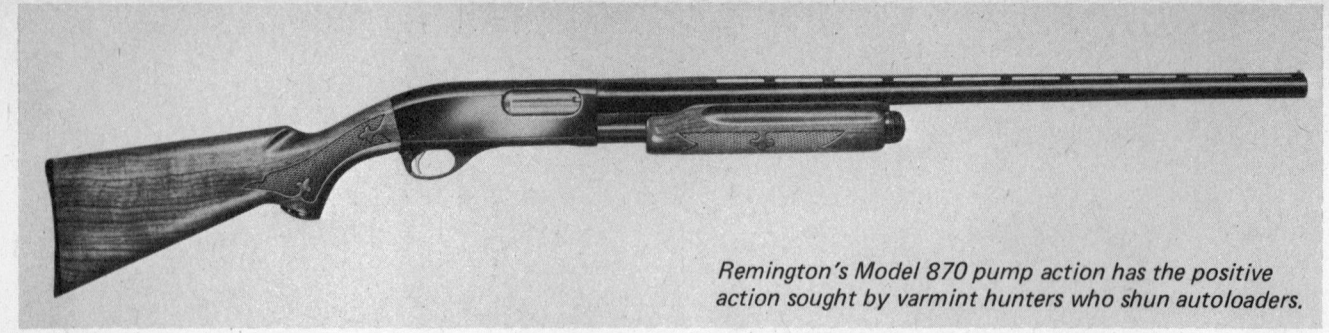

Remington's Model 870 pump action has the positive action sought by varmint hunters who shun autoloaders.

for the duration of that hunt. He zinged a big old dog that evening a full fifty yards away with a load of 2s. When I asked him where he held at fifty yards, he replied "Wherever it feels right."

That's not my type of shotgunning but the point is, the shotgun is a vital piece of the caller's artillery, and while loads seem to vary slightly among hunters, the gauges most prefered are 12s, regardless of the capabilities of Singing Sally, the bent-barrelled 20.

My preference in shotguns runs to twelve bores with 4s or 2s in the hot, short magnum loads like Federal's 1½-ounce boomers. I have used BB-size shot and on several occasions done in close-range critters with 8s. In heavy cover the 4s and 2s get the job done, as will 6s if the ranges are inside of twenty yards. I have seen coyotes rolled up and out at fifty yards many times with 2s, but I suggest that this is too far to be making shotguns effective on any of the varmints.

In most cases the scattergun is selected due to heavy cover, short-range visibility and quick shooting conditions. Shots at fifty yards are not expected; shots at fifty feet are why you're in there with the shotgun to begin with.

Tight chokes are required, the lead must be stacked quickly in the chest and neck region, and the experienced

Because of the shotgun's relatively short range, cover is required to bring the varmint in close for a shot.

With his trusty shotgun at hand for any night varmint, the author uses a flashlight to inspect dinner as it is cooked over a gas stove. Shotguns can be used at night in situations where seeing sights is a problem.

shotgunner will shoot two times, back to back, for double indemnity.

I have had enough experience with 00 buckshot to think it is not worthwhile. No. 4 buck is infinitely better but still not as good under the ranges being considered as the 2s and 4s. Many years ago we had permission to hunt some country inside the city limits of a California city where coyotes were creating a lot of problems with the residents' dogs and cats. We were restricted to shotguns and our first attempt was with 00. I selected a Model 12 Winchester bored skeet, removed the plug and crammed it with five of the heavy loads. In the course of the morning four coyotes ran right through the pattern and only one went down. I was not impressed and from that point went to 2s for instant crunch.

I have seen and made some of the snappiest doubles and triples with a shotgun on tight brushy stands where it is not uncommon to get a group of coyotes up on midmorning efforts. Such results are difficult to accomplish under optimum rifle-shooting conditions, but a fair scattergunner can work wonders at close-order varminting.

When open-country calling slows down about midmorning, the hunting is not necessarily over if the callers can take the hunt right into the critters' living room. Dense riverbed thickets are ideal but a rifle won't get the job done due to the fast action which restricts shooting with scope-sighted rifles and the heavy cover that blows the lightweight high-velocity varmint pills before they make it home. Under such conditions partners should sit close to one another and be ready for the results which will most often be soon in coming. Calling should be subdued. Expect the game to be close at hand and enter the area accordingly, with no talking and careful footwork. Sit in a ready position.

The shotgun is ideal for foxes in brushy, typical grey fox cover at night. While foxes are smaller and lightly constructed when compared to coyotes, I still prefer the 2s and 4s for best knockdown results. The same holds true with bobcats, especially during midday stands which should be in tight cover. While a bobtail will move over open country for distance at night, he is loath to expose his hide during the daytime. He slips in furtively and oftentimes is not observed until he's nothing more than a streak leaving the area. Here the shotgun pays dividends for fast pointing and shooting efficiency.

I've taken many a bobcat as a midday bonus in a bird hunt when a batch of cover looked appealing. Wherever there are good concentrations of quail or chukar in the western states, you can count on some local bobcats being about. It is a matter of being properly equipped to carry a few 4s or 2s and a call anytime a bird safari was organized.

There is a form of coyote hunting that lends itself perfectly to shotgunning. George Wright and I used to call it the Kamikazi Method. In many parts of the country with heavy hunting pressure, coyotes become extremely cautious when being called at night with a light. Before the days of the red light which we started using — and keeping to ourselves — in the early Sixties, the plan was to call coyotes while sitting back to back in the open white-sanded washes on a full-moon night without a light. These were eerie stands. There is something slightly hair-raising about being out there in the dark, no matter how bright the moon and blowing on your wooden whistle. Owls would dive bomb our heads. Subtle sounds made us goosey and a hard-charging coyote suddenly bearing down at us from close quarters most definitely got our complete attention. Usually there was never enough time to warn your companion snuggled up close to your back as much for mental security as physical safety. The sudden eruption of the shotgun going off, belching about three feet of fire invariably caused your companion to start. We experimented with lights taped to the guns, the plan being to leave the light off until it was time to shoot. This defeated the plan. Using the light too soon fouled up the reason for trying it in the first place, but mostly it boiled down to the fact that there just really wasn't enough time.

Most any type of shotgun will do, but my preference runs to autoloaders and that old Browning for two quick shots and fast reloading capabilities. The shotgun does not blow up critters — something I personally have never cared for — and in this age of the increased value of fur on the market, that's another good reason for keeping one handy when the cover gets thick and the calling gets good.

Shotguns that will handle both magnum and standard-length shells offer added versatility. For most varmints, Dougherty favors Number 2 or 4 shot.

There is any number of types of shells and loads that can be used on various varmint species. The shotshell reloader has a lot going for him, as he can tailor his loads to the type of predator that he is trying to take.

Chapter 17

A Look At The Optics Needed For Long-Range Shooting.

An Idaho rock chuck, viewed at the 9X setting of a 3X-9X Leupold scope with Duplex reticle.

TELESCOPIC SIGHTS FOR firearms are not particularly new. Primitive versions were in use at least as early as the War Between the States: they had thin tubes, about the same length as the king-sized barrels of that era, offering extremely limited fields of view. The early scopes were employed primarily for rifles used by snipers, and with remarkably deadly effect, it should be noted.

The intent, then as now and for years yet to pass, was to secure more precise alignment between the trajectory of the projectile and the intended point of impact. Through the magnification of the optical system of the scope, minor angular divergences could be detected and corrected.

To the uninitiated, it seems logical that the most powerful scope sight would be the best one to use — a deluded fancy comparable to the belief that the heaviest bullet available in a given diameter is the automatic logical choice.

COPING WITH SCOPES

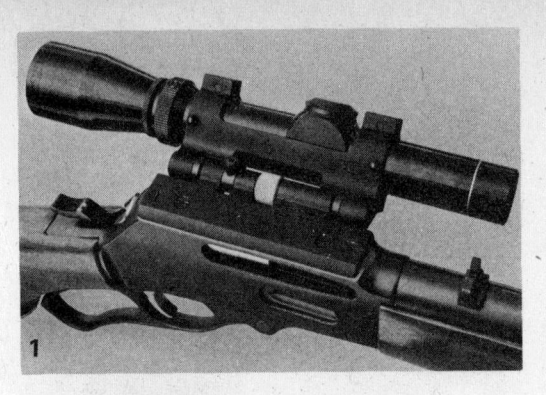

1. Pachmayr Lo-Swing mount permits alternate use of open iron sights at will. 2. Coin-slotted turret screws, here on a Redfield 3X-9X Royal scope, offer ease of adjustment in windage or elevation. 3. Eyepiece end of the Redfield 3X-9X, showing ring for adjusting power and rotating eyepiece with locking ring, as discussed here. 4. Mounting rings from B-Square are designed for attaching to Weaver-type bases. 5. Colt scope attaches to AR-15 handle. 6. Mauser scope is supplied with rings to fit the tapered dovetail bases that are integral to the action of the Interarms Mark X rifle.

Just as in the general field of ballistics, optical sighting equipment selection involves a chain of compromises between opposing sets of desired qualities. The more magnification you have, the narrower the field of view becomes. Given a thirty-power — customarily written as 30X — scope, it is extremely difficult to locate an intended target, particularly from the offhand stance. Likewise it's hard to keep it in the scope's image while taking aim. The image may be magnified by thirty diameters, but the natural tremors inherent in the human body are amplified by the same factor and the effect is demoralizing.

As an approximate rule of thumb, 6X constitutes about as much magnification as can be utilized effectively from the offhand position, and 4X will give approximately the same degree of accuracy, meanwhile affording the advantage of a wider field of viewing.

Many fixed-power scope sights remain in use and large numbers continue to be sold year after year. Coming up to overtake, however, are the variable scopes, capable of changing their magnification by a simple rotation of the graduated ring usually located just ahead of the eyepiece. Commonly, variable scope sights are made in 3X-9X magnification range, although several other combinations — 1.5X-4.5X, 4X-12X, et al. — are offered, as well.

It is an easy and simple matter, given access to a variable scope sight on a rifle, to determine the exact extent to which scope magnification can deliver superior accuracy. Merely fire a few test groups, with all possible care and accuracy, from a steady aim off the benchrest at paper targets, using the same ammunition and two or three settings of magnification. Compare the sizes of the resulting groups. Most shooters will be surprised by the trifling gain of the higher settings.

It is by no means unlikely that groups fired at the higher magnifications may be larger than the low-power settings. This may be especially true if the scope has a large amount of parallax at the distance between bench and target. Let's define that term, for the sake of clarity. From

VARMINT HUNTER'S DIGEST

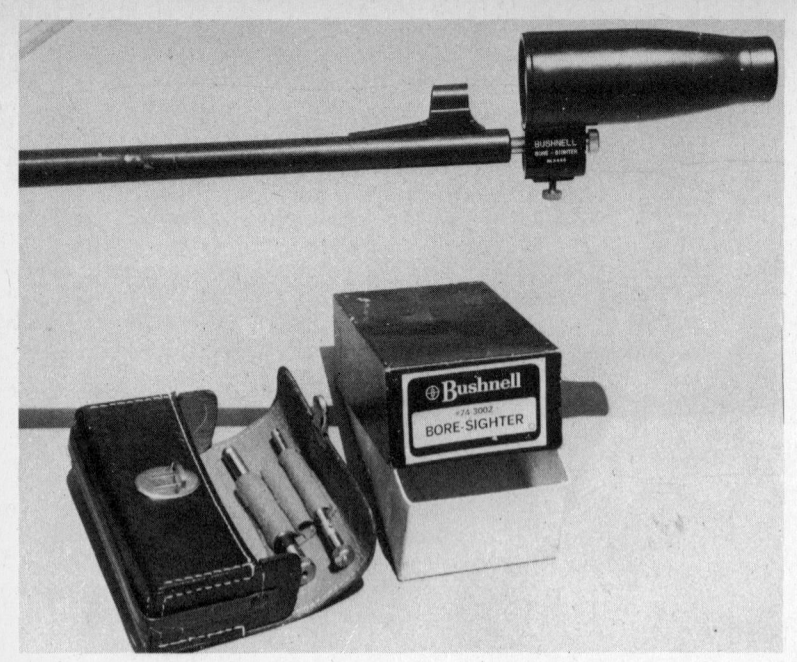

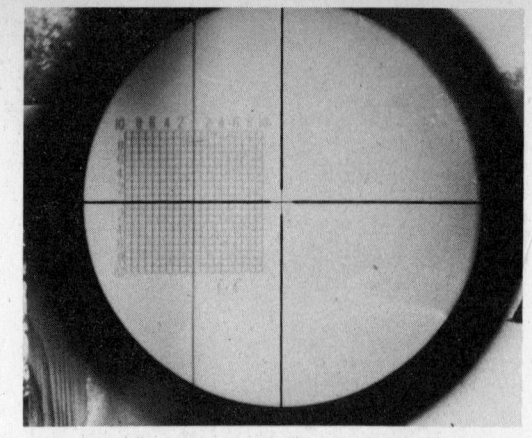

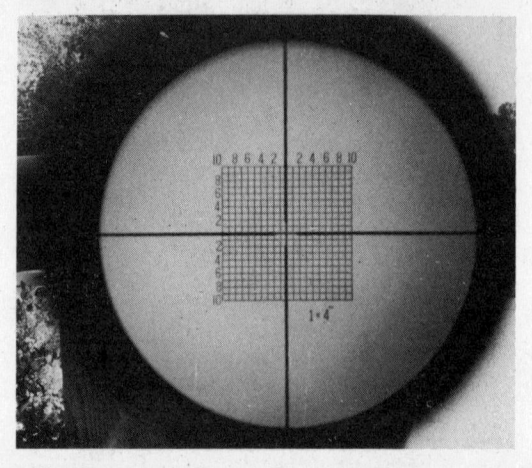

Bushnell's optical bore sighter is supplied in carrying case with three adjustable collets to fit most rifles. Upper right photo shows view through scope before adjusting for windage and, lower right, after adjusting scope reticle to center of bore sighter grid image.

a standpoint of observed symptoms, parallax is present if the rifle is held totally motionless and the center of the reticle — the intersection of the crosshairs — does not remain superimposed over the same aiming point when the aiming eye is moved, up and down/side to side, through the exit pupil of the scope.

Many of the scopes affording higher levels of magnification have an adjustable objective lens — the objective lens is in the front of the scope — to provide correction for parallax at any given distance. The usual arrangement is a ring or collar that can be rotated until the center of the reticle stays on target, regardless of movement of the eye.

The exit pupil of a scope sight is the diameter of the image it delivers to the aiming eye at the normal aiming distance — which, in turn, is called the eye relief. Scopes with higher magnification tend to have smaller exit pupils, hence are more demanding of precise eye placement and a steady hold to avoid losing the image.

Scopes designed for use with .22 rimfire rifles customarily have a short eye relief, since recoil is not a serious consideration on such rifles. Designing for a short eye relief permits the use of lenses and barrels that are smaller in diameter and this, in turn, helps hold cost to competitive levels. Typical .22 scopes have tubes that are .75-inch in diameter, while center-fire designs usually employ 1.00-inch tubes and mounting rings to match, with correspondingly longer eye relief to minimize the risk of injury from recoil.

Scopes used on handguns have — or should have — eighteen to twenty-four inches of eye relief, so as to provide a comfortable extension of the arm when aiming. The Bushnell Phantom, Thompson/Center Lobo and Leupold M8-2X scopes are the three models in widest current use for handguns, as well as for extended mounting on long guns such as the Model 94 Winchester, where conventional mounting is impractical.

Contrary to popular belief, magnification of the image is not the sole advantage of the optical sighting system. There have been some remarkably effective scopes of 1X power — i.e., no magnification beyond normal, unaided vision — and their particular virtue lay in the fact that the reticle was viewed by the aiming eye in precisely the same plane of focus as the target. This eliminated the impossible challenge of trying to focus the eye upon target, front sight and rear sight simultaneously, offering a great boon to those hampered by visual handicaps. Even shooters with perfect vision experience moderate difficulty in reconciling eye focus between three rather widely separated distances and the compromise of focusing upon the front sight leaves much to be desired.

It has been suggested that the numerical magnification of the scope is a subordinate factor in obtaining optimum precision of bullet placement and this is an easy point to verify empirically. A 2X scope on an accurate gun, firing loads that have been winnowed for superior performance in that gun, should have little trouble outpointing a rifle of dubious accuracy and/or a load not compatible with that gun, even though the latter combination mounts a scope sight of the highest magnifying power and ultimate intrinsic precision.

Given a rifle/ammunition combination possessing inherent potential for fine accuracy, a good scope will do well and a better scope will beat it. The pertinent point is that magnification, as such, is not the ruling consideration that many believe it to be. A myriad of factors contribute toward — or degrade from — the minimization of group spread, and scope capability tends to place among the least of these.

At least one informal match was held between two shooters, one firing an as-issued Springfield '03 A3, with a two-groove barrel and issue iron sights, the other firing a prized, sporterized '03 Springfield, with the supposedly superior four-groove barrel, equipped with a 10X scope sight of excellent quality. Alas for logical expectations, the two-groover kept winning — even after the shooters

Herringshaw Maxi-Mount is available for either the Thompson/Center Contender or Auto Mag, here with the former and M8-2X Leupold.

swapped rifles, through practically all of several runs with different batches of ammunition. At the risk of disturbing the placid ruminations of revered sacred cows, such things can happen, and do.

All of which is not intended to denigrate the value of high-quality optical sighting equipment on varmint rifles or handguns. Far from it, a good scope sight offers joy to the heart and balm to the soul. On a good gun, with the right loads, it is the keystone that makes desirable events occur, with implacable predictability. It is not the intent of this discourse to put down scope sights but, rather, to relegate them to their realistic niche in the hierarchy of things, their proper plinth in the collonade, or whatever.

As in many other fields of consumer goods, one tends to get what one pays for. True, enduring, outstanding quality demands a price and delivers value received. That is not to imply that the scope that costs the most will deliver the tightest groups because, as attempts have been made to clarify, many other factors affect the end result and most of them do so more powerfully. There is an aphorism popular among Kentucky colonels to the gist that there is no such thing as a really bad mint julep and, within limits, the same can be said of scope sights. True mediocrity and submediocrity tends toward being self-weeding, due to the inexorable force of consumer reaction.

Vastly inferior scope sights have been made and have been sold. The type supposedly used by Lee Harvey Oswald comes to mind in this context and any experienced shooter who has examined such an instrument is apt to experience profound skepticism toward the conclusions of the Warren Report — but enough of that. A decade or so later, suffice to say, the median quality of all offered scope sights trends toward a level of excellence that is gratifying to the objective observer. Some examples are better than others — and most are priced accordingly — but, like the traditional julep, it becomes ever harder to come upon a really bad one.

A lens brush can be packed along for field cleaning of scope lenses.

Most shoppers for a scope sight settle upon the selection of their choice after examining several samples in a dealer's showroom and that particular consideration poses a modest problem to all users; a point to be expanded upon shortly. For now, let it be noted that it is hard to evaluate scope sight performance in a dealer's showroom.

If it is held that magnifying power is not the *sine qua non* of scope sight performance, it should be conceded that magnifying capability offers one tangible advantage not to be discounted lightly. Moderate magnifying power can enable the scope sight to serve in lieu of a spotting scope and it can be most useful in this respect. A good pair of binoculars or an all-out spotting scope can be extremely useful to the varmint hunter, but capability of using the scope sight for the same purpose effectively can be of about equal value. With this in mind, one can make a good case for choosing a scope sight of 4X magnification or better. You can — to employ a dreadfully footsore cliche — glass the slopes without putting down your rifle.

Most makers of scope sights offer a choice of reticle designs. Some years ago, Leupold introduced a version they call the Duplex, having fairly heavy quadrant lines through most of the image perimeter, tapering to fine crosshairs in the center. This enables speedy alignment with the target, together with useful precision of final aim. Most makers now offer nominally identical reticle patterns, under a bewildering assortment of terms, each with his own. The

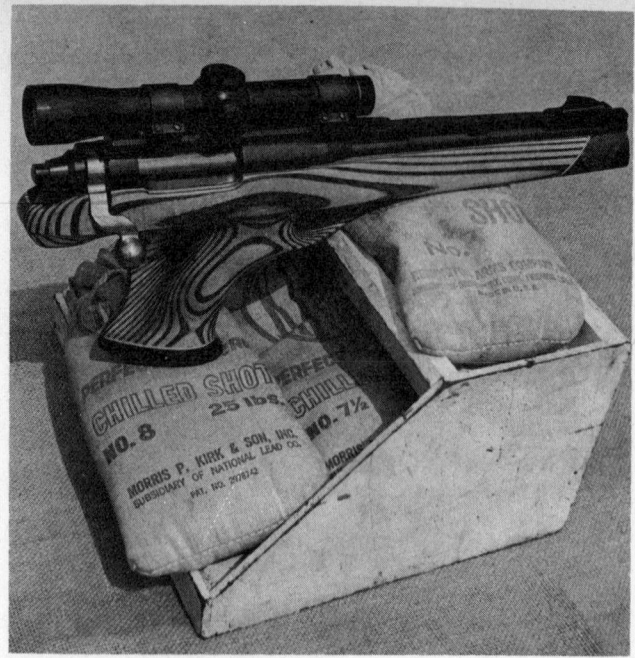

Simple shooting box carries shot bags filled with sand to serve as a portable benchrest for Remington XP-100 .221 Fire Ball single-shot, here with laminated Fajen stock.

The shooting box in use: Two spare sandbags are used to steady and brace the wrists. High-intensity report of the .221 Fire Ball cartridge makes ear protection — such as these David Clark muffs — an excellent idea. Fajen thumb hole stock is comfortable, accurate and handsome, though it prevents use of pistol in the left hand. The XP-100 is capable of 1MOA groups when topped with a good scope, such as this M8-2X Leupold, from a rest with carefully selected handloaded ammo.

Duplex reticle — call it by any term you wish — has won vast popularity in a short time by reason of its manifest convenience and efficiency. It merits your thoughtful consideration before settling upon another choice.

If sheer magnification is arbitrarily relegated to a picayune position in the scheme of things, the same cannot be said of the mounting arrangements. A good installation of mounts and rings can make a lot of yardage toward the desired goal. A bad job of mounting can lose even more in the opposite direction. Mounting a scope sight is not complex nor difficult, as will be seen shortly, but it falls among those activities about which the observation is valid: if it's to be done, 'twere best done properly!

Most modern rifles — and some handguns — carry drilled and tapped holes for installation of scope mounting bases, or alternate arrangements. Some, such as the Model 77 Ruger or certain models from British Small Arms (BSA) incorporate tapering dovetails to accept special rings. Older rifles, lacking this feature, require drilling and tapping before a scope sight can be installed. Such drilling and tapping is not a project for any but the most gifted of amateurs.

Two basic systems for scope sight mounting are in wide use in this country: the Redfield and the Weaver QD — for quick detachable. Several other manufacturers offer bases and rings that are reasonably compatible with one or the other of these; some offer hardware for both systems. Briefly, the Redfield uses one long bridge mount, secured at front and rear, with a front ring having a lower tang that is locked into a matching hole in the front of the base by a tight interference fit after ninety degrees of clockwise rotation.

The Weaver QD system uses rings that clamp onto a dovetail base and the base may consist of two short lengths,

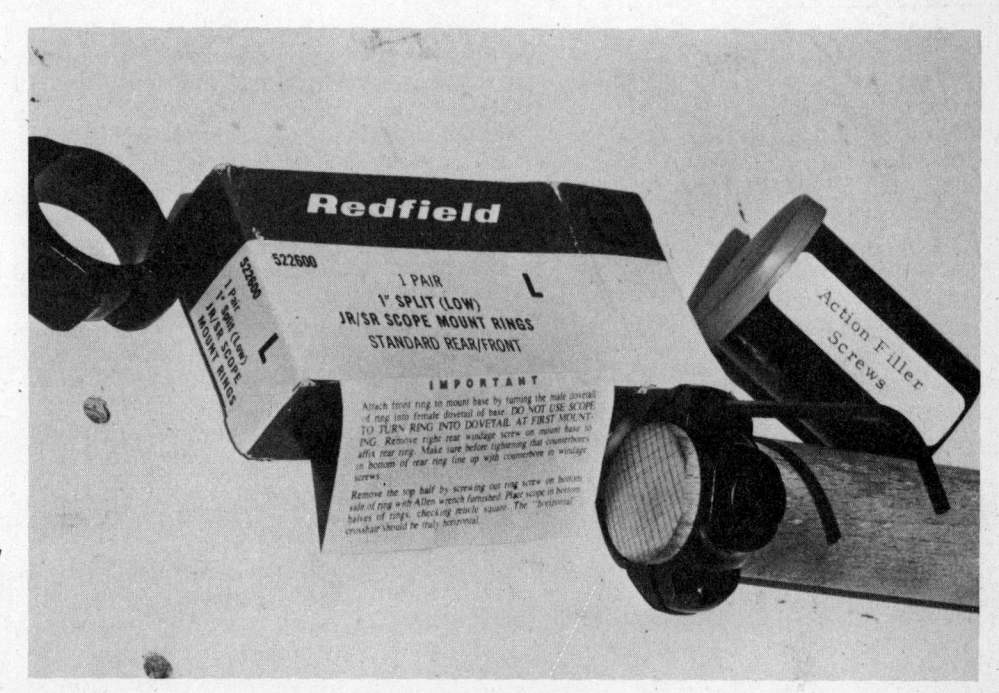

A one-inch hardwood dowel has been secured in Redfield front ring, preparatory to turning its tang into mount.

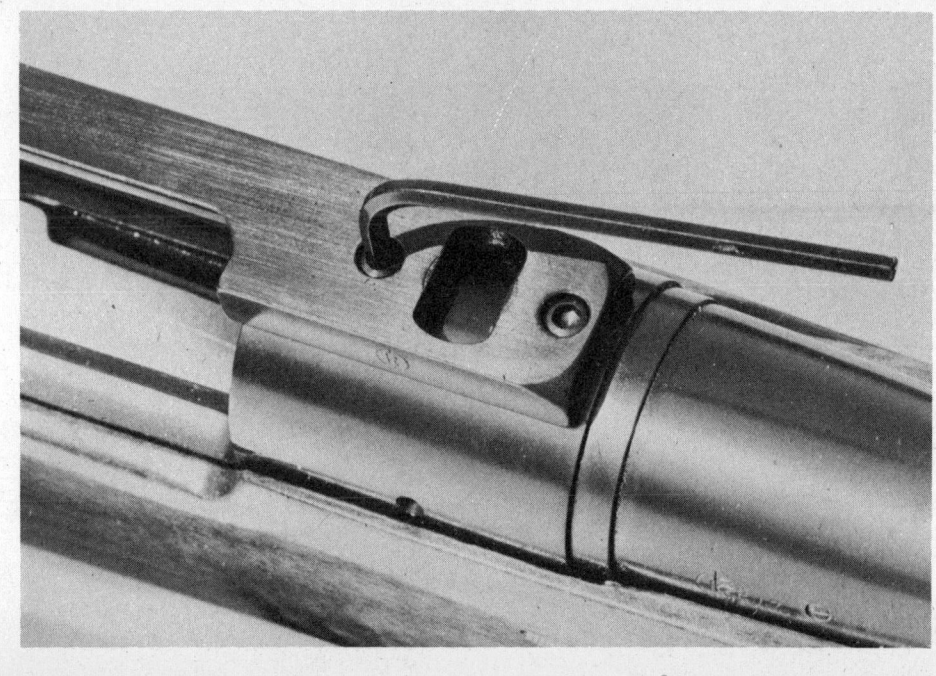

Redfield base attaches to the receiver with hex-socket screws. Recess for front ring tang can be seen here.

one front, one rear, or one long strip, depending upon the gun involved and/or the customer's choice. The Weaver QD rings are two-piece, with an upper segment that hooks into a mating groove of the lower segment at one end and secures at the other end with a pair of screws.

A third basic system is the Conetrol type, with a solid bridge base or front and rear base lugs. Into recesses, a pair of three-piece rings are locked by conical-nosed set screws that match conical recesses in the ring base segments. The Conetrol system may try the patience of the installer, but it results in a remarkably neat and sleek installation, when executed properly.

The Weaver QD system has the virtue of low cost and easy interchangeability of the same scope between several rifles. It has the minor disadvantage that torquing down the holding screws may rotate the scope slightly in the rings, so that the installer must loosen things, make another trial setting and try again, for as many repetitions as may prove necessary, before getting the reticle vertical and horizontal in relation to the rifle.

The Redfield system results in a notably solid installation and solidity is a valued virtue, particularly if heavy recoil of the rifle is apt to be a factor. At the same time, the Redfield system offers the option of a generous correction of misaligned azimuth — azimuth is right/left adjustment, synonymous with windage — which can be quite helpful. Even the most prestigious makers of rifles let one go through now and then that has the scope mounting holes at an angle to the axis of the bore.

Midge Dandridge, with a pair of desert jackrabbits taken with .25/06 Ruger Model 77 topped with 3X-9X Leupold.

The Conetrol mounting system uses three-piece rings. Set screws with conical points engage mating recesses in the bases of the rings to lock the assembled rings in place.

182

VARMINT HUNTER'S DIGEST

Using a 35mm SLR camera, as described here, to adjust eyepiece of scope. Pencil points to four-foot setting, typical focus as supplied.

With camera set at infinity, scope gives blurred image shown in photo above.

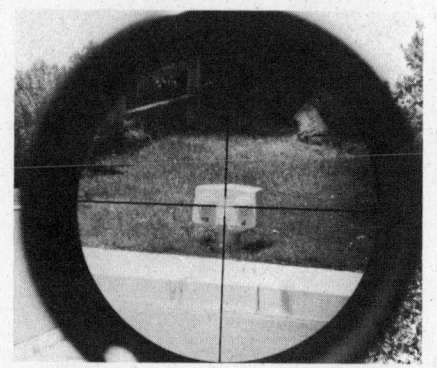

After adjustment, scope reticle and target are seen clearly.

View through same scope, at 3X setting, covers wider field than 9X.

With bases and rings installed, torqued to a light frictional hold of the scope, the rifle should be put to the shoulder in normal firing position and final adjustments made to square up the reticle and move the scope forward or rearward until the eye relief corresponds to comfortable aiming with the shooter's eye in accustomed position. At this point, tighten the holding screws in the rings, but do not do so with undue and injudicious savagery. Excessive tightening of the rings can collapse the walls of the scope tube, causing serious damage and faulty performance.

The scope can be aligned by bore sighting, or by the use of an optical bore sighter. Most scope sights are shipped with their internal adjustments set at midpoint and, if the mounting system permits external adjustment, it's better to use such facilities, rather than compensating by extreme travel of internal adjustments.

It was noted earlier that shoppers for scope sights tend to judge them by peering through samples at nearby objects. With this hard fact in mind, most manufacturers ship their scope out, set to give a clear, sharp image on objects close to the observer. As a direct result, most scope sights need recalibration of the eyepiece focus and they need it desperately.

The popular single lens reflex 35mm camera can be used as a quick and positive means for recalibrating scope sight eyepieces for accurate focus on objects at typical distances. By viewing through the scope and turning the camera focusing ring until the scope reticle is at its sharpest in the camera viewfinder, reference to the focusing scale on the barrel of the camera lens will give an equivalent distance. In most cases, this will be from two to four feet. For shooters with fairly normal vision, it needs to be changed so that the equivalent focus is from fifteen feet to infinity. With most scopes, the adjustment involves backing the eyepiece outward — that is, loosening the lock ring and rotating the eyepiece counterclockwise, as viewed in normal firing mode.

Minor vagaries of personal vision may give best results if the scope is camera-focused at some other distance. Once the distance is determined, the same procedure offers speedy and precisely positive adjustment for all other scope sights. No instrument is readily available at economical cost for calibrating scope sights exclusively, but the 35mm SLR camera — almost universally accessible today, either owned or on short-term loan — can handle the operation decisively, meanwhile performing its nominal functions.

Chapter 18

OUT OF THE NIGHT...

Some Of Calling's Greatest Surprises Lurk There In The Darkness!

Having called, the night varmint hunter must make proper use of light for positive identification of his prey before letting fly.

ONE OF THE most perplexing problems that faces a beginning caller is how he should go about hunting at night.

Successful night hunting is an art in itself; closely related to daytime hunting, it has enough strategic variations to make it a demanding pastime.

Of all the problems that face a beginning night caller, nothing seems to be quite as confusing or prompt more questions than how to properly use a light.

Not only is the proper use of light a problem, but selection of the right type is also a key to success. There are a great many good lights for night hunting; even a common three-cell flashlight can be effective, but is not recommended. Head lamps are also used extensively and can be very effective when calling in country that will put the game at close quarters.

The best lights are the more high-powered variety such as sealed beam spotlights, aircraft landing lights and 6 or 12-volt car headlights. Some of the best lights I have used over the years are standard car headlights available from automotive supply houses. These have the high and low beam advantage as well as being both durable and compact. A good portable light can be constructed easily from a headlight, using a coffee can for a shroud and a homemade handle of wood and a couple of hose clamps. The battery usually can be rigged in a carrying case with a handle. Heavy canvas works well. The light is connected to the battery with at least twenty feet of cord for sufficient maneuverability.

Although somewhat heavy, they are not difficult to pack over the short distances that night callers move and the weight is distributed evenly over a two or three-man calling team that is a must for efficient night hunting anyhow.

These lights — more powerful than the smaller dry cells — provide plenty of power for positive illumination and identification for night calling activities. Positive identification is one of the most important factors in night hunting. Powerful lights, coupled with good scopes that gather even more illumination, provide the hunter with the ability to see clearly what and where he is shooting.

Strong lights will allow the shooter to identify his target

positively before the shot. Further, they illuminate the entire animal's body, eliminating a shot that is taken only at reflecting eyes; a smaller target area that could be a mistake. Serious callers protective of their sport and their own position never shoot at eyes only. If the light does not allow the shooter to see exactly what his target is, a shot should not be taken.

Another reason for powerful lights concerns finding downed game in the dark. The stronger light allows the holder and the shooter to read the country, identify positive landmarks in the vicinity of the target, which will help in locating a bagged bobcat taken at long yardage. Always note the area of your target in detail before taking the shot. Once you go out to make a recovery, everything will appear in a different perspective and it is necessary to have a good mental picture of the location.

This night varmint hunter has strapped his light to his head, permitting the use of both hands. Correct light handling is vital.

It is not the light, but how to use it that concerns most beginning callers. To the newcomer, it is difficult to conceive a coyote coming in to a call, while the light is on, but they do it readily, if the light is handled competently.

Effective night hunting is a two-man operation, at least; one holder, who generally calls, and a shooter. Three men are also effective, as there can be plenty to do, but more than that gets confusing and reduces your chances of success.

The major problem facing those who call at night is not an inability to lure the animals within shooting range, but a lack of a chance to shoot once the varmint is upon the callers.

An overall diagnosis would point out one major cause of not getting a shot: poor light handling and poor lighting equipment. Assuming that the callers have taken the necessary precautions of watching the wind, minimum noise and the other little refinements that a conscientious hunter normally would do by habit, and assuming that they are indeed getting some eyeballs to reflect wickedly occasionally, I will lay the blame on the light and its handling.

It has been my experience that coyotes and foxes are the subjects most often bothered by the light, while the bobcat seems to be less concerned with a poorly handled beam.

Who calls is unimportant. I prefer to call my own stands up to the moment just before the shot will be taken. The partner works the light and, when a varmint shows up, is also ready to hold him with coaxer-type calling, while the shooter-caller takes advantage of his opportunity.

Author Dougherty finds a warm campfire comforting during one of his night varmint hunts.

VARMINT HUNTER'S DIGEST

187

Nighttime varmint hunter...

...demonstrates method of solo varminting...

If you have a good light, a good scope on your rifle and a good call, start your series of calls in a normal manner with perhaps a little less volume than you normally use on a daytime stand. After a minute on the clock, point the light straight up and turn on the switch. With the light pointed up, the edge glow of the beam will fall in a halo around your position. Any animal within this area will have eyes that are easily visible.

If there is nothing within the ring of light, the light is lowered to a position approximately forty-five degrees above the horizon. The coffee can provides a good shroud that extends beyond the front of the light and prevents glow back that will light up the callers and also make it difficult for them to see. With the light at forty-five degrees, make a slow complete circle around the stand, while calling softly. This extends the distance that eyes will reflect, from a short

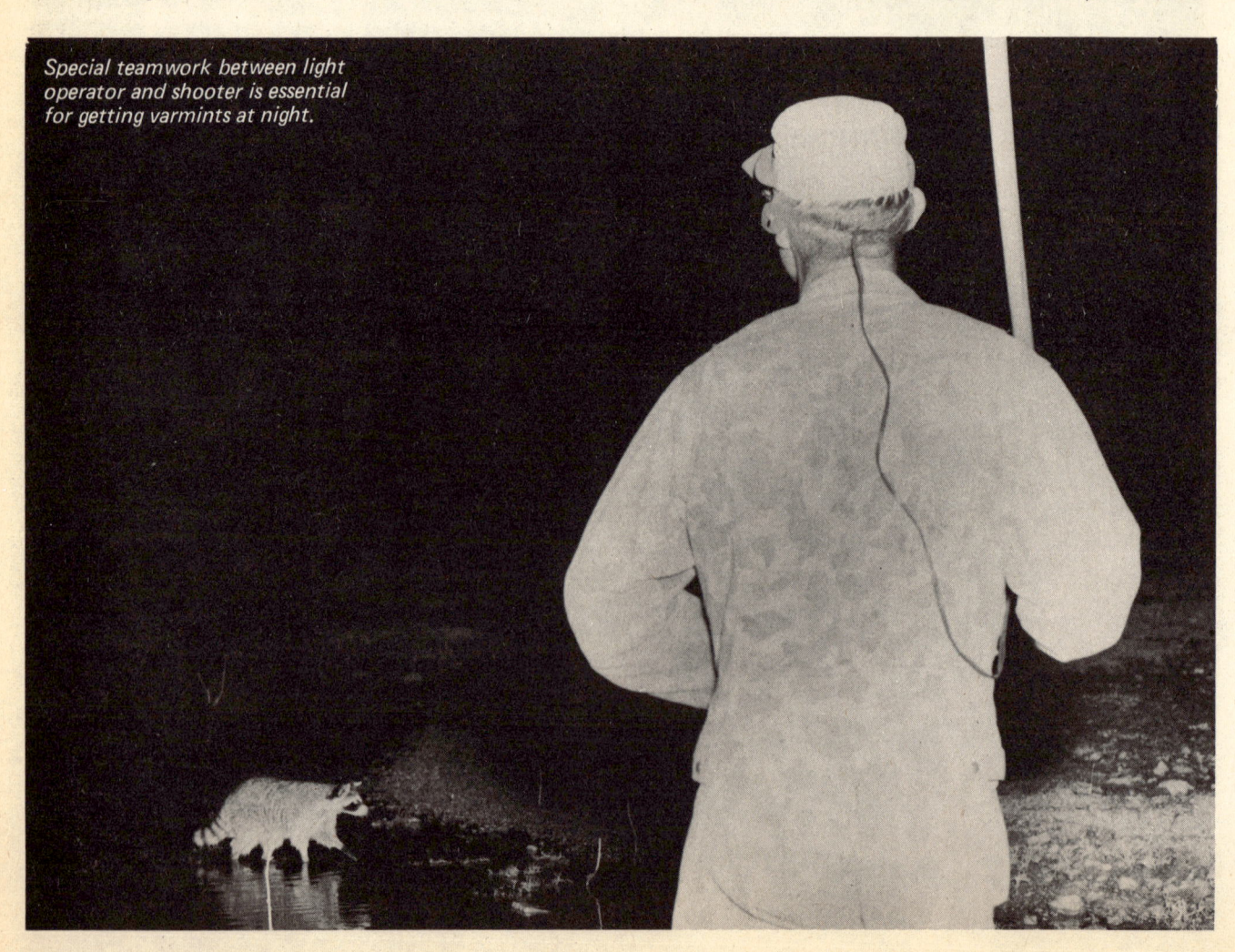

Special teamwork between light operator and shooter is essential for getting varmints at night.

188 VARMINT HUNTER'S DIGEST

...with varmint call in his mouth...

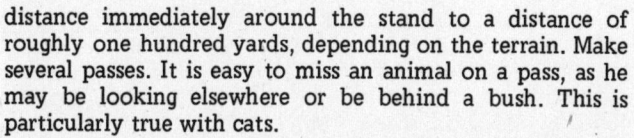

...holding rifle and flashlight in hands.

distance immediately around the stand to a distance of roughly one hundred yards, depending on the terrain. Make several passes. It is easy to miss an animal on a pass, as he may be looking elsewhere or be behind a bush. This is particularly true with cats.

Generally, we will shut the light off after a minute of searching the area to conserve battery power. After another minute or so, the maneuver is repeated, starting with the light straight up for a quick closer-range check. Continue this pattern until eyes are located.

Once an animal is spotted, the game becomes an exercise in teamwork. The caller should be the light holder from this point on, if he hasn't been calling all the time. The shooter must get into a comfortable, steady position, lining up on the eyes, as the caller keeps those eyes on the very edge of the light ring. Presumably the animal will continue his approach and the shooter should be able to line up the eye in the scope and track the approach. The light must be held in front of the scope's objective lens. The best method for this is to have the caller leaning over the shoulder of the shooter, extending the light in front of the objective lens.

Keep the animal coming as long as you possibly can. Once he stops and cannot be moved, the shooter should then indicate his choice to try and take him in that position or continue to work on him for a better position.

If the choice is to take a shot, the light holder suddenly will drop the entire force of the beam on the animal. This should completely illuminate the animal and the area around him, particularly if he is within a range of 150 yards. The shooter, who already has lined up the target, will be able to center his crosshairs further to make a positive identification. If the animal is a bobcat, he will have plenty of time to squeeze off a shot; if a coyote, he still should have ample time to line up his sights and squeeze off a careful round. Coyotes will not hold for a light as long as bobcats, nor will foxes.

When the shot is made, and if it is a hit, both the shooter and the light holder should carefully line up the area in

Through the years, Dougherty has found that the bobcat is the least affected by lights at night. This specimen was called into close range before nightfall.

VARMINT HUNTER'S DIGEST

Correct operation of a light, no matter what type, may help bring in many a varmint, including raccoon.

order that they may recover the animal easily. If the distance is over seventy-five yards, this becomes a problem and care should be taken not to lose the animal. If the shot is taken at close yardage, this is not as necessary.

It takes a lot of practice and teamwork to become effective at night calling. The secret, of course, is in the proper handling of the light and care should always be taken to avoid burning the animal with the full force of the light until it is time to take the shot.

Back about 1970, several guys down in Texas decided to improve the lighting situation. That idea of lugging around a headlight and the power for it seemed to bug them.

Hours of work on a night stand are likely to go for naught, says Dougherty, if light is used improperly.

They came up with an item they called the Mini Gun Light. As far as I know, the invention has passed into oblivion, but that doesn't mean it wasn't a good idea. I suspect, however, that the reason for it being dropped — if that's what has happened — is that too many of them were getting into the hands of poachers who were interested in jacklighting something besides varmints.

The Mini Gun Light solved the problem of the shooter and light man being in tune, when the critical time to take the shot comes along. Extremely lightweight at 4½ ounces, the patented clamp allowed mounting on virtually any gun in a variety of positions. For instance, the clamp would allow direct contact with the barrel, mounting the light ahead of the forearm in a trouble-free position. The same setup also could be mounted atop the scope. This in my opinion, was the least handy of the two, but ideal if the shooter had a Mannlicher stock or over/under barrel conformation.

My first exposure to practical application with the light came after Jim O'Connor of A-1 Manufacturing dropped one off with a suggestion that I give it a try. I had a place to go where the coyotes had been harassing an acquaintance's poultry operation. They weren't getting many chickens, as he had a fairly varmint-proof setup, but their midnight maraudings were getting the dogs uptight and he was losing precious sleep.

I had been promising a friend a coyote hunt, so the situation was opportune. I clamped the unit on my tried-and-true Sako, noting the compactness of a three hundred-yard shooting light with only ounces in weight. The alkaline-type battery of 4.5 volts mounted behind the swivel arrangement that allowed the reflector 360 degrees of movement. Equipped with a switch applied with pressure

There are times when the night hunter must wait until the first light of dawn to get a crack at his game.

sensitive tape, the light was turned on when the switch was depressed with the thumb on the rifle's forearm.

At dark, we turned on the light and made the corrections necessary to line up the beam neatly centered by the crosshairs on my scope. The power of the little light was amazing. There were no wires to interfere, no weight; just complete freedom, with the rifle directing a beam of light straight down the path of the bullet.

The Mini Light was designed to be used only for shooting and not for the normal light work of checking the area, locating an animal and keeping him under surveillance as he is lured to a good shooting position. It wasn't that the light wouldn't work, but the small battery only produced ten minutes of straight burning time at full power. This was enough, however, as burning time generally is measured in seconds, when shooting.

The full value of the light was evident on our third stand, when a double on coyotes was struck. Both animals bore down on our stand at full speed, coming into close range. My partner, completely unfamiliar with how to handle the spotting light I handed him as the coyotes came close, was unable to get it positioned properly in front of my scope. I had forgotten the new light, being conditioned to rely on the skills of my light man. Now I switched on the light with firm pressure from my thumb, illuminating the coyote that collapsed at the whop of the little rifle. The second coyote made tracks, while being tracked with the shooting light. It was a perfect setup; once on target, gun and light were one, making an easy situation out of a tough one.

Those who have tried to track a running varmint at night, while relying on the timing of a partner with the light, realize the advantages. A smooth relationship between gunner and light man is built up over many hunts, overcoming obstacles, blowing stands and becoming frustrated on more than one occasion. The Mini Light did not eliminate the need for a companion, although solo night hunting would certainly be possible.

But the demise of the Mini Gun Light only proves that out of the bad, some good usually comes.

This brings to mind another outing in which a light played an important part.

The coyote came hard across the long, crackly dry sagebrush-studded flat on a course that had him on a collision bearing.

He was closing the distance between us rapidly in that characteristic, mile-eating lope, obviously unaware of the light that was directed straight at his eyes. He was completely oblivious to the three of us standing upright behind the light, one ready with the rifle, one ready with another light, the caller holding the light in use.

The area around us was swathed in the soft glow from the light pointed now straight at the coyote that had slowed to a trot twenty yards away. Still he came on, stopping finally no more than ten yards from the three of us who made no sound, didn't move, only watched.

It was behavior not normal for a nighttime coyote. Sure, we get them to ten yards at night on occasion, but usually they stop out a bit farther, say about fifty to seventy yards which is good for a quick rifleman who has a good light man to rely on.

This coyote, however, had the light full on him since we first cut his eyes, two hundred yards out from our calling position — it never was taken off those bouncing eyes as he crossed the flat.

The reason was obvious; the coyote could not see the light, because the light was red.

This was a good many years ago. Since that time, the red light has been a fairly well-kept secret among nighttime callers in the same manner that a red hot bass angler keeps his pet secret lures to himself or perhaps shares with only a few members of his inner circle.

Knowledge of the application of a red light for hunting nocturnal critters had not been widespread at that time, but certain progressive calling types across the country had been aware of it for many years.

The first time I ever saw it used was in 1965 and, to the best of my knowledge, the guy who discovered it in our area was a fellow named Thumper McDowell. How he stumbled on it I'm not sure, but the concept immediately made sense and practical application proved its effectiveness.

Originally we used lenses made of a transparent red plastic replacing the clear lenses on the Holdstock Critter-Getter, a varmint light then manufactured by my old varmint hunting partner, Ron Holdstock. Not too many callers in the Southern California area were privy to McDowell's discovery and those of us familiar with the red light never used it in the company of outsiders. It was a calling secret selfishly contained among a relatively small group.

Then the so-called secret was out; commercially, that is. The gang that makes the Mini-Lite put a red light on the market and the famed Burnham Brothers did likewise. I'm

A camouflaged bow, arrows at the ready and battery-operated light attached. Use of a filter to produce red light results in seeing without being seen.

The Burnham Brothers of Marble Falls, Texas, market this varmint hunter's spotlight which is designed to plug into a vehicle cigarette lighter. Thirty-watt lamp at just over a pound seems ideal for night hunting.

The caller/bowhunter in this case is Winston Burnham, who is bringing the raccoon well within light range.

sure that the Burnham Brothers had been aware of the value of the red light for many years and I recall discussing it briefly with them years ago, when we hunted together in Texas.

The Burnham light still is being marketed, incidentally. The red light provides ample illumination to pick up eyes as far out as the regular white light spotlights. The theory that seems to make the most sense is that the red light is nearly invisible or appears black to the color-blind predators, hence there is no bright glow to spook them. Red illumination has been used by zoos to change the schedule of nocturnal animals for a good many years, forcing them to appear in daylight hours where visitors could watch them in action. Sufficient light is provided with the red light to facilitate shooting at close range. It is a good practice, however, to have a regulation-type white light handy to put on the target when the shooter is ready; this is particularly true if the varmint is over forty yards away.

The obvious advantage to the red light is its apparent invisibility, particularly in hunting the light-shy coyote. Using the red light, it is no longer necessary to point the spot in the air, relying on only the glow from the outer ring of light to pick up eyes, then dropping the main spot on the target when it is time to shoot.

With the red glow, the light man can scan the country on a level and pick up incoming animals much easier, while fewer critters will escape detection.

Some callers think that eyes show up even better with the red light; I'm not convinced this is true, but they certainly show up plenty hot enough to see even at long ranges. If you're having trouble with extra-shy coyotes, fox or bobcat, the red light could solve the problem.

This would be especially true in areas where only shotguns are allowed and nighttime ranges have to be substantially reduced from the fifty to seventy-five yard norm of night distances.

Chapter 19

Getting Your Critter With Bow And Arrow Requires Skill And Strict Camouflage Practices

Jim Dougherty has called and hunted varmints for more than twenty years. Since he began with a bow and arrow, he still favors the challenge bowhunting offers.

VARMINT BOWHUNTING

I CALLED UP my first coyote at the age of 16 in country that isn't even there now. Many things have changed since that long-past day. The country, our equipment, calls and even the coyote all have been altered by time. I suppose you could say that the country has changed some and the equipment a lot.

When I called up that first critter I was armed with a relatively new high-performance laminated bow of pretty good recurve design. Folks who shot aluminum arrows were considered well heeled and generally were careful of the background before they let fly. Bowquivers were mostly on drawing boards and guys with sights were verbally maligned as pinheads. In retrospect, about the only thing that hasn't changed is the coyote's penchant for what sounds like a free pass at the chow line.

I vividly recall missing that coyote with a considerable

Left-handed, Dougherty draws back recurve bow while using tree trunk as a backrest to steady his aim.

amount of wood. I can't recall how many shots, but by current standards, it would be counted as a bunch. The coyote was as new to the game as I, which contributed to his interest in what was going on all around him. Patience acquired over the years no doubt has contributed more to whatever success I've enjoyed as a bowhunter than real expertise as a whiz-bang archer. The event of that first big miss was repeated with regularity in those beginning months of calling. If it wasn't for the fact that calling critters in was so much fun, I might well have given up the activity.

Occasionally, I equalized conditions with a well-placed missile from my Marlin .22 just to keep things in perspective and avoid any misunderstanding among the coyote population. The first coyote I ever took fell to a hollow-point, as he peered yellow-eyed at me over a clump of orange-laced chemise. Lugging him back to the car was good for the spirit.

In the twenty-odd years that have passed since I first started calling — much of it for profit as an occupation — I have been reminded often that the many hours calling as a bowhunter have contributed significantly to what I feel is a better understanding of the game.

When it comes to the use of calls, blowing a varmint call properly is the easiest calling form to master. Over the years, it has been my good fortune to hunt with those considered to be the best at the game. With few exceptions their calling styles vary, yet their levels of success in the field are consistently productive. Generally, they all agree that the key is not in how you blow so much as where and when.

I've found that individual styles of calling are equally productive no matter where one hunts geographically.

Many varmint varieties may be taken with bow and arrow, although the importance of better camouflage and good calling techniques is paramount for success.

VARMINT HUNTER'S DIGEST

195

Years of practicing calling techniques and expertise with bow and arrow may get the hunter a bobcat such as this one. Dougherty used recurve bow here.

Murray and Winston Burnham are perhaps the two most famous game callers in the country. Their styles are slow and low-keyed compared to those of California and Arizona callers, yet they do well wherever they happen to travel.

Some callers feel that technique or styles develop based on the type of terrain they first begin to hunt. To some degree, I believe this is true. Wide-open spaces of low desert such as the vast expanses of Arizona and Nevada seem to produce callers of particular stamina in wind and volume. By most standards, Texas is big and open, yet most callers I've hunted with from the Lone Star State follow the easy-going pattern of the Burnhams. An opposite would be Wayne Weems, a Texan who was the first true-to-life varmint-calling expert I ever got acquainted with. He has a talent for leaning on a call and covering four counties at once. He did well, too, as you may have heard.

In the midst of all the hubbub that developed during the late Fifties and early Sixties, when varmint calling became a competitive pastime for those of us who traveled the calling contest circuit, volume became a factor and a resultant hunting style beyond proportion to its true value.

Arizona callers in the Sixties had a reputation for being double tough in any calling contest. They were reknown for their loudness. Calling was taking on some serious proportions for a lot of us with key competitors usually boiling down to a few regulars from California and Arizona. Doug Kittredge was always one to be reckoned with.

Calling contests actually got us off on what I came to

believe was the wrong foot for hunting in the field, particularly if you're going to do it with bow and arrow. The real tip-off to this was all wrapped up in Sam Dudley, a good friend of mine, who many, myself included, consider to be the finest caller ever. Dudley would enter a contest on occasion and he could play the game by the rules, one of which was to blow the call as loud and hard as you can. A lot of money points ride on volume.

But things were different when you made a stand with Sam Dudley in the field. Volume wasn't as important as subtle technique; a good bit of perfected coaxing style and a natural talent for knowing in just which bush to set himself before the party got started. I suspect that calling styles, like shooting styles and equipment preference, always will be a matter of individual taste. What works for a fellow pretty much becomes gospel to his way of thinking.

Any newcomer to the sport is well advised to purchase a record or team up with an experienced caller for a spell. What he really gleans from either approach is an opportunity to mimic a proven calling technique. Proving it in the field becomes a matter of application and perseverance.

Patience and observation are two keys to any form of bowhunting success. It comes back in a sense to what old

At left, Dougherty used a compound bow to take this large, nearly fifty-pound coyote. Dougherty believes compound bows are boon to varmint hunter. Below, bowhunters survey their take in desert.

VARMINT HUNTER'S DIGEST

197

Dudley showed us. His many years of experience in the field is what really paid off. This was not so much his calling style, which could be altered considerably, as mentioned, but his real understanding of the game he was hunting.

Based on the terrain, the weather and to some degree the time of year, experience reveals a pattern of animal behavior. It took a while for me to develop a hard, fast set of conditions that, in the long haul, generally will pay off. Obviously, there are always variations but proven theories are hard to beat, as long as they're tempered with a little thought when things aren't going quite right.

For instance, I feel strongly about hunting washes and prominent wandering thickets during midday hours, particularly when bowhunting is the game and the shooting opportunities have to be close range. With a rifle, it's obviously not so important. One can suck a coyote to the edge of cover and take him comfortably from a distance. With a bow, the call should be taken as close to the critter as possible.

I recall a recent calling expedition in Texas. The country was just starting to turn golf course green and the coyotes were beginning to rut; a time of year which is perfect for calling. Weather conditions also were perfect for day-long hunting. Light, cool breezes stirred the country, making it easy to plot constant wind direction which is of paramount importance to a caller. We began on the flats, as the sky was coloring up, and got in a bit of action at close-range dogs. The pattern was short-lived. After full daylight, either we blanked on the stand or the sightings were of distant coyotes who wouldn't cross the relatively open terrain.

We changed our tactics quickly, forsaking the open flats, where visibility was in our favor and moved quietly into the wandering riverbed-like thicket of tangled mesquite and thorny flora that gouged severely. We walked farther from the vehicles to each calling site as stealthily as if we were stalking a whitetail. We set up in a ready position and called in subdued patterns. The action was brisk and a good many mesquite trees were wounded. Trying to thread needles is tough even when the game is close.

I recall one stand where three coyotes came in single file about a minute apart. Each loped down the same trail,

Successful varmint bowhunting depends on the time of day, weather, season, terrain, cover, camouflage and calling techniques. Each must fit situation.

Dougherty says that knowledge and understanding of the game animal's habits — knowing where and when to call — is more important than calling technique.

turned in a little clearing at the exact same place and skedaddled into the brush, shifting gears as he went.

Two arrows placed behind the turning little wolves provided an education in timing for the third. The broadhead nailed him fairly and his lights went out within three strides. Two days of this action, in a clearly defined pattern, provided us with plenty of shooting, a bit of game brought down and an arrow supply that eventually was rendered defunct.

Wind is the most critical factor that affects calling and calling success. As most of us know, periods of high wind affect all animals, and predators are no exception. Most important is how wind, on callable days, is filtered over the area you are hunting. Try to lure something out of

Bobcat and coyote have succumbed to electronic calling. Physical movement on bowhunter's part may spoil shot at skittish varmints unless done properly.

good-looking cover on your downwind side and you might as well lay back and enjoy the scenery; nothing much is likely to happen.

Always call upwind or crosswind even if you have to alter your approach to calling country. Scent helps. A bit of rabbit or buck scent sprinkled on the clothes works, according to some. To my way of thinking, it can't hurt.

An animal coming to a call relies heavily on scent and sight. Being concealed is doubly important with a bow, and getting set right for comfort and concealed movement before the caller starts means a better opportunity.

Not too long ago, I took a fellow coyote hunting. It was for serious hunting, with coyote hides being worth enough on today's fur market to make hunting them a profitable venture. We made several midday stands in country not far from home on a stark, clear winter day with a five-mile breeze in thick, blackjack oak country, knee-deep in tawny, coyote-colored grass.

My friend got too comfortable on three occasions, deep set on his butt, awkwardly positioned for good, smooth reactions. We never saw any of the coyotes that came in until they materialized tight to our position. They were all starry-eyed, muscles tensed, ready to bolt, which they all did into nothing when my partner tried to react with complete body movement. He shot his first coyote late that afternoon in a little clump-covered grassy draw. The setup was right with the sun at our backs. The coyote was six feet away.

The use of sunlight can be important to a bowhunter. Keeping it at your back on early morning and later afternoon stands gives you a positive edge. The sun also helps in highlighting the fur of a moving animal as he becomes easier to see than you do and that's almighty important. The elements of keen sight naturally indicate that camouflage is important. That's a true statement. Even more important is taking advantage of shadows for cover with blowdowns and tangles as background to conceal slow, deliberate movement.

Perhaps the greatest disadvantage to hunting anything with a bow is the amount of physical movement required to bring the weapon into play. Think out just how and from where you will shoot before you start to call. If you have to suddenly face up to this problem with a critter in your pocket, you've just met the second-place winner in the contest.

A fellow told me the other day he was taking more critters now with a compound with a fifty percent relaxed weight. His theory is that he can get it up and ready well in

Keeping the sun at his back during early morning and late afternoon stands will give an edge to the bowhunter. Technique brought this varmint close enough.

VARMINT HUNTER'S DIGEST

201

advance of the critter getting into shootable position. The theory will carry some water, but I suspect it's as much circumstantial conditions as credit to the bow. A fifty percent reduction on a compound is great for comfort, but I'd rather have less drop-off and more bow efficiency in terms of speed, which is plenty important when dealing with nervous coyotes and foxes. Besides, with an ultra-high drop-off, my fingers seem to come off the string one at a time; not too good for the accuracy department. The subject is good fodder for conversation around campfires.

A homemade or commercial portable shooting blind can be an aid to the bowhunter. Ron Holdstock pops out of his blind with partially camouflaged bow for shot.

This bowhunter is using camouflage clothing and face makeup but the bow should be less conspicuous.

Bowhunters who do not wish to use camouflage face makeup may opt for face net. Net serves dual purpose in mosquito country. Note how unpainted hands stand out.

More important than the bow is what is attached to the business end of the arrow. Some years back, I ran into a fellow in the jumbled, black-rock, lava-flow country on the east side of California's Owens Valley. That the guy could call there was not a doubt and he apparently could shoot a pretty wicked stick, but he was playing hell putting the critters on the grass.

His broadheads were the little Bod-Kin cut-back models and not one had ever been inside of five feet of file or stone. These ingredients don't add up to success on a species of animal life that are fierce for tenacity. A rifle-hunting, coyote-busting buddy of mine once said that "pound for pound, coyotes can carry more lead than a junk wagon." Broadheads have to be plenty ready for the job, be it coyote or a bull elk. It's all the same. While I personally am not too much on the recently popular head designs that incorporate razor blades on a relatively blunt ferrule, I do feel these would be excellent for animals of the size and construction of fox, coyotes and bobcats. Their overall value to me on big stuff has yet to be proven, but, again, opinions are based on personal and witnessed experience.

Anticipation is probably the single-most force that drives us to hunt and fish. It's the wondering and planning, the sleepless nights and daydream days as we work up to a particular outing or major safari. If there was ever a sport that carried anticipation to the last degree, it's calling before the hunt, during the stand, then on to the next one. Indeed, calling is the ultimate in anticipation and I'm not so sure it's not the ultimate in excitement, too.

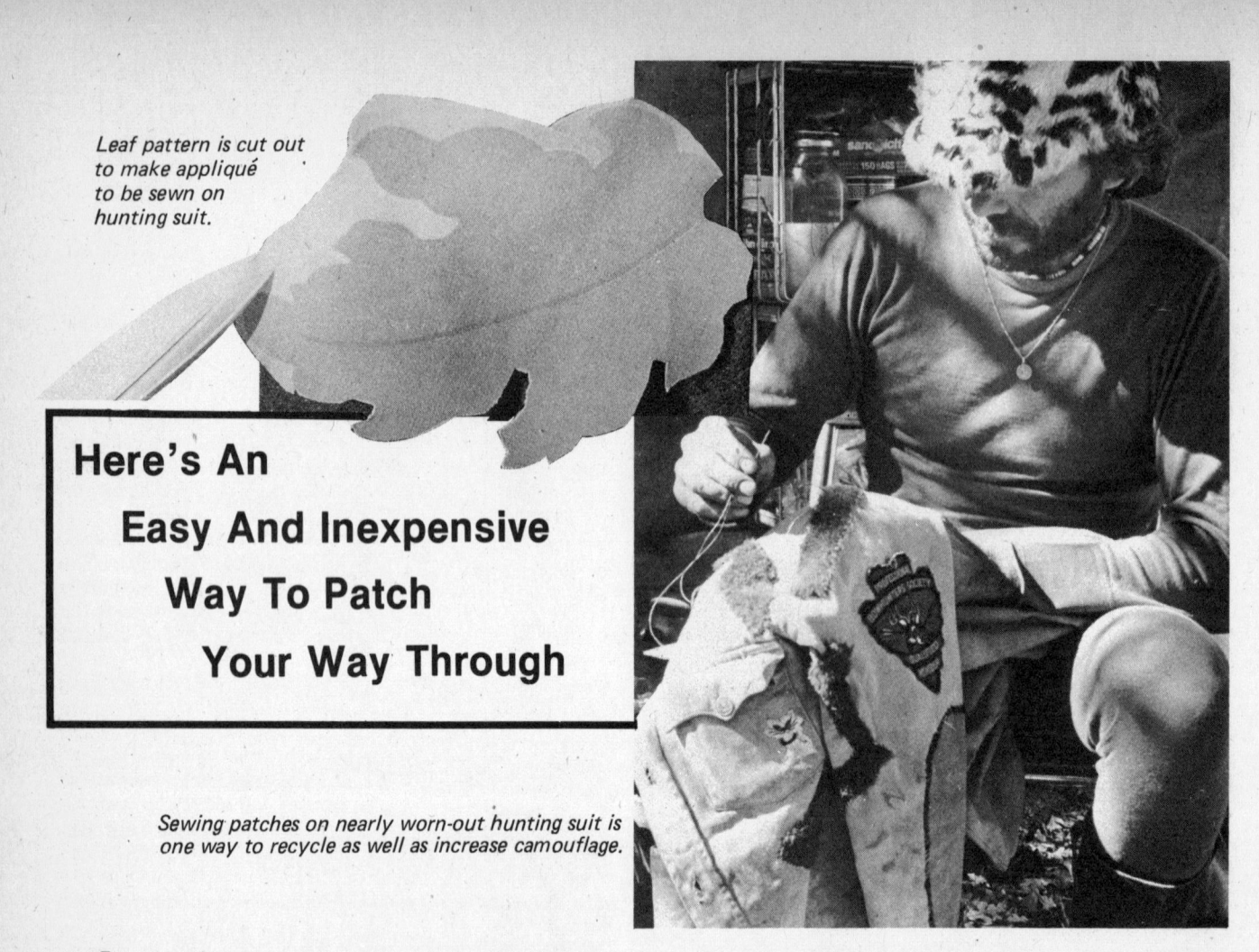

Leaf pattern is cut out to make appliqué to be sewn on hunting suit.

Here's An Easy And Inexpensive Way To Patch Your Way Through

Sewing patches on nearly worn-out hunting suit is one way to recycle as well as increase camouflage.

AN EMBARRASSING THING happened to Jerry Gentellalli, noted outdoor writer/photographer of La Jolla, California, on a recent hunting expedition to the Navajo Reservation. As he reached down to pick up the small forked-horned buck he had just arrowed, ripppppppp went the seat of his pants. His hunting buddy laughed heartily and reminded him that he was going to be rather cool the next day when they planned to hunt varmints. Because he had left for the bowhunting trip in such a hurry, Gentellalli had not brought an extra camouflage suit and was not prepared for this catastrophe. He searched frantically in his Catquiver pouch and luckily found a needle and thread which had been tucked away in there for several seasons. That night, by the dancing light and warmth of the campfire, the bowhunter set about the task of repairing the rather large hole in his pants.

Upon close inspection he realized that his trusty and comfortable tie-die hunting suit, which had served well through many seasons, was showing its age. There were several worn and faded spots in addition to more than a few strategically placed holes. This was his favorite suit, his good luck suit, and the idea of tossing it in the rag pile was like losing a good old friend. At this point Gentellalli realized that it could be saved with a variety of patches of different colors and shapes to produce a camouflage effect. It could last him indefinitely through the use of camouflage patchwork!

As he patched his suit, Gentellalli told how he experimented with patches of different colors and shapes.

"How do you like my patched suit?" he asked his buddy.

"You mean appliquéd suit," his partner corrected. He was obviously quite impressed!

On the way home Gentellalli decided it would be a great

Gentellalli added patched denim flap to his fatigue hat which helps protect hunter's neck in all weather.

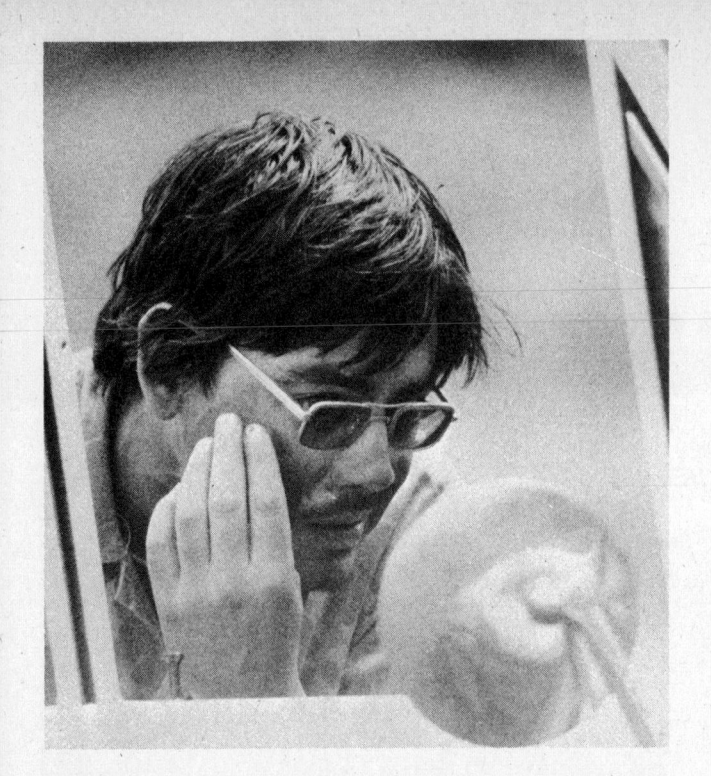

Applying a good pattern of camouflage paint to hands and face is as important as wearing proper hunting clothing to the successful varmint hunter.

idea to use patchwork as an addition to all camouflage suits, both new and old. The idea of elaborating on camouflage suits to give them a custom-made effect was appealing.

Gentellalli checked the local yardage store to find the best methods of doing patchwork. There are three easy methods. The first and quickest is the iron-on method. In this you use a material that adheres to other material when applied with a hot iron. These patches are permanent bond, the kind that are used to patch holes in kids' pants. This is the easiest method.

For the second method the do-it-yourselfer uses a sewing machine. The third method involves a little more time and ingenuity and the ability to work with a needle and thread — here, a simple straight stitch is all you need to know to design your own custom-made camouflage outfits.

Gentellalli used all these methods in designing a suit and the techniques are simple. For the sew-on methods choose a soft material that will be silent when stalking through brush. Felt is good. It comes in assorted colors, is available at yardage stores and costs about thirty cents for a 12x12-inch square. Cotton is stronger but the bowhunter might like felt for its softness. Earth colors such as yellow, brown, green and beige are available. Add a little black and red for accent.

Choose a pattern or motif for the patches such as leaves, branches or grass or invent your own designs. The important factor is the total camouflage effect, keeping it as close to nature as possible. For the camouflage to be successful, the hunter must blend into the natural surroundings. The hunting terrain determines the size of patch to use. Small, close patterns at long distances are seen as solid objects. In heavy foilage the tight close patterns are best, and in open range the larger broken pattern works better.

Patches can be used to renovate old, worn camouflage suits or as additions to new suits. When buying a new suit be certain that the material is comfortable and washable. Choose a solid background color, preferably a shade of tan or green. If the suit is a dark shade, then lighter patches would provide a contrast and create the camouflage effect you want.

There's no need to throw away your favorite hunting suit, especially if you feel it brings you confidence and luck on the stand. By recycling your suit, you could possibly recycle your luck.

Patched and recycled camouflage hunting suit seems to blend well with terrain. Hunter's hands and face should be painted and bow may be coated with nonreflecting black spray paint such as product below.

VARMINT HUNTER'S DIGEST

Chapter 20

BACKYARD SAFARI...

Dougherty's genuine African safari hat plays host to a Daisy Buck Jones Special BB gun. The gun was produced about 1933 and has since become a collectors' item. The cartridge beside the BB carton is a .460 Weatherby magnum.

I STUMBLED on a unique and exciting hunting experience not long ago, completely by accident, while stalking a hairy arachnid.

I was crouched to silhouette my target, a particularly large trophy specimen, against the waning rays of the sun setting behind a cinder block wall. I crept along, taking full advantage of the lengthening shadows, and finally made it within shooting range.

The shot was an anti-climax after the harrowing stalk, because we all know spiders are quite edgy and hard to slip up on, but I succeeded in spilling his hydraulic fluid and was congratulating myself on a job well done when far above me I caught a shadow of flickering movement.

Deep dusk had fallen over the hunting zone by then and I waited, kneeling tense and eager behind a low shrub, for the game to approach. Then suddenly scuttling down a high line came a big fat double-ugly rat with a tail about — would you believe ten feet long? I felt I was undergunned: the Daisy Model 25 pump was fine for the fast and furious

...A Tongue-In-Cheek Look At The Home Varmint Scene

VARMINT HUNTER'S DIGEST

As with most big game, care must be exercised when stalking trophies.

action on running arachnids, but this was serious shooting.

Nevertheless I drew a bead on the beast and squeezed off a round. (And in this case, it really IS round!) To my surprise the missile nearly totaled the rat, which growled horribly and plummeted down straight at me.

As I lacked a back-up gunner, it did not seem prudent to press on into the dense brush along the back fence looking for a wounded animal with a gun that wasn't big enough to finish him off in the first place, so I repaired to the garage for a flashlight and swapped the pump gun for a Model 200 Daisy CO_2 pistol, which I felt might suffice for close-in rat shooting.

The big rat blast was the new shooting discovery, but it was just a segment of the exhilarating adventure that led up to a really true discovery. Armed only with a pistol, a light and raw courage, I returned to the dark area where the rat had fallen, flicked on the flashlight and polished off the beast as he was preparing to charge. Then, with the light illuminating the whole jungly scene, I made the big discovery.

From left, the Daisy Model 26 Masterpiece, 1894 Spittin' Image, Model 25 pump, and Model 102 Daisy Cub; BB guns used during backyard safari.

All along the back wall there were bugs of a beetlelike nature with long, waving antennae. They varied in length from about three-quarters of an inch to almost two inches, and at the glare of the light they ran like the very devil for the sanctuary of the hollow wall. Wood roaches!

You might scoff, but until you have tried to hit a high-balling wood roach at twenty feet, you haven't tried anything. I've seen strong men reduced to tears as one of these orthopterous anthropods evaded a whole fusillade and scurried to safety under the wall with a derisive wave of his antennae. Potting the runners was much like shooting jackrabbits, while the sneakers — the ones that merely peeped from holes — offered tricky head shots not unlike sniping at ground squirrels or chucks with long-range equipment.

The whole idea so intrigued my fancy that I called a neighbor, Jan Schreck, and together we went roach gunning. We developed a plan to waylay the cagey roaches, which quickly became wary under too much gunning pressure. Lights were set up to cover the area and a tasty assortment of bait was left at a tantalizing distance from the wall, forcing the roaches to cross an open area that would give us a shot. It was quite like baiting tigers, as the blind was at an elevated point some distance away (the two deck chairs on each side of a beer-laden card table, to be exact).

When the game was on the bait — they could be heard rustling around in the dark — the light switch was thrown and the copper started flying. Such a degree of skill was developed by some shooters who were invited to try their luck that consistent running hits at thirty feet became the rule.

It got to be quite the "in" thing to be invited to "a roach shoot over at the Doughertys." Invitations came to be highly prized and much sought after. The shooting was fast and furious, with BBs whining angrily off the back wall while roaches that hadn't made it to safety spun crazily through the dust raised by a hail of shot. Trophy roaches were highly prized, and "I got a two-incher last night" became words on a par with "thirty-inch buck" and "grand

Neighbor Thumper McDowell takes careful aim at game. Note that shooter is appropriately clad in camouflage gear.

slam" in sheep. Anyone can go on a deer or bighorn sheep hunt, but not everyone got in on the roach action.

The events leading up to the discovery that BB-gun hunting is a ball were not outstanding. A group of us were sitting on my back porch one September day bemoaning the fact that a morning's vigil in the nearby dove fields had been dismal. Four lone doves, freshly picked, lay stark naked at our feet, and four doves just aren't enough.

As we gurgled a cooling brew and reflected morosely on the failure of the morning's hunt, around the corner came my son, Jim, clutching his Daisy carbine model BB gun. I remember when he got that gun from his proud papa — he was about three days old, as I recall. There for a while he didn't use it much, and his aiming practice was limited to getting a nursing bottle into his mouth, a practice at which he became unerring.

Time marches on, however, and when Jim got old enough to lift the BB gun, he began to shoot. The man who wishes to teach his son the art of gun handling should look to the BB gun. At 9, my oldest son could handle with intelligence any gun in the family cabinet. He realized both the joy that could be taken from them and the danger if

One of the selling points of the Buck Jones Special was built-in compass and sundial. Great for backyard safari.

210

VARMINT HUNTER'S DIGEST

Famed hunter Dougherty takes a steely (coppery?)-eyed look at .177 caliber BB as compared to .460 magnum. Each may be deadly and safety precautions are mandatory no matter where safari is.

not properly handled.

As I pondered the fact that Christmas was approaching and that BB guns make admirable Christmas gifts, a couple of resident doves had the temerity to sail over our heads and drop lightly on the wires of Pacific T&T over my garage. They stayed just long enough to raise the frustration level five full points, then sailed off to flaunt their city limits immunity elsewhere. Their place was taken by an obnoxious starling, fat and sassy from raiding my fig tree. As he sat there smugly I heard the sound of a refreshment glass being set down very hard on the patio floor. The glass was held by my hunting partner, Ron Holdstock, and it naturally was made of glass whereas the patio floor is of concrete. You can guess which one broke.

"Give me that gun, Dougherty," said Holdstock, whose frustration had plainly outlived his patience. Naturally thinking that he had created some foul breach of socializing in an adult world, young Dougherty surrendered the gun with trepidation, only to discover that Holdstock's ire was directed not at him but at the bird world.

The enormity of the deed Holdstock prepared to perform hit the group of shotgunners around the table all at once. He fully intended to bag a bird with a BB gun! With a cold and deliberate eye he brought the stubby gun to his cheek, sighted and released the spring-powered miniature mini ball at the unsuspecting starling. Fairly swatted, the pesky bird power-dived to the concrete at the group of men's feet, raising their spirits in delight, their voices in a glad shout and their bag of birds by a full twenty percent.

Before the day was out the group bagged uncounted flies, several other nondescript insects and the starling. They discovered, on that memorable day, the pleasure that can be afforded by a safari through your own backyard with your trusty BB gun.

Take birds, now. I like birds just fine, when they stay the hell out of my fruit trees. Sparrows I have somewhat less than no use for, since they descend in whirring hordes on my peach and fig trees, and take one large bite out of every ripe fruit. I wouldn't mind if they ate their fair share, but when they get through marauding there is usually nothing unbitten left for me.

Prior to rediscovery of the BB gun we had tried a variety of bird dissuaders, ranging from tin can lids tied on the limbs to importing cats. The lids didn't work, and the cats didn't work very hard either. One, in fact, shared his food nose to nose with all the sparrows on the block. Having ravaged my fruit trees to destruction, the birds decided a switch to minced tuna balls would aid their diet, and the cat didn't seem to mind.

The BB gun altered the bird picture a bit. They still ate

all my fruit, but now they ate an occasional BB as well, for in peppering the tree, a few stray BBs got imbedded in the fruit.

I know they did, because my wife found one at breakfast, and the dentist's bill was forty dollars. Oh well, you can't win 'em all.

Being an enthusiast for this sort of thing, I dove into the BB gun scene with great gusto. First I noted that a whale of a variety of pill pushers is available, and having acquired a catalog, I upped the accounts payable of my sporting goods emporium quite a bit by ordering one of everything that looked good. Holdstock, with similar enthusiasm, had done the same thing. Would you believe being overstocked on BB guns? We solved this problem by inviting all the gang over for a backyard safari. Shotguns and deer rifles having somewhat more horsepower than necessary, they all had to buy BB guns. But then, business is business.

Today's BB guns are a far cry from the models of yesteryear. The range of price and model is fascinating, and you can buy everything from a gun fit for living room target shooting all the way to an arm suitable for the biggest backyard game going — mice, bats, crickets, etc.

I admit that I don't know much about air gun collecting and was using some antiquated pieces in my backyard safaris that would make the average collector drool, since one of the guns brought into play was the Buck Jones Special manufactured in the early Thirties and now much sought by the collecting fraternity.

As a training arm, the BB gun is remarkably flexible. A Christmas BB gun can be used all Winter in indoor practice by using one of the many traps designed to catch the pellets safely. Every member of the family can join in the fun: my family and I have shot literally thousands of BBs into a trap located in our fireplace.

But the biggest thrill of all awaits you afield, when you pit your skill and cunning against the denizens of nature twenty feet from your back door.

For instance, there is the fine and highly dangerous art of sniping at yellow jackets or wasps. Here is a sport steeped in adventure and doubly invigorating from the danger standpoint. Cool nerves and a steady hand are called for, and a back-up partner must cover you in case of a

Not satisfied with the few game birds at his feet, this backyard Batman waits for more.

Bore of a .458 caliber magnum muzzle, at left, compared to .177 caliber air rifle. The safety procedures for each gun are same, despite size difference.

BB guns and boys have gone together for many years. Air guns are a great way to teach children correct gun use.

charge. Hunting dangerous backyard game calls for specialized equipment. We discovered, after several hair-raising episodes, that the best back-up weapon is a badminton racquet.

The technique is this: the hunter makes his stalk, takes aim and fires. If he incurs the wrath of the prey, trouble is the order of the day and the intended victim generally peels off and begins a strafing run. At this point the back-up man leaps heroically into the fray, swinging mightily with his badminton racquet while the shooter runs like hell. It sometimes helps to station your wife on the outskirts of the fray with a bug bomb and Band-Aids, in case the hornet calls in reinforcements. Wing shots, of course, are out of the question.

Exotic game, such as garden spiders, can provide a whole afternoon of diverting activity, and if you make it sporting and shoot only at spiders in webs being swayed by the breeze, it gets pretty tricky. I have a thing about spiders. At an early age, I was running pell-mell late in the evening and one met me smack dab between the eyes, a gray beast fully eight feet across the beam and intent on devouring me then and there. Talk about trauma! To this day I'll take six rattlers to one spider — though not with a BB gun. The pellet pusher does fine on spiders, however.

Several other areas of sport were investigated for such backyard safaris. Bat shooting offered a challenge that eventually had to be given up as unrewarding — not enough bats and most are far too fast!

We did develop a good moth shoot during the summer months when the giant sphinx moths make their appearance. These were lured into the area with a strong, high light and as the bird-size moths danced around it, we opened up. Invariably some overly enthusiastic clod would blast out the light at the heat of the action and end the shoot. We finally had to give up sphinx moths for financial reasons.

Mice, of course, fall into the big-game category, but too few of us are blessed (blessed?) with a mouse population. We did discover one area, but overgunning resulted in annihilation of the resource and an end to the hunting.

In spite of all of the tomfoolery the entire affair of backyard safari is conducted with caution and a degree of intelligence. The BB gun is not a toy and should not be treated as one. Although my son sees grown men acting rather simple in their games of backyarding it, he never sees them handling guns in a sloppy manner.

The kids shoot the guns under adult control, and watch enviously as the adults shoot bugs. They can hardly wait to be invited out for a roach shoot. What it all boils down to is a chance to do what we like to do — shoot. To some of you it probably sounds a little silly, which it is — with a point. The point is that shooting is fun, and a silly safari in your own backyard can sharpen your shooting eye on hard-to-hit moving game, pass a few hours of time, and maybe even bag you a world's record locust, earwig or *Blatella germanica*. Cockroach, to you.

Chapter 21

MISADVENTURES OF A VARMINT HUNTER

All Was Not Sweetness And Success During The Author's Participation In The Annual California-Arizona Varmint Hunts.

THERE I WAS, in the midst of what was supposed to be a fierce, competitive shooting event, walking knee-deep in water and towing a boat down the so-called mighty Colorado River.

The sparkling propeller of the potent Johnson outboard motor had yet to bite into sufficient water to do its duty and all the while, I envisioned our landlubber buddies rolling coyotes and snookering bobcats, forging on to victory, while I forged through six inches of water with a half-ton boat at the end of a one-inch rope.

At the helm — I believe this is the proper nautical terminology — Ron Holdstock, my varmint hunting partner, was a pillar of strength as he directed me down-river to the channel he insisted had to be there.

If you've ever been fortunate enough to witness that epic celluloid, *The African Queen*, and the trials of Humphrey Bogart, you will appreciate the next three hours spent by my cohort and myself.

Sledge hammer and hatchet hardly can be considered ideal gear for the varmint hunter who wants to cover a lot of ground and travels light, but such items can be found useful if one doesn't want to starve in the field.

Dougherty and his hunting partner consider potential of rifle before taking to the field for wily varmints.

It had all started as something of a brainstorm where we had been discussing means by which we might — by fair means or foul — cop the crown for the annual varmint hunting contest between Arizona Varmint Calling Association champions and the California Varmint Calling Association. It was agreed that we needed a secret weapon.

The appointed day dawned bright in Blythe, California. Residents, used to an influx of sportsmen, nonetheless were somewhat dazzled by the parade of hardy souls invading their fair city from both sides of the Colorado River, boundary between Arizona and California. The highway was filled with a variety of sturdy rigs designed for easy desert travel, each loaded with two men and enough equipment to stock several large sporting goods firms.

As then-president of the California State Varmint Callers, I had made prior arrangements with Pete Ogden, president of the Blythe Chamber of Commerce, to set up a group breakfast for the visiting coyote crunchers and arrange suitable headquarters for the event. When I picked Pete up at 8 a.m., he expressed amazement at the participation and enthusiasm for our project.

Californians had hit Blythe like a plague of famished locusts, each one wanting an Arizonian for breakfast. Vengeance was foremost in their minds, the taste of defeat the previous year still metallic in their collective mouths.

The spirit of competition was thick in the air, but staunch friendships had been formed in the past, and the hunt was a chance to renew these acquaintances.

Amid the clatter of breakfast dishes, varmint hunting talk filled the room with a low roar. Greetings and jibes were exchanged and hands were clasped across the tables. Seated among all the confusion, forking a platter of hotcakes and greeting one and all in the mild manner of the gentleman that he is, was Sam Dudley. If coyotes talk, the name of this man has been passed from state to state and den to den.

In my opinion, Dudley is the finest field varmint caller in the world. I've seen a lot of them the country over and some damn good ones, but this man is tops. George Wright, a top California caller, had declared before this event my own summation of this man's ability. Said George, "We may beat Arizona, but we won't beat Sam Dudley."

In years, Sam is no kid. He was more than sixty-five then and still held an active job. With a twinkle in his eye, he'll relate how many jobs have come and gone because they interfered with his hunting.

I've hunted with Sam on too few occasions, but we try to make it at least once a year. Seeing him in action, I come away filled with increased admiration of the man's ability to read and understand the sign and habits of his quarry. If Sam tells me to hold my rifle sight on one spot and shoot "the ole dog that steps in it," I'll slip my safety. One's going to coyote heaven right there.

Although every Californian probably secretly hoped Sam would not be able to make the hunt, each realized that, without him, it would not be the same. I heard someone say, "Oh, hell, Sam Dudley's here. Better shoot for second place."

VARMINT HUNTER'S DIGEST

The hunt was set up as a twenty-four-hour, two-man team affair, beginning Saturday at noon and terminating at noon on Sunday. My partner, Ron Holdstock, given the opportunity to get out, would be a tough one to beat by any caller — maybe even Dudley.

We had commandeered that secret weapon that we hoped would be the key to doing our part in the event for California.

Neatly trailered behind Ron's pickup was a sleek, sixteen-foot boat powered by a seventy-five-horsepower Johnson outboard motor. The manufacturer had been quite enthusiastic about our project, after I explained to their personnel just what a varmint caller is. I guess they understood.

Our plan was to get down the river far enough to leave the landlocked callers behind, enter virgin country and reap the harvest. The country along the Colorado is accessible by roads only for a short distance. Beyond, we would skim off the cream and emerge victorious. A real milk run. Or so it seemed at the time.

As the callers assembled at the Blythe marina, which had been designated as headquarters, Ron and I were treated to a variety of advice — of dubious value and intent — as we loaded the craft with gasoline, warm clothes, hip boots, mucho ammo, food, booze and the other necessities of survival in the wilderness. Our armament consisted of a .243, a .222 magnum, a Winchester Model 1200 pump gun in 12 gauge and a Browning A-5 12 gauge. Each of us had Arizona licenses as well as the tickets of our home state, which would enable us to strike down the enemy on both sides of the river.

At this point, we noted with some dismay that the river was pretty low. As a matter of fact, I imagine that I could probably have run across it at this point without getting my sneakers wet. Undaunted, we planned to continue with our project. There has to be enough water in the Colorado to float a boat — doesn't there?

In seeking the varmint hunting title during annual California-Arizona competition, Dougherty used all of the basics of cover and concealment, but found that these practices didn't always help greatly.

The team of Ron Holdstock and Jim Dougherty, often dubbed the Dubious Brothers, found there were added benefits when they procured a boat to cruise up and down length of the Colorado River in search of eligible varmints.

As zero hour approached, the callers broke into smaller groups, comparing notes as to where to go and what to do. Sign-ins complete, it was noted that California had fielded ninety-four men, Arizona twenty-four. The rules were read again by George Allison, then state vice-president for California, and Jack Naperella of the Cactus Staters. Tails were to be brought in with at least six inches of the back hide attached. One of the contestants, majoring in game biology at the University of Arizona, had requested that all foxes taken be brought in to help him in his study of the little beasties.

With these final comments, the hunters were dismissed to travel their respective ways. Ron and I swaggered toward our little craft. My brother-in-law, Holt Dandridge, came down to wish us well and help us embark. His parting words were that, should I fail to return, he would take possession of my Browning over-and-under.

Our amphibious attack started well enough, but then the Blythe marina had water. It was the rest of the Colorado River that didn't. We were barely out of sight of our array of well-wishers when we ran aground. It was over the side for me to tug on a rope, pulling our gallant vessel over the sandbar, as Ron offered sage advice (while rattling a pair of ball bearings in the palm of his hand) from his position in the bow. He looked a little like George Washington crossing the Delaware, except that in that escapade, no one had to get out and walk.

Hell, if General George had run into our problems, the country would still belong to the Redcoats and bobcats!

Eventually we made deep water. I was cognizant of this as I suddenly slipped from sight beneath the rippling surface and returned to the top, clawing frantically for the bow, uttering four-letter phrases amid the bubbles. Unsympathetic, Ron ventured, "Now we can start the motor." Three hours had elapsed since the beginning of the hunt and we had yet to make a stand.

In the channel at last, we started the big seventy-five and headed downstream on the way to making a hunt out of what was beginning to look like another weekly chapter of *Sea Hunt.* I lit a cigarette, scanning the shore for suitable hunting grounds.

The first game we sighted were three deer watering at the shoreline. Minutes later, we rounded a bend and came upon a small flock of magnificent Canada geese. Laws prohibiting shooting from a power boat saved a couple of lives.

Our first stand was on the Arizona side of the river, where we got our initial look at the game sign in the area. Almost immediately after stepping ashore, we jumped six deer. Before the stand was complete, we had seen ten more and the ground was tromped with deer tracks. We failed to call in any shootable game and continued downstream, seeking another suitable location for beaching.

All along the river, the sound of shotguns being discharged at the variety of local game birds reached our

VARMINT HUNTER'S DIGEST 217

When the opening of the annual hunting competition was sounded, the rush by varmint hunters to find likely looking hunting grounds had some of the aspects of a full-scale demolition derby, Dougherty soon learned.

ears. We had yet to get away from the easily accessible areas. We made one more stand before dark and both of us were quite surprised that this too was a blank, as coyote and cat signs were thick.

In the last hour of legal shotgunning, the sporadic shooting turned to a barrage, as flights of widgeon, pintails, mallards and teal wheeled and whirred overhead. The shooting was annoying, as this could prove a bad scene where high-strung coyotes are concerned. It didn't annoy us enough, though, to curtail the stoning of a nice drake mallard that soared by as Ron prepared to cook dinner on a sandbar. I dropped him and the current swept him swiftly away. I caught him just two steps after I went into water over my boots. Things still were not quite working out.

Running a boat down a river of the magnitude of the Colorado is not a thing to be taken lightly, especially after the sun has set so gloriously in the West. I was glad to have Ron as a partner. His years of chartering and fishing the high seas and his familiarity with all sizes of boats in all types of water instilled confidence. The fact that you die clean by drowning isn't enough to make me a willing candidate.

With the coming of the moon, the air took on a chill and the shivers down our backs were increased by the gabble and cluck of great honkers flying high overhead to feed. The sound of wild geese is ample reward to me for getting out into the open spaces and we discussed the hopeful possibility of snagging a couple before we returned on the morrow.

The moon brightened the dark sky to give us light enough to travel and, with the equipment repacked as neatly as possible, Ron turned the big mill to life with a flick of the electric starter. The big engine purred like a contented kitten as we slid downstream. It was as though we were in another world in the center of this mighty river.

Along the shore, the brush grew close and thick. Calling would be a problem. The best apparent bet would be to call the larger sandbars that lay along the waterway in hopes of suckering the critters into these openings. As night varmint hunting was legal only in California, we could eliminate scrutinizing the Arizona side. We picked a bar and slid ashore to make a stand.

Night hunting is tricky business and in such cramped quarters I selected the Winchester pump gun, while Ron grabbed up his .243. For loads, I shoved three Mark 5 No. 4 buckshot into the smoothbore and we settled down to wait for things to quiet.

After five minutes I began wailing away on my Weems All Call.

After about three minutes, Ron began to work the light and we picked up the eyes of a bobcat.

He was quite eager for something and, at ten yards, I gave it to him, the roar of the shotgun destroying the night — and the cat.

Two hours later we had bagged the cat's big brother and a fox, both taken by Ron with two of the finest rifle shots I've ever witnessed. Things were looking pretty fair for the *African Queen's* crew — then we ran out of water.

For some reason, I had the only pair of waders, which were too big for Ron and thus eliminated the possibility of his having to use them. Back to the rope. For a course in instant physical fitness, I suggest that you try towing a sixteen-foot vessel, one dry varmint hunter, three varmints and the necessary paraphernalia around one of the country's largest rivers, looking for water.

About sunup, we found enough to float in and began to pick our way back upstream. Almost the entire night had been lost to us and we hoped to recoup on coyotes in the early daylight hours. We had just tapped the beginning of the good country and now we had to leave it behind.

With plenty of water it would have been no problem, as the big Johnson will push the boat along at forty

When the annual series was ended and the varmint count made, properly designed trophies were handed out to the winners, but the author found himself among the winners only on rare occasions, despite his inventive approaches.

A bearded and dirty Jim Dougherty appears rather hopeless as he surveys the desert terrain for likely varmint sign.

miles per hour, but with no water, feeling out the channels was time-consuming work. We made as many stands as we dared and never got a strike.

We collected a bonus on our last stand. As we sat on a slight outcropping of rocks, Ron's warning hiss caused me to look in the pointed direction. Wings set in a tight formation came a flock of about a dozen snow geese. They were high, but possibly I could scratch one with the big No. 4 buck. As they passed overhead, I got into action with Ron's Browning and was pleasantly surprised as the first two shots brought down the two lead birds.

With our bag of two cats, one fox, one mallard and two geese, we reached headquarters at 11:30 and collapsed on shore as those who had arrived before us came down to view the spent seamen.

"Here comes Dudley!" Sam and his partner, Harold Thompson, had collected eight coyotes and one fox. I could hear someone swear. I closed my eyes and laughed, while George Wright looked down at the ground, toed a rock and just shook his head.

So it came to pass that while California had beaten Arizona, possibly by force of numbers, Invincible Sam remained invincible. Scores were taken from the top ten returning teams from each side. The big ticket was bobcats, as the Arizonians had failed to score on one kitty. Of the forty-seven California teams, twenty-seven had blanked out completely. The bag was pretty equally distributed, with coyotes holding a bit of an edge over fox and cats.

The Arizona biologist who was collecting foxes had a field day as he gleefully loaded his truck with the critters and interrogated the hunters as to where, how and so on, jotting it all down in his notebook.

The .243 was the big gun for the hunt and has to be given the number one cartridge position among these varmint hunters. The rest ran to many extremes, but there was a surprising number of shotguns.

The hunt over, Ron and I loafed in the shade, resting from our amphibious ordeal.

"You know, Dougherty, I never believed I'd see the day when you couldn't call one coyote." So we made a stand and promptly busted a dog that boiled in to give a look.

As I lifted him up, I said to Ron, "See, just like Sam Dudley."

"Not quite," said my partner, slinging his rifle. "Dudley does it when it counts."

The man had a point.

Gun World Magazine's staff meetings are conducted with dignity and some ceremony. The field men are expected to make quick, accurate replies to the questions of the chief. And since this magazine had been sponsoring my participation in varmint calling contests, I was expected to have answers.

Jack Lewis tossed a hard look down the length of the table at me through the V created by his crossed cowboy boots propped on the conference table. "The Savage 110-MCL, what have you done with her?"

"Shot it, sir," I quavered.

"We didn't expect you to row a boat with it. What does it do?"

I felt like replying that it made a loud noise when the trigger was pulled, but curbed my tongue and reported crisply that it "holds minute of angle groups easily; factory ammo first rate; handloads of 37.5 grains 4895 with 55-grain Speer bullets excellent, but not necessarily superior to Remington factory 55-grain s.p. bullets. Excellent on animals in varmint category. Four coyotes, one cat taken on the last field operation, all one-shot kills, normal .22-250."

"We are not talking calibers. What about the gun itself? What's different about it? Come, James, I'm a busy man."

"Weight, six and three-quarters; barrel length, twenty-four inches; safety, top tang model; left-hand design; fully enclosed bolt head with double front locking lugs, five-shot capacity, makes a loud noise when the trigger is pulled...sir!"

I stood. One must use all the diplomacy and salesmanship at his disposal in moments such as this. Besides, I wanted to be able to move quickly. "Last year you procured a boat for Ron Holdstock and myself, so we might go down to the river in boats for the big varmint hunting contest.

"Well, the boat deal didn't work and I thought I'd take the Savage and nip off to the latest hunt to continue the field test, but first off...could you get me an airplane?"

"An airplane," Lewis repeated.

"Yes, sir, an airplane. I have another plan."

So, it came to be that Holdstock and I once more were entered for the annual Arizona vs. California championships. The boys at the office titled it Operation Critterclobber.

On one occasion, Dougherty attempted to steal a march on competitors by hiring an airplane to get him into neglected area where he expected to find hunting good.

VARMINT HUNTER'S DIGEST 221

Besides the big bash between two large varmint calling organizations, the California State Field Championships would be decided during the same twenty-four-hour hunt. On paper, the plan looked better than perfect: get into a prime area, away from the crowd, and reap the harvest. I had made arrangements to fly into the Swink Ranch some three hundred-plus miles north of the contest headquarters in Blythe, California, and hunt out of a vehicle that ranch foreman Bob Walls promised to have ready to go. The timetable was laid out to be minute perfect, as a late arrival at the headquarters area on Sunday would be disqualification grounds.

The last days before the big event Holdstock and I spent in readying our gear and rechecking the arsenal. I was taking the Savage 110-MCL and a Ruger Blackhawk .357 magnum. Ron chose his custom .243 and also took along a handgun, a Ruger Single Six .22 magnum. On the range, I tacked in the rifle again with a Weaver six-power scope to hold one-inch high at a hundred yards. We cut the gear down to a minimum of two lights, camera, ammo, calls and warm clothes, as any desert in January is cold; even the edge of Death Valley, where we figured to be. Two Thermos jugs for black coffee were a must and for eats we took a dozen sandwiches, apples and candy bars.

The Blythe marina had been offered as headquarters once again for the hunt. It was from here that, a year earlier, we had launched our boat into the mighty Colorado, then spent twenty hours looking for enough water to float it. When we pulled into the marina, after eating breakfast in Blythe, I was appalled. Never before have so many varmint callers assembled at one time. Trucks, jeeps, cars and desert buggies were parked row upon row and we had trouble finding a place to park our truck.

The list of those present was a real Who's Who in varmint calling, ranging from the legendary Sam Dudley and famed call-maker Jack Cain, through top-flight competitors in world and national calling events with whom I had knocked heads through more than one occasion, beating a few, losing to others. Don Williams is the fifth Arizonian to take a mountain lion by calling, while California's sole claim to lion killing fame is held by Stubby Dills of the Orange County chapter of the CVCA. When you see callers of their caliber lined up for a hunt, you begin to wonder how in hell you can ever hope to beat them.

George Allison, president of the South Bay Chapter, made a surprise announcement with presentation of the Dudley Cup. Suitably inscribed to the *Grand Old Man of Varmint Calling*, it was to be presented on Sam Dudley's behalf from this hunt on to the best showing by an individual chapter. We of California had all seven of our chapters represented, while Arizona had four.

Tension and excitement mounted as noon rolled up. Engines were started and 284 callers got ready to roll out. There was a surprising number of gals making the hunt. One was Dixie Lee Kitts of Arizona, one of the few if not only woman to complete the rugged Arizona Big Ten. This feat includes taking the bighorn sheep, mountain lion, buffalo, elk, mule deer, whitetail, bear and others.

Allison yelled, "Let's go!" into the loud-speaker and the resulting rush would have made the grand dash of the Cherokee Strip look like a kiddie car parade. The mass of vehicles screaming like bats out of hell for a one-lane road was a beautiful sight.

There was no particular rush to get out, as there was a traffic jam that would do credit to the Hollywood Freeway. We made sure we had everything from food to stay-awake pills; ammo to camo and even a few trinkets for luck, like owl feathers and old bear teeth.

We were four minutes late and our pilot was waiting for us with a warmed-up Cessna 210 at the Blythe Airport. Neale Perkins, a top-notch private pilot with close to 3000 hours of air time, heads up Safariland, a custom leather-working operation that makes shooting accessories. Neale's talk about the weather didn't set well as we loaded up. High winds, some rain and getting worse was the forecast. It looked bad in Blythe and wasn't expected to be better anyplace else. If anything wrecks calling, it's the wind.

At seven thousand feet we could see the problem and feel it, as the 210 bounced through rough air. The ground looked a long way down but considerably more stable. We talked about guns, bullets and flying experiences and looked over the California desert from our spectacular vantage point. It was unique to see all the country that we knew firsthand from the ground from this perspective, to note how much of it was virtually inaccessible from the ground.

Bucking headwinds cut our time down a bit and Perkins stated that this was about as bad as anything he had previously encountered. Ron began to look as though he hoped he could find a long rope as we bounced, dipped and, once in awhile, fell a little. That was all right, though, since once in awhile we'd bounce up a little bit.

The windsock on the strip, cut out of the desert, was spinning around like a runaway second hand as Perkins circled several times, trying to figure the wind.

"Well, we'll one-wheel it," he decided and began a descent that was like a greenwing teal bombing into a decoy set, side-slipped, rocked her back and forth and slipped the plane onto the runway without raising a puff of dust.

"What about that, Holdstock?" I asked. "Pretty, huh?"

"I had my eyes closed."

I stepped out of the Cessna and damned near became airborne. The wind was hitting forty knots and rising. Simply grand.

An hour later found us in a truck, driving through the bush. The wind grew worse and tumbleweeds blew by, thirty feet in the air.

"Well, here's another mess you got me into," was about all Ron could come up with. Things really didn't look too bright, but I could have been pulling him around the river in that damn boat again.

When I decided to make a stand in a thick run of dead mesquite, Ron thought I was a bit dinged in the cranial cavity, but it didn't figure we would make any points sitting in the cab of the truck.

You couldn't really say it was a stand, as I don't think five seconds had passed before a coyote hurled himself down the barrel of the Savage. A real tricky accuracy test at ten feet!

I hit the call again and chuckled as Ron asked softly, "What kept ya?" Another coyote appeared downwind, but as soon as the hard wind cut his nose, he wheeled and vanished. One couldn't ask for a better start than that, though — a double in on the first stand; one down and we weren't even warmed up.

VARMINT HUNTER'S DIGEST

"Must have some luck things going for us," said Ron as we dragged the big dog back to the truck.

We got in one more stand before dark, then settled down to wait for a bit and have a sandwich topped off with coffee and a candy bar.

It was a couple of hours before any further action. This stand got us up a cat. It was about ten yards away when I saw him, just sitting there out of the soft edge of the light I had pointed well up. I leaned forward and whispered to Ron, who was facing away. "There's a bob-

To sharpen his shooting eye, Dougherty engages in a bit of instinctive shooting, aiming at a ration can that has been tossed in the air by his hunting partner. He found he was better on cans than he was on proper game!

While cruising the Colorado River in search of varmints, the team of Dougherty and Holdstock soon found themselves lost in the heavy fog.

cat trying to get in my pocket. Would you mind terribly shooting him?"

When he turned around, I hit the cat with the full spot and he was still walking forward. At the shot, the cat went four feet up, then ran straight at us, turning off a few short feet away into the brush. He was nicked, but apparently not hit hard. A close shot can be real tricky with a scoped rifle at night.

Somewhere in the vicinity of two in the freezing morning, we got up a fox that galloped in like there was no tomorrow and stopped. Ron was ready but didn't shoot.

"I think it's a kit fox." Kits are protected and we didn't want to take a chance, so passed.

An hour later, we got up another cat. Unfortunately, it was clear across a meadow and wouldn't come out to give Ron a good shot. We waited and coaxed, using about umpteen calls. He would stare until Ron was about one pound on the trigger away from blowing off his head, then would duck. Finally he was gone.

At five o'clock exactly, the wind died. Six minutes later, a cat appeared and sashayed right in to about fifty yards. Ron lowered the boom with the .22-250 and that was that. At ten after five, the wind started again, only harder.

Bullet performance on the last cat was interesting. It hit straight-on, didn't exit and made no mark on the handsome hide; unusual for a 55-grain soft-point. With the coyote, the same type of bullet had created a three-inch exit hole. There was, of course, about 49½ yards difference in distance.

Always placing high in the varmint hunting sequence were the individuals who had done well in the world varmint calling championships. The 1960 world titlists were (from right) Bill Dudley, Arizona, first; Doug Kittredge, California, second; and Dave Niehuis, Arizona, third.

By eight-thirty, when it was time to quit and fly back to Blythe, we had the definite feeling that no matter what — angles, attack, planning, good luck charms, rabbit scent, good calls, good calling or voodoo fetishes — Somebody Up There just didn't like us.

To go prancing into headquarters with only a cat and a coyote galled us to the core.

"We'll probably crash in the middle of the desert," was Ron's final prediction, as we climbed into the plane where he promptly fell asleep.

We rolled into headquarters fifteen minutes before noon and noted that the main body of varmint busters was in ahead of us. We didn't have a chance to place, but it appeared the wind had affected the calling for most teams as seriously as it had us.

The Arizona point system had been used which gives twenty for cats, seven for coyotes and five for fox. Lions and wolves, which weren't lying around in heaps, each are worth one hundred. The scorekeepers were busy tallying the points, but I created no mathematical problems for them with our offering of a whopping twenty-seven. By the final count, California had emerged victorious with 476 to Arizona's 269. The breakdown on animals went like this: California — fifteen bobcats, thirty-two coyotes, fifteen foxes, to Arizona's five bobcats, twenty-three coyotes and three foxes. From a statistical angle, only twenty-five percent of each side's teams scored. From the looks on the faces of the callers, many of them had put in some hard hours. The driving times of some were equal to the hunting time, with many going clear into Mexico where, I learned the wind did not blow.

The hunt was not as hard on the critters as on the hunters.

"Well, buddy," I said, "there's always next year."

Holdstock gave me a rather sorry look. "You always say that."

It was another year and the council fires burned brightly in the Great Lodge of the Gun World tribe. The distant stacatto of electric typewriters rumbled faintly under the polished nails of lithe, sloe-eyed maiden secretaries. The warriors were plotting. The Great Chief spoke.

"Once again the time of year comes when the Long Knife coyote hunters gather and our war chief" (with an

226   VARMINT HUNTER'S DIGEST

inclining nod in my direction) "requests aid from his leaders."

There were a few suppressed groans.

The Great Chief resumed, "We have supplied you with boats, with the big bird that flies in the sky, guns and ammunition, even expense accounts. What is it that you wish us to do this time?"

Each member leaned a little closer, there was a tensing of muscles, all eyes were riveted on me as I carefully laid aside the firearm whose scope mounts I had been adjusting and cleared my throat.

"It is true, you have in the past answered all my requests for equipment to aid in my cunning schemes, as I battle against the vast gathering of coyote hunters. True, indeed, that you gave me a boat when there was no water to float it, truer still that a great sky-bird was at my disposal when there was too much wind to fly it. Once again they gather on the shores of the mighty Colorado, an estimated three hundred strong, and it is true that once again there is something that I need." I paused for dramatic effect. A war chief must raise a fever pitch in any council.

"I need three boxes of 12-gauge, three-inch magnum shells, one box each of 2s, Oh and Double Oh buck." I sat down. The uncomprehending pause that followed lasted for several minutes. Finally the silence was broken. "That's all? No tanks? Light cannon? No aircraft carrier? How about a blimp? Just three boxes of shotgun shells?"

I nodded calmly, having already returned my attention to the troublesome mount on the rifle. As if it were an omen, I stripped a screw.

And so the annual Arizona-California Varmint Callers hunt was begun on a wonderful, clean and bright day on the shores of the Colorado River out of Needles, California. The Needles marina was jammed with vehicles when our little caravan of three trucks pulled into the meeting area. My partner again was that famed, legendary hero of previous sagas of despair and defeat, Ron "Lone Buzzard" Holdstock. We had, in true war party tradition, spent a portion of the previous evening in one of Needles' more sedate big medicine lodges. The front door was easy to find; we simply backtracked the blood trail from the parking lot to the swinging doors of this most unique haven of primitive native dance.

In spite of our own previous thrashings of a personal nature, Lone Buzzard and I again were confident we had

Jerry Mills, considered one of the more knowledgeable of the California-based hunters, poses with his take of one coyote and two bobcats taken during a night of hunting and calling in reaches of the California desert.

VARMINT HUNTER'S DIGEST

the answer to the problem of how to succeed on this hunt.

By pulling a few strings, we had succeeded in obtaining permission to hunt on a great piece of highly protected real estate and we would have it all to ourselves. There should be critters in profusion, waiting to hurl themselves upon us. The country was extremely brushy, being right on the river's edge, justification for the powerful request I had made at the council meeting. A rifle in this cover would be out of the question, while three-inch magnums would be fast-pointing and devastating under these conditions. We had high hopes, great confidence and a sure feeling that this time it was our turn.

The meeting area was a picture of activity, particularly in the lines where teams stood waiting to pay their fee of entry. California's Dick Graham grinned broadly from under a pile of the long green, as over a hundred California two-man teams already had signed in. Each team signed up with its chapter affiliation, as each team also was in competition for the state field championships, the top ten in the interstate hunt, various chapter functions and each chapter from both sides was in competition for the prestige trophy, the Dudley Cup.

Loud-speakers called attention to various important items, assembled callers for sign-up, repeated points of information and the fact that coffee was available.

(Left) Members of the first organized California club hoist their colors at beginning of interstate contest.
(Below) A variety of clothing, headgear is favored by serious varmint hunters who dote on individualism.

The contests would not have been complete without a few friendly wagers involving the outcome of two-state hunts.

Banners of each chapter flew in the gusty breeze, while over it all flew the flag of the United States and the California state flag signifying that we were hosts for this event. Representatives of the Fish and Wildlife Service were on hand to brief callers as to closed areas along the river and to answer questions.

At ten to noon, George Allison, then California president, and Jack Naperella, the Arizona leader, climbed to the top of the command post and began their instructions. Extreme emphasis was placed on the penalties against any team observed spotlighting from a moving vehicle and a breakdown of each state's game laws and regulations as they apply to our sport. Introductions were made of the Federal officers and mention was made of the California Highway Patrol's requests for prudence while in the area. A final roll call of all signed-in teams was made to insure against any eager beavers who might have slipped away in order to get a head start.

We were advised of what was required in the form of proof of kill and at 12:15 the great varmint callers' landrush took place as almost three hundred vehicles roared forward into one great ball-up that would have put the ill-famed Hollywood Freeway to shame.

Wild Bill Koutnik was shipping out from the marina in a pontoon boat properly decked out in flying pennants, camouflage rigging and poop deck, while he strode fore and aft complete in a camo admiral's hat and full dress sword. Such cries of command to his one-man crew, Stan Germain, as "jibe the anchor, furl your rudder and jettison the poopdeck" were extremely nautical in sound if not in authenticity. The last I saw was Captain Bill wildly waving his sword and screaming, "Mr. Germain!" as Ron and I made our way out of the area in his four-wheel-drive Toyota.

One could assume that with so many callers, the area would be overcrowded, hunting would be dangerous — not to mention confusing — and the animals within this area would suffer heavily. This is not the case. From the Needles rendezvous, caller teams scattered out as far as four hundred miles in every direction, some as far as Mexico to the south and Utah to the northwest.

Our destination was not too far south and our plans called for the sacking of perhaps a half-dozen coyotes before dark, some leisurely night hunting and a grand coup in the early morning hours preceding our casual, victorious drive back to headquarters by the following noon. It goes without saying that this did not occur.

By dark, we both lay gasping in the sand drawing air into tortured lungs after expending breath into reeded instruments we both believed to be infallible. Not a single critter had we seen, much less tallied, and my three boxes of shells still counted up to seventy-five rounds.

To the south, deep in Mexico, George Allison and Don Carper were just beginning to hunt, having driven deep into the country and planning to hunt back. Their strategy called for all-night hunting and it began to pay off immediately. In the course of their night's hunt only a few stands failed to produce a varmint and the majority of these were nailed with shooting of what

Dougherty holds his rifle where it can be brought into action quickly if his call brings in a coyote.

At the end of the contest, author takes in his bag to be tallied by the judges and final announcement.

Allison referred to as "about a hundred-percent increase in our normal efficiency."

LeRoy Janulewicz and his partner, Ralph Whited, got involved in some rather stimulating action themselves. The big event came when the two, armed only with Ralph's .243, made a stand along a rocky ridge in the late afternoon. LeRoy called and soon observed a large coyote standing out some 150 yards. Watching the dog in his binoculars, LeRoy instructed Ralph to shoot him. Eyes glued to the lenses, our boy watched and waited for the report and the coyote to fall. At the shot he loudly proclaimed, "You missed! Shoot! Shoot again!"

Ralph, in the meantime, was somewhat perplexed in that the big coyote that lay flopping not six feet from LeRoy certainly didn't look nor act as though it had been missed.

At this point, LeRoy became aware that something wasn't quite as it should be and lowered his glasses. He looked at the coyote, at Ralph, then out to the original subject of his interest. With a squawk, he grabbed the rifle from a startled partner and proceeded to chase the first coyote off with a whizzing torrent of 100-grain pills.

Somewhere in the high country of Nevada, an unidentified caller looked up in time to see three bears bearing down on his location at a pace that could not by any manner be considered casual. According to the report, the pace set by the caller back to his vehicle also was not to be considered casual.

While all about these callers were getting into the thick of things, Lone Buzzard and I still had yet to score. Our campfire lit up the dark of the desert as we burned a couple of venison steaks to an edible point, then topped them off with a piece of cake and some scalding coffee. The aroma of burning meat drifted downwind, the barking of coyotes some fifty yards away brought us scrambling for our lights and shootum sticks. No coyotes could see through the thick cover of the salt cedar, so Ron began his eerie chant to the desert dogs. Yipping and howling, he soon had the desert alive with answering coyotes, from a half to four miles away. They were here after all, but why couldn't we get any in?

It wasn't too long after that we caught on. From the sound of things, the coyotes were in the midst of the rut. The snarling bark of several males could be heard throughout the night. The coyotes were not interested in what we had going for them when there was more serious action taking place.

I've seen this happen before. On one occasion it happened to Sam Dudley and me in southern Arizona. We had one good day of calling and the next was a dud. The dogs were running together and overnight their interest in calls, food and other less-earthy matters vanished. Ron and I could only assume that this was the problem now.

Naturally, it had to figure that, with another good plan going for us, something would have to go wrong. It could also well be that there was a definite lack of talent involved but this is too drastic an assumption. We are content to lay the blame at the feet of the unpredictable gods that govern such things and the shattering fact that this hunt for us is nothing less than a vast disaster. By ten o'clock, we had succeeded in knocking off two gray foxes for a grand total of eight points. Not a coyote had we seen, save one fleeting glimpse of a dog crossing a desolate road in our headlights. We may have collected him as we made a stand close by, but it was here that one fox came slamming in and four points in hand is better than a now-dubious eight. I clobbered the fox without hesitation.

Nothing is as dull nor as frustrating as stand upon stand of unrewarded effort. We tried every trick in the bag and even invented a few. I personally changed calls and calling styles five times. We used scent, we howled at the coyotes and called them names. We climbed trees and called under a full, golden moon in sandy washes without a light, hoping that maybe one would run over us in the dark.

By one in the cold, freezing morning, I was angry, Ron was sore and the critters were unconcerned. I cannot recall ever going hunting when I reached such a point as to be one hundred percent full out and totally mad. We moved into better-looking bobcat country and made stands up to forty minutes long. In the distance, great horned owls could be heard. Even the owls which will always give a call several hair-raising passes would not be lured and not a bobcat did we see.

It points out that no matter what you think you may know of this calling of game you will never fully understand it all and you are always vulnerable to a face-losing smash.

(Right) Exhausted after the weekend ordeal of sleeplessness, Dougherty catches a few winks in the shade of a convenient tree.

Proper rifle and ammunition combo is subject to same individualism as the mode of dress affected by the contestants at the big hunt.

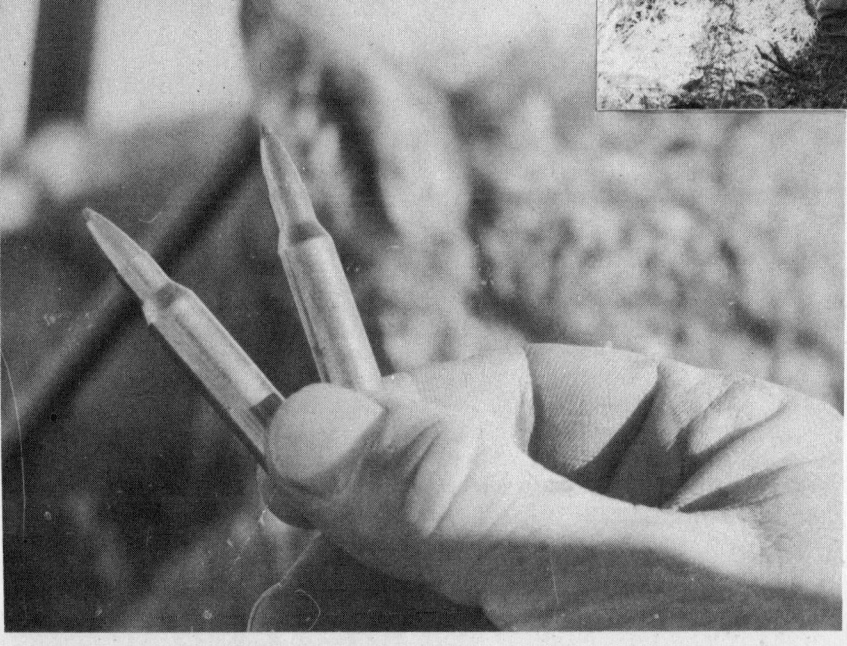

VARMINT HUNTER'S DIGEST

Dougherty checks tooth wear on one of the coyotes he downed during annual hunt to gain some idea of its age.

I by no means claim to be the all-knowing varmint caller, but I do have enough confidence in my ability and in the combination of Ron's and mine to enter any calling event with more than a little confidence.

You begin to lose it after twenty empty stands with the weather knifing through your heavy clothes and toes so cold that walking becomes a hardship. You also begin to wish that you had requested a blimp. At least, we could be doing something unusual.

If our luck was bad, Captain Koutnik's luck would have to be considered really rotten. Sometime in the late afternoon, this fearless leader eased his ponderous craft into a shallow lagoon and stood by to drop anchor. He made fast and led his party of one ashore to hunt. Upon returning to the vessel some hours later, the stalwart captain and his crew stood aghast on the bank of the mighty Colorado. There high and dry, a full quarter-mile from the river, stood the good ship *Bountyhunter*. The receding and unpredictable waters of the Colorado had drained their little lagoon and left the noble craft in the center of two acres of slimy, bottomless, stinking mud. The hunt ended at noon the following day, Sunday. The crew of two finally made it home Monday night, a little late for check-in time.

For some, the hunt was a bundle of action and activity. A team from the San Diego chapter laid into the critters with a whoop and a holler and, when the dust had settled, they counted up seven bobcats, one coyote and a total of 113 points. The Orange County outfit nailed up an impressive two cats, nine coyotes and one fox for 106 points, while another San Diego team clinched third with 101 points for three cats, four coyotes and six fox.

Allison and Carper, way down South of the Border, did in two cats, seven coyotes and two fox for ninety-four to tie with another San Diego group that tallied six bobcats and one fox. Down about thirty-second came Lone Buzzard and Gut Shot with their three foxes, for somehow we managed to add another big four points at nine the following morning.

This final fox bears mentioning, though, in that Holdstock did him in on the dead run with his Smith & Wesson .22 Jet at thirty yards and it made a total of seven straight running shots that Lonely has pulled off with his adept handgun handling.

The varminting partners await announcement of the winners in the contest.

As we limped into Needles at a little after eleven, we noticed two callers carrying a coyote back to their truck parked on the shoulder of the road. Wanting to see what a coyote looked like, we stopped to pass the time of day. The infectious enthusiasm of one caller about tore it. He reported that in the last hour they had dumped three big dogs, all within a half hour of town in wide-open, arid desert that was fast growing hot. He went further to report that many teams had experienced considerable action within a forty-mile radius of town on the way back in.

Many teams failed to score at all and a number came in with only one or two critters, but even one cat is still better than three foxes. The Federal people were on hand at the grand tally and expressed considerable interest in the accomplishments, indicating that the varmint callers have a place in the control of predators. A total of 150 varmints were bagged over several thousand miles of country.

One could wonder what possibly could go wrong to add a final fitting note to such a dismal performance. Ron was wondering just that and had no more than put this thought into words than, with a great clatter, over a hundred miles from home, the engine in the Toyota gave up and died with an anguished scream.

As we coasted to a halt, I looked to my partner who was close to tears and asked, "Does that answer your question?"

In dusk of the final day, trophies go to the winners, while members of various clubs hear the results.

VARMINT HUNTER'S DIGEST

RIFLES FOR VARMINTS

Generally speaking, the varmint calling enthusiast with experience in the field tends to favor a bolt-action center-fire rifle. The calibers, of course, tend to differ with individual preference.

These days, the .30-30 is not considered the ideal deer rifle by many. In fact, there are many serious hunters who tend to look down on it. But the fact still remains that there probably have been more deer brought down with the .30-30 rifle than any other cartridge.

This is true, too, of the varmint rifle. The serious callers of coyotes, bobcats, et al., tend to favor the smaller calibers with their fast, flat trajectory bullets. But as indicated in this volume, in the course of history, chances are that the venerable .30/06 probably has downed more varmints in the past seventy-five years than any other caliber.

The same is true of the slide-action, the lever-action and semiautomatic rifles. At any gathering of varmint callers, one will find a smattering of these designs among the populace. Those that are felt to fit the game to be hunted are included in this listing. Prices are those of 1978.

BOLT ACTION CENTERFIRE RIFLES

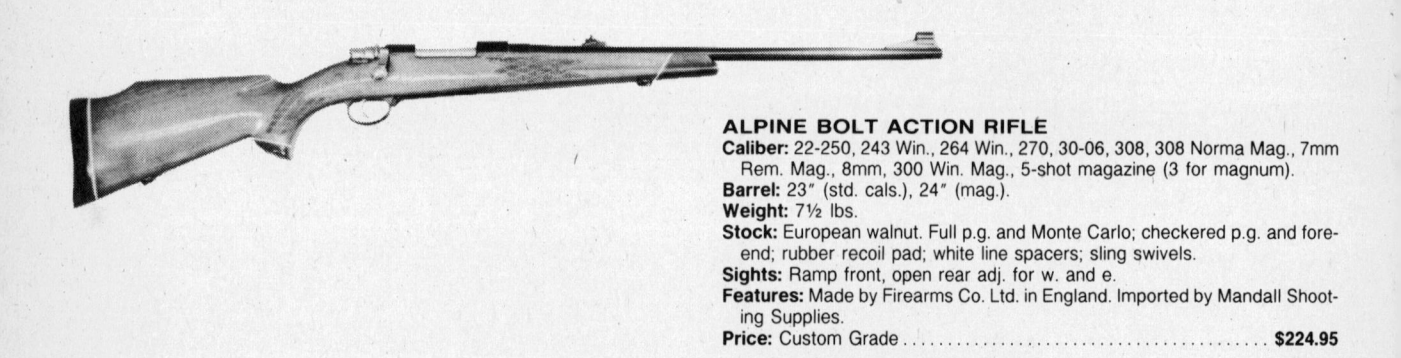

ALPINE BOLT ACTION RIFLE
Caliber: 22-250, 243 Win., 264 Win., 270, 30-06, 308, 308 Norma Mag., 7mm Rem. Mag., 8mm, 300 Win. Mag., 5-shot magazine (3 for magnum).
Barrel: 23" (std. cals.), 24" (mag.).
Weight: 7½ lbs.
Stock: European walnut. Full p.g. and Monte Carlo; checkered p.g. and fore-end; rubber recoil pad; white line spacers; sling swivels.
Sights: Ramp front, open rear adj. for w. and e.
Features: Made by Firearms Co. Ltd. in England. Imported by Mandall Shooting Supplies.
Price: Custom Grade $224.95

CHAMPLIN RIFLE
Caliber: All std. chamberings, including 458 Win. and 460 Wea. Many wildcats on request.
Barrel: Any length up to 26" for octagon. Choice of round, straight taper octagon, or octagon with integral quarter rib, front sight ramp and sling swivel stud.
Length: 45" over-all. **Weight:** About 8 lbs.
Stock: Hand inletted, shaped and finished. Checkered to customer specs. Select French, Circassian or claro walnut. Steel p.g. cap, trap buttplate or recoil pad.
Sights: Bead on ramp front, 3-leaf folding rear.
Features: Right or left hand Champlin action, tang safety or optional shroud safety, Canjar adj. trigger, hinged floorplate.
Price: From $1,780.00

COLT SAUER RIFLE
Caliber: 25-06, 270, 30-06, (std.), 7mm Rem. Mag., 300 Wea. Mag., 300 Win. Mag. (Magnum).
Barrel: 24", round tapered.
Length: 43¾" over-all. **Weight:** 8 lbs. (std.).
Stock: American walnut, cast-off M.C. design with cheekpiece. Fore-end tip and p.g. cap rosewood with white spacers. Hand checkering.
Sights: None furnished. Specially designed scope mounts for any popular make scope furnished.
Features: Unique barrel/receiver union, non-rotating bolt with cam-actuated locking lugs, tang-type safety locks sear. Detachable 3- and 4-shot magazines.
Price: Standard cals. ...... **$599.95**   Magnum cals. **$599.95**

Colt Sauer Short Action Rifle
Same as standard rifle except chambered for 22-250, 243 and 308 Win. 24" bbl., 43" over-all. Weighs 7½ lbs. 3-shot magazine. **$599.95**

DUMOULIN BOLT ACTION RIFLE
Caliber: All commercial calibers.
Barrel: 25".
Weight: 7 lbs. **Length:** 43".
Stock: French walnut with rosewood p.g. cap and fore-end tip, standard or skip line checkering, recoil pad.
Sights: Optional, available at extra cost.
Features: Made to customer requirements using Sako or FN action, with or without engraving (3 grades available). Imported from Belgium by Firearms Center.
Price: .... From **$950.00**

HARRINGTON & RICHARDSON 300 BOLT ACTION
Caliber: 30-06.
Barrel: 22" round, tapered.
Weight: 7¾ lbs. **Length:** 42½" over-all.
Stock: American walnut, hand checkered p.g. and fore-end, Monte Carlo, roll-over cheekpiece.
Sights: Adjustable rear, gold bead ramp front.
Features: Hinged floorplate; sliding side safety; sling swivels, recoil pad. Receiver tapped for scope mount. Sako action.
Price: **$321.50**

HERTER'S MARK J9 RIFLE
Caliber: 22-250, 25-06, 243, 6mm, 270, 308, 30-06, 264, 7mm mag., 300 Win. Mag.
Barrel: 23½".
Weight: 8 lbs. **Length:** 42½".
Stock: Black walnut, rollover cheek piece, ebonite p.g. cap and butt plate.
Sights: Ramp front, rear adj. for w. and e.
Features: Also available w/o sights, with Mannlicher or beavertail style stocks. Three grades (Hunter's, Supreme, Presentation) differ stock finish, style. Also available as actions or barreled actions. Imported from Yugoslavia by Herter's.
Price: Supreme Grade **$200.95**
Price: Presentation Grade **$207.98**

ITHACA LSA-55 STANDARD BOLT ACTION RIFLE
Caliber: 222, 243, 308, 22-250, 6mm Rem.
Barrel: 23" round tapered, full-floating.
Weight: About 6½ lbs. **Length:** 41½" over-all
Stock: Hand checkered walnut, Monte Carlo with built-in swell on p.g.
Sights: Removable rear adj. for w. & e. ramp front.
Features: Detachable 3-shot magazine, adj. trigger, top tang safety. Receiver tapped for scope mounts.
Price: 243, 308, 22-250, 6mm & 222 .... **$329.95**
Price: 270, 30-06 & 25-06 (LSA-65 Deluxe) **$369.95**
Price: 222 heavy bbl. **$399.95**
Price: Heavy Bbl., 22-250 .... **$399.95**

Ithaca LSA-55 Deluxe Bolt Action
Same as the std. except rollover cheekpiece, fore-end tip and pistol grip cap of rosewood with white spacers. Scope mount rings supplied. Sling swivels installed.
Price: 222, 243, 308, 22-250 & 6mm **$369.95**

VARMINT HUNTER'S DIGEST

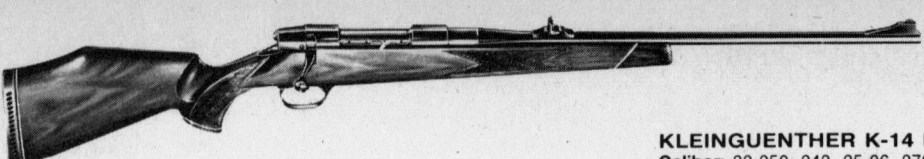

KLEINGUENTHER K-14 INSTA-FIRE RIFLE
Caliber: 22-250, 243, 25-06, 270, 7x57, 7mm Rem. Mag., 30-06, 300 Win. Mag., 308 Win., 308 Norma, 375 H&H, 458 Win.
Barrel: 24", 26".
Weight: 7⅛ lbs. **Length:** 43½" over-all.
Stock: Available in light, medium or dark European walnut. Monte Carlo, hand checkered, cheekpiece, rosewood fore-end tip, rosewood p.g. cap with diamond inlay.
Sights: None furnished. Drilled and tapped for scope mounts. Iron sights optional.
Features: Ultra fast lock/ignition time. Rubber recoil pad, hidden clip, external trigger adj., recessed bolt face, 60° bolt lift. Lifetime warranty. Imported from Germany by Kleinguenther's.
Price: Std. cals. .... $521.00   Mag. cals. $521.00

MANNLICHER-SCHOENAUER M-72 MODEL L/M
Caliber: 22-250, 5.6x57, 6mm Rem. 243, 6.5x57, 270, 7x57, 7x64, 30-06, 308 Win.
Barrel: 20" (full stock), 23½" (half stock).
Weight: 7¼ lbs. (full stock). **Length:** 40" over-all (full stock).
Stock: Full Mannlicher or standard half stock, oil or varnish finish. Rubber recoil pad, hand checkered walnut, Monte Carlo cheekpiece.
Sights: Ramp front, open U-notch rear.
Features: 6 forward locking lugs. 60° bolt throw, wing-type safety. Choice of interchangeable single or double set triggers. Drilled and tapped for scope mounting. Imported by Steyr-Daimler-Puch of America.
Price: Rifle $650.00
Price: Carbine version $689.95

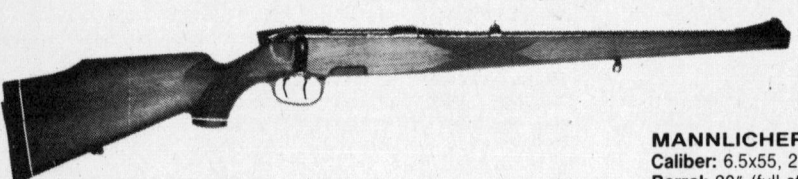

Mannlicher Model L Varmint
Same as Model M except available only in 22-250, 5.6x57, 6mm Rem., 243, 308 Win. Custom hand engraving and stock carving as well as heavy barrel varmint version available $459.95

MANNLICHER MODEL SSG
Caliber: 308 Win.
Barrel: 25½".
Weight: 8½ lbs. **Length:** 44½" over-all.
Stock: Walnut or synthetic.
Sights: Hooded blade front, folding leaf rear or Walther diopter match sight.
Features: Extra magazine included with rifle. 6 rear locking lugs, 60° bolt throw. Adj. trigger. Optional 10-shot magazine available. Imported by L.E.S.
Price: Synthetic stock $475.00
Price: Walnut $525.00

MANNLICHER-SCHOENAUER M-72 MODEL S
Caliber: 6.5x68, 7mm Rem. Mag., 8x68S, 9.3x64, 375 H&H Mag.
Barrel: 25½".
Weight: 8½ lbs. **Length:** 46" over-all.
Stock: Walnut half-stock style, varnished or oil finish. Rubber recoil pad, hand checkered. Monte Carlo cheekpiece.
Sights: Hooded ramp front, U-notch open rear.
Features: 6 forward locking lugs. 60° bolt throw. Wing-type safety. Choice of interchangeable single or double set triggers. Drilled and tapped for scope mounts. Custom engraving and stock carving avail. Imported by Steyr-Daimler-Puch of America.
Price: $750.00

MANNLICHER MODEL M
Caliber: 6.5x55, 270, 7x57, 7x64, 30-06, 8x57JS, 9.3x62, 5-shot.
Barrel: 20" (full stock).
Weight: 6½ lbs. (full stock). **Length:** 39" over-all (full stock).
Stock: Full Mannlicher or standard half stock. Rubber recoil pad, hand checkered walnut. Monte Carlo cheekpiece.
Sights: Ramp front, open U-notch rear.
Features: Extra magazine included. Choice of interchangeable double set or single trigger. Detachable 5-shot rotary magazine. 6 rear locking lugs. Drilled and tapped for scope mounting. Imported by Steyr-Daimler-Puch of America.
Price: $499.00

MANNLICHER MODEL SL
Caliber: 222, 222 Rem. Mag., 223, 5.6x50 Mag.
Barrel: 20" (full stock), 23½" (half stock).
Weight: 5½ lbs. **Length:** 38¼" over-all (20" bbl.).
Stock: Hand checkered walnut with Monte Carlo cheekpiece. Either full Mannlicher or half stock.
Sights: Ramp front, open U-notch rear.
Features: Choice of interchangeable single or double set triggers. Extra magazine included. Detachable "Makrolon" rotary magazine. 6 rear locking lugs. Drilled and tapped for scope mounts. Custom hand engraving and stock carving avail. Imported by Steyr-Daimler-Puch of America.
Price: $449.95
Price: Carbine $459.95
Price: Varmint (222 Rem. only) $449.95

Mannlicher Model S
Same as Model SL except available in 6.5x68, 257 Weatherby Mag., 264 Win. Mag., 7mm Rem. Mag., 300 H&H, 308 Norma Mag., 8x68S, 338 Win. Mag., 9.3x64, 375 H&H Mag. Avail. only with half-stock. Extra magazine fits in buttstock recess $585.00

MANNLICHER-SCHOENAUER M-72 MODEL T
Same as Model S except weighs 9¼ lbs., available in 9.3x64, 375 H&H Mag., and 458 Win. Mag. only $800.00

MARK X RIFLE
Caliber: 22-250; 243, 270, 308 Win.; 30-06; 25-06; 7×57; 7 mm Rem. Mag; 300 Win. Mag.
Barrel: 24".
Weight: 7½ lbs. **Length:** 44".
Stock: Hand checkered walnut, Monte Carlo, white line spacers on p.g. cap, buttplate and fore-end tip.
Sights: Ramp front with removable hood, open rear adj. for w. and e.
Features: Sliding safety, quick detachable sling swivels, hinged floorplate. Also available as actions or bbld. actions. Imported from Europe by Interarms.
Price: With adj. trigger and sights $234.00
Price: With adj. trigger, no sights $222.00

MARK X VISCOUNT RIFLE
Caliber: 22-250; 243; 25-06; 270; 7×57; 7mm Rem. Mag.; 308 Win.; 30-06; 300 Win. Mag.
Barrel: 24".
Weight: 7½ lbs. **Length:** 44".
Stock: Genuine Walnut stock, hand checkered with 1" sling swivels.
Sights: Ramp front with removable hood, open rear sight ajustable for windage and elevation.
Features: One piece trigger guard with hinged floor plate, drilled and tapped for scope mounts and receiver sight, hammer-forged chrome vanadium steel barrel. Imported by Interarms.
Price: From $199.00

MARK X MANNLICHER-STYLE CARBINE
Caliber: 270, 7x57, 30-06, 308 Win.
Barrel: 20".
Weight: 7½ lbs. **Length:** 40" over-all.
Stock: Hand checkered European walnut.
Sights: Ramp front with removeable hood; open rear adj. for w. and e.
Features: Quick detachable sling swivels; fully adj. trigger; blue steel fore-end cap; white line spacers at p.g. cap and buttplate. Mark X Mauser action. Imported by Interarms.
Price: $274.00

MARK X CAVALIER RIFLE
Caliber: 22-250; 243; 25-06; 270; 7×57; 7mm Rem. Mag.; 308 Win.; 30-06; 300 Win. Mag.
Barrel: 24".
Weight: 7½ lbs. **Length:** 44".
Stock: Checkered Walnut with Rosewood fore-end tip and pistol grip cap, Monte Carlo cheek piece and recoil pad.
Sights: Ramp front with removable hood, open rear adjustable for windage and elevation.
Features: Contemporary-styled stock with sculptured accents; roll over cheek piece and flat bottom fore-end. Adjustable trigger and quick detachable sling swivels, standard. Receiver drilled and tapped for receiver sights and scope mounts. Also available without sights. Imported by Interarms.
Price: From $262.00

MOSSBERG 800 SERIES BOLT ACTION RIFLE
Caliber: 22-250, 243 and 308. 4-shot magazine.
Barrel: 22" AC-KRO-GRUV round tapered.
Weight: 6½ lbs. **Length:** 42" over-all.
Stock: Walnut, Monte Carlo, checkered p.g. and fore-end.
Sights: Gold bead ramp front, adj. folding-leaf rear.
Features: Top tang safety, hinged floorplate, 1" sling swivels installed. Receiver tapped for scope mounts.
Price: $184.95

Mossberg 800 CVT Varmint Target Rifle
Model 800 with heavy 24" bbl, target scope bases, no iron sights. Cals. 243 and 22-250 only. 44" overall, wgt. about 9½ lbs. $193.95

MOSSBERG 810 AH BOLT ACTION RIFLE
Caliber: 30-06, 5-shot magazine.
Barrel: 22", straight taper.
Weight: 8 lbs. **Length:** 43½" over-all.
Stock: Walnut Monte Carlo with checkered fore-end and capped p.g. recoil pad and sling swivels installed.
Sights: Gold bead on ramp front, folding-leaf rear.
Features: Receiver tapped for metallic sight or scope mounts. Top tang safety. Detachable box magazine.
Price: $192.95
Price: 270 cal. as Model 810CH $192.95

> Consult our Directory pages for the location of firms mentioned.

VARMINT HUNTER'S DIGEST

NIKKO GOLDEN EAGLE MODEL 7000 RIFLE
Caliber: 22-250, 243, 25-06, 270 Win., 270 Wea. Mag., 7mm Rem. Mag., 30-06, 300 Win. Mag., 300 Wea. Mag., 338 Win. Mag., 375 H&H, 458 Win. Mag.
Barrel: 24" or 26".
Weight: 7¾ lbs. (8¾ lbs. in 338 and 375, 10½ lbs. in 458) **Length:** 43½" over-all (24" barrel).
Stock: American walnut, Monte Carlo, hand checkered p.g. and fore-end. Vent. recoil pad.
Sights: None furnished. Drilled and tapped for scope mounting.
Features: Removeable clip, tang safety, five bolt locking lugs, grip cap with Golden Eagle head by Sid Bell. Four-shot capacity for 22-250, 2-shot in 458, rest 3-shot. Comes with hard luggage type gun case.
Price: Std. cals. $379.00
Price: Mag. cals. $379.00
Price: African cals. $399.50

PARKER-HALE SUPER 1200 BOLT ACTION RIFLE
Caliber: 22-250, 243 Win., 6mm Rem., 25-06, 270 Win., 30-06, 308 Win., 7mm Rem. Mag., 300 Win. Mag.
Barrel: 24".
Weight: 7¼ lbs. **Length:** 45".
Stock: 13.5" x 1.8" x 2.3". Hand checkered walnut, rosewood p.g. and fore-end caps, fitted rubber recoil pad with white line spacers.
Sights: Bead front, folding adj. rear. Receiver tapped for scope mounts.
Features: 3-way side safety, single-stage adj. trigger, hinged mag. floorplate. Varmint Model (1200V) has glass-bedded action, free-floating bbl., avail. in 22-250, 6mm Rem., 25-06, 243 Win., without sights. Imported from England by Jana.
Price: .... $259.95 ($274.95, mag. cals.)
Price: 1200V $274.95

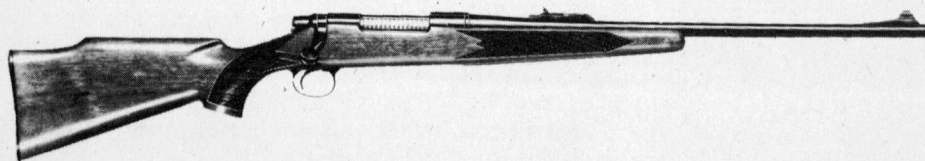

Remington 700 BDL Bolt Action Rifle
Same as 700-ADL, except: fleur-de-lis checkering; black fore-end tip and p.g. cap, white line spacers. Matted receiver top, quick release floorplate. Hooded ramp front sight. Q.D. swivels and 1" sling **Price:** $259.95
Available also in 17 Rem., 7mm Rem. Mag., 264 and 300 Win. Mag., 8mm Rem. Mag., caliber. 44½" over-all, weight 7½ lbs. $274.95
Peerless Grade .... $950.00   Premier Grade $1,900.00

Remington 700 BDL Varmint
Same as 700 BDL, except: 24" heavy bbl., 43½" over-all, wgt. 9 lbs. Cals. 222, 223, 22-250, 6mm Rem., 243, 25-06, and 308. No Sights. . $274.95

REMINGTON 700 ADL BOLT ACTION RIFLE
Caliber: 222, 22-250, 6mm Rem., 243, 25-06, 270, 308 and 30-06.
Barrel: 22" or 24" round tapered.
Weight: 7 lbs. **Length:** 41½" to 43½"
Stock: Walnut, RKW finished p.g. stock with impressed checkering, Monte Carlo (13⅜"x1⅝"x2⅜").
Sights: Gold bead ramp front; removable, step-adj. rear with windage screw.
Features: Side safety, receiver tapped for scope mounts.
Price: $229.95
Price: 7mm Rem. Mag., 17 Rem., 264 Win. Mag., 300 Win. Mag., 8mm Rem. Mag. $244.95

Remington 700BDL Left Hand
Same as 700 BDL except: mirror-image left-hand action, stock. 270, 30-06 $264.95; 7mm Rem. Mag. $279.95

Remington 700 C Custom Rifle
Same as the 700 BDL except choice of 20", 22" or 24" bbl. with or without sights. Jewelled bolt, with or without hinged floor plate. Select American walnut stock is hand checkered, rosewood fore-end & grip cap. Hand lapped barrel. 16 weeks for delivery after placing order $525.00

REMINGTON 788 BOLT ACTION RIFLE
Caliber: 222 (5-shot), 22-250, 223 Rem., 6mm Rem., 243, and 308 (4-shot).
Barrel: 22" round tapered (24" in 222, 223 and 22-250).
Weight: 7-7½ lbs. **Length:** 41⅝" over-all.
Stock: Walnut finished hardwood with Monte Carlo and p.g. (13⅝"x1⅞"x2⅝").
Sights: Blade ramp front, open rear adj. for w. & e.
Features: Detachable box magazine, thumb safety, receiver tapped for scope mounts.
Price: $159.95
Sling strap and swivels, installed $8.25
Model 788 with Universal Model UE 4x scope, mounts and rings in cals. 6mm Rem., 243 Win., 308 and 22-250 .... $184.95

Remington 788 Left Hand Bolt Action
Same as 788 except cals. 6mm & 308 only and left hand stock and action.
Price: $164.95

238   VARMINT HUNTER'S DIGEST

RUGER 77 BOLT ACTION RIFLE
Caliber: 22-250, 243, 6mm, (5-shot).
Barrel: 22" round tapered.
Weight: 6¾ lbs. **Length:** 42" over-all.
Stock: Hand checkered American walnut (13¾"x1⅝"x2⅛"), p.g. cap, sling swivel studs and recoil pad.
Sights: Optional gold bead ramp front, folding leaf adj. rear, or scope rings.
Features: Integral scope mount bases, diagonal bedding system, hinged floorplate, adj. trigger, tang safety. Scope optional.
Price: With Ruger steel scope rings $230.00
Price: With rings and open sights $245.00

RUGER MODEL 77 VARMINT
Caliber: 22-250, 220 Swift, 243, 6mm, 25-06.
Barrel: 24" heavy straight tapered, 26" in 220 Swift.
Weight: Approx. 9 lbs. **Length:** Approx. 44" over-all.
Stock: American walnut, similar in style to Magnum Rifle.
Sights: Barrel drilled and tapped for target scope blocks. Integral scope mount bases in receiver.
Features: Ruger diagonal bedding system, Ruger steel 1" scope rings supplied. Fully adj. trigger. Barreled actions available in any of the standard calibers and barrel lengths.
Price: $230.00
Price: Barreled action only all cals. except 338, 458 ..... $172.50
Price: Bbld. action, 338 .... $185.00
Price: Bbld. action, 458 .... $237.50

Ruger Model 77 Magnum Rifle
Similar to Ruger 77 except: magnum-size action. Calibers 25-06, 270, 7x57, 30-06 (5-shot), 7mm Rem. Mag., 300 Win. Mag., 338 Win. Mag., 458 Win. Mag. (3-shot). 270 and 30-06 have 22" bbl., all others have 24". Weight and length vary with caliber.
Price: With rings only, 338 Win. Mag. $245.00
Price: With rings only, all cals. except 458 .... $230.00
Price: With rings and sights, 338 .... $250.00
Price: With rings and sights, 458 .... $303.00
Price: With rings and sights, other cals. $245.00
Price: With rings and sights, 458, Circassian walnut $370.00

Ruger Model 77 Magnum Round Top
Same as Model 77 except: round top receiver, drilled and tapped for standard scope mounts. Open sights are standard equipment. Calibers 25-06, 270, 30-06, 7mm Rem. Mag., 300 Win. Mag., 338 Win. Mag.
Price: All cals. except 338 .... $230.00
Price: 338 .... $245.00

SAKO MODEL 74 SUPER SPORTER
Caliber: 222, 22-250, 220 Swift, 223, (short action); 243, (medium action); 25-06, 270, 30-06, 7mm Mag., 300 Mag., 338 Mag., 375 H&H Mag. (long action).
Barrel: 23" (222, 223, 243), 24" (other cals.).
Weight: 6¾ lbs. (short); 6¾ lbs. (med.); 8 lbs. (long).
Stock: Hand-checkered European walnut.
Sights: None furnished.
Features: Adj. trigger, hinged floorplate. 222 and 223 have short action, 243 has medium action, others are long action. Imported from Finland by Garcia.
Price: Short action, about $380.00
Price: Medium action, about $380.00
Price: Long action, about $385.00
Price: Magnum cals., about $385.00

Sako Model 74 Deluxe Sporter
Same action as M-74 except has select wood, Rosewood p.g. cap and fore-end tip. Fine checkering on top surfaces of integral dovetail bases, bolt sleeve, bolt handle root and bolt knob. Vent. recoil pad, skip-line checkering, mirror finish bluing.
Price: 222 or 223 cals., about $505.00
Price: 22-250, 243, 308, about $505.00
Price: 270, 30-06, about $505.00
Price: 7mm Rem. Mag. 375 H&H, 338 Mag., about $510.00

Sako Heavy Barrel
Same as std. Super Sporter except has beavertail fore-end; available in 222, 223 (short action), 22-250, 243, (medium action); 25-06, 7mm Mag. (long action). Weight from 8¼ to 8½ lbs. 5-shot magazine capacity.
Price: 222, 223 (short action), about $385.00
Price: 22-250, 243 (medium action), about $385.00
Price: 25-06, 7mm Mag. (long action), about $385.00

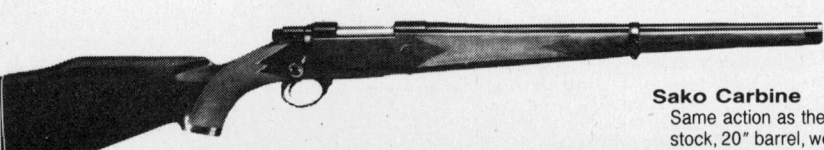

Sako Carbine
Same action as the standard Model 74 except has full "Mannlicher" style stock, 20" barrel, weighs 7½ lbs. 30-06 only. Introduced 1977. From Garcia.
Price: 30-06 only, about $490.00

VARMINT HUNTER'S DIGEST

SAKO MODEL 78 BOLT ACTION
Caliber: 22 LR or 22 Hornet.
Barrel: 22½".
Weight: 6¾ lbs.
Stock: Hand checkered European walnut.
Sights: None furnished; receiver has rail-type scope mount bases.
Features: New action design with tapered sporter weight barrel, adjustable trigger, detachable box magazine (5 shots in 22 LR, 4 shots in Hornet). Shrouded bolt, silent sliding safety, low bolt uplift. Introduced 1977. Imported by Garcia.
Price: 22 LR, about $250.00
Price: 22 Hornet, about $280.00

SAVAGE 110E BOLT ACTION RIFLE
Caliber: 30-06, 243, 4-shot.
Barrel: 22" round tapered.
Weight: 6¾ lbs. **Length:** 43" (22" barrel).
Stock: Walnut finished hardwood with Monte Carlo, checkered p.g. and fore-end, hard rubber buttplate.
Sights: Gold bead removable ramp front, step adj. rear.
Features: Top tang safety, receiver, tapped for peep or scope sights.
Price: $165.00

Savage 110B, 110BL Bolt Action Rifle
Same as 110E except chambered for 30-06, 270 and 243, and has internal magazine.
Price: Right hand 110B $194.00
Price: Left hand 110BL $199.50

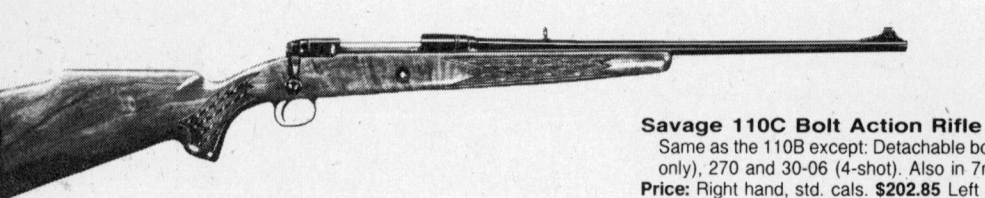

Savage 110C Bolt Action Rifle
Same as the 110B except: Detachable box magazine. Cals. 243 (right-hand only), 270 and 30-06 (4-shot). Also in 7mm Rem. (3-shot).
Price: Right hand, std. cals. $202.85 Left hand (110 CL), std. cals. $210.00
Price: Right hand, mag. cals. $219.00 Left hand, mag. cals. $225.00

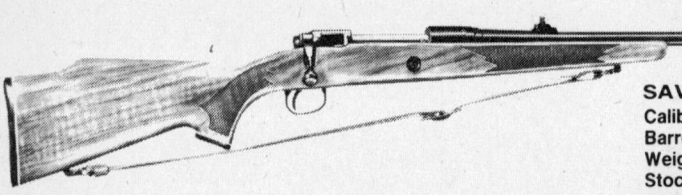

SAVAGE MODEL 111 CHIEFTAIN BOLT ACTION RIFLE
Caliber: 30-06, 243, 7x57, 270 (5-shot), 7mm Rem. Mag. (4-shot).
Barrel: 22" (standard cals.), 24" (mag. cals.). Free floating.
Weight: 7½ lbs. (std.), 8¼ (mag.) **Length:** 43" over-all, 45" for mag.
Stock: Walnut, Monte Carlo, hand checkered fore-end and p.g., p.g. cap, white spacers.
Sights: Removeable hooded ramp front, open rear adj. for w. and e.
Features: Top tang safety, ejector clip magazine, teardrop design bolt handle. Drilled and tapped for scope mounts.
Price: Standard calibers $240.00
Price: Magnum calibers $250.00

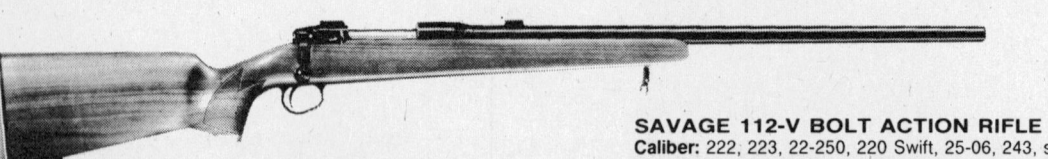

SAVAGE 112-V BOLT ACTION RIFLE
Caliber: 222, 223, 22-250, 220 Swift, 25-06, 243, single shot.
Barrel: 26" tapered, 13/16" at muzzle.
Weight: 9¼ lbs. **Length:** 47" over-all.
Stock: Walnut. Free floating varmint stock with high, deeply fluted comb, Wundhammer swell at p.g., Hand checkered (20 l.p.i.). White spacer at recoil pad, 1¼" q.d. swivels.
Sights: None. Drilled and tapped for scope mounting.
Features: Designed expressly for varmint shooting. Recessed bolt face; 2 gas ports; top tang safety; chrome moly steel barrel. Stock measures 13½", drop at comb and heel 9/16" (measured from barrel centerline).
Price: $245.00

SAVAGE 340 CLIP REPEATER
Caliber: 22 Hornet, 222 Rem., 223 (4-shot) and 30-30 (3-shot).
Barrel: 24" and 22" respectively.
Weight: About 6½ lbs. **Length:** 40"-42"
Stock: Walnut, Monte Carlo, checkered p.g. and fore-end white line spacers.
Sights: Gold bead ramp front, folding-leaf rear.
Features: Detachable clip magazine, sliding thumb safety, receiver tapped for scope mounts.
Price: **$131.50**

SAVAGE/ANSCHUTZ 1433-1533 Sporter
Caliber: 22 Hornet, 222 Rem.
Barrel: 19¾".
Weight: 6½ lbs. **Length:** 39¾" over-all.
Stock: European walnut, Mannlicher type with European-style cheekpiece.
Sights: Hooded ramp front, folding leaf rear. Receiver grooved for scope mount.
Features: Double set or single stage trigger. Magazine capacity in 222 is 4-shots. Blue steel nose cap; sling swivels. Imported by Savage Arms.
Price: 1433 (22 Hornet) **$517.00**
Price: 1533 (222 Rem.) **$517.00**
Price: 1432 Custom Sporter (22 Hornet) **$449.75**

TRADEWINDS HUSKY MODEL 5000 BOLT RIFLE
Caliber: 270, 30-06, 308, 243, 22-250.
Barrel: 23¾".
Weight: 6 lbs. 11 oz.
Stock: Hand checkered European walnut, Monte Carlo, white line spacers on p.g. cap, fore-end tip and butt plate.
Sights: Fixed hooded front, adj. rear.
Features: Removeable mag., fully recessed bolt head, adj. trigger. Imported by Tradewinds.
Price: **$295.00**

WEATHERBY MARK V BOLT ACTION RIFLE
Caliber: All Weatherby cals., 22-250 and 30-06.
Barrel: 24" or 26" round tapered.
Weight: 6½-10½ lbs. **Length:** 43¼"-46½"
Stock: Walnut, Monte Carlo with cheekpiece, high luster finish, checkered p.g. and fore-end, recoil pad.
Sights: Optional (extra).
Features: Cocking indicator, adj. trigger, hinged floorplate, thumb safety, quick detachable sling swivels.
Price: Cals. 224 and 22-250, std. bbl. **$449.50**
With 26" semi-target bbl. **$459.50**
Cals. 240, 257, 270, 7mm, 30-06 and 300 (24" bbl.) **$469.50**
With 26" No. 2 contour bbl. **$479.50**
Cal. 340 (26" bbl.) **$479.50**
Cal. 378 (26" bbl.) **$479.50**
Cal. 460 (26" bbl.) **$479.50**

Weatherby Mark V Rifle Left Hand
Available in all Weatherby calibers except 224 and 22-250 (and 26" No. 2 contour 300WM). Complete left handed action; stock with cheekpiece on right side. Prices are $10 higher than right hand models except the 378 and 460WM are unchanged.

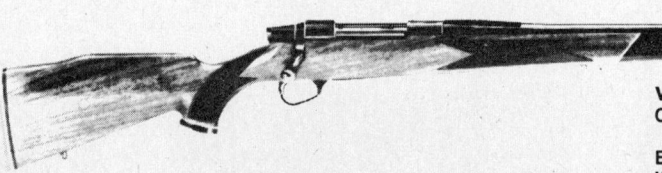

WEATHERBY VANGUARD BOLT ACTION RIFLE
Caliber: 25-06, 243, 270, 30-06 and 308 (5-shot), 7mm Rem. and 300 Win. Mag. (3-shot).
Barrel: 24" hammer forged.
Weight: 7⅞ lbs. **Length:** 44½" over-all.
Stock: American walnut, p.g. cap and fore-end tip, hand inletted and checkered, 13½" pull.
Sights: Optional, available at extra cost.
Features: Side safety, adj. trigger, hinged floorplate, receiver tapped for scope mounts.
Price: **$299.50**

VARMINT HUNTER'S DIGEST

WESTERN FIELD MODEL 732 BOLT ACTION RIFLE
Caliber: 7mm (4-shot), 30-06 (5-shot).
Barrel: 22".
Weight: 8½ lbs. (30-06). **Length:** 43½" over-all.
Stock: Walnut. Monte Carlo cheekpiece, checkered p.g. and fore-end.
Sights: Gold bead front, adj. folding leaf rear.
Features: Adjustable trigger. Rubber recoil pad, p.g. cap. Receiver drilled and tapped for scope mounts. 1" sling swivels. Top receiver safety.
Price: 7mm $199.99
Price: 30-06 .... $189.99

WESTERN FIELD 780 BOLT ACTION RIFLE
Caliber: 243, 308, 5-shot mag.
Barrel: 22" round tapered.
Weight: 6½ lbs. **Length:** 42" over-all.
Stock: Walnut, Monte Carlo, checkered p.g. and fore-end.
Sights: Ramp, gold bead front; rear adj. for e.
Features: Recessed bolt head, top tang safety, hinged magazine floorplate, Receiver tapped for scope mount.
Price: $179.99

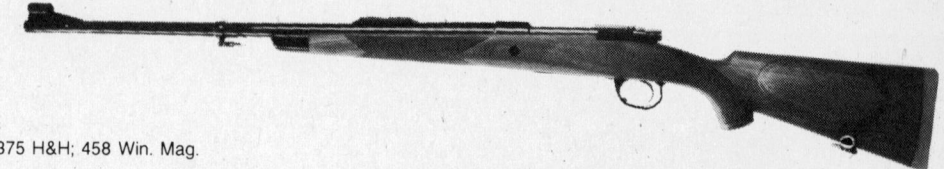

WHITWORTH EXPRESS RIFLE
Caliber: 7mm Rem. Mag., 300 Win. Mag., 375 H&H; 458 Win. Mag.
Barrel: 24".
Weight: 7½-8 lbs. **Length:** 44".
Stock: Classic English Express rifle design of hand checkered, select European Walnut.
Sights: Three leaf open sight calibrated for 100, 200, 300 yards on ¼-rib, ramp front with removable hood.
Features: Solid rubber recoil pad, barrel mounted sling swivel, adjustable trigger, hinged floor plate, solid steel recoil cross bolt. Imported by Interarms.
Price: $425.00

Winchester 70 Varmint Rifle
Same as M70 Standard except: 222, 22-250, and 243 only, target scope blocks, no sights, 24" heavy bbl., 14" twist in 22-250, 10" twist in 243. 44½" over-all, 9¾ lbs. Stock measures 13½"x$^{9}/_{16}$"x$^{15}/_{16}$"x$^{3}/_{8}$" from bore line.
Price: $280.00

WINCHESTER 70A BOLT ACTION RIFLE
Caliber: 222, 22-250, 243, 25-06, 270, 30-06, 308.
Barrel: 22" (25-06, has 24").
Weight: 7⅛ to 7½ lbs. **Length:** 42½" (22" bbl.).
Stock: Monte Carlo, checkering at p.g. and fore-end.
Sights: Removeable hooded ramp front, adj. open rear.
Features: Sling swivels installed, three position safety, deep cut checkering.
Price: $229.95

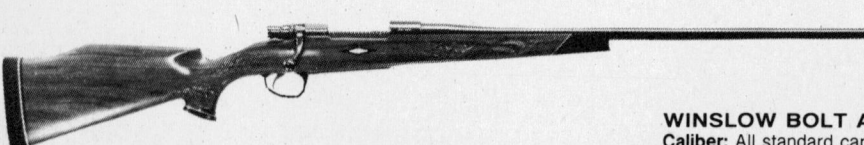

WINCHESTER 70 STANDARD RIFLE
Caliber: 222, 22-250, 25-06, 243, 270, 308 and 30-06, 5-shot.
Barrel: 22" swaged, floating. 10" twist (222 & 22-250 have 14" twist, 308 is 12").
Weight: 7½ lbs. **Length:** 42½" over-all.
Stock: Walnut, Monte Carlo, (13½"x1¾"x1½"x2⅛") checkered p.g. and fore-end.
Sights: Removable hooded bead ramp front, adj. open rear.
Features: Sling swivels installed, steel p.g. cap, hinged floorplate, receiver tapped for scope mounts.
Price: $265.00

WINSLOW BOLT ACTION RIFLE
Caliber: All standard cartridges (magnum add $10)
Barrel: 24" Douglas premium. (Magnums 26")
Weight: 7-7½ lbs. **Length:** 43" over-all.
Stock: Hand rubbed black walnut, choice of two styles
Sights: None. Metallics available at extra cost.
Features: Receivers tapped for scope mounts, QD swivels and recoil pad installed. 4-shot blind mag.
Price: Regal Grade $550.00
Price: Regent Grade $675.00
Price: Regimental Grade $850.00
Price: Crown, Emperor, Imperial grades .. **Price on request from factory**

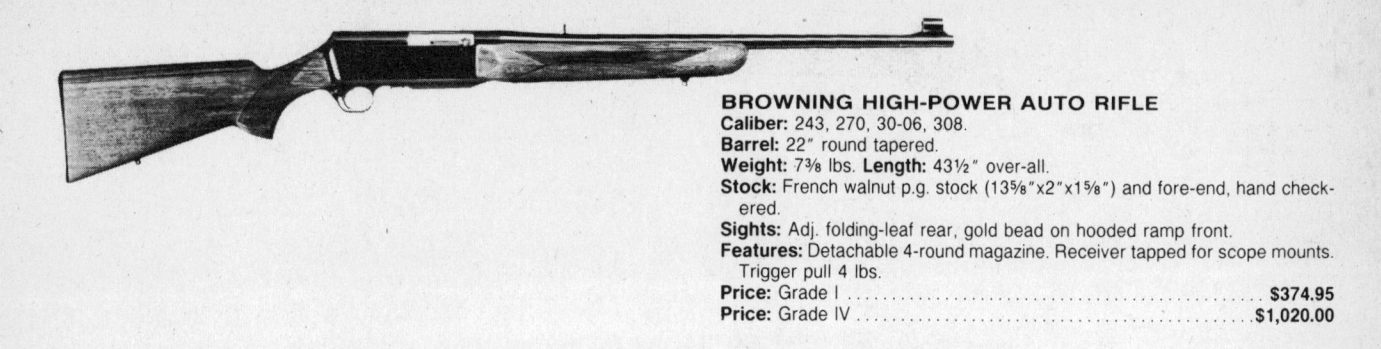

AUTOLOADING & SLIDE ACTION CENTERFIRE RIFLES

BROWNING HIGH-POWER AUTO RIFLE
Caliber: 243, 270, 30-06, 308.
Barrel: 22" round tapered.
Weight: 7⅜ lbs. **Length:** 43½" over-all.
Stock: French walnut p.g. stock (13⅝"x2"x1⅝") and fore-end, hand checkered.
Sights: Adj. folding-leaf rear, gold bead on hooded ramp front.
Features: Detachable 4-round magazine. Receiver tapped for scope mounts. Trigger pull 4 lbs.
Price: Grade I $374.95
Price: Grade IV $1,020.00

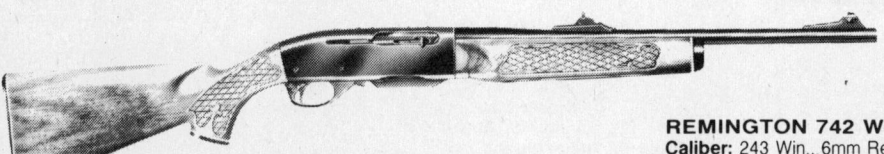

REMINGTON 742 WOODSMASTER AUTO RIFLE
Caliber: 243 Win., 6mm Rem., 280 Rem., 308 Win. and 30-06.
Barrel: 22" round tapered.
Weight: 7½ lbs. **Length:** 42" over-all
Stock: Walnut (13¼"x1⅝"x2¼") deluxe checkered p.g. and fore-end.
Sights: Gold bead front sight on ramp; step rear sight with windage adj.
Features: Positive cross-bolt safety. Receiver tapped for scope mount. 4-shot clip mag.
Price: $257.95
Extra 4-shot clip magazine $7.95
Sling strap and swivels (installed) $13.75
Peerless (D) and Premier (F) grades .... $1,200.00 and $2,400.00
Premier with gold inlays $3,600.00

Remington 742 BDL Woodsmaster
Same as 742 except: "stepped" receiver, Monte Carlo with cheekpiece (right or left), whiteline spacers, basket-weave checkering on p.g. and fore-end, black fore-end tip, RKW finish (13⁵⁄₁₆"x1⅝"x1¹³⁄₁₆"x2½"). Cals. 30-06, 308 .... $277.95

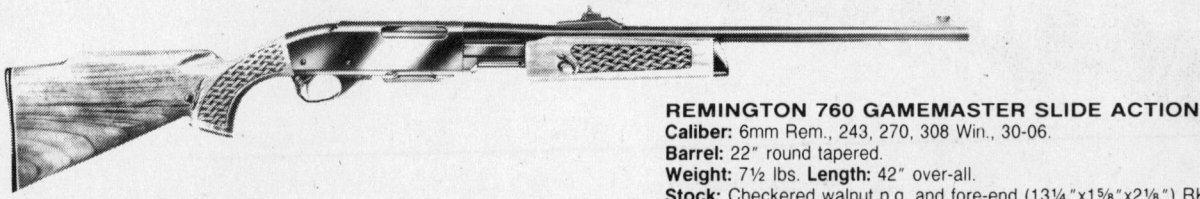

REMINGTON 760 GAMEMASTER SLIDE ACTION
Caliber: 6mm Rem., 243, 270, 308 Win., 30-06.
Barrel: 22" round tapered.
Weight: 7½ lbs. **Length:** 42" over-all.
Stock: Checkered walnut p.g. and fore-end (13¼"x1⅝"x2⅛") RKW finish
Sights: Gold bead front sight on matted ramp, open step adj. sporting rear.
Features: Detachable 4-shot clip. Cross-bolt safety. Receiver tapped for scope mount.
Price: $224.95
Sling strap and swivels (installed) $13.75
Extra 4-shot clip $7.25

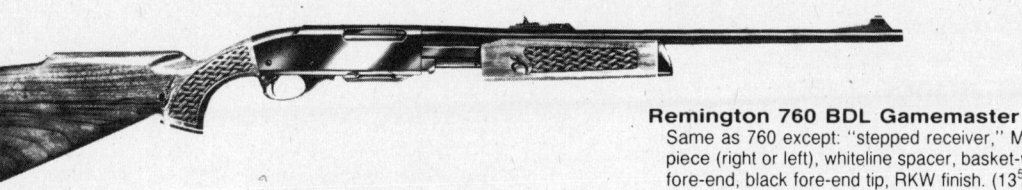

Remington 760 BDL Gamemaster
Same as 760 except: "stepped receiver," Monte Carlo stock with cheekpiece (right or left), whiteline spacer, basket-weave checkering on p.g. and fore-end, black fore-end tip, RKW finish. (13⁵⁄₁₆"x1⅝"x1¹³⁄₁₆"x2½"). Cals. 270, 30-06, 308 .... $244.95
Also in Peerless (D) and Premier (F) grades ... $1,200.00 and $2,400.00
(F), with gold inlay $3,600.00

RUGER MINI-14 223 CARBINE
Caliber: 223 Rem., 5-shot detachable box magazine.
Barrel: 18½".
Weight: 6.4 lbs. **Length:** 37¼" over-all.
Stock: Walnut, steel reinforced.
Sights: Ramp front, fully adj. rear.
Features: Fixed piston gas-operated, positive primary extraction. 10 and 20-shot magazines available from Ruger dealers, 30-shot magazine available only to police departments.
Price: $200.00

VARMINT HUNTER'S DIGEST

LEVER ACTION CENTERFIRE RIFLES

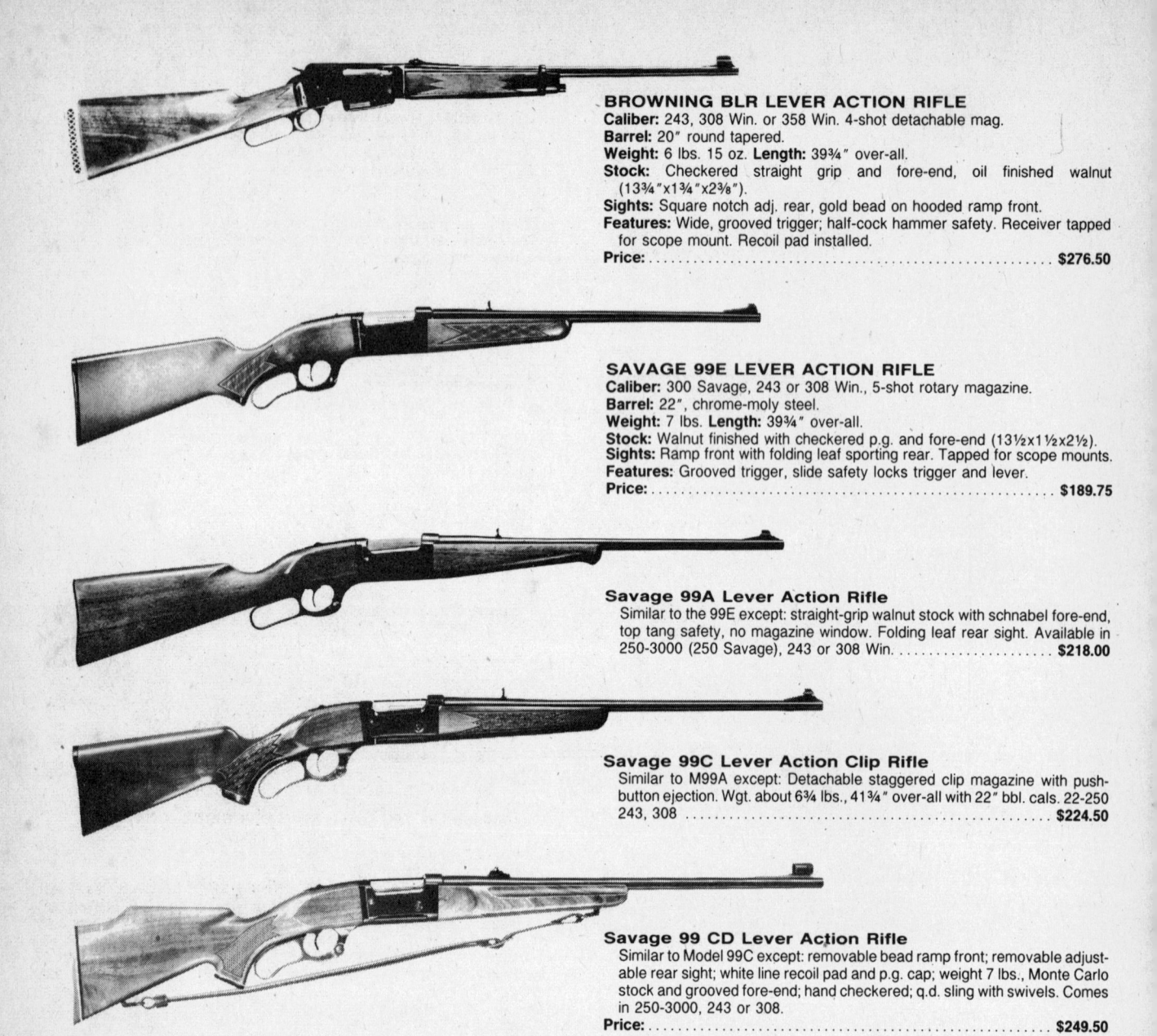

BROWNING BLR LEVER ACTION RIFLE
Caliber: 243, 308 Win. or 358 Win. 4-shot detachable mag.
Barrel: 20″ round tapered.
Weight: 6 lbs. 15 oz. **Length:** 39¾″ over-all.
Stock: Checkered straight grip and fore-end, oil finished walnut (13¾″x1¾″x2⅜″).
Sights: Square notch adj. rear, gold bead on hooded ramp front.
Features: Wide, grooved trigger; half-cock hammer safety. Receiver tapped for scope mount. Recoil pad installed.
Price: $276.50

SAVAGE 99E LEVER ACTION RIFLE
Caliber: 300 Savage, 243 or 308 Win., 5-shot rotary magazine.
Barrel: 22″, chrome-moly steel.
Weight: 7 lbs. **Length:** 39¾″ over-all.
Stock: Walnut finished with checkered p.g. and fore-end (13½x1½x2½).
Sights: Ramp front with folding leaf sporting rear. Tapped for scope mounts.
Features: Grooved trigger, slide safety locks trigger and lever.
Price: $189.75

Savage 99A Lever Action Rifle
Similar to the 99E except: straight-grip walnut stock with schnabel fore-end, top tang safety, no magazine window. Folding leaf rear sight. Available in 250-3000 (250 Savage), 243 or 308 Win. $218.00

Savage 99C Lever Action Clip Rifle
Similar to M99A except: Detachable staggered clip magazine with push-button ejection. Wgt. about 6¾ lbs., 41¾″ over-all with 22″ bbl. cals. 22-250 243, 308 .... $224.50

Savage 99 CD Lever Action Rifle
Similar to Model 99C except: removable bead ramp front; removable adjustable rear sight; white line recoil pad and p.g. cap; weight 7 lbs., Monte Carlo stock and grooved fore-end; hand checkered; q.d. sling with swivels. Comes in 250-3000, 243 or 308.
Price: $249.50

SINGLE SHOT CENTERFIRE RIFLES

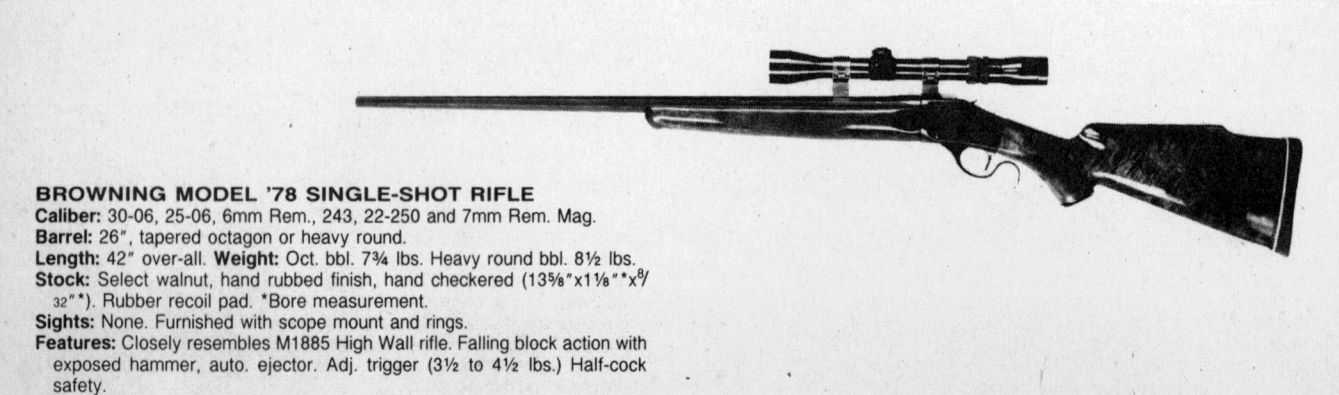

BROWNING MODEL '78 SINGLE-SHOT RIFLE
Caliber: 30-06, 25-06, 6mm Rem., 243, 22-250 and 7mm Rem. Mag.
Barrel: 26″, tapered octagon or heavy round.
Length: 42″ over-all. **Weight:** Oct. bbl. 7¾ lbs. Heavy round bbl. 8½ lbs.
Stock: Select walnut, hand rubbed finish, hand checkered (13⅝″x1⅛″*x⁹/₃₂″*). Rubber recoil pad. *Bore measurement.
Sights: None. Furnished with scope mount and rings.
Features: Closely resembles M1885 High Wall rifle. Falling block action with exposed hammer, auto. ejector. Adj. trigger (3½ to 4½ lbs.) Half-cock safety.
Price: $362.95

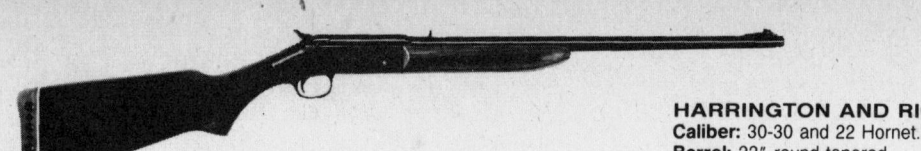

HARRINGTON AND RICHARDSON 158 TOPPER RIFLE
Caliber: 30-30 and 22 Hornet.
Barrel: 22" round tapered.
Weight: 5¼ lbs. **Length:** 37½"
Stock: Walnut finished stock and fore-end.
Sights: Lyman folding adj. rear and ramp front sights.
Features: Side lever break-open action with visible hammer. Easy takedown. Converts to 20 ga. Shotgun with accessory bbl. ($20 extra).
Price: 22 Hornet or 30-30 .... $69.50
Price: Rifle/shotgun combo $89.50

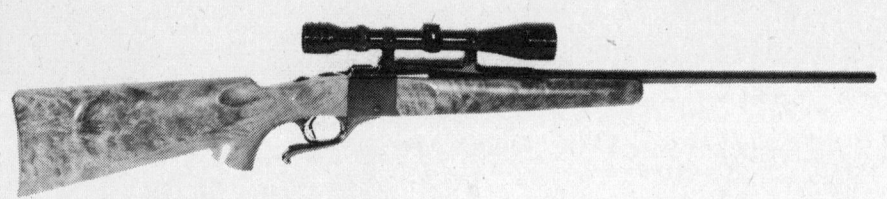

HYPER-SINGLE RIFLE
Caliber: All calibers, standard and wildcat.
Barrel: Choice of maker, weight, length (std. twist and contours).
Length: To customer specs. **Weight:** To customer specs.
Stock: To customer specs. AA fancy American black walnut is standard.
Sights: None furnished. Drilled and tapped for scope mounts.
Features: Falling block action. Striker rotates on bronze bearing and is powered by dual coil springs. Trigger adj. for weight, pull and travel. Tang safety. Octagon receiver on special order (same price).
Price: Complete Rifle ..... $1,750.00   Barreled action $1,100.00
Price: Action only (blank extractor) $850.00
Price: Stainless steel barrel (extra) $75.00
Price: Fluted or octagon barrel (extra) $75.00

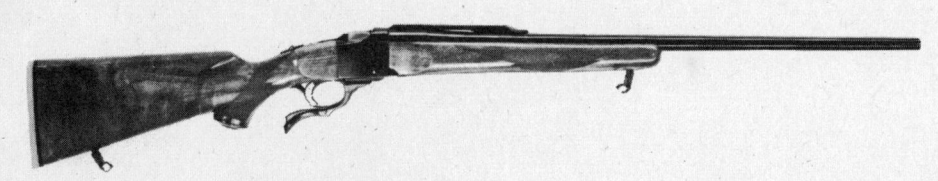

RUGER NUMBER ONE SINGLE SHOT
Caliber: 22-250, 243, 6mm Rem., 25-06, 270, 7x57mm, 30-06, 7mm Rem. Mag., 300 Win., 45-70, 458 Win. Mag., 375 H&H Mag.
Barrel: 26" round tapered with quarter-rib (also 22" and 24", depending upon model).
Weight: 8 lbs. **Length:** 42" over-all.
Stock: Walnut, two-piece, checkered p.g. and fore-end (either semi-beavertail or Henry style).
Sights: None, 1" scope rings supplied for integral mounts. 3 models have open sights.
Features: Under lever, hammerless falling block design has auto ejector, top tang safety. Standard Rifle 1B illus.
Price: $295.00
Available also as Light Sporter, Medium Sporter, Special Varminter or Tropical Rifle $295.00
Price: Barreled action, blued only $170.00

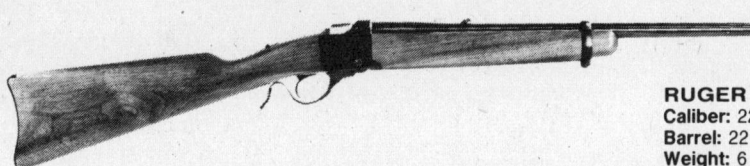

RUGER NO. 3 CARBINE SINGLE SHOT
Caliber: 22 Hornet, 30-40 Krag, 45-70.
Barrel: 22" round.
Weight: 6 lbs. **Length:** 38½".
Stock: American walnut, carbine-type.
Sights: Gold bead front, adj. folding leaf rear.
Features: Same action as No. 1 Rifle except different lever. Has auto ejector, top tang safety, adj. trigger.
Price: $175.00

WICKLIFFE '76 FALLING BLOCK RIFLE
Caliber: 22 Hornet, 223, 22-250, 243, 25-06, 270, 308, 45-70; single-shot.
Barrel: 26", heavy sporter weight; 22" lightweight in 22 Hornet, 243 and 308 only (Standard Grade), 22" in 30-06 only for Deluxe.
Weight: 8½ lbs. (26" bbl.), 6¾ lbs. (22" bbl.).
Stock: Select American walnut, dull finish (Std. grade); fancy figured walnut, high-gloss finish (Deluxe grade). Monte Carlo buttstock with p.g., semi-beavertail fore-end.
Sights: Scope mounts on barrel, with extensions and 1" rings.
Features: Single-shot, falling block action. Adjustable extractor-ejector for extraction only or complete ejection; trigger adjustable for over-travel and sear engagement; diamond lapped 4140 chrome-moly barrel. Full 5 year warranty Deluxe Grade has nickel silver grip cap, engine-turned breech block, better wood and metal finish.

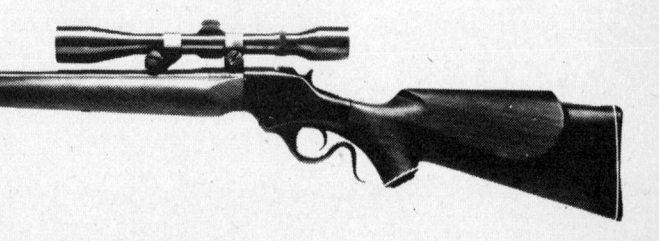

Price: Standard Grade $298.00
Price: Deluxe Grade $372.00
Price: Barreled action $205.00

VARMINT HUNTER'S DIGEST

Varmint Hunter's Trade Directory

AMMUNITION (Commercial)

Alcan Shells, (See: Smith & Wesson Ammunition Co.)
Cascade Cartridge Inc., (See Omark)
DWM (see RWS)
Dynamit Nobel of America, Inc., 910, 17 St. NW, Suite 709, Washington DC 20006
Federal Cartridge Co., 2700 Foshay Tower, Minneapolis, Minn. 55402
Frontier Cartridge Co., Inc., Box 1848, Grand Island, Neb. 68801
Lee E. Jurras & Assoc., Inc., P.O. Box 846, Roswell, NM 88201 (Auto Mag only)
Omark-CCI, Inc., Box 856, Lewiston, Ida. 83501
RWS (see Dynamit Nobel)
Remington Arms Co., Bridgeport, Conn. 06602
Service Armament, 689 Bergen Blvd., Ridgefield, N.J. 07657
Smith & Wesson Ammunition Co., 2399 Forman Rd., Rock Creek, OH 44084
Weatherby's, 2781 E. Firestone Blvd., South Gate, Calif. 90280
Winchester-Western, East Alton, Ill. 62024

AMMUNITION (Custom)

Ed Agramonte, Inc., 41 Riverdale Ave., Yonkers, NY 10701
Bill Ballard, P.O. Box 656, Billings, MT 59103 (ctlg. 25¢)
Beal's Bullets, 170 W. Marshall Rd., Lansdowne, PA 19050
Bell's Gun & Sport Shop, 3309-19 Mannheim Rd., Franklin Park, IL 60131
Brass Extrusion Labs. Ltd. (see Bell's)
Russell Campbell, 219 Leisure Dr., San Antonio, Tex. 78201
Collectors Shotshell Arsenal, 365 S. Moore, Lakewood, CO 80226
Crown City Arms, P.O. Box 1126, Cortland, NY 13045
Cumberland Arms, 1222 Oak Dr., Manchester, Tenn. 37355
E. W. Ellis Sport Shop, RFD 1, Box 139, Corinth, N.Y. 12822
Ellwood Epps (Orillia) Ltd., Hwy. 11 North, Orillia, Ont., Canada
David J. Gaida, 1109 S. Millwood, Wichita, KS 67203
Gussert Bullet & Cartridge Co., 1868 Lenwood Ave., Green Bay, WI 54303
Hutton Rifle Ranch, 619 San Lorenzo St., Santa Monica, CA 90402
J-4, Inc., 1700 Via Burton, Anaheim, CA 92806 (custom bullets)
R. H. Keeler, 1304 S. Oak, Port Angeles, Wash. 98362
KTW Inc., 710 Foster Park Rd., Lorain, OH 44053 (bullets)
Dean Lincoln, P.O. Box 1886, Farmington, NM 87401
Lomont Precision Bullets, 4421 S. Wayne Ave., Ft. Wayne, IN 46807 (custom bullets)
Pat B. McMillan, 1828 E. Campo Bello Dr., Phoenix, Ariz. 85022
Mansfield Gunshop, Box 83, New Boston, N.H. 03070
Numrich Arms Corp., 203 Broadway, W. Hurley, N.Y. 12491
The Outrider, Inc., 3288 LaVenture Dr., Chamblee, GA 30341
Robert Pomeroy, Morison Ave., Corinth, ME 04427 (custom shells)
A. F. Sailer, P.O. Box L, Owen, WI 54460
Sanders Cust. Gun Serv., 2358 Tyler Lane, Louisville, Ky. 40205
Shotshell Components, 365 S. Moore, Lakewood, CO 80226
Geo. Spence, P.O. Box 222, Steele, MO 63877 (box-primed cartridges)
H. Winter Cast Bullets, 422 Circle Dr., Clarksville, TN 37040

AMMUNITION (Foreign)

Canadian Ind. Ltd. (C.I.L.), Ammo Div., Howard House, Brownsburg, Que., Canada, J0V 1A0
Colonial Ammunition Co., Box 8511, Auckland, New Zealand
Dynamit Nobel of America, Inc., 910, 17 St. NW, Suite 709, Washington DC 20006
Eastern Sports Distributors Co., Inc., P.O. Box 28, Milford, NH 03055 (RWS; Geco)
Gevelot of Canada, Box 1593, Saskatoon, Sask., Canada
Hirtenberger Patronen-, Zündhütchen- & Metallwarenfabrik, A.G., Leobersdorfer Str. 33, A2552 Hirtenberg, Austria
Hy-Score Arms Co., 200 Tillary, Brooklyn, N.Y. 11201
Paul Jaeger Inc., 211 Leedom St., Jenkintown, Pa. 19046
S. E. Laszlo, 200 Tillary, Brooklyn, N.Y. 11201
NORMA-Precision, Lansing, NY 14882
Oregon Ammo Service, Box 19341, Portland, Ore. 97219
The Outrider, Inc., 3288 LaVenture Dr., Chamblee, GA 30341
RWS (Rheinische-Westfälische Sprengstoff) see: Eastern

AMMUNITION COMPONENTS—BULLETS, POWDER, PRIMERS

Alcan, (see: Smith & Wesson Ammunition Co.)
Ammo-O-Mart, P.O. Box 66, Hawkesbury, Ont., Canada (Curry bullets)
Bahler Die Shop, Rte. 1, Box 412 Hemlock, Florence, OR 97439 (17 cal. bull.)
Joe J. Balickie, 6108 Deerwood Pl., Raleigh, NC 27607
Ballistic Research Industries, see: S & W (12 ga. Sabot bullets)
B.E.L.L., Bell's Gun & Sport Shop, 3309-19 Mannheim Rd., Franklin Pk., IL 60131
Bitterroot Bullet Co., Box 412, Lewiston, Ida. 83501
The Bullet Boys, Box 367, Jaffrey, NH 03452 (cast bullets)
Centrix, 2116 N. 10th Ave., Tucson, Ariz. 85705
Kenneth E. Clark, 18738 Highway 99, Madera, CA 93637 (Bullets)
Colorado Custom Bullets, Rt. 1, Box 507-B, Montrose, Colo. 81401
Curry Bullets Canada, P.O. Box 66, Hawkesbury, Ont., Canada
Division Lead, 7742 W. 61 Pl., Summit, Ill. 60502
DuPont, Explosives Dept., Wilmington, Del. 19898
Eastern Sports Distributors Co., Inc., P.O. Box 28, Milford, NH 03055 (RWS percussion caps)
Elk Mountain Shooters Supply, 1719 Marie, Pasco, WA 99301 (Alaskan bullets)
Farmer Bros., see: Lage Uniwad
Federal Cartridge Co., 2700 Foshay Tower, Minneapolis, MN 55402 (nickel cases)
Forty Five Ranch Enterprises, 119 S. Main, Miami, Okla. 74354
Godfrey Reloading Supply, R.R. 1, Box 688, Brighton, Ill. 62012 (cast bullets)
Lynn Godfrey, see: Elk Mtn. Shooters Supply
Green Bay Bullets, 233 No. Ashland, Green Bay, Wis. 54303 (lead)
Gussert Bullet & Cartridge Co., 1868 Lenwood Ave., Green Bay, WI 54303
Hercules Powder Co., 910 Market St., Wilmington, Del. 19899
Herter's Inc., Waseca, Minn. 56093
Hodgdon Powder Co. Inc., 7710 W. 50th Hwy., Shawnee Mission, KS 66202
Hornady Mfg. Co., Box 1848, Grand Island, Neb. 68801
N. E. House Co., Middletown Rd., E. Hampton, Conn. 06424 (zinc bases only)
J-4, Inc., 1700 Via Burton, Anaheim, CA 92806 (custom bullets)
L. L. F. Die Shop, 1281 Highway 99 North, Eugene, Ore. 97402
Lage Uniwad Co., 1102 Washington St., Eldora, IA 50627
Ljutic Ind., Inc., Box 2117, Yakima, WA 98902 (Mono-wads)
Lomont Precision Bullets, 4421 S. Wayne Ave., Ft. Wayne, IN 46807
Lyman Gun Sight Products, Middlefield, Conn. 06455
Markell, Inc., 4115 Judah St., San Francisco, Calif. 94112
Meyer Bros. Mfgrs., Wabasha, Minn. 55981 (shotgun slugs)
Miller Trading Co., 20 S. Front St., Wilmington, N.C. 28401
Norma-Precision, Lansing, NY 14882
Northridge Bullet Co., P.O. Box 1208, Vista, Ca. 92083
Nosler Bullets, P.O. Box 688, Beaverton, OR 97005
Old West Gun Room, 3509 Carlson Rd., El Cerrito, CA 94530 (RWS)
Oregon Ammo Service, Box 19341, Portland, Ore. 97219
Robert Pomeroy, Morison Ave., East Corinth, ME 04427
Remington-Peters, Bridgeport, Conn. 06602
Sanderson's, 724 W. Edgewater, Portage, Wis. 53901 (cork wad)
Sierra Bullets Inc., 10532 Painter Ave., Santa Fe Springs, CA 90670
Sisk Bullet Co., Box 874, Iowa Park, TX 76367
Smith & Wesson Ammunition Co., 2399 Forman Rd., Rock Creek, OH 44084
Speedy Bullets, Box 1262, Lincoln, Neb. 68501
Speer Products Inc., Box 896, Lewiston, Ida. 83501
C. H. Stocking, Rte. 3, Box 195, Hutchinson, Minn. 55350 (17 cal. bullet jackets)
Taylor Bullets, P.O. Box 21254, San Antonio, Tex. 78221
Vitt & Boos, 11 Sugarloaf Dr., Wilton, CT 06897 (shotgun slugs)
Winchester-Western, New Haven, Conn. 06504
F. Wood, Box 386, Florence, Ore. 97439 (17 cal.)
Xelex Ltd., Hawksbury, Ont., Canada (powder, Curry bullets)
Zero Bullet Co., P.O. Box 1012, Cullman, AL 35055

BULLET & CASE LUBRICANTS

Birchwood-Casey Co., Inc., 7900 Fuller Rd., Eden Prairie, Minn. 55343 (Anderol)
Chopie Mfg. Inc., 531 Copeland, La Crosse, Wis. 54601 (Black-Solve)
Cooper-Woodward, Box 972, Riverside, Cal. 92502 (Perfect Lube)
D. R. Corbin, P.O. Box 44, North Bend, OR 97459
Green Bay Bullets, 233 N. Ashland, Green Bay, Wis. 54303 (EZE-Size case lube)
Gussert Bullet & Cartridge Co., 1868 Lenwood Ave., Green Bay, WI 54303 (Super Lube)
Herter's, Inc., Waseca, Minn. 56903 (Perfect Lubricant)
IPCO (Industrial Products Co.), Box 14, Bedford, MA 01730
Javelina Products, Box 337, San Bernardino, Cal. 92402 (Alox beeswax)
Jet-Aer Corp., 100 Sixth Ave., Paterson, N.J. 07524
Lenz Prod. Co., Box 1226, Sta. C, Canton, O. 44708 (Clenzoil)
Lyman Gun Sight Products, Middlefield, Conn. 06455 (Size-Ezy)
Marmel Prods., P.O. Box 97, Utica, MI 48087 (Marvelube, Marvelux)
Micro Shooter's Supply, Box 213, Las Cruces, N. Mex. 88001 (Micro-Lube)
Mirror Lube, P.O. Box 693, San Juan Capistrano, CA 92675
Pacific Tool Co., P.O. Drawer 2048, Ordnance Plant Rd., Grand Island, NB 68801
Phelps Rel. Inc., Box 4004, E. Orange, N.J. 07019
RCBS, Inc., Box 1919, Oroville, Calif. 95965
SAECO Rel. Inc., P.O. Box 778, Carpinteria, CA 93103
Scientific Lubricants Co., 3753 Lawrence Ave., Chicago, Ill. 60625
Shooters Accessory Supply (SAS), see D. R. Corbin
Testing Systems, Inc., 2832 Mt. Carmel, Glenside, PA 19038

BULLET SWAGE DIES AND TOOLS

Bahler Die Shop, Box 386/412 Hemlock St., Florence, OR 97439
Belmont Products, Rte. #1, Friendsville, TN 37737
C-H Tool & Die Corp., P.O. Box L, Owen, WI 54460

Clymer Mfg. Co., 14241 W. 11 Mile Rd., Oak Park, MI 48237
Lester Coats, 416 Simpson St., North Bend, OR 97459 (lead wire cutter)
D. R. Corbin, P.O. Box 44, North Bend, OR 97459
Herter's Inc., Waseca, MN 56093
Hollywood, Whitney Sales Inc., P.O. Box 875, Reseda, CA 91335
Independent Machine & Gun Shop, 1416 N. Hayes, Pocatello, ID 83201 (TNT)
L.L.F. Die Shop, 1281 Highway 99 North, Eugene, OR 97402
Rorschach Precision Products, P.O. Box 1613, Irving, TX 75060
SAS Dies, see: D. R. Corbin
Robert B. Simonson, Rte. 2, 2129 Vanderbilt Rd., Kalamazoo, MI 49002
TNT (see Ind. Mach. & Gun Shop)

CASES, CABINETS AND RACKS—GUN

Alco Carrying Cases, 601 W. 26th St., New York, N.Y. 10001
Artistic Wood Specialties, 923-29 W. Chicago Ave., Chicago, Ill. 60622
Morton Booth Co., Box 123, Joplin, Mo. 64801
Boyt Co., Div. of Welsh Sportg. Gds., Box 1108, Iowa Falls, Ia. 50126
Browning, Rt. 4, Box 624-B, Arnold, MO 63010
Cap-Lex Gun Cases, Capitol Plastics of Ohio, Inc., 333 Van Camp Rd., Bowling Green, OH 43402
Castle Westchester Prods. Co., Inc., 498 Nepperhan Ave., Yonkers, N.Y. 10701
Challanger Mfg. Co., 118 Pearl St., Mt. Vernon, NY 10550
E & C Enterprises, 9582 Bickley Dr., Huntington Beach, CA 92646 (gun socks)
East-Tenn Mills, Inc., Box 1030, Johnson City, TN 37601 (gun socks)
Ellwood Epps (Orillia) Ltd., Hwy. 11 North, Orillia, Ont., Canada
Flambeau Plastics Corp., 801 Lynn, Baraboo, Wis. 53913
Gun-Ho Case Mfg. Co., 110 East 10th St., St. Paul, Minn. 55101
Harbor House Gun Cabinets, 12508 Center St., South Gate, CA 90280
B. E. Hodgdon, Inc., 7710 W. 50 Hiway, Shawnee-Mission, Kans. 66202
Ithaca Gun Co., Terrace Hill, Ithaca, N.Y. 14850
J-K Imports, Box 403, Novato, Cal. 94947 (leg 'o mutton case)
Jumbo Sports Prods., P.O. Box 280-Airport Rd., Frederick, MD 21701
Kolpin Mfg., Inc., Box 231, Berlin, WI 54923
Marble Arms Corp., 420 Industrial Park, Gladstone, Mich. 49837
Bill McGuire, Inc., 10324 Valmay Ave., NW, Seattle, WA 98177 (custom cases)
W. A. Miller Co., Inc. (Wamco), Mingo Loop, Oguossoc, ME 04964 (wooden handgun cases)
National Sports Div., 19 E. McWilliams St., Fond du Lac, Wis. 54935
Nortex Co., 2821 Main St., Dallas, Tex. 75226 (automobile gun rack)
North Star Devices, Inc., P.O. Box 2095, North St., Paul, MN 55109 (Gun-Slinger portable rack)
Paul-Reed, Inc., P.O. Box 227, Charlevoix, Mich. 49720
Penguin Industries, Inc. Box 97, Parkesburg, Pa. 19365
Pistolsafe, Dr. L., N. Chili, NY 14514 (handgun safe)
Precise Imp. Corp., 3 Chestnut, Suffern, N.Y. 10901
Protecto Plastics, Inc., 201 Alpha Rd., Wind Gap, Pa. 18091 (carrying cases)
Richland Arms Co., 321 W. Adrian, Blissfield, Mich. 49228
San Angelo Die Castings, Box 984, San Angelo, Tex. 76901
Buddy Schoellkopf, 4100 Platinum Way, Dallas, Tex. 75237
Security Gun Chest, Div. of Tread Corp., P.O. Box 5497, Roanoke, VA 24012
Sile Distr., 7 Centre Market Pl., New York, N.Y. 10013 (leg o'mutton case)
Stearn Mfg. Co., Div. & 30th St., St. Cloud, Minn. 56301
Sundance Prods., 255 W. 200 S., Salt Lake City, UT 84101
Tread Corp., P.O. Box 5497, Roanoke, VA 24012 (security gun chest)
Woodstream Corp., Box 327, Lititz, Pa. 17543
Yield House, Inc., RFD, No. Conway, N.H. 03860

CHRONOGRAPHS AND PRESSURE TOOLS

B-Square Co., Box 11281, Ft. Worth, Tex. 76110
Chronograph Specialists, P.O. Box 5005, Santa Ana, Calif. 92704
Delta Technology, Inc., Lewisburg, TN 37091
Display Electronics, Box 1044, Littleton, CO 80120
Diverter Arms, Inc., 6520 Rampart St., Houston, TX 77036 (press. tool)
Herter's, Waseca, Minn. 56093
Micro-Sight Co., 242 Harbor Blvd., Belmont, Calif. 94002 (Techsonic)
Oehler Research, P.O. Box 9135, Austin, Tex. 78756
Scharon Fabricators, 2145 East Dr., St. Louis, MO 63131
Schmidt-Weston Co., Box 9, West Islip, NY 11795
Sundtek Co., P.O. Box 744, Springfield, Ore. 97477
Telepacific Electronics Co., Inc., P.O. Box 2210, Escondido, CA 92025
M. York, 19381 Keymar Way, Gaithersburg, MD 20760 (press. tool)

CLEANING & REFINISHING SUPPLIES

ADSCO, Box 191, Ft. Kent, Me. 04743 (stock finish)
A 'n A Co., Box 571, King of Prussia, PA 19406 (Valet shotgun cleaner)
Allied Products Co., 734 N. Leavitt, Chicago, Ill. 60612 (Cor-O-Dex)
Armite Labs., 1845 Randolph St., Los Angeles, CA 90001 (pen oiler)
Armoloy, 206 E. Daggett St., Ft. Worth, TX 76104
Ber Big Enterprises, Box 291, Huntington, CA 90255 (gunsoap)
Birchwood-Casey Chem. Co., 7900 Fuller Rd., Eden Prairie, Minn. 55343 (Anderol, etc.)
Bisonite Co., Inc., P.O. Box 84, Kenmore Station, Buffalo, NY 14217
Blue and Gray Prods., Inc., 817 E. Main St., Bradford, PA 16701
Jim Brobst, 299 Poplar St., Hamburg, Pa. 19526 (J-B Compound)
GB Prods. Dept., H & R, Inc., Industrial Rowe, Gardner, MA 01440

Browning Arms, Rt. 4, Box 624-B, Arnold, Mo. 63010
J. M. Bucheimer Co., Airport Rd., Frederick, MD 21701
Burnishine Prod. Co., 8140 N. Ridgeway, Skokie, Ill. 60076 (Stock Glaze)
Caddie Products Corp., Div. of Jet-Aer, Paterson, NJ 07524 (the Cloth)
Cherry Corners Mfg. Co., 11136 Congress Rd., Lodi, Ohio 44254 (buffing compound)
Chopie Mfg. Inc., 531 Copeland, La Crosse, Wis. 54601 (Black-Solve)
Clenzoil Co., Box 1226, Sta. C, Canton, O. 44708
Clover Mfg. Co., 139 Woodward Ave., Norwalk, CT 06856 (Clover compound)
Craftsman Wood Serv. Co., 2729 S. Mary, Chicago, Ill. 60608 (ctlg. 50¢)
Dri-Slide, Inc., Industrial Park, Fremont, Mich. 49412
Forty-Five Ranch Enterpr., 119 S. Main St., Miami, Okla. 74354
Garcia Sptg. Arms Corp., 329 Alfred Ave., Teaneck, N.J. 07666
Gun-All Products, Box 244, Dowagiac, Mich. 49047
Frank C. Hoppe Div., P.O. Box 97, Parkesburg, Pa. 19365
J & G Rifle Ranch, Box S 80, Turner, MT 59542
Jet-Aer Corp., 100 Sixth Ave., Paterson, N.J. 07524 (blues & oils)
Kellog's Professional Prods., Inc., Sandusky, OH 44870
K.W. Kleinendorst, 48 Taylortown Rd., Montville, N.J. 07045 (rifle clg. cables)
LPS Res. Labs. Inc., 2050 Cotner Ave., Los Angeles, Calif. 90025
LEM Gun Spec., Box 31, College Park, Ga 30337 (Lewis Lead Remover)
Liquid Wrench, Box 10628, Charlotte, N.C. 28201 (pen. oil)
Lynx Line Gun Prods. Div., Protective Coatings, Inc., 20626 Fenkell Ave., Detroit, MI 48223
Marble Arms Corp., 420 Industrial Pk., Gladstone, Mich. 49837
Micro Sight Co., 242 Harbor Blvd., Belmont, Ca. 94002 (bedding)
Mill Run Prod., 1360 W. 9th, Cleveland, O. 44113 (Brite-Bore Kits)
Mirror-Lube, P.O. Box 693, San Juan Capistrano, CA 92675
Mistic Metal Mover, Inc., R.R. 2, P.O. Box 336, Princeton, Ill. 61356
Mitchell Chemical Co., Wampus Lane, Milford, CT 06460 (Gun Guard)
New Method Mfg. Co., Box 175, Bradford, Pa. 16701 (gun blue)
Northern Instruments, Inc., 4643 No. Chatsworth St., St. Paul, MN 55112 (Stor-Safe rust preventer)
Numrich Arms Co., West Hurley, N.Y. 12491 (44-40 gun blue)
Ordnance Parkerizing, 1511 Waverly Ave., Florence, SC 29501
Outers Laboratories, Box 37, Onalaska, Wis. 54650 (Gunslick kits)
Radiator Spec. Co., 1400 Independence Blvd., Charlotte, N.C. 28201 (liquid wrench)
Realist Inc., N. 93 W. 16288 Megal Dr., Menomonee Falls, Wis. 53051
Reardon Prod., 103 W. Market St., Morrison, IL 61270 (Dry-Lube)
Rice Gun Coatings, 1521-43rd St., West Palm Beach, FL 33407
Riel & Fuller, 423 Woodrow Ave., Dunkirk, N.Y. 14048 (anti-rust oil)
Rig Products Co., Box 279, Oregon, Ill. 61061 (Rig Grease)
Rocket Chemical Co., Inc., 5390 Napa St., San Diego, Calif. 92110 (WD-40)
Rusteprufe Labs., 605 Wolcott St., Sparta, Wis. 54656
Saunders Sptg. Gds., 338 Somerset, No. Plainfield, NJ 07060 (Sav-Bore)
Schultea's Gun String, 67 Burress, Houston, TX 77022 (pocket-size rifle cleaning kit)
Service Armament, 689 Bergen Blvd., Ridgefield, N. J. 07657 (Parker-Hale)
Silicote Corp., Box 359, Oshkosh, Wis. 54901 (Silicone cloths)
Silver Dollar Guns, P.O. Box 489, Franklin, NH 03235 (Silicone oil)
A. D. Soucy, Box 191, Ft. Kent, Me. 04743 (ADSCO stock finish)
Southeastern Coatings, Ind., (SECOA), Bldg. 132, P.B.I. Airport, W. Palm Beach, Fla. 33406 (Teflon Coatings)
Sportsmen's Labs., Inc., Box 732, Anoka, Minn. 55303 (Gun Life lube)
Surcon, Inc., P.O. Box 277, Zieglerville, Pa. 19492
Taylor & Robbins, Box 164, Rixford, Pa. 16745 (Throat Saver)
Testing Systems, Inc., 2832 Mt. Carmel, Glenside, PA 19038 (gun lube)
Texas Platers Supply Co., 2453 W. Five Mile Parkway, Dallas, TX 75233 (plating kit)
C. S. Van Gorden, 120 Tenth Ave., Eau Claire, Wis. 54701 (Instant Blue)
WD-40 Co., 1061 Cudahy Pl., San Diego, CA 92110
West Coast Secoa, Inc., Rt. 5, Box 138, Lakeland, FL 33801 (Teflon coatings)
Williams Gun Sight, 7389 Lapeer Rd., Davison, Mich. 48423 (finish kit)
Winslow Arms Co., P.O. Box 578, Osprey, Fla. 33595 (refinishing kit)
Wisconsin Platers Supply Co., see: Texas Platers Supply Co.
Woodstream Corp., P.O. Box 327, Lititz, Pa. 17543 (Mask)

CUSTOM GUNSMITHS

Abe and Van Horn, 5124 Huntington Dr., Los Angeles, CA 90032
P. O. Ackley, 2235 Arbor Lane, Salt Lake City, UT 84117
Ed Agramonte, Inc., 41 Riverdale Ave., Yonkers, NY 10701
Ahlman Cust. Gun Shop, R.R. 1, Box 20, Morristown, Minn. 55052
Anderson's Guns, Jim Jares, 706 S. 23rd St., Laramie, WY 82070
Dale P. Andrews, 3572 E. Davies, Littleton, CO 80122
Antique Arms, D. F. Saunders, 1110 Cleveland Ave., Monett, MO 65708 (Hawken copies)
R. J. Anton, 874 Olympic Dr., Waterloo, IA 50701
Atkinson Gun Co., P.O. Box 512, Prescott, AZ 86301
Bacon Creek Gun Shop, Cumberland Falls Rd., Corbin, Ky. 40701
Bain and Davis Sptg. Gds., 599 W. Las Tunas Dr., San Gabriel, Calif. 41776
Joe J. Balickie, 6108 Deerwood Pl., Raleigh, N.C. 27607
Wm. G. Bankard, 4211 Thorncliff Rd., Baltimore, MD 21236 (Kentuckys)
Barta's, Rte. 1, Box 129-A, Cato, Wis. 54206
Bayer's Gun Shop, 213 S. 2nd, Walla Walla, Wash. 99362
Bennett Gun Works, 561 Delaware Ave., Delmar, N.Y. 12054
Irvin L. Benson, Saganaga Lake, Pine Island Camp, Ontario, Canada
Fred M. Bergen, 6 Longview Rd., High Crest Lake, Butler, NJ 07405
Gordon Bess, 708 River St., Canon City, Colo. 81212
Bruce Betts Gunsmith Co., 100 W. Highway 72, Rolla, MO 65401

VARMINT HUNTER'S DIGEST

John Bivins, Jr., 200 Wicklow Rd., Winston-Salem, NC 27106
Edwin T. Blackburn, Jr., 474 E. McKinley, Sunnyvale, CA 94086 (precision metal work)
Ralph Bone, 806 Ave. J, Lubbock, TX 79401
Boone Mountain Trading Post, Averyville Rd., St. Marys, Pa. 15857
T. H. Boughton, 410 Stone Rd., Rochester, N.Y. 14616
Kay H. Bowles, Pinedale, Wyo. 82941
Breckheimers, Rte. 69-A, Parish, NY 13131
L. H. Brown, Rte. 2, Airport Rd., Kalispell, Mont. 59901
Lenard M. Brownell, Box 25, Wyarno, WY 82845
David Budin, Margaretville, NY 12455
George Bunch, 7735 Garrison Rd., Hyattsville, Md. 20784
Samuel W. Burgess, 25 Squam Rd., Rockport, MA 01966 (bluing repairs)
Tom Burgess, 180 McMannamy Draw, Kalispell, MT 59901 (metalsmithing only)
Leo Bustani, P.O. Box 8125, W. Palm Beach, Fla. 33407
Gus Butterowe, 10121 Shoreview Rd., Dallas, TX 75238
Cameron's Guns, 16690 W. 11th Ave., Golden, Colo. 80401
Carpenter's Gun Works, Gunshop Rd., Plattekill, N.Y. 12568
Carter Gun Works, 2211 Jefferson Pk. Ave., Charlottesville, VA 22903
Cassell Gun Shop, 403 West Lane, Worland, Wyo. 82401
Ray Chalmers, 18 White Clay Dr., Newark, Del. 19711
N. C. Christakos, 2832 N. Austin, Chicago, IL 60634
Gene Clark, P.O. Box 26087, New Orleans, LA 70186
Jim Clark, Custom Gun Shop, 5367 S. 1950 West, Roy, UT 84067
Kenneth E. Clark, 18738 Highway 99, Madera, Calif. 93637
Cloward's Gun Shop, J. K. Cloward, 4023 Aurora Ave. N., Seattle, WA 98102
Crest Carving Co., 14849 Dillow St., Westminster, Ca. 92683
Philip R. Crouthamel, 513 E. Baltimore, E. Lansdowne, PA 19050
Custom Rifle Shop, 4550 E. Colfax Ave., Denver, Colo. 80220
Jim Cuthbert, 715 S. 5th St., Coos Bay, Ore. 97420
Dahl's Gunshop, 6947 King Ave., Billings, MT 59102
Davis Gun Shop, 7213 Lee Highway, Falls Church, VA 22046
Dee Davis, 5658 So. Mayfield, Chicago, Ill. 60638
Jack Dever, 8520 N.W. 90, Okla. City, OK 73132 (S. S. Work)
Dominic DiStefano, 4303 Friar Lane, Colorado Springs, CO 80907
Drumbore Gun Shop, 119 Center St., Lehigton, PA 18235
Charles Duffy, Williams Lane, W. Hurley, N.Y. 12491
Gerald D. Eisenhauer, Rte. #3, Twin Falls, Ida. 83301
Bill English, 4411 S. W. 100th, Seattle, Wash. 98146
Ken Eyster, Heritage Gunsmiths Inc., 6441 Bishop Rd., Centerburg, O. 43011
N. B. Fashingbauer, Box 366, Lac Du Flambeau, Wis. 54538
Ted Fellowes, Beaver Lodge, 9245-16th Ave., S.W., Seattle, Wa. 98106 (muzzle loaders)
The Fergusons, R.F.D. #1, Box 143, Hillsboro, NH 03244
H. J. and L. A. Finn, 12565 Gratiot Ave., Detroit, MI 48205
Loxley Firth Firearms, 8563 Oswego Rd., R. D. 4, Baldwinsville, N.Y. 13027
Marshall F. Fish, Westport, N.Y. 12993
Jerry Fisher, 1244—4th Ave. West, Kalispell, Mont. 59901
Flagler Gun Clinic, Box 8125, West Palm Beach, Fla. 33407 (Win. 92 & 94 Conv.)
Flynn's Cust. Gunsmithing, 3309 Elliott, Apt. B, Alexandria, LA 71301
Frazier's Custom Guns, Box 3, Tyler, WA 99035
Clark K. Frazier/Matchmate, RFD 1, Rawson, OH 45881
Freeland's Scope Stands, 3737—14th Ave., Rock Island, Ill. 61201
Fred's Gun Shop, Box 725, Juneau, Alaska 99801
Frederick Gun Shop, 10 Elson Drive, Riverside, R.I. 02915
Frontier Arms, Inc., 420 E. Riding Club Rd., Cheyenne, Wyo. 82001
Fuller Gunshop, Cooper Landing, Alas. 99572
Geo. M. Fullmer, 2499 Mavis St., Oakland, Cal. 94501 (metal work, precision chambering only)
Georgia Gun & Smith, 5170 Thistle Rd., Smyrna, GA 30080
Ed Gillman, 116 Upper High Crest Rd., Butler, NJ 07405
Dale Goens, Box 224, Cedar Crest, NM 87008
A. R. Goode, R.D. 1, Box 84, Thurmont, MD 21788
G. T. Gregory, P.O. Box 162, Plymouth, CA 95669 (saddle rifles)
Griffin & Howe, 589-8th Ave., New York, N.Y. 10017
H. L. Grisel, Rte. 1, Box 925, Bend, OR 97701 (rifles)
Dale M. Guise, Rt. 2, Box 239, Gardners, Pa. 17324 (Rem. left-hand conversions)
The Gunshop, Inc., Jack First, 44633 Sierra Highway, Lancaster, CA 93534
H & R Custom Gun Serv., 68 Passaic Dr., Hewitt, N.J. 07421
Paul Haberly, 2364 N. Neva, Chicago, IL 60635
Chas. E. Hammans, Box 788, Stuttgart, AR 72160
Harkrader's Cust. Gun Shop, 111 No. Franklin St., Christiansburg, Va. 24073
Rob't W. Hart & Son, 401 Montgomery St., Nescopeck, Pa. 18635 (actions, stocks)
Hal Hartley, 147 Blairs Fork Rd., Lenoir, NC 28654
Hubert J. Hecht, 55 Rose Mead Circle, Sacramento, CA 95831
Edw. O. Hefti, 300 Fairview, College Sta., Tex. 77840
Iver Henriksen, 1211 So. 2nd, Missoula, Mont. 59801
Wm. Hobaugh, Box 657, Philipsburg, Mont. 59858
Richard Hodgson, 9081 Tahoe Lane, Boulder, Colo. 80301
Hoenig-Rodman, 853 So. Curtis Rd., Boise, ID 83705
Hollis Gun Shop, 917 Rex St., Carlsbad, N.M. 88220
Hurt's Specialty Gunsmithing, Box 1033, Muskogee, Okla. 74401
Hyper-Single Precision SS Rifles, 520 E. Beaver, Jenks, OK 74037
Independent Machine & Gun Shop, 1416 N. Hayes, Pocatello, Ida. 83201
Jackson's, Box 416, Selman City, TX 75689
Paul Jaeger, 211 Leedom, Jenkintown, Pa. 19046
J. J. Jenkins, 462 Stanford Pl., Santa Barbara, CA 93105
Jerry's Gun Shop, 9220 Ogden Ave., Brookfield, Ill. 60513
Johnson's Gun Shop, 1316 N. Blackstone, Fresno, Calif. 93703

John Kaufield Small Arms Eng. Co., P.O. Box 306, Des Plaines, IL 60018 (restorations)
Kennedy Gun Shop, Rt. 6, Clarksville, Tenn. 37040
Monte Kennedy, P.O. Box 214, Kalispell, MT 59901
Kennon's Custom Rifles, 5408 Biffle, Stone Mtn., Ga. 30083
Kerr Sport Shop, Inc., 9584 Wilshire Blvd., Beverly Hills, Calif. 90212
Kess Arms Co., 12515 W. Lisbon Rd., Brookfield, Wis. 53005
Kesselring Gun Shop, 400 Pacific Hiway 99 No., Burlington, Wash. 98233
Vern Kitzrow, 2504 N. Grant Blvd., Milwaukee, WI 53210 (single shots)
K. W. Kleinendorst, 48 Taylortown Rd., Montville, NJ 07045
Knights Gun Store, Inc., 103 So. Jennings, Ft. Worth, Tex. 76104
Ward Koozer, Box 18, Walterville, Ore. 97489
Lacy's Gun Service, 1518A West Blvd., Charlotte, N.C. 28208
Sam Lair, 520 E. Beaver, Jenks, OK 74037
R. H. Lampert, Rt. 1, Box 61, Guthrie, MN 56451 (metalsmithing only)
LanDav Custom Guns, 7213 Lee Highway, Falls Church, VA 22046
Harry Lawson Co., 3328 N. Richey Blvd., Tucson, Ariz. 85716
John G. Lawson, 1802 E. Columbia, Tacoma, Wa. 98404
Gene Lechner, 636 Jane N. E., Albuquerque, NM 87123
LeDel, Inc., Main and Commerce Sts., Cheswold, Del. 19936
Art LeFeuvre, 1003 Hazel Ave., Deerfield, Ill. 60015
LeFever Arms Co., R.D. 1, Lee Center, N.Y. 13363
Max J. Lindauer, R.R. 1, Box 114, Washington, Mo. 63090
Robt. L. Lindsay, 9416 Emory Grove Rd., Gaithersburg, Md. 20760 (services only)
Ljutic Ind., Box 2117, Yakima, WA 98902 (Mono-Wads)
Llanerch Gun Shop, 2800 Township Line, Upper Darby, Pa. 19083
Ned McCandless, Box 126, Meriden Rte., Cheyenne, WY 82001
McCormick's Gun Bluing Service, 4936 E. Rosecrans Ave., Compton, Calif. 90221
Bill McGuire, Inc., 10324 Valmay Ave., Seattle, WA 98177
Pat B. McMillan, 1828 E. Campo Bello Dr., Phoenix, Ariz. 85022
R. J. Maberry, 511 So. K, Midland, Tex. 79701
Harold E. MacFarland, Star Route, Box 84, Cottonwood, Ariz. 86326
Marquart Precision Co., Box 1740, Prescott, AZ 86301
Martel's Custom Guns, 4038 S. Wisteria Way, Denver, CO 80237
E. H. Martin's Gun Shop, 937 S. Sheridan Blvd., Denver, CO 80226
Maryland Gun Exchange, RD 5, Rt. 40 W., Frederick, MD 21701
Mashburn Arms Co., 1020 N.W. 6th St., Oklahoma City, OK 73102
Seely Masker, 261 Washington Ave., Pleasantville, NY 10570
Mathews & Son, 10224 S. Paramount Blvd., Downey, Calif. 90241
Maurer Arms, 2366 Frederick Dr., Cuyahoga Falls, Ohio 44221 (muzzleloaders)
Maxson's Gun Shop, 122 E. Franklin, Box 145, Clinton, MO 64735
Middaugh's Nodak, 318 2nd St., Bismarck, N.D. 58501
Miller Gun Works, P.O. Box 7326, Tamuning, Guam 96911
C.D. Miller Guns, St. Onge, SD 57779
Earl Milliron, 1249 N.E. 166th Ave., Portland, Ore. 97230
Mills (D.H.) Custom Stocks, 401 N. Ellsworth, San Mateo, Calif. 94401
Mitchell's Gun Repair, Rt. 1, Perryville, Ark. 72126
Thurman Nation, Rte. 1, Box 236, Hiway 60 & 84, Clovis, NM 88101
Natl. Gun Traders, Inc., 225 S.W. 22nd Ave., Miami, Fla. 33135
Clayton N. Nelson, R.R. #3, Box 119, Enid, OK 73701
Newman Gunshop, 119 Miller Rd., Agency, Ia. 52530
Nu-Line Guns, Inc., 3727 Jennings Rd., St. Louis, Mo. 63121
Oak Lawn Gun Shop, Inc., 9618 Southwest Hwy., Oak Lawn, Ill. 60453
O'Brien Rifle Co., 324 Tropicana No. 128, Las Vegas, Nev. 89109
The Outrider, Inc., 3288 LaVenture Dr., Chamblee, GA 30341
Pachmayr Gun Works, 1220 S. Grand Ave., Los Angeles, Calif. 90015
Charles J. Parkinson, 116 Wharncliffe Rd. So., London, Ont., Canada N6J2K3
Pendleton Gunshop, 1210 S. W. Haley Ave., Pendleton, Ore. 97801
C. R. Pedersen & Son, Ludington, Mich. 49431
Al Petersen, Box 8, Riverhurst, Sask., Canada S0H3P0
A. W. Peterson Gun Shop, 1693 Old Hwy. 441 No., Mt. Dora, FL 32757 (ML rifles, also)
Ready Eddie's Gun Shop, 501 Van Spanje Ave., Michigan City, IN 46360
Marion Reed Gun Shop, 1522 Colorado, Bartlesville, Okla. 74003
R. Neal Rice, Box 12172, Denver, CO 80212
Ridge Guncraft, Inc., 234 N. Tulane, Oak Ridge, Tenn. 37830
Riedl Rifles, 15124 Weststate St., Westminster, CA 92683
Rifle Shop, Box 657, Philipsburg, Mont. 59858
Riflemen's Hdqs., Rte. 3, RD 550-E, Kendallville, IN 46755
W. Rodman, 6521 Morton Dr., Boise, ID 83705
Carl Roth, P.O. Box 2593, Cheyenne, WY 82001
Royal Arms, Inc., 10064 Bert Acosta, Santee, Calif. 92071
Murray F. Ruffino, Rt. 2, Milford, ME 04461
Rush's Old Colonial Forge, 106 Wiltshire Rd., Baltimore, MD 21221 (Ky.-Pa. rifles)
Sanders Custom Gun Serv., 2358 Tyler Lane, Louisville, Ky. 40205
Sandy's Custom Gunshop, Rockport, Ill. 62370
Saratoga Arms Co., R.D. 3, Box 387, Pottstown, Pa. 19464
Roy V. Schaefer, 965 W. Hilliard Lane, Eugene, Ore. 97402
N.H. Schiffman Cust. Gun Serv., 963 Malibu, Pocatello, ID 83201
Schuetzen Gun Works, 1226 Prairie Rd., Colorado Springs, Colo. 80909
Schumaker's Gun Shop, 208 W. 5th Ave., Colville, Wash 99114
Schwab Gun Shop, 1103 E. Bigelow, Findlay, O. 45840
Schwartz Custom Guns, 9621 Coleman Rd., Haslett, Mich. 48840
Schwarz's Gun Shop, 41-15th St., Wellsburg, W. Va. 26070
Jim Scott, Hiway 2-East, Leon, IA 50144
Scotty's Gun Shop, 534 E. Hwy. 190, Harker Heights, TX 76541 (ML)
Joseph M. Sellner, 1010 Stelton Rd., Piscataway, N.J. 08854
Shaw's, Rt. 4, Box 407-L, Escondido, CA 92025
Shell Shack, 113 E. Main, Laurel, MT 59044
George H. Sheldon, P.O. Box 489, Franklin, NH 03235 (45 autos & M-1 carbines only)
Shilen Rifles, Inc., 205 Metropark Blvd., Ennis, TX 75119
Harold H. Shockley, Box 355, Hanna City, Ill. 65126 (hot bluing & plating)

Walter Shultz, R.D. 3, Pottstown, Pa. 19464
The Sight Shop, 1802 E. Columbia Ave., Tacoma, Wa. 98404
Silver Dollar Guns, P.O. Box 489, Franklin, NH 03235 (45 autos & M-1 carbines only)
Simmons Gun Spec., 700 Rogers Rd., Olathe, Kans. 66061
Simms Hardward Co., 2801 J St., Sacramento, Calif. 95816
Skinner's Gun Shop, Box 30, Juneau, Alaska 98801
Markus Skosples, c/o Ziffren Sptg. Gds., 124 E. Third St., Davenport, IA 52801
Jerome F. Slezak, 1290 Marlowe, Lakewood (Cleveland), OH 44107
Small Arms Eng., P.O. Box 306, Des Plaines, IL 60018 (restorations)
John Smith, 912 Lincoln, Carpentersville, Ill. 60110
Smitty's Gunshop, 308 S. Washington, Lake City, Minn. 55041
Snapp's Gunshop, 6911 E. Washington Rd., Clare, Mich. 48617
R. Southgate, Rt. 2, Franklin, Tenn. 37064 (new Kentucky rifles)
Sport Service Center, 2364 N. Neva, Chicago, IL 60635
Sportsman's Den, 1010 Stelton Rd., Piscataway, N.J. 08854
Sportsmens Equip. Co., 915 W. Washington, San Diego, Calif. 92103
Sportsmen's Exchange & Western Gun Traders, Inc., P.O. Box 603, Oxnard, CA 93030
Jess L. Stark, 12051 Stroud, Houston, TX 77072
Keith Stegall, Box 696, Gunnison, Colo. 81230
Victor W. Strawbridge, 6 Pineview Dr., Dover Point, Dover, NH 03820
W. C. Strutz, Rte. 1, Eagle River, WI 54521
Suter's House of Guns, 332 N. Tejon, Colorado Springs, Colo. 80902
Swanson Custom Firearms, 1051 Broadway, Denver, Colo. 80203
A. D. Swenson's 45 Shop, P.O. Box 606, Fallbrook, CA 92028
T-P Shop, 212 E. Houghton, West Branch, Mich. 48661
Talmage Ent., 43197 E. Whittier, Hemet, CA 92343
Taylor & Robbins, Box 164, Rixford, Pa. 16745
Daniel Titus, 119 Morlyn Ave., Bryn Mawr, PA 19010
Tom's Gunshop, 600 Albert Pike, Hot Springs, Ark. 71901
Dave Trevallion, 3442 S. Post Rd., Indianapolis, IN 46239
Trinko's Gun Serv., 1406 E. Main, Watertown, Wis. 53094
Herb. G. Troester's Accurizing Serv., Cayuga, ND 58013
Doc Ulrich, 2511 S. 57th Ave., Cicero, IL 60650
Brent Umberger, Sportsman's Haven, R.R. 4, Cambridge, OH 43725
Upper Missouri Trading Co., Inc., Box 181, Crofton, MO 68730
Roy Vail, R. 1, Box 8, Warwick, N.Y. 10990
VanHorn-Abe, 5124 Huntington Dr., Los Angeles, CA 90032
J. W. Van Patten, Box 145, Foster Hill, Milford, Pa. 18337
Herman Waldron, Box 475, Pomeroy, WA 99347 (metalsmithing)
Walker Arms Co., R. 2, Box 73, Selma, AL 36701
Harold Waller, 1288 Camillo Way, El Cajon, CA 92021
R. A. Wardrop, Box 245, Mechanicsburg, Pa. 17055
Weatherby's, 2781 Firestone Blvd., South Gate, Calif. 90280
Wells Sport Store, 110 N. Summit St., Prescott, Ariz. 86301
R. A. Wells, 3452 N. 1st, Racine, Wis. 53402
Robert G. West, Rte. 1, Box 941, Eugene, OR 97402 (L.H. conversions)
Western Gunstocks Mfg. Co., 550 Valencia School Rd., Aptos, CA 95003
Duane Wiebe, 426 Creekside Dr., Pleasant Hill, CA 94563
M. C. Wiest, 234 N. Tulane Ave., Oak Ridge, Tenn. 37830
W. C. Wilber, 400 Lucerne Dr., Spartanburg, SC 29302
Williams Gun Sight Co., 7389 Lapeer Rd., Davison, Mich. 48423
Williams Gunsmithing, 1706 E Rosslynn, Fullerton, CA 92631
Bob Williams, c/o Hermans-Atlas Custom Guns, 800 E St. N.W., Washington, DC 20004
Williamson-Pate Gunsmith Service, 6021 Camp Bowie Blvd., Ft. Worth, TX 76116
Wilson Gun Store Inc., R.D. 1, Rte. 225, Dauphin, Pa. 17018
Robert M. Winter, Box 484, Menno, SD 57045
Lester Womack, Box 17210, Tucson, AZ 85710
Yale's Gun Shop, 2618 Conowingo Rd., Bel Air, MD 21014 (ML work)
York County Gun Works, RR 4, Tottenham, Ont., Canada (muzzleloaders)
G. A. Yorks, Rte. 3, Box 135, Newaygo, MI 49337
Russ Zeeryp, 1601 Foard Dr., Lynn Ross Manor, Morristown, TN 37814
R. E. Zellmer, W180 N8996 Leona Ln., Menomonee Falls, WI 53051

GAME CALLS

Burnham Bros., Box 100-C, Marble Falls, Tex. 78654
Faulk's, 616 18th St., Lake Charles, La. 70601
Lohman Mfg. Co., 320 E. Spring, Neosho, Mo. 64850
Edward J. Mehok, 1737 Davis Ave., Whiting, IN 46394
Phil. S. Olt Co., Box 550, Pekin, Ill. 61554
Penn's Woods Products, Inc., 19 W. Pittsburgh St., Delmont, Pa. 15626
Sport-Lore, Inc., 1757 Cherry St., Denver, Colo. 80220
Johnny Stewart Wildlife Calls, Box 7954, Waco, Tex. 76710
Thomas Game Calls, P.O. Box 336, Winnsboro, TX 75494
Weems Wild Calls, 500 S. 7th, Fort Smith, AR 72901
Wightman Electronics, Box 989, Easton, Md. 21601
Tex Wirtz Ent., Inc., 1925 W. Hubbard St., Chicago, Ill. 60622

GUNS (Foreign)

Abercrombie & Fitch, Madison at 45th, New York, N.Y. 10017
Alaskan Rifles, Box 30, Juneau, Alaska 99801
American Import Co., 1167 Mission St., San Francisco, Calif. 94103
American International, 103 Social Hall Ave., Salt Lake City, UT 84111
Armi Fabbri, Casella 206, Brescia, Italy 25100
Armi Famars, Via Cinelli 33, Gardone V.T. (Brescia), Italy 25063
AYA (Aguirre y Aranzabal) see: Ventura Imports (Spanish shotguns)
Armoury Inc., Rte. 25, New Preston, Ct. 06777
Bretton, Soc. Gen. de Mecanque, 21 Rue Clement Forissier, 42-St. Etienne, France
Browning, Rt. 4, Box 624-B, Arnold, Mo. 63010

Centennial Arms Corp., 3318 W. Devon, Chicago, (Lincolnwood) Ill. 60645
Century Arms Co., 3-5 Federal St., St. Albans, Vt. 05478
Champlin Firearms, Inc., Box 3191, Enid, OK 73701 (Gebruder Merkel)
Connecticut Valley Arms Co., Saybrook Rd., Haddam, CT 06438 (CVA)
Continental Arms Corp., 697 Fifth Ave., New York, N.Y. 10022
W. H. Craig, Box 927, Selma, Ala. 36701
Creighton & Warren, P.O. Box 15723, Nashville, TN 37215 (Krieghoff combination guns)
Morton Cundy & Son, Ltd., 413 6th Ave. E., Kalispell, MT 59901
Daiwa, 14011 Normandie Ave., Gardena, CA 90247
Charles Daly (see: Sloan's Sptg. Gds.)
Davidson Firearms Co., 2703 High Pt. Rd., Greensboro, N.C. 27403 (shotguns)
Davis Gun Shop, 7213 Lee Highway, Falls Church, VA 22046 (Fanzoj, Ferlach; Spanish guns)
Diana Co., 842 Vallejo St., San Francisco, CA 94133 (Benelli, Breda shotguns)
Dixie Gun Works, Inc., Hwy 51, South, Union City, Tenn. 38261 ("Kentucky" rifles)
Eastern Sports Distributors Co., Inc., P.O. Box 28, Milford, NH 03055 (Rottweil; Geco)
Euroarms, Via Solferino 13/A, 25100 Brescia, Italy
J. Fanzoj, P.O. Box 25, Ferlach, Austria 9170
Ferlach (Austria) of North America, P.O. Box 143435, S. Miami, FL 33143
R. C. Fessler & Co., 1634 Colorado Blvd., Los Angeles, Calif. 90041
Firearms Center Inc. (FCI), 113 Spokane, Victoria, TX 77901
Firearms Imp. & Exp. Co., 2470 N.W. 21st St., Miami, Fla. 33142
Firearms International Corp., 515 Kerby Hill Rd., Washington, DC 20022
Flaig's Lodge, Millvale, Pa. 15209
Florida Firearms Corp., 5555 N.W. 36th Ave., Hialeah, FL 33142
Freeland's Scope Stands, Inc., 3737 14th Ave., Rock Island, Ill. 61201
J. L. Galef & Son, Inc., 85 Chambers, New York, N.Y. 10007
Renato Gamba, Fabbrica d'Armi, via Metteotti, 81-ang. via Castelli, 29, 25063 GardoneV.T. (Brescia), Italy
Armas Garbi, Fundidores 4, Eibar, Spain (shotguns)
Garcia Sptg. Arms Corp., 329 Alfred Ave., Teaneck, N.J. 07666
Gevelot of Can. Ltd., Box 1593, Saskatoon, Sask., Canada
Georges Granger, 66 Cours Fauriel, 42 St. Etienne, France
Hawes Firearms Co., 8224 Sunset Blvd., Los Angeles, Calif. 90046
Healthways, Box 45055, Los Angeles, Calif. 90061
Gil Hebard Guns, Box 1, Knoxville, IL 61448 (Hammerli)
A. D. Heller, Inc., Box 268, 2322 Grand Ave., Baldwin, NY 11510
Herter's, Waseca, Minn. 56093
Husqvarna, see FFV Sports Inc.
Interarmco, see: Interarms (Walther)
Interarms Ltd., 10 Prince St., Alexandria, Va. 22313 (Mauser, Valmet M-62/S)
Intercontinental Arms, 2222 Barry Ave., Los Angeles, Calif. 90064
International Distr., Inc., 7290 S.W. 42nd St., Miami, FL 33155 (Taurus rev.)
Ithaca Gun Co., Terrace Hill, Ithaca, N.Y. 14850 (Perazzi)
Italguns, Via Leonardo da Vinci 36, 20090 Zingoni Di Trezzano, Milano, Italy
JBL Arms Co., 156 Terrace Way, Camillus, NY 13031 (AYA)
J-K Imports, Box 403, Novato, Cal. 94947 (Italian)
Paul Jaeger Inc., 211 Leedom St., Jenkintown, Pa. 19046
Jana Intl. Co., Box 1107, Denver, Colo. 80201 (Parker-Hale)
J. J. Jenkins, 462 Stanford Pl., Santa Barbara, CA 93105
Guy T. Jones Import Co., 905 Gervais St., Columbia, S. Car. 29201
Kanematsu-Gosho USA Inc., 543 W. Algonquin Rd., Arlington Heights, IL 60005 (Nikko)
Kassnar Imports, P.O. Box 3895, Harrisburg, PA 17105
Kerr's Sport Shop, Inc., 9584 Wilshire Blvd., Beverly Hills, CA 90212
Kimel Industries, P.O. Box 335, Matthews, NC 28105
Kleinguenther's, P.O. Box 1261, Seguin, TX 78155
Knight & Knight, 5930 S.W. 48 St., Miami, FL 33155 (made-to-order only)
Krieghoff Gun Co., P.O. Box 48-1367, Miami, FL 33148
L. A. Distributors, 4 Centre Market Pl., New York, N.Y. 10013
L.E.S., 3640 Dempster, Skokie, IL 60076 (Steyr, Mannlicher-Schonauer
S. E. Laszlo, 200 Tillary St., Brooklyn, N.Y. 11201
Lever Arms Serv. Ltd., 771 Dunsmuir, Vancouver, B.C., Canada V6C 1M9
Liberty Arms Organization, Box 306, Montrose, Calif. 91020
McKeown's Guns, R.R. 1, Pekin, Ill. 61554
McQueen Sales Co. Ltd., 1760 W. 3rd Ave., Vancouver, B.C., Canada V6J 1K5
Mandall Shooting Supplies Corp., 7150 E. 4th St., Scottsdale, AZ 85252
Manu-Arm, St. Etienne, France
Manufrance, 100-Cours Fauriel, 42 St. Etienne, France
Marietta Replica Arms Co., 706½ Mongomery St., Marietta, OH 45750
Mars Equipment Corp., 3318 W. Devon, Chicago, Ill. 60645
Mauser Amerika, 1721 Crooks Rd., Troy, MI 48084
Navy Arms Co., 689 Bergen Blvd., Ridgefield, N.J. 07657
Nikko Sporting Firearms, 543 W. Algonquin Rd., Arlington Heights, IL 60005
Omnipol, Washingtonova 11, Praha 1, Czechoslovakia
Harry Owen, P.O. Box 774, Sunnyvale, Ca. 94088.
Pachmayr Gun Works, 1220 S. Grand Ave., Los Angeles, CA 90015
Pacific Intl. Merch. Corp., P.O. Box 8022, Sacramento, CA 95818
Parker-Hale, Bisleyworks, Golden Hillock Rd., Sparbrook, Birmingham 11, England
Ed Paul Sptg. Goods, 172 Flatbush Ave., Brooklyn, N.Y. 11217 (Premier)
Picard-Fayolle, 42-rue du Vernay, 4200 Saint Etienne, France
Precise Imp. Corp. (PIC), 3 Chestnut, Suffern, N.Y. 10901
Premier Shotguns, 172 Flatbush Ave., Brooklyn N.Y. 11217
RG Industries, Inc., 2485 N.W. 20th St., Miami, FL 33142 (Erma)
Richland Arms Co., 321 W. Adrian St., Blissfield, Mich. 49228
Rottweil, see: Eastern
Sanderson's, 724 W. Edgewater, Portage, Wis. 53901

VARMINT HUNTER'S DIGEST

Savage Arms Corp., Westfield, Mass. 01085 (Anschutz)
Security Arms Co., 1815 No. Ft. Myer Dr., Arlington, VA 22209 (Heckler & Koch)
Service Armament, 689 Bergen Blvd., Ridgefield, N.J. 07657 (Greener Harpoon Gun)
Sherwood Dist., Inc., 18714 Parthenia St., Northridge, CA 91324
Simmons Spec., Inc., 700 Rogers Rd., Olathe, Kans. 66061
Skinner's Gun Shop (see Alaskan Rifles)
Sloan's Sprtg. Goods, Inc., 10 South St., Ridgefield, CT 06877
Franz Sodia Jagdgewehrfabrik, 9170 Ferlach, Austria
Steyr, A4400 Steyr, Austria
Stoeger Arms Co., 55 Ruta Ct., S. Hackensack, N.J. 07606
Tradewinds, Inc., P.O. Box 1191, Tacoma, Wash. 98401
Twin City Sptg. Gds., 217 Ehrman Ave., Cincinnati, OH 45220
Uberti, Aldo & Co., Via G. Carducci 41 or 39, Ponte Zanano (Brescia), Italy
Ignacio Ugartechea, Eibar, Spain
Universal Sporting Goods Co., Inc., 3746 E. 10th Ct., Hialeah, FL 33013
Valor Imp. Corp., 5555 N.W. 36th Ave., Miami, FL 33142
Ventura Imports, P.O. Box 2782, Seal Beach, CA 90740 (Spanish shotguns)
Verney-Carron, 17 Cours Fauriel, 42010 St. Etienne Cedex, France
Waffen-Frankonia, Box 380, 87 Wurzburg, W. Germany
Weatherby's, 2781 Firestone Blvd., So. Gate, Calif. 90280 (Sauer)
Dan Wesson Arms, 293 So. Main, Monson, Mass. 01057
Zavodi Crvena Zastava, 29 Novembra St., No. 12, Belgrade, Yugosl.

GUN PARTS, U. S. AND FOREIGN

Badger Shooter's Supply, Box 397, Owen, WI 54460
Shelley Braverman, Athens, N.Y. 12015
Philip R. Crouthamel, 513 E. Baltimore, E. Lansdowne, Pa. 19050
Charles E. Duffy, Williams Lane, West Hurley, N.Y. 12491
Federal Ordnance Inc., 9634 Alpaca St., So. El Monte, CA 91733
Greg's Winchester Parts, P.O. Box 8125, W. Palm Beach, FL 33407
The Gunshop, Inc., 44633 Sierra Highway, Lancaster, CA 93534
Hunter's Haven, Zero Prince St., Alexandria, Va. 22314
International Sportsmen's Supply Co., Inc., Arapaho-Central Park, Suite 311, Richardson, TX 75080 (bbld. actions)
Numrich Arms Co., West Hurley, N.Y. 12491
The Outrider, Inc., 3288 LaVenture Dr., Chamblee, GA 30341
Pacific Intl. Merch. Corp., P.O. Box 8022, Sacramento, CA 95818
Potomac Arms Corp. (see Hunter's Haven)
Martin B. Retting, Inc., 11029 Washington, Culver City, Cal. 90230
Ruvel & Co., 3037 N. Clark, Chicago, IL 60614
Sarco, Inc., 192 Central, Stirling, N.J. 07980
Sherwood Distr. Inc., 18714 Parthenia St., Northridge, CA 91324
Simms, 2801 J St., Sacramento, CA 95816
Clifford L. Smires, R.D., Box 39, Columbus, NJ 08022 (Mauser rifles)
N. F. Strebe, 4926 Marlboro Pike, S.E., Washington, D.C. 20027
Triple-K Mfg. Co., 568-6th Ave., San Diego, CA 92101

GUNS, SURPLUS PARTS AND AMMUNITION

Century Arms, Inc., 3-5 Federal St., St. Albans, Vt. 05478
W. H. Craig, Box 927, Selma, Ala. 36701
Cummings Intl. Inc., 41 Riverside Ave., Yonkers, N.Y. 10701
Eastern Firearms Co., 790 S. Arroyo Pkwy., Pasadena, Calif. 91105
Hunter's Lodge, 200 S. Union, Alexandria, Va. 22313
Lever Arms Serv. Ltd., 771 Dunsmuir St., Vancouver, B.C., Canada V6C IM9
Mars Equipment Corp., 3318 W. Devon, Chicago, III. 60645
National Gun Traders, 225 S.W. 22nd, Miami, Fla. 33135
The Outrider, Inc., 3288 LaVenture Dr., Chamblee, GA 30341
Pacific Intl. Merch. Corp., P.O. Box 8022, Sacramento, CA 95818
Plainfield Ordnance Inc., Box 447, Dunellen, N.J. 08812
Potomac Arms Corp., Box 35, Alexandria, Va. 22313
Ruvel & Co., 3037 N. Clark St., Chicago, Ill. 60614
Service Armament Co., 689 Bergen Blvd., Ridgefield, N.J. 07657
Sherwood Distrib. Inc., 18714 Parthenia St., Northridge, CA 91324

GUNS, U.S.-made

ArmaLite, 118 E. 16th St., Costa Mesa, Calif. 92627
Apollo Custom Rifles, Inc., 1235 Cowles St., Long Beach, CA 90813
Artistic Arms, Inc., Box 23, Hoagland, IN 46745 (Sharps-Borchardt)
Bauer Firearms, 34750 Klein Ave., Fraser, MI 48026
Bortmess Gun Co., Inc., RD #1, Box 199A, Scenery Hill, PA 15360
Challanger Mfg. Corp., 118 Pearl St., Mt. Vernon, NY 10550 (Hopkins & Allen)
Champlin Firearms, Inc., Box 3191, Enid, Okla. 73701
Charter Arms Corp., 430 Sniffens Ln., Stratford, CT 06497
Clerke Products, 2219 Main St., Santa Monica, Ca. 90405
Colt, 150 Huyshope Ave., Hartford, CT 06102
Commando Arms, Inc., Box 10214, Knoxville, Tenn. 37919
Cumberland Arms, 1222 Oak Dr., Manchester, Tenn 37355
Day Arms Corp., 7515 Stagecoach Ln., San Antonio, Tex. 78227
Falling Block Works, P.O. Box 22, Troy, MI 48084
Firearms Imp. & Exp. Corp., 2470 N.W. 21st St., Miami, FL 33142 (FIE)
Firearms Intl. Corp., (see: Garcia)
4 Ace Mfg. Inc., P.O. Box 3820, Brownsville, TX 78520
Golden Age Arms Co., 14 W. Winter St., Delaware, OH 43015
Greyhawk Arms Corp., 1900 Tyler Ave., Unit 15, South El Monte, CA 91733

H & N Minicraft, Inc., 1066 E. Edna Pl., Covina, CA 91722 (Thomas auto pistol)
Gyrojet (see Intercontinental Arms)
Harrington & Richardson, Industrial Rowe, Gardner, MA 01440
A. D. Heller, Inc., Box 268, Grand Ave., Baldwin, NY 11510
Hi-Shear Corp., 2600 Skypark Dr., Torrance, CA 90509 (Omega rifle)
High Standard Mfg. Co., 1817 Dixwell Ave., Hamden, Conn. 06514
Hopkins & Allen, see: High Standard
Hyper-Single Precision SS Rifles, 520 E. Beaver, Jenks, OK 74037
Indian Arms Corp., 13503 Joseph Campar, Detroit, MI 48212
Intercontinental Arms, Inc., 2222 Barry Ave., Los Angeles, Ca. 90064
Int'l. Sportsmen's Supply Co., Inc., Arapaho-Central Park, Suite 311, Richardson, TX 75080 (Santa Barbara bbld. actions)
Ithaca Gun Co., Ithaca, N.Y. 14850
Iver Johnson Arms & Cycle Works, Fitchburg, Mass. 01420
J & R carbine, (see: PJK Inc.)
Lee E. Jurras & Assoc., Inc., P.O. Box 846, Roswell, NM 88201 (Auto Mag)
Ljutic Ind., Inc., P.O. Box 2117, Yakima, WA 98902 (Mono-Gun)
MBAssociates (see Intercontinental Arms)
Manchester Arms, Inc., 6858 Manchester Rd., Rt. 2, Clinton, OH 44216
Marlin Firearms Co., 100 Kenna Dr., New Haven, Conn. 06473
Merrill Co. Inc., Box 187, Rockwell City, IA 50579
O. F. Mossberg & Sons, Inc., 7 Grasso St., No. Haven, Conn. 06473
W. L. Mowrey Gun Works, Inc., Box 28, Iowa Park TX 76367
Natl. Ordance Inc., 9643 Alpaca, S. El Monte, CA 91733
Navy Arms Co., 689 Bergen Blvd., Ridgefield, N.J. 07657
Norarmco, 41471 Irwin, Mt. Clemens, MI 48043 (D.A. 25 auto)
North American Arms Co., 3303 Old Conejo Rd., Newbury Park, CA 91320
North Star Arms, R.2, Box 74A, Ortonville, MN 56278 (The Plainsman)
Numrich Arms Corp., W. Hurley, N.Y. 12491
Omega (see Hi-Shear Corp.)
PJK, Inc., 1527 Royal Oak Dr., Bradbury, Ca 91010 (J&R Carbine)
Pedersen Custom Guns, Div. of O. F. Mossberg & Sons, Inc., 7 Grasso Ave., North Haven, CT 06473
Plainfield Machine Co., Inc., Box 447, Dunellen, N.J. 08812
Plainfield Ordnance Co., P.O. Box 251, Middlesex, NJ 08846
Potomac Arms Corp., P.O. Box 35, Alexandria, Va. 22313 (ML replicas)
R G Industries, 2485 N.W. 20th SE., Miami, FL 33142
Remington Arms Co., Bridgeport, Conn. 06602
Riedl Rifles, 15124 Weststate St., Westminster, CA 92683 (S.S.)
Ruger (see Sturm, Ruger & Co.)
Savage Arms Corp., Westfield, Mass. 01085
Sears, Roebuck & Co., 825 S. St. Louis, Chicago, Ill. 60607
Security Industries of America, Inc., 31 Bergen Turnpike, Little Ferry, NJ 07643
Seventrees Ltd., 315 W. 39th St., New York, N.Y. 10018
Smith & Wesson, Inc., 2100 Roosevelt Ave., Springfield, MA 01101
Sporting Arms, Inc., 9643 Alpaca St., So. El Monte, CA 91733 (M-1 carbine)
Springfield Armory, Div. of RSI, 218 N. State St., Geneseo, IL 61254
Sterling Arms Corp., 4436 Prospect St., Gasport, NY 14067
Sturm, Ruger & Co., Southport, Conn. 06490
Thompson-Center Arms, Box 2405, Rochester, N.H. 03867
Tingle, 1125 Smithland Pike, Shelbyville, Ind. 46176 (muzzleloader)
Trail Guns Armory, 2115 Lexington, Houston, TX 77006 (muzzleloaders)
Universal Firearms Corp., 3746 E. 10th Ct., Hialeah, Fla. 33013
Unordco, P.O. Box 15723, Nashville, TN 37215
Ward's, 619 W. Chicago, Chicago, Ill. 60607 (Western Field brand)
Weatherby's, 2781 E. Firestone Blvd., South Gate, Calif. 90280
Dan Wesson Arms, 293 So. Main St., Monson, Mass. 01057
Winchester Repeating Arms Co., New Haven, Conn. 06504
Winslow Arms Co., P.O. Box 578, Osprey, Fla. 33595

GUNSMITH SUPPLIES, TOOLS, SERVICES

Alamo Heat Treating Co., Box 55345, Houston, Tex. 77055
Albright Prod. Co., P.O. Box 1027, Winnemucca, NV 89445 (trap buttplates)
Alley Supply Co., Carson Valley Industrial Park, Gardnerville, NV 89410
Ames Precision Machine Works, 5270 Geddes Rd., Ann Arbor, MI 48105 (portable hardness tester)
Anderson & Co., 1203 Broadway, Yakima, Wash. 98902 (tang safe)
Armite Labs., 1845 Randolph St., Los Angeles, Cal. 90001 (pen oiler)
B-Square Co., Box 11281, Ft. Worth, Tex. 76110
Jim Baiar, Rt. 1-B, Box 352, Columbia Falls, Mont. 59912 (hex screws)
Al Biesen, W. 2039 Sinto Ave., Spokane, WA 99201 (grip caps, buttplates)
Bonanza Sports Mfg. Co., 412 Western Ave., Faribault, Minn. 55021
Brookstone Co., 16 Brookstone Bldg., Vose Farm Rd., Peterborough, NH 03458
Brown & Sharpe Mfg. Co., Precision Pk., No. Kingston, R.I. 02852
Bob Brownell's, Main & Third, Montezuma, Ia. 50171
W. E. Brownell, 1852 Alessandro Trail, Vista, Calif. 92083 (checkering tools)
Maynard P. Buehler, Inc., 17 Orinda Hwy., Orinda, Calif. 94563 (Rocol lube)
Burgess Vibrocrafters, Inc. (BVI), Rte. 83, Grayslake, Ill. 60030
M. H. Canjar, 500 E. 45th, Denver, Colo. 80216 (triggers, etc.)
Chapman Mfg. Co., Rte. 17, Durham, CT 06422
Chase Chemical Corp., 3527 Smallman St., Pittsburgh, PA 15201 (Chubb Multigauge)
Chubb (see Chase Chem. Corp.)
Chicago Wheel & Mfg. Co., 1101 W. Monroe St., Chicago, Ill. 60607 (Handee grinders)
Christy Gun Works, 875-57th St., Sacramento, Calif. 95819
Clover Mfg. Co., 139 Woodward Ave., Norwalk, CT 06856 (Clover compound)

Clymer Mfg. Co., 14241 W. 11 Mile Rd., Oak Park, Mich. 48237 (reamers)
Colbert Industries, 10107 Adella, South Gate, Calif. 90280 (Panavise)
A. Constantine & Son, Inc., 2050 Eastchester Rd., Bronx, N.Y. 10461 (wood)
Cougar & Hunter, G 6398 W. Pierson Rd., Flushing, Mich. 48433 (scope jigs)
Alvin L. Davidson, 1215 Branson, Las Cruces, NM 88001 (action sleeves)
Dayton-Traister Co., P.O. Box 593, Oak Harbor, Wa. 98277 (triggers)
Dem-Bart Hand Tool Co., 6807 Hwy 2, Snohomish, WA 98290 (checkering tools)
Ditto Industries, 527 N. Alexandria, Los Angeles, Cal. 90004 (clamp tool)
Dixie Diamond Tool Co., Inc., 6875 S.W. 81st St., Miami, Fla. 33143 (marking pencils)
Dremel Mfg. Co., 4915-21st St., Racine, WI 53406 (grinders)
Chas. E. Duffy, Williams Lane, West Hurley, N.Y. 12491
E-Z Tool Co., P.O. Box 3186, 25 N.W. 44th Ave., Des Moines, Ia. 50313 (lathe taper attachment)
Edmund Scientific Co., 101 E. Glouster Pike, Barrington, N.J. 08007
F. K. Elliott, Box 785, Ramona, Calif. 92065 (reamers)
Forster Products, Inc., 82 E. Lanark Ave., Lanark, Ill. 61046
Keith Francis, 8515 Wagner Creek Rd., Talent, Ore. 97540 (reamers)
G. R. S. Corp., Box 1157, Boulder, Colo. 80302 (Gravermeister)
Gager Gage and Tool Co., 27509 Industrial Blvd., Hayward, CA 94545 (speedlock triggers f. Rem. 1100 & 870 pumps)
Gilmore Pattern Works, 1164 N. Utica, Tulsa, Okla. 74110
Gold Lode, Inc., 181 Gary Ave., Wheaton, IL 60187 (gold inlay kit)
Grace Metal Prod., 115 Ames St., Elk Rapids, MI 49629 (screw drivers, drifts)
Gopher Shooter's Supply, Box 246, Faribault, Minn. 55021 (screwdrivers, etc.)
Gunline Tools Inc., 719 No. East St., Anaheim, CA 92805
H. & M. 24062 Orchard Lake Rd., Farmington, Mich. 48024 (reamers)
Half Moon Rifle Shop, Rt. 1B, Box 352, Columbia Falls, MT 59912 (hex screws)
Hartford Reamer Co., Box 134, Lathrup Village, Mich. 48075
O. Iber Co., 626 W. Randolph, Chicago, Ill. 60606
Paul Jaeger Inc., 211 Leedom St., Jenkintown, Pa. 19046
Jeffredo Gunsight Co., 1629 Via Monserate, Fallbrook, CA 92028 (trap buttplate)
Kasenite Co., Inc., 3 King St., Mahwah, N.J. 07430 (surface hrdng. comp.)
LanDav Custom Guns, 7213 Lee Highway, Falls Church, VA 22046
John G. Lawson, 1802 E. Columbia Ave., Tacoma, WA 98404
Lea Mfg. Co., 237 E. Aurora St., Waterbury, Conn. 06720
Lock's Phila. Gun Exch., 6700 Rowland Ave., Philadelphia, Pa. 19149
Marker Machine Co., Box 426, Charleston, Ill. 61920
Michaels of Oregon Co., P.O. Box 13010, Portland, Ore. 97213
Viggo Miller, P.O. Box 4181, Omaha, Neb. 68104 (trigger attachment)
Miller Single Trigger Mfg. Co., RD1, Box 69, Millersburg, PA 17061
Frank Mittermeier, 3577 E. Tremont, N.Y., N.Y. 10465
Moderntools Corp, Box 407, Dept. GD, Woodside, N.Y. 11377
N&J Sales, Lime Kiln Rd., Northford, Conn. 06472 (screwdrivers)
Karl A. Neise, Inc., 5602 Roosevelt Ave., Woodside, N.Y. 11377
Palmgren, 8383 South Chicago Ave., Chicago, Ill. 60167 (vises, etc.)
Panavise, Colbert Industries, 10107 Adelia Ave., South Gate, CA 90280
C. R. Pedersen & Son, Ludington, Mich. 49431
Ponderay Lab., 210 W. Prasch, Yakima, Wash. 98902 (epoxy glass bedding)
Redford Reamer Co., Box 40604, Redford Hts. Sta, Detroit, MI 48240
Richland Arms Co., 321 W. Adrian St., Blissfield, Mich. 49228
Riley's Supply Co., 121 No. Main St., Avilla, Ind. 46710 (Niedner buttplates, caps)
Ruhr-American Corp., So. Hwy #5, Glenwood, Minn. 56334
A. G. Russell, 1705 Hiway 71N, Springdale, AR 72764 (Arkansas oilstones)
Schaffner Mfg. Co., Emsworth, Pittsburgh, Pa. 15202 (polishing kits)
Schuetzen Gun Works, 1226 Prarie Rd., Colo. Springs, Colo. 80909
Shaw's, Rt. 4, Box 407-L, Escondido, CA 92025
A. D. Soucy Co., Box 191, Fort Kent, Me. 04743 (ADSCO stock finish)
L. S. Starrett Co., Athol, Mass. 01331
Texas Platers Supply Co., 2453 W. Five Mile Parkway, Dallas, TX 75233 (plating kit)
Timney Mfg. Co., 5624 Imperial Hwy., So. Gate, Calif. 90280 (triggers)
Stan de Treville, Box 33021, San Diego, Calif. 92103 (checkering patterns)
Twin City Steel Treating Co., Inc., 1114 S. 3rd, Minneapolis, Minn. 55415 (heat treating)
Ward Mfg. Co., 500 Ford Blvd., Hamilton, O. 45011
Will-Burt Co., P.O. Box 160, Orrville, O. 44667 (vises)
Williams Gun Sight Co., 7389 Lapeer Rd., Davison, Mich. 48423
Wilson Arms Co., 63 Leetes Island Rd., Branford, CT 06405
Wilton Tool Corp., 9525 W. Irving Pk. Rd., Schiller Park, Ill. 60176 (vises)
Wisconsin Platers Supply Co., see: Texas Platers
W. C. Wolff Co., Box 232, Ardmore, PA 19003 (springs)
Woodcraft Supply Corp., 313 Montvale, Woburn, MA 01801

HANDGUN ACCESSORIES

A. R. Sales Co., 9624 Alpaca St., South El Monte, CA 91733
Baramie Corp., 6250 E. 7 Mile Rd., Detroit, MI 48234 (Hip-Grip)
Bar-Sto Precision Machine, 633 S. Victory Blvd., Burbank, CA 91502
B. L. Broadway, Rte. 1, Box 381, Alpine, CA 92001 (machine rest)
C'Arco, P.O. Box 2043, San Bernardino, CA 92406 (Ransom Rest)
Case Master, 4675 E. 10 Ave., Miami, Fla. 33013
Central Specialties Co., 6030 Northwest Hwy., Chicago, Ill. 60631
John Dangelzer, 3056 Frontier Pl., N.E., Albuquerque, N.M. 87106 (flasks)
Bill Dyer, 503 Midwest Bldg., Oklahoma City, Okla. 73102 (grip caps)
R. S. Frielich, 396 Broome St., New York, N.Y. 10013 (cases)
R. G. Jensen, 16153½ Parthenia, Sepulveda, Calif. 91343 (auxiliary chambers)
Lee E. Jurras & Assoc., Inc., P.O. Box 846, Roswell, NM 88201 (Auto Mag only)
Lee Prec. Mfg., 46 E. Jackson, Hartford, WI 53027 (pistol rest holders)
Los Gatos Grip & Specialty Co., P.O. Box 1850, Los Gatos, CA 95030 (custom-made)
Marcon, 1720 Marina Ct., Suite D, San Mateo, CA 94403 (Mellmark pistol safe)
Matich Loader, Box 958, So. Pasadena, Calif. 91030 (Quick Load)
W. A. Miller Co., Inc., Mingo Loop, Oguossoc, ME 04964 (cases)
No-Sho Mfg. Co., 10727 Glenfield Ct., Houston, TX 77035
Pachmayr, 1220 S. Grand, Los Angeles, Calif. 90015 (cases)
Pistolsafe, Dr. L., N. Chili, NY 14514 (handgun safe)
Platt Luggage, Inc., 2301 S. Prairie, Chicago, Ill. 60616 (cases)
Sportsmen's Equipment Co., 415 W. Washington, San Diego, Calif. 92103
M. Tyler, 1326 W. Britton, Oklahoma City, Okla. 73114 (grip adaptor)

HANDGUN GRIPS

Beckelhymer's, Hidalgo & San Bernardo, Laredo, Tex. 78040
Belmont Prods., Rte. #1, Friendsville, TN 37737
Cloyce's Gun Stocks, Box 1133, Twin Falls, Ida. 83301
Crest Carving Co., 8091 Bolsa Ave., Midway City, CA 92655
Custom Combat Grips, 148 Shepherd Ave., Brooklyn, N.Y. 11208
Fitz, Box 49697, Los Angeles, Calif. 90049
Herrett's, Box 741, Twin Falls, Ida. 83301
Hogue Custom Combat Grips, c/o Gateway Shooters' Supply, Inc., 991 Gun Club Dr., Jacksonville, FL 32218
J. R. Grips, 1601 Wilt Rd., Fallbrook, CA 92028
Mershon Co., Inc., 1230 S. Grand Ave., Los Angeles, Calif. 90015
Mustang Custom Pistol Grips, 28030 Del Rio Rd., Temecula, CA 92390
Safety Grip Corp., Box 456, Riverside St., Miami, Fla. 33135
Sanderson Custom Pistol Stocks, 17695 Fenton, Detroit, Mich. 48219
Jay Scott, 81 Sherman Place, Garfield, N.J. 07026
Sile Dist., 7 Centre Market Pl., New York, N.Y. 10013
Sports Inc., P.O. Box 683, Park Ridge, IL 60068 (Franzite)

HEARING PROTECTORS

AO Safety Prods., Div. of American Optical Corp., 14 Mechanic St., Southbridge, MA 01550 (ear valve)
Bausch & Lomb, 635 St. Paul St., Rochester, N.Y. 14602
David Clark Co., 360 Franklin St., Worcester, Mass. 01604
Curtis Safety Prod. Co., Box 61, Webster Sq. Sta., Worcester, Mass. 01603 (ear valve)
EAR Corp., Concord Rd., Billerica, MA 01821
Hodgdon, 7710 W. 50 Hiway, Shawnee Mission, Kans. 66202
Sigma Eng. Co., 11320 Burbank Blvd., No. Hollywood, Ca. 91601 (LeeSonic ear valve)
Safety Direct, P.O. Box 8907, Reno, NV 89507 (Silencio)
Smith & Wesson, 2100 Roosevelt Ave., Springfield, MA 01101
Vector Scientific, P.O. Box 21106, Ft. Lauderdale, FL 33316
Willson Prods Div., P.O. Box 622, Reading, Pa. 19603 (Ray-O-Vac)

HOLSTERS & LEATHER GOODS

American Sales & Mfg. Co., P.O. Box 677, Laredo, Tex. 78040
Andy Anderson, P.O. Box 225, North Hollywood, CA 91603 (Gunfighter Custom Holsters)
Bianchi Holster Co., 100 Calle Cortez, Temecula, CA 92390
Boyt Co., Div. of Welch Sptg., Box 1108, Iowa Falls, Ia. 51026
Brauer Bros. Mfg. Co., 817 N. 17th, St. Louis, Mo. 63106
Browning, Rt. 4, Box 624-B, Arnold, MO 63010
J. M. Bucheimer Co., Airport Rd., Frederick, Md. 21701
Cathey Enterprises, P.O. Box 3545, Chula Vista, CA 92011
Clements Custom Leathercraft, 1245 S. Pennsylvania St., Denver, CO 80203 (Custom-made holsters)
Cole's Acku-Rite, Box 25, Kennedy, N.Y. 14747
Colt's, 150 Huyshope Ave., Hartford, Conn. 06102
Daisy Mfg. Co., Rogers, Ark. 72756
Eugene DeMayo & Sons, Inc., 2795 Third Ave., Bronx, N.Y. 10455
Ellwood Epps (Orillia) Ltd., Hwy. 11 North, Orillia, Ont., Canada
Filmat Enterpr., Inc., 200 Market St., East Paterson, N.J. 07407
Goerg Ent., 3009 S. Laurel, Port Angeles, Wash. 98362
Gunfighter (See Anderson)
Hoyt Holster Co., P.O. Box 1783, Costa Mesa, Cal. 92626
Don Hume, Box 351, Miami, Okla. 74354
The Hunter Co., 3300 W. 71st Ave., Westminster, CO 80030
Jet Sports Prods., 4 Centre Market Pl., New York, N.Y. 10013
Jumbo Sports Prods., P.O. Box 280, Airport Rd., Frederick, MD 21701
George Lawrence Co., 306 S. W. First Ave., Portland, Ore. 97221
Leathercrafters, 710 S. Washington, Alexandria, VA 22314
MMGR Corp., 5710 12th Ave., Brooklyn, N.Y. 11219
S. D. Myres Saddle Co., Box 9776, El Paso, Tex. 79988
Pancake Holsters, Roy Baker, Box 245, Magnolia, AR 71753
Pony Express Sport Shop, 17460 Ventura Blvd., Encino, Calif. 91316
Red Head Brand Co., 4100 Platinum Way, Dallas, Tex. 75237
Rickenbacker's, P.O. Box 532, State Ave., Holly Hill, SC 29059
R. E. Roseberry, 810 W. 38th, Anderson, Ind. 46014
Roy's Custom Leather Goods, Hwy. 132, Rt. 1, Box 245, Magnolia, AR 71753
Safariland Leather Products, 1941 Walker Ave., Monrovia, Calif. 91016
Safety Speed Holster, Inc., 910 So. Vail, Montebello, Calif. 90640
Saguaro Holsters, 1508 Del Carlo Circle, Seagoville, TX 75159 (custom)
Buddy Schoellkopf Products, Inc., 4100 Platinum Way, Dallas, Tex. 75237
Seventrees, Ltd., 315 W. 39 St., New York, N.Y. 10018
Sile Distr., 7 Centre Market Pl., New York, N.Y. 10013

Smith & Wesson Leather Co., 2100 Roosevelt, Springfield, Mass. 01101
Stein Holsters & Accessories, Inc., Drawer B, Wakefield Sta., Bronx, NY 10466
Swiss-Craft Co., Inc., 33 Arctic St., Worcester, MA 01604
Tandy Leather Co., 1001 Foch, Fort Worth, Texas 76107
Tayra Corp., 1529-19th St. N.W., Canton, O. 44709
Torel, Inc., 1053 N. South St., Yoakum, TX 77995 (gun slings)
Triple-K Mfg. Co., 568 Sixth Ave., San Diego, CA 92101
Whitco, Box 1712, Brownsville, Tex. 78520 (Hide-A-Way)

HUNTING AND CAMP GEAR, CLOTHING, ETC.

Eddie Bauer, 1737 Airport Way So., Seattle, Wash. 98134
L. L. Bean, Freeport, Me. 04032
Bear Archery Co., R.R. 1, Grayling, Mich. 49738 (Himalayan backpack)
Bernzomatic Corp., 740 Driving Pk. Ave., Rochester, N.Y. 14613 (stoves & lanterns)
Big Beam, Teledyne Co., 290 E. Prairie St., Crystal Lake, Ill. 60014 (lamp)
Bill Boatman & Co., So. Maple St., Bainbridge, OH 45612
Browning, Rte. 1, Morgan, Utah 84050
Camouflage Mfg. Co., P.O. Box 5437, Pine Bluff, AR 71601
Camp Trails, P.O. Box 14500, Phoenix, Ariz. 85031 (packs only)
Camp Ways, 415 Molino St., Los Angeles, CA 90013
Challanger Mfg. Co., Box 550, Jamaica, N.Y. 11431 (glow safe)
Coleman Co., Inc., 250 N. St. Francis, Wichita, Kans. 67201
Colorado Outdoor Sports Co., 5450 N. Valley Hwy., Denver, Colo. 80216
Converse Rubber Co., 1200 Kirk St., Elk Grove Village, IL 60007 (boots)
Corcoran, Inc., 2 Canton Street, Stoughton, Mass. 02072
Dana Safety Heater, J. L. Galef & Son, Inc., 85 Chamber St., N.Y. N.Y. 10007
DEER-ME Prod. Co., Box 345, Anoka, Minn. 55303 (tree steps)
Dunham's Footwear, RFD 3, Brattleboro, Vt. 05301 (boots)
Filmat Enterpr., Inc., 200 Market St., East Paterson, N.J. 07407 (field dressing kit)
Freeman Ind., Inc., 100 Marblehead Rd., Tuckahoe, N.Y. 10707 (Trak-Kit)
Game-Winner, Inc., 515 Candler Bldg., Atlanta, GA 30303 (camouflage suits)
Gander Mountain, Inc., Box 248, Wilmot, Wis. 53192
Gerry Mountain Sports, Inc. (see Colorado Sports)
Gokey, 94 E. 4th St., St. Paul, Minn. 55101
Gun Club Sportswear, Box 477, Des Moines, Ia. 50302
Gun-Ho Case Mfg. Co., 110 E. 10th St., St. Paul, Minn. 55101
Herter's Inc., Waseca, Minn. 56093
Himalayan Back Packs, P.O. Box 5668, Pine Bluff, AR 71601
Bob Hinman, 1217 W. Glen, Peoria, Ill. 61614
Holubar Mountaineering, Box 7, Boulder, Colo. 80302
Kelty Pack, Inc., Box 3645, Glendale, Calif. 91201
Peter Limmer & Sons, Box 66, Intervale, N.H. 03845 (boots)
Marathon Rubber Prods. Co., 510 Sherman St., Wausau, WI 54401 (rain gear)
Marble Arms Corp., 420 Industrial Park, Gladstone, Mich. 49837
National Sports Div., 19 E. McWilliams St., Fond du Lac, Wis. 54935
Nimrod & Wayfarer Trailers, 500 Ford Blvd., Hamilton, O. 45011
Charles F. Orvis Co., Manchester, Vt. 05254 (fishing gear)
Palco Prods., 15 Hope Ave., Worcester, MA 01603
Paulin Infra-Red Prod. Co., 30520 Lakeland Blvd., Willowick, OH 44094
Primus-Sievert, 354 Sackett Pt. Rd., No. Haven, CT 06473 (stoves)
Ranger Mfg. Co., Inc., P.O. Box 3676, Augusta, GA 30904
Red Head Brand Co., 4100 Platinum Way, Dallas Tex. 75237
Red Wing Shoe Co., Rte. 2, Red Wing, Minn. 55066
Refrigiwear, Inc., 71 Inip Dr., Inwood, L.I., N.Y. 11696
Reliance Prod. Ltd., 1830 Dublin Ave., Winnipeg 21, Man., Can. (tent peg)
W. R. Russell Moccasin Co., 285 S.W. Franklin, Berlin, WI 54923
Buddy Schoellkopf, Inc., 4100 Platinum Way, Dallas, Tex. 75237
Servus Rubber Co., 1136 2nd St., Rock Island, Ill. 61201 (footwear)
The Ski Hut-Trailwise, 1615 University Ave., P.O. Box 309, Berkeley, CA 94701
Snow Lion Corp., P.O. Box 9056, Berkeley, CA 94709 (sleeping bags and parkas)
Stearns Mfg. Co., Division & 30th St., St. Cloud, Minn. 56301
Sterno Inc., 105 Hudson St., Jersey City, N.J. 07302 (camp stoves)
Teledyne Co., Big Beam, 290 E. Prairie St., Crystal Lake, IL 60014
10-X Mfg. Co., 6185 Arapahoe, Boulder, CO 80303
Thermos Div., KST Co., Norwich, Conn. 06361 (Pop Tent)
Norm Thompson, 1805 N.W. Thurman St., Portland, Ore. 97209
Ute Mountain Corp., Box 3602, Englewood, Colo. 80110 (Metal Match)
Utica Duxbak Corp., 815 Noyes St., Utica, N.Y. 13502
Visa-Therm Prod., Inc., P.O. Box 486, Bridgeport, Conn. 06601 (Astro/Electr. vest)
Waffen-Frankonia, Box 380, 87 Wurzburg, W. Germany
Ward Mfg. Co., 500 Ford Blvd., Hamilton, O. 45015 (trailers)
Weinbrenner Shoe Corp., Polk St., Merrill, WI 54452
Wenzel Co., 1280 Research Blvd., St. Louis, MO 63132
Woods Bag & Canvas Co., Ltd., 16 Lake St., Ogdensburg, N.Y. 13669
Woodstream Corp., Box 327, Lititz, Pa. 17543 (Hunter Seat)
Woolrich Woolen Mills, Woolrich, Pa. 17779
Yankee Mechanics, Lacey Place, Southport, CT 06490 (hand winches)

KNIVES, AXES, HATCHETS, KNIFEMAKER'S SUPPLIES—HUNTING

Baker Forged Knives, P.O. Box 514, Hinsdale, IL 60521 (custom-made, folder $1)
L. L. Bean, Freeport, Maine 04032
Bear Archery Co., R.R. 1, Grayling, MI 49738
Lee Biggs, 3816 Via La Silva, Palo Verde, CA 92266 (custom-knives)
Ralph Bone Knife Co., 806 Avenue J, Lubbock, Tex. 79401
H. Gardner Bourne, 1252 Hope Ave., Columbus, O. 43212 (custom-knives)
Bowen Knife Co., P.O. Box 14028, Atlanta, GA 30324
L. E. "Red" Brown, 3203 Del Amo Blvd., Lakewood, CA 90712 (custom-knives)
Buck Knives, Inc., P.O. Box 1267, El Cajon, CA 92022
Busch Custom Knives, 418 Depre St., Mandeville, LA 70448
Pete Callan, 17 Sherline Ave., New Orleans, LA 70124 (custom-knives)
Camillus Cutlery Co., Main St., Camillus, NY 13031
W. R. Case Knives, 20 Russell Blvd., Bradford, Pa. 16701
Challanger Mfg. Co., 118 Pearl St., Mt. Vernon, NY 10550
Clements Custom Leathercraft, 1245 S. Pennsylvania St., Denver, CO 80203 (supplies)
Collins Brothers Div. (belt-buckle knife), see: Bowen Knife Co.
Michael Collins, Rte. 4, Batesville Rd., Woodstock, GA 30188 (custom-knives, scrimshander)
Cooper Knives, P.O. Box 1423, Burbank, CA 91505 (custom, ctlg. 50¢)
Custom Cutlery, 907 Greenwood Pl., Dalton, GA 30720
Custom Knifemaker's Supply, P.O. Box 11448, Dallas, TX 75223 (ctlg. 50¢)
Dan-D Custom Knives, Box 4479, Yuma, AZ 85364
Davis Custom Knives, North 1405 Ash, Spokane, WA 99201
Philip Day, Rte. 1, Box 465T, Bay Minetter, AL 36507 (custom-knives)
J. R. Dennard, 907 Greenwood Pl., Dalton, GA 30720 (custom-knives)
D'Holder Custom Knives, 6808 N. 30th Dr., Phoenix, AZ 85017
Chas. E. Dickey, 803 N.E. A St., Bentonville, AR 72712 (custom-knives)
T. M. Dowell, 139 St. Helen's Pl., Bend, OR 97701 (TMD custom-knives, ctlg. $1)
Rob. Dozier, P.O. Box 58, Palmetto, LA 71358 (custom-knives, ctlg. $1)
John Ek, 1547 NW 119th St., No. Miami, FL 33167
Eze-Lap Diamond Prods., Box 2229, Westminster, CA 92683 (knife sharpeners)
Fischer Custom Knives, Rt. 1, Box 170-M, Victoria, TX 77901
H. H. Frank, Rte. #1 Mountain Meadows, Whitefish, MT 59937 (custom-knives)
Franklin Hand-Made Knives, R.R. #2, Columbus, IN 47201
James Furlow, 2499 Brookdale Dr. N.E., Atlanta, GA 30345 (custom-knives)
Garcia Sptg. Arms Corp., 329 Alfred Ave., Teaneck, NJ 07666
Gault Present. Knives, 1626 Palma Plaza, Austin, TX 78703 (ctlg. 50¢)
Gerber Legendary Blades, 14200 S.W. 72nd St., Portland, OR 99223
Gutman Cutlery Co., Inc., 900 S. Columbus Ave., Mt. Vernon, NY 10550
H & B Forge Co., Rte. 2, Box 24, Shiloh, OH 44837 (tomahawks)
Hale Handmade Knives, 609 Henryetta St., Springdale, AR 72764
C. M. (Pete) Heath, 119 Grant St., Winnecone, WI 54986 (custom-knives)
J. A. Henckels Twinworks, 1 Westchester Plaza, Elmsford, NY 10523
Heritage Custom Knives, 2895 Seneca St., Buffalo, NY 14224
G. H. Herron, 920 Murrah Ave., Aiken, SC 29801 (custom-knives)
Hibben Knives, Box 207, Star Rte. A, Anchorage, AK 99502 (cust ctlg. $1)
Chubby Hueske, 4808 Tamarisk Dr., Bellaire, TX 77401 (custom-knives)
Imel Custom Knives, 945 Jameson Ct., New Castle, IN 47362
Imperial Knife Assn. Co., Inc., 1776 Broadway, New York, NY 10019
Indian Ridge Traders, P.O. Box X-50, Ferndale, MI 48220
Jet-Aer Corp., 100 Sixth Ave., Paterson, NJ 07524 (G96 knives)
LaDow (Doc) Johnston, 2322 W. Country Club Parkway, Toledo, OH 43614 (custom-knives)
KA-BAR Cutlery, Inc., 5777 Grant Ave., Cleveland, OH 44105
Jon W. Kirk, 800 N. Olive, Fayetteville, AR 72701 (custom-knives)
W. Kneubuhler, P.O. Box 327, Pioneer, OH 43554 (custom-knives)
Kustom Made Knives, 418 Jolee, Richardson, TX 75080
Lile Handmade Knives, Rte. 1, Box 56, Russellville, AR 72801
LocKnives, 11717 E. 23rd St., Independence, MO 64050
R. W. Loveless, P.O. Box 7836, Arlington Sta., Riverside, CA 92503 (custom-knives, ctlg. $1)
Bob Ludwig, 1028 Pecos Ave., Port Arthur, TX 77640 (custom-knives)
Marble Arms Corp., 420 Industrial Park, Gladstone, MI 49837
H. O. McBurnette, Jr., Rte. 4, Box 337, Piedmont, AL 36272 (custom knives)
John T. Mims, 620 S. 28th Ave., Apt. 327, Hattiesburg, MS 39401 (custom-knives)
Mitchell Knives, 511 Ave. B, So. Houston, TX 77587 (custom)
W. F. Moran, Jr., Rt. 5, Frederick, MD 21701 (custom-knives, ctlg. 50¢)
Morseth Sports Equip. Co., 1705 Hiway 71N, Springdale, AR 72764 (custom-knives)
Naifeh Knives, Rte. 13, Box 380, Tulsa, OK 74107
Nolen Knives, Box 6216, Corpus Christi, TX 78411 (custom-made, ctlg. 50¢)
Normark Corp., 1710 E. 78th St., Minneapolis, MN 55423
Ogg Custom Knives, Rt. 1, Box 230, Paris, AR 72855
Olsen Knife Co., Inc., 7 Joy St., Howard City, MI 49329
Ramrod Knife & Gun Shop, Route 5, State Road 3 North, Newcastle, IN 47362 (custom-knives)
Randall-Made Knives, Box 1988, Orlando, FL 32802 (ctlg. 25¢)
Razor Edge, Box 203, Butler, WI 53007 (knife sharpener)
F. J. Richtig, Clarkson, NB 68629 (custom-knives)
Rigid Knives, P.O. Box 460, Santee, CA 92071 (custom-made)
Ruana Knife Works, Box 574, Bonner, MT 59823 (ctlg. 50¢)
A. G. Russell, 1705 Hiwy. 71 N., Springdale, AR 72764
Sanders, 2358 Tyler Lane, Louisville, KY 40205 (Bahco)
Jack D. Schmier, 16787 Mulberry Ct., Fountain Valley, CA 92708 (custom-knives)
Bob Schrimsher, Custom Knifemaker's Supply, P.O. Box 11448, Dallas, TX 75223
John J. Schwarz, 41 Fifteenth St., Wellsburg, WV 26070 (custom-knives)
N. H. Schiffman Custom Knives, 963 Malibu, Pocatello, ID 83201
Shaw-Leibowitz, Rt. 1, Box 421, New Cumberland, WV 26047 (blade etchings)
C. R. Sigman, Star Rte., Box 3, Red House, WV 25168
Silver Fox Knives, 4714-44th St., Dickinson, TX 77539 (custom

Skachet, (see: Gyrfalcon Inc.)
Smith & Wesson, 2100 Roosevelt Ave., Springfield, MA 01101
John T. Smith, 6048 Cedar Crest Dr., So. Haven, MS 38671 (custom-knives)
W. J. Sonneville, 1050 Chalet Dr. W., Mobile, AL 36608 (custom-knives)
Bernard Sparks, Box 32, Dingle, ID 83233 (custom-knives)
Stone Knives, 703 Floyd Rd., Richardson, TX 75080
Thompson/Center, P.O. Box 2405, Rochester, NH 03867
Dwight L. Towell, Rt. 1, Midvale, ID 83645 (custom knives)
Track Knives, 1313 2nd St., Whitefish, MT 59937
Tru-Balance Knife Co., 2115 Tremont Blvd., Grand Rapids, MI 49504
True-Temper, 1623 Euclid, Cleveland, OH 44100 (handaxes and hatchets only)
Unique Inventions, Inc., 3727 W. Alabama St., Houston, TX 77027 (throwing knife)
W-K Knives, P.O. Box 327, Pioneer, OH 43554
Western Cutlery Co., 5311 Western Ave., Boulder, CO 80302
W. C. Wilber, 400 Lucerne Dr., Spartanburg, SC 29302 (custom knives)
Ronnie Wilson, P.O. Box 2012, Weirton, WV 26062 (custom-knives)
Don Zaccagnino, P.O. Box Zack, Pahokee, FL 33476 (custom-knives)

LABELS, BOXES, CARTRIDGE HOLDERS

Milton Brynin, Box 162, Fleetwood Station, Mount Vernon, NY 10552 (cartridge box labels)
E-Z Loader, Del Rey Products, P.O. Box 91561, Los Angeles, CA 90009
Jasco, J. A. Somers Co., P.O. Box 49751, Los Angeles, CA 90049 (cartridge box labels)
Peterson Label Co., P.O. Box 186, Redding Ridge, CT 06876 (cartridge box labels; Targ-Dots)
N. H. Schiffman, 963 Malibu, Pocatello, ID 83201 (cartridge carrier)
Shooters Supplies, 1251 Blair Ave., St. Paul, MN 55104 (cartridge and shotshell boxes)

LOAD TESTING & CHRONOGRAPHING

Carter Gun Works, 2211 Jefferson Pk. Ave., Charlottesville, Va. 22903
Custom Ballistics' Lab., 3354 Cumberland Dr., San Angelo, Tex. 76901
Horton Ballistics, North Waterford, Me. 04267
Hutton Rifle Ranch, Box 898, Topanga, CA 90290
Jurras Co., Box 163, Shelbyville, Ind. 46176
Kennon's, 5408 Biffle, Stone Mountain, Ga. 30083
NeSal Enterprises, Box 126, Meriden Rte., Cheyenne, WY 82001
Plum City Ballistics Range, Rte. 1, Box 29A, Plum City, Wis. 54761
H. P. White Lab., Box 331, Bel Air, Md. 21014

MISCELLANEOUS

Accurizing Service, Herbert G. Troester, Cayuaga, ND 58013
Action Sleeves, Alvin L. Davidson, 1215 Branson, Las Cruces, NM 88001
Adhesive Flannel, Forest City Prod., 722 Bolivar, Cleveland, OH 44115
Archery, Bear Co., R.R. 1, Grayling, Mich. 49738
Arms Restoration, J. J. Jenkins, 462 Stanford Pl., Santa Barbara, CA 93105
Barrel Band Swivels, Phil Judd, 83 E. Park St., Butte, Mont. 59701
Bedding Kit, Bisonite Co., P.O. Box 84, Kenmore Station, Buffalo, NY 14217
Bedding Kit, Fenwal, Inc., Resin Systems Div., 400 Main St., Ashland, Mass. 01721
Bootdryers, Baekgaard Ltd., 1855 Janke Dr., Northbrook, Ill. 60062
Breech Plug Wrench, Swaine Machine, 195 O'Connell, Providence, R.I. 02905
Case Gauge, Plum City Ballistics Range, Rte. 1, Box 29A, Plum City, Wis. 54761
Chrome Brl. Lining, Marker Mach. Co., Box 426, Charleston, Ill. 61920
Color Hardening, Alamo Heat Treating Co., Box 55345, Houston, Tex. 77055
Crow Caller, Wightman Elec. Inc., Box 989, Easton, Md. 21601
Distress Flares, Marsh Coulter Co., P.O. Box 333, Tecumseh, MI 49286
E-Z Loader, Del Rey Prod., P.O. Box 91561, Los Angeles, CA 90009
Ear-Valv, Sigma Eng. Co., 11320 Burbank Blvd., N. Hollywood, Cal. 91601 (Lee-Sonic)
Emergency Food, Chuck Wagon, Micro Dr., Woburn, Mass. 01801
Fill N'File, Apsco Packaging Co., 9325 W. Bryon St., Schiller Park, IL 60176
Flares, Colt Industries, Huyshope Ave., Hartford, Conn. 06102
Flares, Intercontinental Arms, 2222 Barry Ave., Los Angeles, Ca. 90064 (MBA)
Flares, Smith & Wesson Chemical Co., 2399 Forman Rd., Rock Creek, OH 44084
Flat Springs, Alamo Heat Treating Co., Box 55345, Houston, Tex. 77055
Game Hoist, Cam Gear Ind., P.O. Box 1002, Kalispell, MT 59901 (Sportsmaster 500 pocket hoist)
Game Hoist, PIC, 3 Chestnut, Suffern, N.Y. 10901
Game Scent, Buck Stop, Inc., 3015 Grow Rd., Stanton, Mi 48888
Game Scent, Pete Rickard, Box 1250, Cobleskill, NY 12043 (Indian Buck lure)
Gun Bedding Kit, Resin Systems Div., Fenwal, Inc., 400 Main St., Ashland, Mass. 01721

Gun Jewelry, Sid Bell Originals, R.D. 2, Tully, NY 13159
Gun Jewelry, Al Popper, 614 Turnpike St., Stoughton, Mass. 02072
Gun Lock, E & C Enterprises, 9582 Bickley Dr., Huntington Beach, CA 92646
Gun Sling, Kwikfire, Wayne Prods. Co., P.O. Box 247, Camp Hill, PA 17011
Gun Slings, Torel, Inc., 1053 N. South St., Yoakum, TX 77995
Hollow Pointer, Goerg Ent., 3009 S. Laurel St., Port Angeles, Wash. 98362
Hugger Hooks, Roman Products, Box 860, Golden, Colo. 80401
Insect Repellent, Armor, Div. of Buck Stop, Inc., 3015 Grow Rd., Stanton, Mich. 48888
Insert Barrels, (22 RF), H. Owen, P.O. Box 774, Sunnyvale, Calif. 94088
Lightnin-Loader, Hunter Mfg. Co., Box 2882, Van Nuys, Cal. 91404
Locks, Gun, Bor-Lok Prods., 105 5th St., Arbuckle, CA 95912
Locks, Gun, Master Lock Co., 2600 N. 32nd St., Milwaukee, WI 53245
Monte Carlo Pad, Frank A. Hoppe Div., P.O. Box 97, Parkesburg, Pa. 19365
Muzzle-Top, Allen Assoc., 7502 Limekiln, Philadelphia, PA 19150 (plastic gun muzzle cap)
Pell Remover, A. Edw. Terpening, 838 E. Darlington Rd., Tarpon Springs, FL 33589
Pockethoist, Cam-Gear Industries, Inc., P.O. Box 1002, Kalispell, MT 59901 (Sportsmaster 500)
Powder Storage Magazine, C & M Gunworks, 2603 41st St., Moline, IL 61265
Pressure Testg. Machine, M. York, 19381 Keymar Way, Gaithersburg, MD 20760
Ransom Handgun Rests, C'Arco, P.O. Box 2043, San Bernardino, CA 92406
Rifle Slings, Bianchi, 212 W. Foothill Blvd., Monrovia, Cal. 91016
Rifle Sling, Ready Sling Co., P.O. Box 536, Delano, CA 93215
RIG, NRA Scoring Plug, Rig Prod. Co., Box 279, Oregon, Ill. 60161
Rubber Cheekpiece, W. H. Lodewick, 2816 N. E. Halsey, Portland, Ore. 97232
Safeties, Williams Gun Sight Co., 7389 Lapeer Rd., Davison, Mich. 48423
Sav-Bore, Saunders Sptg. Gds., 338 Somerset St., N. Plainfield, NJ 07060
Scrimshaw Engraving, C. Milton Barringer, 217-2nd Isle N., Port Richey, FL 33568
Scrimshaw Engraving, A. Douglas Jacobs, Box 1236, Cutchogue, NY 11935
Sharpening Stones, Russell's Arkansas Oilstones, 1705 Hiway 71N., Springdale, AR 72764
Shell Shrinker Mfg. Co., Box 6143, Lubbock, Tex. 79413
Shooting Bench/Porto, Seyferth's, Inc., 926 N. Memorial Dr., Racine, WI 53404
Shooting Coats, 10-X Mfg. Co., 6185 Arapahoe, Boulder, CO 80303
Shooting Ranges, Shooting Equip. Inc., 10 S. LaSalle, Chicago, IL 60603
Shotgun Sight, bi-ocular, Trius Prod., Box 25, Cleves, O. 45002
Silver Grip Caps, Bill Dyer, P.O. Box 75255, Oklahoma City, Okla. 73107
Snap Caps, Filmat, 200 Market, East Paterson, N.J. 07407
Snap Caps, Frank's Mach. Shop, 11529 Tecumseh-Clinton Rd., Clinton, MI 49236
Snowshoes, Sportsmen Prod. Inc., Box 1082, Boulder, Colo. 80302
Springfield Safety Pin, B-Square Co., P.O. Box 11281, Ft. Worth, Tex. 76110
Springs, W. Wolff Co., Box 232, Ardmore, Pa. 19003
Supersound, Edmund Scientific Co., 101 E. Gloucester Pike, Barrington, NJ 08007 (safety device)
Swivels, Michaels, P.O. Box 13010, Portland, Ore. 97213
Swivels, Sile Dist., 7 Centre Market Pl., New York, N.Y. 10013
Swivels, Williams Gun Sight Co., 7389 Lapeer Rd., Davison, Mich. 48423
Targ-It Stamp Co., Box G, Emlenton, PA 16373 (rubber stamp target makers)
Trophies, L. G. Balfour Co., Attleboro, Mass. 02703
Trophies, Blackinton & Co., 140 Commonwealth, Attleboro Falls, Mass. 02763
Trophies, F. H. Noble & Co., 559 W. 59th St., Chicago, Ill. 60621
Universal 3-shot Shotgun Plug, LanDav Custom Guns, 7213 Lee Highway, Falls Church, VA 22046

REBORING AND RERIFLING

P.O. Ackley, 2235 Arbor Lane, Salt Lake City, UT 84117
Atkinson Gun Co., P.O. Box 512, Prescott, AZ 86301
Bain & Davis Sptg. Gds., 559 W. Las Tunas Dr., San Gabriel, Calif. 91776
Carpenter's Gun Works, Gunshop Rd., Plattekill, N.Y. 12568
Fuller Gun Shop, Cooper Landing, Alaska 99572
John Kaufield Small Arms Eng. Co., P.O. Box 306, Des Plaines, IL 60018
Ward Koozer, Box 18, Walterville, Ore. 97489
Les' Gun Shop, Box 511, Kalispell, Mont. 59901
Morgan's Cust. Reboring, 707 Union Ave., Grants Pass, OR 97526
Nu-Line Guns, 3727 Jennings Rd., St. Louis, Mo. 63121
Al Petersen, Box 8, Riverhurst, Saskatchewan, Canada S0H3P0
Schuetzen Gun Works, 1226 Prairie Rd., Colorado Springs, Colo. 80909
Siegrist Gun Shop, 2689 McLean Rd., Whittemore, MI 48770
Small Arms Eng., P.O. Box 306, Des Plaines, IL 60018
Snapp's Gunshop, 6911 E. Washington Rd., Clare, Mich. 48617
R. Southgate, Rt. 2, Franklin, Tenn. 37064 (Muzzleloaders)
J. W. Van Patten, Box 145, Foster Hill, Milford, Pa. 18337
Robt. G. West, Rte. 1, Box 941, Eugene, OR 97402

RELOADING TOOLS AND ACCESSORIES

Advanced Mfg. Co., Inc., 18619 W. 7 Mile Rd., Detroit, MI 48219 (super filler primer tube)
Alcan, (See: Smith & Wesson Arrns Co.)

Anderson Mfg. Co., Royal, Ia. 51357 (Shotshell Trimmers)
Aurands, 229 E. 3rd St., Lewistown, Pa. 17044
B-Square Eng. Co., Box 11281, Ft. Worth, Tex. 76110
B & W Enterprises, 1206 11th Ave. N.E., Rochester, MN 55901 (Meyer shotgun slugs)
Bahler Die Shop, Rte. 1, Box 412, Hemlock, Florence, OR 97439
Bair Co., 4555 N. 48th St., Lincoln, NB 68504
Bill Ballard, P.O. Box 656, Billings, MT 59103 (ctlg. 25¢)
Belding & Mull, P.O. Box 428, Philipsburg, Pa. 16866
Belmont Prods., Rte. 1, Friendsville, TN 37737 (lead cutter)
Blackhawk SAA East, K2274 POB, Loves Park, Ill. 61111
Blackhawk SAA West, Box 285, Hiawatha, KS 66434
Bonanza Sports, Inc., 412 Western Ave., Faribault, Minn. 55021
Gene Bowlin, 3602 Hill Ave., Snyder, Tex. 79549 (arbor press)
Brown Precision Co., 5869 Indian Ave., San Jose, Calif. 95123 (Little Wiggler)
A. V. Bryant, 72 Whiting Rd., E. Hartford, CT 06118 (Nutmeg Universal Press)
C-H Tool & Die Corp., Box L, Owen, Wis. 54460
Camdex, Inc., 23880 Hoover Rd., Warren, MI 48089
Carbide Die & Mfg. Co., Box 226, Covina, CA 91724
Carter Gun Works, 2211 Jefferson Pk. Ave., Charlottesville, Va. 22903
Cascade Cartridge, Inc., (See Omark)
Clymer Mfg. Co., 14241 W. 11 Mile Rd., Oak Park, MI 48237 (½-jack. swaging dies)
Lester Coats, 416 Simpson St., No. Bend, Ore. 97459 (core cutter)
Conevera's Reloading Supplies, 5064 Dialette Dr., Rockford, IL 61102
Container Development Corp., 424 Montgomery St., Watertown, WI 53094
Continental Kite & Key Co., Box 40, Broomall, PA 19008 (primer pocket cleaner)
Cooper-Woodward, Box 972, Riverside, Calif. 92502 (Perfect Lube)
D. R. Corbin, P.O. Box 44, North Bend, OR 97459
Corey Enterprises, Inc., 4838 N. 29th St., Phoenix, AZ 85016 (Tap-It bullet puller)
Diverter Arms, Inc., 6520 Rampart St., Houston, TX 77036 (bullet puller)
Division Lead Co., 7742 W. 61st Pl., Summit, Ill. 60502
Eagle Products Co., 1520 Adelia Ave., So. El Monte, Cal. 91733
W. H. English, 4411 S. W. 100th, Seattle, Wash. 98146 (Paktool)
Farmer Bros., See: Lage
The Fergusons, R.F.D. #1, Box 143, Hillsboro, NH 03244
Fitz, Box 49697, Los Angeles, Calif. 90049 (Fitz Flipper)
Flambeau Plastics, 801 Lynn, Baraboo, Wis. 53913
Forster Products Inc., 82 E. Lanark Ave., Lanark, Ill. 61046
Gene's Gun Shop, 3602 Hill Ave., Snyder, Tex. 79549 (arbor press)
John R. Gillette, 4514 W. 123d Place, Alsip, IL 60658
Goerg Enterprises, 3009 S. Laurel, Port Angeles, WA 98362 (hollow pointer)
Gopher Shooter's Supply, Box 246, Faribault, Minn. 55021
The Gun Clinic, 81 Kale St., Mahtomedi, Minn. 55115
Hart Products, Rob. W. Hart & Son, 401 Montgomery St., Nescopeck, PA 18635
Ed Hart's Gun Supply, U.S. Rte. 15 No., Bath, NY 14810 (Meyer shotgun slugs)
Hensley & Gibbs, Box 10, Murphy, Ore. 97533
Herter's Inc., RR1, Waseca, Minn. 56093
B. E. Hodgdon, Inc., 7710 W. 50 Hiway, Shawnee Mission, Kans. 66202
Hollywood Reloading, see: Whitney Sales, Inc.
Hornady (see: Pacific)
Hulme Firearm Serv., Box 83, Millbrae, Calif. 94030 (Star case feeder)
Hunter Bradlee Co., 2800 Routh St., Dallas, TX 75201 (powder measure)
Independent Mach. & Gun Shop, 1416 N. Hayes, Pocatello, Ida. 83201
Ivy Armament, P.O. Box 10, Greendale, WI 53129 (shell case dispenser for Star and Phelps machines)
JASCO, Box 49749, Los Angeles, Calif. 90049
J & G Rifle Ranch, Box S80, Turner, MT 59542 (case tumblers)
Javelina Products, Box 337, San Bernardino, Cal. 92402 (Alox beeswax)
Kexplore, Box 22084, Houston, Tex. 77027
Kuharsky Bros. (see Modern Industries)
Lachmiller Eng. Co., 11273 Goss St., Sun Valley, CA 91352
Lac-Cum Bullet Puller, Route Box 242, Apollo, PA 15613
Lage Uniwad Co., 1102 N. Washington St., Eldora, IA 50627 (Universal Shotshell Wad)
LanDav, 7213 Lee Highway, Falls Church, VA 22046 (X-15 bullet puller)
Lee Engineering, 46 E. Jackson, Hartford, Wis. 53027
Leon's Reloading Service, 3945 No. 11 St., Lincoln, Neb. 68521
Lewisystems, Container Dev. Corp., 426 Montgomery St., Watertown, WI 53094
L. L. F. Die Shop, 1281 Highway 99 N., Eugene, Ore. 97402
Dean Lincoln, P.O. Box 1886, Farmington, NM 87401 (mould)
Ljutic Industries, 918 N. 5th Ave., Yakima, Wash. 98902
Lock's Phila. Gun Exch., 6700 Rowland, Philadelphia, Pa. 19149
Lyman Gun Sight Products, Middlefield, Conn. 06455
McKillen & Heyer, Box 627, Willoughby, O. 44094 (case gauge)
Paul McLean, 2670 Lakeshore Blvd., W., Toronto 14, Ont., Canada (Universal Cartridge Holder)
Pat B. McMillan, 1828 E. Campo Bello Dr., Phoenix, Ariz. 85022
MTM Molded Prod., 5680 Webster St., Dayton, OH 45414
Magma Eng. Co., P.O. Box 881, Chandler, AZ 85224
Judson E. Mariotti, Beauty Hill Rd., Barrington, NH 03825 (brass bullet mould)
Marmel Prods., P.O. Box 97, Utica, MI 48087 (Marvelube, Marvelux)
Marquart Precision Co., Box 1740, Prescott, AZ 86301 (precision case-neck turning tool)
Mayville Eng. Co., 715 South St., Mayville, Wis. 53050 (shotshell loader)
Merit Gun Sight Co., P.O. Box 995, Sequim, Wash. 98382
Modern Industries, Inc., 613 W-11, Erie, PA 16501 (primer pocket cleaner)
Murdock Lead/RSR Corp., P.O. Box 1695, Dallas, TX 75222
National Lead Co., Box 831, Perth Amboy, N.J. 08861

Normington Co., Box 6, Rathdrum, ID 83858 (powder baffles)
Ohaus Scale Corp., 29 Hanover Rd., Florham Park, N.J. 07932
Omark-CCI, Inc., Box 856, Lewiston, Ida. 83501
Pacific Tool Co., P.O. Drawer 2048, Ordnance Plant Rd., Grand Island, NB 68801
Pak-Tool Co., 4411 S.W. 100th, Seattle, WA 98146
John Palmer, Box 35797, Houston, TX 77035
Perfection Die Co., 1614 S. Choctaw, El Reno, Okla. 73036
Personal Firearms Record Book, Box 201, Park Ridge, Ill. 60068
Ferris Pindell, R.R. 3, Box 205, Connersville, IN 47331 (bullet spinner)
Plum City Ballistics Range, Rte. 1, Box 29A, Plum City, Wis. 54761
Ponsness-Warren, Inc., P.O. Box 861, Eugene, OR 97401
Potter Eng. Co., 1410 Santa Ana Dr., Dunedin, FL 33528 (electric pots only)
Marian Powley, 19 Sugarplum Rd., Levittown, Pa. 10956
Precise Alloys Inc., 69 Kinkel St., Westbury, NY 11590 (chilled lead shot; bullet wire)
Quaco Industries Ltd., St. Martins, St. John Co., New Brunswick, Canada E0G 2Z0 (Echo dies, etc.)
Quinetics Corp., Box 13237, San Antonio, TX 78213 (kinetic bullet puller)
RCBS, Inc., Box 1919, Oroville, Calif. 95965
Redding Inc., 114 Starr Rd., Cortland, NY 13045
Remco, 1404 Whitesboro St., Utica, N.Y. 13502 (shot caps)
Rifle Ranch, Rte. 5, Prescott, Ariz, 86301
Rochester Lead Works, Rochester, N.Y. 14608 (leadwire)
Rorschach Precision Prods., P.O. Box 1613, Irving, Tex. 75060
Rotex Mfg. Co. (see Texan)
Ruhr-American Corp., So. East Hwy. 55, Glenwood, Minn. 56334
SAECO Rel. Inc., P.O. Box 778, Carpinteria, Calif. 93013
Sandia Die & Cartridge Co., Rte. 5, Box 5400, Albuquerque, NM 87123
Saunders Gun & Machine Shop, 145 Delhi Rd., Manchester, IA 52057 (primer feed tray)
Scientific Lubricants Co., 3753 Lawrence Ave., Chicago, Ill. 60625
Shilo Products, 37 Potter St., Farmingdale, NY 11735 (4-cavity bullet mould)
Shooters Accessory Supply, see: D. R. Corbin
Shooters Specialties, 8371 W. Virginia Ave., Denver, CO 80226
Sil's Gun Prod., 490 Sylvan Dr., Washington, Pa. 15301 (K-spinner)
Jerry Simmons, 713 Middlebury St., Goshen, Ind. 46526 (Pope de- & recapper)
Rob. B. Simonson, Rte. 7, 2129 Vanderbilt Rd., Kalamazoo, Mich. 49002
Smith & Wesson Ammunition Co., Inc., 2399 Forman Rd., Rock Creek, OH 44084
J. A. Somers Co., P.O. Box 49751, Los Angeles, CA 90049 (Jasco)
D. E. Stanley, P.O. Box 323, Arvin, CA 93203 (Kake-Kutter)
Star Machine Works, 418 10th Ave., San Diego, Calif. 92101
Texan Reloaders, Inc., P.O. Box 5355, Dallas, Tex. 75222
W. S. Vickerman, 505 W. 3rd Ave., Ellensburg, Wash. 98926
WAMADET, Silver Springs, Goodleigh, Barnstaple, Devon, England
Walker Mfg. Inc., 8296 So. Channel, Harsen's Island, MI 48028 (Berdan decapper)
Weatherby, Inc., 2781 Firestone Blvd., South Gate, Calif. 90280
Webster Scale Mfg. Co., Box 188, Sebring, Fla. 33870
Whits Shooting Stuff, P.O. Box 1340, Cody, WY 82414
Whitney Sales, Inc., P.O. Box 875, Reseda, CA 91335 (Hollywood)
L. E. Wilson, Inc., Box 324, Cashmere, Wash. 98815
Xelex, Ltd., Hawksbury, Ont., Canada (powder)
Zenith Ent., 361 Flagler Rd., Nordland, WA 98358

RESTS—BENCH, PORTABLE, ETC.

Bill Anderson, 551 Fletcher, Wayne, PA 19087
Bausch & Lomb, 635 St. Paul St., Rochester, NY 14602 (rifle rest)
Gene Beecher Prods., 2155 Demington Dr., Cleveland Hgts., OH 44106
Jim Brobst, 299 Poplar St., Hamburg, PA 19526 (bench rest pedestal)
C'Arco, P.O. Box 2043, San Bernardino, CA 92401 (Ransom handgun rest)
Central Specialties Co., 630 Northwest Hwy., Chicago, IL 60631 (portable gun rest)
Cole's Acku-Rite Prod., Box 25, Kennedy, N.Y. 14747
Decker Shooting Products, 1729 Laguna Ave., Schofield, WI 54476 (rifle rests)
F & H Machining, 4645 Cambio Ct., Fremont, CA 94536
The Fergusons, R.F.D. #1, Box 143, Hillsboro, NH 03244 (rifle rests)
Frontier Arms, Inc., 420 E. Riding Club Rd., Cheyenne, Wyo. 82001
The Gun Case, 11035 Maplefield, El Monte, Cal. 91733
GVA Enterprises, Box 725, Garland, TX 75040 (Rif-L-Vise)
Harris Engr., Inc., Box 305, Fraser, Mich. 48026 (bipods)
Rob. W. Hart & Son, 401 Montgomery St., Nescopeck, Pa. 18635
North Star Devices, Inc., P.O. Box 2095, North St. Paul, MN 55109 (Gun Slinger)
Porto/Shooting bench, Seyferth's Inc., 926 N. Memorial, Racine, WI 53404
Rec. Prods. Res., Inc., 158 Franklin Ave., Ridgewood, N.J. 07450 (Butts Pipod)
D. E. Stanley, P.O. Box 323, Arvin, CA 93203 (portable shooting rest)
Suter's, 332 Tejon, Colorado Springs, CO 80902
Basil Tuller, 29 Germania, Galeton, PA 16922 (Protector sandbags)

RIFLE BARREL MAKERS

P.O. Ackley, 2235 Arbor Lane, Salt Lake City, UT 84117
Apex Rifle Co., 7628 San Fernando, Sun Valley, Calif. 91352
Atkinson Gun Co., P.O. Box 512, Prescott, AZ 86301
Christy Gun Works, 875 57th St., Sacramento, Calif. 95819

Clerke Prods., 2219 Main St., Santa Monica, Calif. 90405
Cuthbert Gun Shop, 715 So. 5th, Coos Bay, Ore. 97420
Darr's Rifle Shop, 2309 Black Rd., Joliet, IL 60435
Douglas Barrels, Inc., 5504 Big Tyler Rd., Charleston, W. Va. 25312
Douglas Jackalope Gun & Sport Shop, Inc., 1205 E. Richards St., Douglas, WY 82633
Federal Firearms Co., Inc., Box 145, Oakdale, Pa. 15071 (Star bbls., actions)
A. R. Goode, R.D. 1, Box 84, Thurmont, MD 21788
Hart Rifle Barrels, Inc., RD 2, Lafayette, N.Y. 13084
Wm. H. Hobaugh, Box 657, Philipsburg, Mont. 59858
Intern'l Casting Co., 19453 Forrer, Detroit, Mich. 48235
Gene Lechner, 636 Jane N.E., Albuquerque, NM 87123
Les' Gun Shop, Box 511, Kalispell, Mont. 59901
McGowen Rifle Barrels, Rte. 3, St. Anne, Ill. 60964
D. M. Manley, 295 Main St., Brookville, PA 15825
Marquart Precision Co., Box 1740, Prescott, AZ 86301
Nu-Line Guns, Inc., 3727 Jennings Rd., St. Louis, Mo. 63121
Numrich Arms, W. Hurley, N.Y. 12491
R. Paris & Son, R.D. 5, Box 61, Gettysburg, Pa. 17325
Al Petersen, The Rifle Ranch, Box 8, Riverhurst, Sask., Canada SOH3PO
Rheinmetall (see John Weir)
Sanders Cust. Gun Serv., 2358 Tyler Lane, Louisville, Ky. 40205
Scotty's Gun Shop, 534 E. Hwy 190, Harker Heights, TX 76541
Sharon Rifle Barrel Co., P.O. Box 106, Kalispell, MT 59901
Ed Shilen Rifles, Inc., 205 Metropark Blvd., Ennis, TX 75119
W. C. Strutz, Rte. 1, Eagle River, WI 54521
Titus Barrel & Gun Co., R.F.D. #1, Box 23, Heber City, UT 84032
John E. Weir, 3304 Norton Ave., Independence, Mo. 64052
Wilson Arms, 63 Leetes Island Rd., Branford, CT 06405

SCOPES, MOUNTS, ACCESSORIES, OPTICAL EQUIPMENT

Alley Supply Co., Carson Valley Industrial Park, Gardnerville, NV 89410 (Scope collimator)
American Import Co., 1167 Mission, San Francisco, Calif. 94103
Anderson & Co., 1203 Broadway, Yakima, Wash. 98902 (lens cap)
Avery Corp., P.O. Box 99, Electra, TX 76360 (Mini-Light)
Ball-One Buck Scope Lens Cover, Box 426, Midway City, CA 92655
Bausch & Lomb Inc., 635 St. Paul St., Rochester, N.Y. 14602
Bennett, 561 Delaware, Delmar, N.Y. 12054 (mounting wrench)
Bridge Mount Co., Box 3344, Lubbock, Tex. 79410 (one-piece target mts.)
Browning Arms, Rt. 4, Box 624-B, Arnold, Mo. 63010
Maynard P. Buehler, Inc., 17 Orinda Highway, Orinda, Calif. 94563
Burris Co., 351 E. 8th St., Greeley, CO 80631
Bushnell Optical Co., 2828 E. Foothill Blvd., Pasadena, Calif. 91107
Kenneth Clark, 18738 Highway 99, Madera, Calif. 93637
Clearview Mfg. Co., Inc., 23702 Crossley, Hazel Park, MI 48030 (mounts)
Clear View Sports Shields, P.O. Box 255, Wethersfield, CT 06107 (shooting/testing glasses)
Colt's, Hartford, Conn. 06102
Compass Instr. & Optical Co., Inc., 104 E 25th St., New York, N.Y. 10010
Conetrol, Hwy 123 South, Seguin, Tex. 78155
Continental Arms Corp., 697-5th Ave., New York, N.Y. 10022 (Nickel)
Davis Optical Co., P.O. Box 6, Winchester, Ind. 47934
Del-Sports Inc., Main St., Margaretville, NY 12455 (Habicht)
M. B. Dinsmore, Box 21, Wyomissing, PA 19610 (shooting glasses)
Eder Instrument Co., 5115 N. Ravenswood, Chicago, IL 60640 (borescope)
Flaig's, Babcock Blvd., Millvale, Pa. 15209
Freeland's Scope Stands, Inc. 3734 14th, Rock Island, Ill. 61201
Griffin & Howe, Inc., 589-8th Ave., New York, N.Y. 10017
Jim Herringshaw, 354 So. Hambden St., Chardon, OH 44024
Herter's Inc., Waseca, Minn. 56093
J. B. Holden Co., Box 393, 603 Aurelia, Plymouth, MI 48170
The Hutson Corp., P.O. 1127, Arlington, Tex. 76010
Hy-Score Arms Corp., 200 Tillary St., Brooklyn, N.Y. 11201
Paul Jaeger, 211 Leedom St., Jenkintown, Pa. 19046 (Nickel)
Jana Intl. Co., Box 1107, Denver, Colo. 80201
Jason Empire Inc., 9200 Cody, Overland Park, KS 66214
Jeffredo Gunsight Co., 1629 Via Monserate, Fallbrook, CA 92028
L.E. Jurras & Associates, Drawer F, Hagerman, NM 88232
Kesselring Gun Shop, 400 Pacific Hiway 99 No, Burlington, Wash. 98283
Kris Mounts, 108 Lehigh St., Johnstown, PA 15905
Kuharsky Bros. (see Modern Industries)
Kwik-Site, 27367 Michigan Ave., Inkster, MI 48141 (rings, mounts only)
LanDav, 7213 Lee Highway, Falls Church, VA 22046 (steel leverlock side mt.)
T. K. Lee, Box 2123, Birmingham, Ala. 35201 (reticles)
E. Leitz, Inc., Rockleigh, N.J. 07647
Leupold & Stevens Inc., P.O. Box 688, Beaverton, Ore. 97005
Jake Levin and Son, Inc., 9200 Cody, Overland Park, KS 66214
W. H. Lodewick, 2816 N.E. Halsey, Portland, OR 97232 (scope safeties)
Lyman Gun Sight Products, Middlefield, Conn. 06455
Marble Arms Co., 420 Industrial Park, Gladstone, MI 49837
Marlin Firearms Co., 100 Kenna Dr., New Haven, Conn. 06473
Mitchell's Shooting Glasses, Box 539, Waynesville, MO 65583
Modern Industries, Inc., 613 W-11, Erie, PA 16501
O. F. Mossberg & Sons, Inc., 7 Grasso Ave., North Haven, Conn. 06473
Normark Corp., 1710 E. 78th St., Minneapolis, Minn. 55423 (Singlepoint)
Numrich Arms, West Hurley, N.Y. 12491
Nydar Div., Swain Nelson Co., Box 45, Glenview, Ill. 60025 (shotgun sight)
PGS, Peters' Inc., 622 Gratiot Ave., Saginaw, Mich. 48602 (scope shields)
Pachmayr Gun Works, 1220 S. Grand Ave., Los Angeles, Calif. 90015
Pacific Tool Co., P.O. Drawer 2048, Ordnance Plant Rd., Grand Island, NB 68801
Ed Paul's Sptg. Goods, Inc., 172 Flatbush Ave., Brooklyn, N.Y. 11217 (Tops)

Precise Imports Corp., 3 Chestnut, Suffern, N.Y. 10901 (PIC)
Ranging Inc., P.O. Box 9106, Rochester, N.Y. 14625
Ray-O-Vac, Willson Prod. Div., P.O. Box 622, Reading, PA 19603 (shooting glasses)
Realist, Inc., N. 93 W. 16288, Megal Dr., Menomonee Falls, Wis. 53051
Redfield Gun Sight Co., 5800 E. Jewell Ave., Denver, Colo. 80222
S & K Mfg. Co., Box 247, Pittsfield, Pa. 16340 (Insta-mount)
Sanders Cust. Gun Serv., 2358 Tyler Lane, Louisville, Ky. 40205 (MSW)
Saunders Gun & Machine Shop, 145 Delhi Rd., Manchester, IA 52057 (lens caps)
Savage Arms, Westfield, Mass. 01085
Sears, Roebuck & Co., 825 S. St. Louis, Chicago, Ill. 60607
Sherwood Distr., Inc., 18714 Parthenia St., Northridge, CA 91324 (mounts)
W. H. Siebert, 22720 S.E. 56th Pl., Issaquah, WA 98027
Singlepoint (see Normark)
Southern Precision Inst. Co., 3419 E. Commerce St., San Antonio, TX 78219
Spacetron Inc., Box 84, Broadview, IL 60155 (bore lamp)
Stoeger Arms Co., 55 Ruta Ct., S. Hackensack, N.J. 07606
Supreme Lens Covers, Box GG, Jackson Hole, WY 83001 (lens caps)
Swift Instruments, Inc., 952 Dorchester Ave., Boston, Mass. 02125
Tasco, 1075 N.W. 71st, Miami, Fla. 33138
Thompson-Center Arms, P.O. Box 2405, Rochester, N.H. 03867 (handgun scope)
Tradewinds, Inc., Box 1191, Tacoma, Wash. 98401
John Unertl Optical Co., 3551-5 East St., Pittsburgh, Pa. 15214
United Binocular Co., 9043 S. Western Ave., Chicago, Ill. 60620
Universal Firearms Corp., 3746 E. 10th Ct., Hialeah, Fla. 33013
Vissing (see: Supreme Lens Covers)
H. P. Wasson, P.O. Box 1286, Homestead, FL 33030 (eyeglass apertures)
Weatherby's, 2781 Firestone, South Gate, Calif. 90280
W. R. Weaver Co., 7125 Industrial Ave., El Paso, Tex. 79915
Wein Prods. Inc., 115 W. 25th St., Los Angeles, CA 90007 (Cronoscope)
Williams Gun Sight Co., 7389 Lapeer Rd., Davison, Mich. 48423
Willrich Precision Instrument Co., 37-13 Broadway, Rte. 4, Fair Lawn, NJ 07410 (borescope)
Carl Zeiss Inc., 444 Fifth Ave., New York, N.Y. 10018 (Hensoldt)

SIGHTS, METALLIC

B-Square Eng. Co., Box 11281, Ft. Worth, Tex. 76110
Bo-Mar Tool & Mfg. Co., Box 168, Carthage, Tex. 75633
Maynard P. Buehler, Inc., 17 Orinda Highway, Orinda, Calif. 94563
Christy Gun Works, 875 57th St., Sacramento, Calif. 95819
Cornwall Bridge Gun Shop, P.O. Box 67, Cornwall Bridge, CT 06754 (vernier)
E-Z Mount, Ruelle Bros., P.O. Box 114, Ferndale, MT 48220
Firearms Dev. Lab., 360 Mt. Ida Rd., Oroville, CA 95965 (F. D. L. Wondersight)
Freeland's Scope Stands, Inc., 3734-14th Ave., Rock Island, Ill. 61201
Paul T. Haberly, 2364 N. Neva, Chicago, IL 60635
Paul Jaeger, Inc., 211 Leedom St., Jenkintown, PA 19046
Lyman Gun Sight Products, Middlefield, Conn. 06455
Marble Arms Corp., 420 Industrial Park, Gladstone, Mich. 49837
Merit Gunsight Co., P.O. Box 995, Sequim, Wash. 98382
Micro Sight Co., 242 Harbor Blvd., Belmont, Calif. 94002
Miniature Machine Co., 212 E. Spruce, Deming, N.M. 88030
Modern Industries, Inc., 613 W-11, Erie, PA 16501
C. R. Pedersen & Son, Ludington, Mich. 49431
Poly Choke Co., Inc., P.O. Box 296, Hartford, CT 06101
Redfield Gun Sight Co., 5800 E. Jewell St., Denver, Colo. 80222
Schwarz's Gun Shop, 41 - 15th St., Wellsburg, W. Va. 26070
Simmons Gun Specialties, 700 Rodgers Rd., Olathe, Kans. 66061
Slug Site Co., Box 268, Nesswa, MN 56468
Sport Service Center, 2364 N. Neva, Chicago, IL 60635
Tradewinds, Inc., Box 1191, Tacoma, WA 98401
Williams Gun Sight Co., 7389 Lapeer Rd., Davison, Mich. 48423

STOCKS (Commercial and Custom)

Abe and VanHorn, 5124 Huntington Dr., Los Angeles, CA 90032
Adams, Custom Gun Stocks, 13461 Quito Rd., Saratoga, CA 95070
Ahlman's Inc., R.R. 1, Box 20, Morristown, MN 55052
Anderson's Guns, Jim Jares, 706 S. 23rd St., Laramie, WY 82070
Dale P. Andrews, 3572 E. Davies, Littleton, CO 80122
R. J. Anton, 874 Olympic Dr., Waterloo, IA 50701
Austrian Gunworks Reg'd., P.O. Box 136, Eastman, Que., Canada, J0E 1P0
Jim Baiar, Rt. 1-B, Box 352, Columbia Falls, Mont. 59912
Joe J. Balickie, Custom Stocks, 6108 Deerwood Pl., Raleigh, N.C. 27607
Bartas, Rte. 1, Box 129-A, Cato, Wis. 54206
John Bianchi, 212 W. Foothill Blvd., Monrovia, Calif. 91016 (U. S. carbines)
Al Biesen, West 2039 Sinto Ave., Spokane, Wash. 99201
Stephen L. Billeb, Rte. 3, Box 163, Bozeman, MT 59715
E. C. Bishop & Son Inc., Box 7, Warsaw, Mo. 65355
Nate Bishop, Box 334, Minturn, CO 81645
Kay H. Bowles, Pinedale, Wyo. 82941
Brown Precision, Co., 5869 Indian Ave., San Jose, CA 95123
Lenard M. Brownell, Box 25, Wyarno, WY 82845
Calico Hardwoods, Inc., 1648 Airport Blvd., Windsor, Calif. 95492 (blanks)
Dick Campbell, 1445 So. Meade, Denver, Colo. 80219
Winston Churchill, 55 High St., Ludlow, VT 05149
Cloward's Gun Shop, 4023 Aurora Ave. N., Seattle, WA 98102
Mike Conner, Box 2383, Juneau, AK 99803
Crane Creek Gun Stock Co., 25 Shephard Terr., Madison, WI 53705
Crest Carving Co., 8091 Bolsa Ave., Midway City, CA 92655

VARMINT HUNTER'S DIGEST

Charles De Veto, 1087 Irene Rd., Lyndhurst, O. 44124
Custom Gunstocks, 1445 So. Meade, Denver, Colo. 80219
Reinhart Fajen, Box 338, Warsaw, Mo. 65355
N. B. Fashingbauer, Box 366, Lac Du Flambeau, Wis. 54538
Ted Fellowes, Beaver Lodge, 9245 16th Ave. S. W., Seattle, Wash. 98106
Clyde E. Fischer, Rt. 1, Box 170-M, Victoria, Tex. 77901
Jerry Fisher, 1244-4th Ave. W., Kalispell, MT 59901
Flaig's Lodge, Millvale, Pa. 15209
Donald E. Folks, 205 W. Lincoln St., Pontiac, IL 61764
Horace M. Frantz, Box 128, Farmingdale, N.J. 07727
Freeland's Scope Stands, Inc., 3734 14th Ave., Rock Island, Ill. 61201
Aaron T. Gates, 3229 Felton St., San Diego, Calif. 92104
Dale Goens, Box 224, Cedar Crest, N.M. 87008
Gary Goudy, 263 Hedge Rd., Menlo Park, CA 44025
Gould's Myrtlewood, 1692 N. Dogwood, Coquille, Ore. 97423 (gun blanks)
Rolf R. Gruning, 315 Busby Dr., San Antonio, Tex. 78209
Gunwoods (N.Z.) Ltd., Box 18505, New Brighton, Christchurch, New Zealand, (blanks)
Half Moon Rifle Shop, Rte. 1B, Box 352, Columbia Falls, MT 59912
Harper's Custom Stocks, 928 Lombrano St., San Antonio, Tex. 78207
Harris Gun Stocks, Inc., 12 Lake St., Richfield Springs, N.Y. 13439
Hal Hartley, 147 Blairsfork Rd., Lenoir, NC 28654
Hayes Gunstock Service Co., 914 E. Turner St., Clearwater, Fla. 33516
Hubert J. Hecht, 55 Rose Mead Circle, Sacramento, CA 95831
Edward O. Hefti, 300 Fairview, College Sta., Tex. 77840
Herter's Inc., Waseca, Minn. 56093
Klaus Hiptmayer, P.O. Box 136, Eastman, Que., Canada
Richard Hodgson, 9081 Tahoe Lane, Boulder, CO 80301
Hollis Gun Shop, 917 Rex St., Carlsbad, N.M. 88220
Jack's Walnut Woods, 10333 San Fernando Rd., Pacoima, CA 91331 (English and Claro blanks)
Jackson's, Box 416, Selman City, Tex. 75689 (blanks)
Paul Jaeger, 211 Leedom St., Jenkintown, Pa. 19046
I. D. Johnson, Rt. 1, Strawberry Point, Ia. 52076 (blanks)
Johnson's Gun Shop, 1316 N. Blackstone, Fresno, CA 93703
Monte Kennedy, P.O. Box 214, Kalispell, MT 59901
Leer's Gun Barn, Rt. 3, Sycamore Hills, Elwood, Ind. 46036
LeFever Arms Co., Inc., R.D. 1, Lee Center, N.Y. 13363
Bill McGuire, Inc., 10324 Valmay Ave., N.W., Seattle, WA 98177
Maryland Gun Exchange, Rd., 5, Rt. 40 W., Frederick MD 21701
Maurer Arms, 2366 Frederick Dr., Cuyahoga Falls, O. 44221
Leonard Mews, Spring Rd., Box 242, Hortonville, WI 54944
Robt. U. Milhoan & Son, Rt. 3, Elizabeth, W. Va. 26143
C. D. Miller Guns, St. Onge, S.D. 57779
Mills (D.H.) Custom Stocks, 401 N. Ellsworth Ave., San Mateo, Calif. 94401
Nelsen's Gun Shop, 501 S. Wilson, Olympia, Wash. 98501
Oakley and Merkley, Box 2446, Sacramento, CA 95811 (blanks)
Maurice Ottmar, Box 657, Coulee City, WA 99115
Pachmayr Gun Works, 1220 S. Grand Ave., Los Angeles, CA 90015 (blanks and custom jobs)
Ernest O. Paulsen, Rte. 71, Box 11, Chinook, MT 59523 (blanks)
Peterson Mach. Carving, Box 1065, Sun Valley, Calif. 91352
Andrew Redmond, Inc., No. Anson, Me. 04958 (birchwood blanks)
R. Neal Rice, Box 12172, Denver, CO 80212
Richards Micro-Fit Stocks, P.O. Box 1066, Sun Valley, CA. 91352 (thumbhole)
Roberts Gunstocks, 1400 Melody Rd., Marysville, Calif. 95901
Carl Roth, Jr., P.O. Box 2593, Cheyenne, Wy. 82001
Royal Arms, Inc., 10064 Bert Acosta Ct., Santee, Calif. 92071
Sanders Cust. Gun Serv., 2358 Tyler Lane, Louisville, Ky. 40205 (blanks)
Saratoga Arms Co., R.D. 3, Box 387, Pottstown, Pa. 19464
Roy Schaefer, 965 W. Hilliard Lane, Eugene, Ore. 97402 (blanks)
Shaw's, Rt. 4, Box 407-L, Escondido, CA 92025
Hank Shows, The Best, 1202 N. State, Ukaih, CA 95482

Walter Shultz, R.D. 3, Pottstown, Pa. 19464
Sile Dist., 7 Centre Market Pl., New York, N.Y. 10013
Ed Sowers, 8331 DeCelis Pl., Sepulveda, Calif. 91343
Sportsmen's Equip. Co., 915 W. Washington, San Diego, Calif. 92103 (carbine conversions)
Keith Stegall, Box 696, Gunnison, Colo. 81230
Stinehour Rifles, Box 84, Cragsmoor, N.Y. 12420
Surf N' Sea, Inc., 62-595 Kam Hwy., Box 268, Haleiwa, HI 96712 (custom gunstocks blanks)
Swanson Cust. Firearms, 1051 Broadway, Denver, Colo. 80203
Talmage Enterpr., 43197 E. Whittier, Hemet, CA 92343
Trevallion Gunstocks, 3442 S. Post Rd., Indianapolis, IN 46239
Brent L. Umberger, Sportsman's Haven, R.R. 4, Cambridge, OH 43725
Roy Vail, Rt. 1, Box 8, Warwick, N.Y. 10990
Harold Waller, 1288 Camillo Way, El Cajon, CA 92021
Weatherby's, 2781 Firestone, South Gate, Calif. 90280
Frank R. Wells, 2832 W. Milton Rd., Tucson, AZ 85706 (custom stocks)
Western Gunstocks Mfg. Co., 550 Valencia School Rd., Aptos, CA 95003
Joe White, Box 8505, New Brighton, Christchurch, N.Z. (blanks)
Duane Wibe, 426 Creekside Dr., Pleasant Hill, CA 94563
Bob Williams, c/o Hermans-Atlas Custom Guns, 800 E St. N.W., Washington, DC 20004
Williamson-Pate Gunsmith Service, 6021 Camp Bowie Blvd., Ft. Worth, TX 76116
Robert M. Winter, Box 484, Menno, S.D. 57045
Fred Wranic, 6919 Santa Fe, Huntington Park, Calif. 90255 (mesquite)

TAXIDERMY

Jack Atcheson & Sons, Inc., 3210 Ottawa St., Butte, MT 59701
Clearfield Taxidermy, 603 Hanna St., Clearfield, PA 16830
Jonas Bros., Inc., 1037 Broadway, Denver, CO 80203 (catlg. $2)
Knopp Bros., N. 6715 Division St., Spokane, WA 99208
Mac's Taxidermy, 1316 West Ave., Waukesha, WI 53186

TRIGGERS, RELATED EQUIP.

M. H. Canjar Co., 500 E. 45th Ave., Denver, CO 80216 (triggers)
Dayton-Traister Co., P.O. Box 593, Oak Harbor, WA 98277 (triggers)
Flaig's, Babcock Blvd. & Thompson Run Rd., Millvale, PA 15209 (trigger shoe)
Gager Gage & Tool Co., 27509 Industrial Blvd., Hayward, CA 94545 (speedlock triggers f. Rem. 1100 and 870 shotguns)
Michaels of Oregon Co., P.O. Box 13010, Portland, OR 97213 (trigger guards)
Viggo Miller, P.O. Box 4181, Omaha, NB 68104 (trigger attachment)
Ohaus Corp., 29 Hanover Rd., Florham Park, NJ 07932 (trigger pull gauge)
Pachmayr Gun Works, 1220 S. Grand Ave., Los Angeles, CA 90015 (trigger shoe)
Pacific Tool Co., P.O. Drawer 2048, Ordnance Plant Rd., Grand Island, NB 68801 (trigger shoe)
Richland Arms Co., 321 W. Adrian St., Blissfield, MI 49228 (trigger pull gauge)
Schwab Gun Shop, 1103 E. Bigelow, Findlay, OH 45840 (trigger release)
Sport Service Center, 2364 N. Neva, Chicago, IL 60635 (release triggers)
Melvin Tyler, 1326 W. Britton Ave., Oklahoma City, OK 73114 (trigger shoe)
L. H. Waltersdorf, 29 Freier Rd., Quakertown, PA 18951 (release trigger)
Williams Gun Sight Co., 7389 Lapeer Rd., Davison, MI 48423 (trigger shoe)